writers.net
▼▼▼

There's a cool web of language winds us in.
—ROBERT GRAVES

writers.net

Every Writer's Essential Guide to Online Resources and Opportunities

GARY GACH

PRIMA PUBLISHING

© 1997 by Gary Gach

All rights reserved. No part of this book may be reproduced or transmitted in any form or by any means, electronic or mechanical, including photocopying, recording, or by any information storage or retrieval system, without written permission from Prima Publishing, except for the inclusion of brief quotations in a review.

PRIMA PUBLISHING and colophon are registered trademarks of Prima Communications, Inc.

The title of this book is not intended to suggest any affiliation or sponsorship of any particular Internet/Web site. It should be noted, however, that *Writers.Net* is a trademark of Internet Concepts, an Internet hosting and content provider. This book is not affiliated with, sponsored or licensed by Internet Concepts.

Glossary of Internet Terms ©1995 by Internet Advertising Southwest, reproduced with permission.

Library of Congress Cataloging-in-Publication Data

Gach, Gary.
Writers.net : every writer's essential guide to online resources and opportunity.
p. cm.
Includes index.
ISBN 0-7615-0641-1
1. Authorship — Data processing. 2. Internet (Computer network).
3. Social networks. 4. Information networks. I. Title.
PN171.D37G33   1996
025.06'80802 — dc20   96-43378
                                                        CIP

97 98 99 00 01 DD 10 9 8 7 6 5 4 3 2 1
Printed in the United States of America

HOW TO ORDER

Single copies may be ordered from Prima Publishing, P.O. Box 1260BK, Rocklin, CA 95677; telephone (916) 632-4400. Quantity discounts are also available. On your letterhead, include information concerning the intended use of the books and the number of books you wish to purchase.

Visit us online at http://www.primapublishing.com

CONTENTS

Acknowledgments xiii

INTRODUCTION: GETTING ORIENTED xvii

1 NET LEARNING 1

▼ Online Learning, for Free 6
Online Learning for a Fee 8
Teaching Writing Through Distance Learning 11
Megasource Jumpstations 12

2 NETWORKING — REACHING OUT AND GETTING AHEAD 15

▼ Forums 16
Commercial Online Services 22
Internet Relay Chat (IRC) 25
Megasource Jumpstations 26

v

3 NET SCIENCE FICTION/FANTASY WRITERS 31

▼ Forums 32
Online Magazines and Newsletters 34
Bookstores 35
Publishers 36
Games and Online Collaborators 37
Authors' Home Pages 39
Miscellaneous 40

4 NET ROMANCE WRITERS 45

▼ Forums 45
Magazines and Newsletters 48
Publishers 48
Reviews 49
Authors' Home Pages 50
Miscellaneous 50
Megasource Jumpstations 52

5 NET MYSTERY WRITERS 55

▼ Forums 56
Magazines and Newsletters 57
Bookstores 58
Publishers 58
Authors' Home Pages 59

       Miscellaneous 59
       Megasource Jumpstations 60

6   NET POETS   65

▼   Forums and Online Critiques 66
       Magazines 67
       Publishers 70
       Poets' Home Pages 71
       Miscellaneous 73
       Megasource Jumpstations 75

7   NET CHILDREN'S WRITERS   77

▼   Forums 78
       Personalized Literature 78
       Books and Magazines 78
       For Kids by Kids 79
       Adult Authors' Home Pages 80
       Miscellaneous 81
       Megasource Jumpstations 81

8   NET SCREENWRITERS   83

▼   Forums 84
       Cyber Mentoring 84
       Nuts and Bolts of Screenwriting 86

Screenplays and Shooting Scripts 87
Film Reviews 87
Authors' Home Pages 88
Megasource Jumpstations 88

9 NET PLAYWRIGHTS 91

▼ Forums 91
Nuts and Bolts of Playwriting 92
Magazines 92
Scripts 93
Megasource Jumpstations 93

10 NET TECHNICAL WRITERS 95

▼ Forums 95
Periodicals 96
Bookstores 97
Authors' Home Pages 97
Miscellaneous 98
Megasource Jumpstations 99

11 CYBERSOAPS AND WEBISODIC SITES 101

▼ How the Genre Began 101
Sampling the Web Serials 103

12 NET MONEY 107

- For Free or for Fee? 108
- Unpaid Self-Promotion 108
- Subscriptions, Sales, and Fees 109
- Sponsors and Advertisers 110
- Micropayment 111

13 NET JOURNALISM 115

- Making the Transition to Digital News 116
- Two Case Studies 118
- Forums 125
- Journalists' Research Resources 130
- Feeds and Leads 132
- Trends to Watch 136
- Self-Publishing the News 145
- Professional Organizations 148
- Online Newsstands 149
- Job Banks 150
- Miscellaneous Resources 151
- Megasource Jumpstations 153

14 NET RESEARCH 157

- Locating People 157
- Conducting Research via Forums 163

FTP 166
Telnet 166
Gopher 167
WAIS 168
Conducting Research on the Web 169
Online Reference Shelf 182
For More Information 183
Megasource Jumpstations 186

15 NET MAGAZINES 191

▼ Five Case Studies 192
Other Webzines 200
E-Zines 202

16 NET BOOKS 215

▼ Book Publishing and the Internet: Two Case Studies 216
Paperless Books 225
Online Bookstores for Bound Books 233
Resources for Book Lovers 237
Megasource Jumpstations 241

17 NET SELF-PUBLISHING AND SELF-PROMOTION 245

▼ Net Self-Publishing 246
Net Self-Promotion 253

Creating Your Own Web Site   255
Miscellaneous Resources for Self-Publishers   269
Megasource Jumpstations   271

18   NET WRITING   273

▼   Collaboration   274
The Art of Hypertext   281
Megasource Jumpstations   289

19   NET CENSORSHIP AND COPYRIGHT   293

▼   Net Censorship   294
Net Copyright   297
Additional Resources   304

APPENDIX: AN INTERNET PRIMER FOR WRITERS   311

▼   What Is the Internet and How Can I Get There?   311
What's Out There? — A Guided Tour   316
Putting the Net in Perspective   322

Bibliography   335
Glossary   339
Index   355

ACKNOWLEDGMENTS

*In this net it's not just the strings that count
but the air too, flying out through the mesh*
— Pablo Neruda

Right off, I must thank the Learning Annex and U.C. Berkeley Extension, where I initially developed "Internet for Writers" as a class, and my many fine students there, whose input and feedback kept my feet on the path. Such an opportunity proved an invaluable preliminary to the construction of this book.

Then comes Greg Aaron. He honored me by looking up my name in the phone book. He said he'd noticed I was teaching a class and wondered if I was interested in developing a book for Prima Publishing, where he was an editor. I'll never forget our brainstorming session over lunch. To the degree that the result merits any praise, credit is due to that memorable afternoon.

Then there are the many pairs of eyes and hands of the Prima team, each of whose work is evident: Jennifer Basye Sander, Susan Silva, Dan Foster, Paula Lee, Steve Martin, Susie Bell, Mary Beth Gallagher, Jonna Pedrioli, Linda Shapiro, Janet Hansen, Mary Jane Mahoney, and Katherine Stimson. My literary agent, Jack Scovil, dispensed valuable wisdom from Publishers' Row. Additional thanks to Rose Nelli, too, at Command Central.

I am grateful to Alex Swain's FAQ for the section on zines; to Ken Auletta for his May 16, 1996 *New Yorker* profile of Michael Kinsley; to Barbara Croll Fought at Syracuse University and Bill Knowles at the University of Montana for calling to my attention many of the journalist forums cited herein; to David Fischer and Victor Gray of the World Affairs Council for inviting me to participate in their fiftieth annual Asilomar retreat, "Media and Foreign Affairs," where my thoughts on journalism had occasions for fine-tuning, and to the presentations there by Hodding Carter, Barrie Dunsmore, Haynes Johnson, and Gerald Warren; to Mark Hull, Barry Parr (now with C|NET), John Murrell, and Bob Ryan for assistance with the case study of *Mercury Center*; to Joe Shea for the case study of his paper, *American Reporter*. Of many parties at Simon & Schuster too numerous to name, Kate Fischer's assistance stands out in the construction of that case study. The generosity of other subjects of case studies and sidebars is acknowledged and appreciated as well.

Thanks to Craig Jackson and Lucinda Walker, at The Mechanics' Institute's reference desk. Thanks are also due for the professional courtesies of May A. and Nasib Naser, Aaron Lehmer, and the whole crew at Compu-Tyme, and Ed Allendorf and Nam Fei Ho at Mailboxes, Etc., for diminishing the arduousness of manuscript construction and transportation. For Nasib, that applies doubly, for checking all the 750-plus URLs. A number of people at the Well's expert support line helped, notably Orion Letizi.

Next, how can I thank the Internet? Easier, perhaps, to scoop up the moon in a bucket of water. This is a book not only written about the Net but also by way of the Net. So, to the wizards who stayed up late and made the Net a reality, and to the many, many Netizens who demonstrated the courtesy and generosity that makes the Net such a vibrant place, I thank you, too.

The authors, teachers, editors, publishers, and entrepreneurs of the writing community who gave a vote of confidence in the form of interviews, articles, and research are equally deserving of unmitigated praise. Particular thanks go to Daniel Dern, John Levine, and Stephen Spencer. A tip of the hat goes to the resources, support, and understanding of *AsianWeek*, City Lights Bookstore, the Community of Mindful Living, Flashback Books, the Kamal Palace Alton Appreciation Society, Little Al, Mechanics' Institute Library's reference desk, San Francisco State University's Multimedia Studies Department, San Francisco Bay Area Book Council, and the Washington Research Institute — plus various houseguests who tiptoed around the disaster zones.

Maybe you have to live in San Francisco (or Paris) to understand why I say this, but I really have to thank my landlord. In thanking my family and friends, I am honored to count my landlord in that category too.

And, last but not least, I thank my parents for raising me in a cultured, loving environment, for having faith in me, and for merely being.

Thanks one and all. This book is a mere teacup of the ocean of gratitude I bear each and all of you. May it merit the sweet kindnesses you have shown it. And may it enable writers everywhere to thrive.

All attempts have been made to attribute sources of information, wherever possible. If any errors of omission have been made, they will be corrected in future editions.

❄ ❄ ❄

The Internet Road Map to Books was presented at the San Francisco Bay Area Book Festival by Daniel Kehoe <http://www.bookfair.com> and Simon Hayes <http://www.glasscat.com> and is used with their permission. Laura Fillmore's sidebar is taken from *Publishers Weekly*, November 22, 1993, "Like a Book on a Wire." Robert Ingle's journalism epigraph is from Rob French's article entitled "Where Is Publishing Headed?" in the May/June, 1996, issue of *Adobe*. Patrick Lee's statement on the Internet and reporting is taken from a response he made online in CARR-L, in response to a query from another member. Melinda McAdams' sidebar is reprinted from *Interpersonal Computing and Technology: an Electronic Journal for the 21st Century (IPCT)*, III:3, with the author's permission. David Talbot is quoted from the August, 1996, issue of *NetGuide*. The quote from Sherry Turkle is posted in the Mind To Mind section of Howard Rheingold's home page, Brainstorms <http://www.well.com/users/hlr>, and used with permission. And the epigraph to the Appendix, attributed to Kate Muldoon, was cited in the StudioB mailing list <http://www.StudioB.com> by Sean Cavanaugh, who, in turn, cited Dick Vinocur's *Footprints*, quoting from Dick Gorelick's newsletter. The Glossary of Internet Terms is reproduced with kind permission from Internet Advertising Southwest.

INTRODUCTION: GETTING ORIENTED

*The line of words is a fiber optic, flexible as wire;
it illuminates the path just before its fragile tip.*
— ANNIE DILLARD, *The Writing Life*

Welcome to the writer's Internet — a realm of unbound potential. You are embarking on a journey that can transform the way you write, the way you relate with other writers, and the means by which your creative works find their audience.

In this book you'll find out about the special things the Internet holds in store for you as a writer — no matter what your literacy level is as to writing or computers. The good news is: the Internet is easier to use than a word processor or a VCR. And it's tremendously useful for writers across the board.

How are writers using the Internet?

- to learn how to write better
- to find writing assignments and jobs
- to do research
- to hang out with other writers (and readers)
- to find new publishing outlets (including electronic submission and self-publishing)

Writers.net is your comprehensive manual for those uses, and more. Whatever kind of writing you fancy, you'll find useful connections. You can best fill in what's missing in your understanding by going online and seeing for yourself. And take your time. Just because the Internet is electric, don't expect to get through it in a hurry. You'll grow to like it better if you let it breathe as you do.

WHAT IS THE INTERNET?

If you're new to the Internet, take a look at the Appendix, "An Internet Primer for Writers," which will make much of this book easier for you to understand. Even if you're somewhat familiar with the Internet, you might wish to refer to the Appendix to further your grasp of its features. Meanwhile, here's a quick gloss.

The Internet is simply a lot of computers hooked up to each other. There are three important aspects of the Internet to understand:

1. It doesn't matter what kind of screen and keyboard you use (personal computer, network computer, or TV), or what kind of transmission media (satellite, cable, radio, phone); the Net internetworks all these networks into one (hence the name "Internet").

2. The Net began and remains decentralized; there is no single main computer — plug into any part and you can plug into the whole.

3. A truly global medium, the Net is like one big 800 number. Well, almost: once you're connected, there's no *extra* toll You call a *local* number for access to the Net and communicate anywhere in the world. You pay only for local phone charges for the time you're connected plus the base rates of your Internet Service Provider. And once information is posted to the Net, it becomes available to anyone in the world with Internet access.

The most popular Internet access providers are America Online (AOL), CompuServe, Prodigy, and The Microsoft Network (MSN). There are also Mindspring, Netcom, Earthlink, and others, in addition to the phone companies' services, such as AT&T WorldNet and MCI-Mail.

As of this writing, there are at least 60,000 computer networks connected to each other via the Internet, across 2.2 million host computers in 159 countries. The Net hosts an estimated twenty-five to fifty million people and grows at a rate of ten to fifteen percent every month. A new online network is connected to the Internet every thirty minutes. The average user spends one to two hours online each day.

The three most popular Internet features are:

- e-mail (electronic mail);
- forums enabling discussion among people with shared interests; and
- the World Wide Web (WWW)

A Web Within a Net

The Web is part of the Internet, but not the whole. In one sentence, the Web is an interactive multimedia network that can link to anywhere else on the Internet, and whose most common programming — Hypertext Markup Language (HTML) — anyone can learn.

The Web's unique *interactive* aspect is a breakthrough known as "hypertext" — a nonlinear presentation whereby anything can be linked to anything else. Clicking on a highlighted word or phrase can summon up a picture or supplemental text from within the document or from anywhere on the Internet. One way of grasping it at first is to imagine a huge mall in which every room has doors leading directly to any other room, or to other parts of the neighborhood. Because it supports pictures as well as text, the software used to access the Web (called a "browser"; Netscape Navigator or Internet Explorer, for example) provides an easy interface to the Internet; instead of being keyboard-driven, it enables you to manipulate the cursor (the portable tracking spot on your computer monitor) to "point and click." And this *multimedia* aspect — merging graphics, video, and sound with text — seems to point toward a convergence of computers, telephones, and TV. Already it's possible to conduct videoteleconferencing over the Net.

Customizing your browser with "bookmarks" means saving direct links to any of the resources out there, so you can map your own personal Internet usage and favorite locations with a simple point-and-click. And the ease of making your own Web pages is now as simple as turning over your palm. (Creating HTML Web pages is far easier than creating desktop graphics!)

The Power and Pitfalls of the Internet

The Net is still in its formative stages but is already clearly different than other major media, such as broadcast (mass market print as well as radio and TV). Instead, the Net is "narrowcast." Users of online networks are producers as well as consumers of information (as with the telephone we become both speakers and listeners). To continue the analogy, the Net enables us to hold conference calls with no limit to the number of people on either side of the sending or receiving end of the communication, and no central gatekeeper who determines where a person can travel in cyberspace.

But be mindful that there are potential pitfalls, too. For example, the Internet has proven addictive to some. An Internaut might have to remember to "keep a life," as they say. There's a tendency to look for everything online, but the online world is but one realm. True community involves direct, personal contacts. Some interviews are best done face-to-face. Having access to so much information doesn't neccessitate using it all.

But the possible powers truly outweigh the potential pitfalls, and the Internet can be quite profitable, as well as a lot of fun!

WHAT YOU'LL FIND IN WRITERS.NET

In Chapter 1, "Net Learning," you'll discover academic Online Writing Labs (OWLs) and other "distance-learning" environments where you can learn how to write and edit better. You'll also learn how distance learning (once known as correspondence courses) is not only a new vehicle for lifelong learning but also for teaching — a profession practiced by many a writer.

Chapter 2, "Networking — Reaching Out and Getting Ahead," will give you a taste of "internetworking" as an activity of a literary community that exchanges ideas and information. Here you'll learn about workshops where writers gather to make new contacts, find an agent, editor, publisher, or freelance writing assignment, figure out how to deal with a thorny contract clause, check out possible contacts, cope with an irrational editor, get feedback on work in progress, celebrate a manuscript sale, brainstorm, or just take a break at a twenty-four-hour "virtual watercooler."

In subsequent chapters, you'll find more specific resources. There are several chapters covering genres: science fiction/fantasy, romance, mystery, poetry, children's writing, screenwriting, plays, technical writing, and serials. Here too, you'll learn where to find resources to improve your writing, find contacts and companions, and submit proposals and drafts, and how to stay abreast of the latest news in the field.

Then, in Chapter 12, "Net Money," we'll answer the question: "Who's Paying for All This Stuff?" Every writer will want to peruse this chapter's study of the financial models for online publishing — whether you're considering going into Net self-publishing, or just because you want to know who's paying for your check, so you can watch out for the *quid pro quo* and such-like. Along the way, you'll also learn a new angle on catching a publisher's eye.

Chapter 13, "Net Journalism," is fertile turf for all nonfiction writers. But fiction writers will find valuable tools here, as well, for building atmospheric background, character traits, verisimilitude of detail, and so on. And if you're a card-carrying journalist (foreign correspondent, local beats, freelance, etc.), you'll find out how the Internet is affecting your career.

Chapter 14 covers "Net Research." After touring such potent Internet features as Usenet and gopher, you'll be brought up to speed about the difference between search engines (narrow searching) and subject guides (broad), and you'll learn how you can further refine your search with such techniques as "operators."

In Chapter 15, "Net Magazines," you'll find numerous outlets for marketing your work, both paying and non-paying. You may even be inspired to publish your own e-zine — a new avenue for expression and recognition.

Chapter 16 covers the world of "Net Books," beginning with two case studies that contrast big and little business. Then you'll learn about the Internet as a library of books for reading and research; as a bookstore for increasing sales and revenues of your books; and as a means of publishing original works, for free or for fee.

Chapter 17, "Net Self-Publishing and Self-Promotion," surveys the merger of writing, printing, point-of-purchase, warehouse, distribution, and PR all into one place: a computer. After a look at using the Net for digital short-run printing, we'll look at paperless self-publishing online. You'll learn the rudiments of "webtop" and e-mail publishing, and I'll cover some of the basic ins and outs of publicizing yourself and your work on the Net.

The Internet is not only a place to find jobs, do research, hang out with other writers, gain instruction, and find new outlets, but also a place to discover new ways to work. Chapter 18, "New Writing," surveys two forms of new writing: collaborative and interactive. Mixing fun and profit, you'll learn how you can network your way into the multimedia business. And you'll get a taste for the art of hypertext in criticism, poetry, drama, and fiction in general.

Chapter 19 zeroes in on the fine points of "Net Censorship and Copyright," both tremendous challenges in a telenetworked society, and of particular interest to writers. You'll learn about censorship and copyright affinity groups both on and off the Net.

And, as mentioned earlier, I've concocted "An Internet Primer for Writers," which you will find as an Appendix. Feel free to turn to it at any time. You'll learn what the Internet is and how to connect to it; you'll tour the basic applications, such as FTP for sending large drafts as opposed to e-mail for short text; and you'll get a sense of perspective about incorporating it all into your own life. Plus, there's a glossary.

NOTES ON FORMAT

Although this book is arranged sequentially, and each chapter has at least a little something for *everyone*, individual readers will probably hop and skip first to sections of immediate interest. Before you do so, here are some guideposts that pertain to everyone.

Internet Addresses and Commands

Please note that I've placed angle brackets ("<" and ">") around Internet "addresses" so that your eye can pick them out easily. But when you're using them, please don't type the brackets!

When an address occurs at the end of a line and spills over to the next, I have not hyphenated it; that way, you'll know that if you see a hyphen, it's intended to be there.

Commands to be entered are often shown in quotation marks, such as "Send me more information." Here too, don't type the quotation marks. If an instruction says "*YourFirstName YourLastName*," then insert your name (italics are not needed; I use them here to indicate a variable to fill in).

Computers are very unsubtle. If you don't enter something exactly as written, according to the "rules," your message may bounce back or just do nothing at all.

Tip: some Web browsers, such as Netscape Navigator, Internet Explorer, and Lynx, don't require you to key in the prefixes "http://" or "gopher://".

By the way, don't be alarmed if you look for a site and get a message saying that it can't be found. It may have moved or merely changed its address. Just do a search for the name of the item using one of the search tools named in Chapter 14, such as AltaVista or HotBot.

Why Contents of Sites Are Listed

Rather than my just telling you, "Hey, go visit Mergatroyd's Web Site for Children's Writers, because it's really neat," I'll often provide a partial description of what's there. This will give you some idea of whether you want to visit the site at all. And if you do, you'll have a printed guide right beside your computer. You might think of these lists and descriptions as a grocery list or a map.

After you've cruised a number of sites, you may want to use *writers.net* as your personal log book of voyages in cyberspace. Please feel free to annotate and refine this book as you go; *writers.net* is designed for you to customize — to fit your experience and needs as a writer.

The other reason I list the contents of Web sites is because there's inevitable overlap, which brings us to the last of my housekeeping hints.

Megasource Jumpstations and Bookmarking

If a given resource pertains to a number of different topics, I usually list it only once, according to its primary value. Please be aware that the overlap among informational categories on the Internet often makes it difficult to neatly categorize sites. This is especially the case at the sites on the Internet that are huge inventories of other sites — what I call "megasource jumpstations." Consider them as atlases for charting the terrain.

Expect to find overlap and duplication from one site to another. But keeping track of where you've been and where you've yet to go will make you a happier camper.

Simple. But let me say that again two different ways, just to make sure.

The Internet is often compared to a library. Well, imagine a library where different teams of librarians are arranging the same collection of stuff, but each according to a different system. One group is lumping everything together — books, magazines, records, sheet music — and arranging it all by subject. Another group is separating books out and cataloging magazines, records, and sheet music later. Meanwhile, another committee is arranging the books according the Dewey Decimal System, while another battalion is stacking books according to how often they've been checked out.

So *The Hobbyist's Journal of Idiopathic Endocrinology* might be only found in the first group's index, whereas John Grisham's latest novel will turn up in all three. That's a fair picture of the Internet's often chaotic art of arrangement.

On the following page is a picture of a megasource jumpstation, to help you visually get a handle on how this works. It's recreated from a diagram created by Daniel Kehoe, who maintains a mega-resource called Internet Bookfair.

Writers.net lists this site in Chapter 16 ("Net Books"), but please note that it also includes resources for writers. Similarly, other book megasources on the Net have overlaps, gaps, and unique resources.

Note, too, that this megasource includes other megasources, in the center. (*writers.net* calls such sites megasource jumpstations; Kehoe calls them "meta" sites, as in "metaphysical.") Expect this kind of overlap as well.

And note that Reviews and Reading Lists (at about 1:00 on the circle) both link to each other; an overlap of a finer degree of granularity, but of absolute interest to book reviewers.

You'll find that this kind of overlap also occurs within and between *writers.net* chapters. Thus a megasource jumpstation — or just a small, particular site —

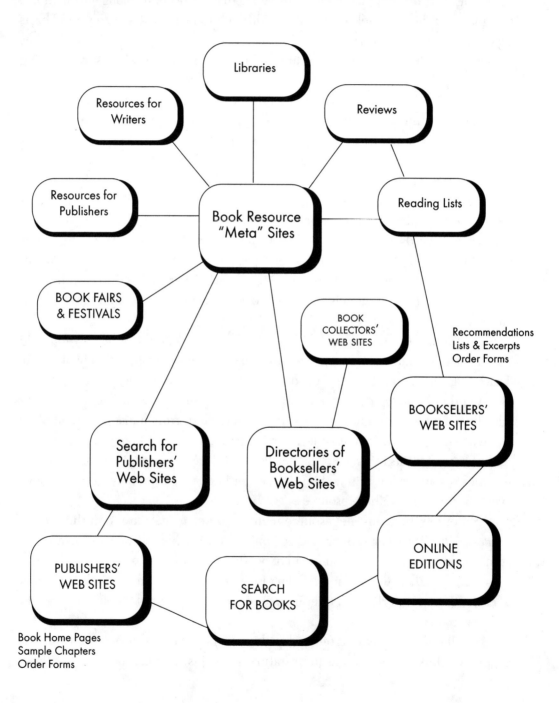

mentioned in a chapter on a genre might also have listings for books but won't necessarily be mentioned again in the chapter on books. In such cases, I picked what I felt was the strong suit, but I invite you to visit and explore each megasource fully for yourself.

In practical terms, I recommend that you bookmark sites to explore: individual sites, as well as megasource jumpstations and the sites on them. For example:

WordSmith's WebBook
<http://www.physplt.wsu.edu/info.html>

This megasource jumpstation, maintained by writer Althea Sexton, has all sorts of fascinating links (new users, tips, publishers, agents, etc.), plus other megasource jumpstation sites.

Vocabulary

The Appendix is a tutorial and primer that will fill in the major gaps in an average writer's Internet vocabulary. Otherwise, when I've used possibly unfamiliar technical terminology (also known as "nerd words," "geek speak," and "tech talk"), I've defined them or supplied some synonyms to clue you in through context and usage.

Online, you'll find an abundance of glossaries for the Internet and for computerese. One such glossary, from Internet Advertising Southwest, is reprinted in the back of this book. You might also try the Glossary of Internet Terms, <http://www.matisse.net/files/glossary.html>, created by Internet consultant Matisse Enzer (who cut his teeth on answering support questions at the WELL). There's also Net Lingo, a pretty good glossary defining hundreds of Internet-related terms: <http://www.netlingo.com>.

Writers.net Online

Visit Prima Publishing's Web site, <http://www.primapublishing.com/life/76150641.html>, and watch for additional *writers.net* material, links, and updates online. We'll be putting up excerpts from our chapter on Net research, as an active, all-purpose navigation tool for the Net. If you want to write me personally with comments, news, or haiku, my mail box is: <writersnet@hotmail.com>. I love getting mail!

1

Net Learning

If you ask someone, "Can you play the violin?" and he says, "I don't know, I haven't tried, perhaps I can," you'd laugh. Whereas about writing, people always say: "I don't know, I haven't tried," as though one had only to try and one would become a writer.
—Leo Tolstoy

In the second half of the twentieth century, writers' workshops at American colleges and elsewhere blossomed on a grand scale, serving both as incubators for a large percentage of today's new writers and as workbenches for professional writers to refine their craft.

In this chapter, you'll discover how to take the next leap and learn the craft of writing — and teaching — from the comfort of your home. You'll learn about:

- the Online Writing Labs (OWLs) of a few dozen creative writing programs
- courses and workshops that are online-only
- one-on-one online mentoring
- distance education as a viable profession for writers who teach

ONLINE LEARNING, FOR FREE

The Internet offers a number of educational options. These range from a twenty-four-hour rack of handouts to courses offered for credit via e-mail and/or the Web.

OWLs

Many academic writing programs maintain online writing laboratories (OWLs) — exchanges between students and writing tutors, mediated over the Internet — which began with e-mail and have since branched out onto the Web. Some even offer multi-user spaces (a.k.a. MOOs, for "Multi-Object Oriented") — where students can interact with tutors in virtual worlds (simulated classrooms, libraries, etc.).

While most OWLs deal only with work submitted by registered students, many can respond to direct questions from nonstudents about writing, writing strategies, formats, grammar, research resources, and so on. For example, questions may be addressed via e-mail to the Purdue University OWL: <owl@cc.purdue.edu>. And, of course, you always have the option of enrolling as a student for full service.

Besides tutors, these OWLs sometimes have on hand an array of useful texts, plus a jumpstation to further Internet links. For example:

The Writing Center at Virginia Tech
<http://athena.english.vt.edu/OWL_WWW/OWL.html>

This Web site, besides maintaining an OWL, also offers a gopher chock-full of handouts (Mac, DOS, and text) on a wide range of writing-related issues, from action words, commas, and nonsexist language to run-on sentences, transitions, and writer's block. (Other sites might offer tips on brainstorming, preparing a resumé, and the principles of revising, as well as the plurals of Greek- and Latin-derived nouns.) And its jumpstation connects you to eight other OWLs, as well as to such other libraries and reference texts as the Library of Congress, the Virtual Computer Library, *Webster's Dictionary, Roget's Thesaurus, Bartlett's Familiar Quotations,* Project Gutenberg, and the Human Languages Page. (Other sites might link to the *Encyclopedia Britannica* and *Elements of Style.*)

Or you might wish to get assistance with ideas and drafts in real time ("live") via a MOO, or some other form of "chat," as well as via e-mail ("lists"):

The University of Missouri's Writery
<http://www.missouri.edu/~wleric/email.html>

Has many useful resources.

George Mason University
<http://coyote.gmu.edu/cgi-bin/webx.cgi>

You may wish to register for free Creative Writing Web Forums. Look for "GMU Creative Writing Forum."

Virtual Writing Courses

In addition to providing a forum where existing land-based institutions can instruct students, the Internet is evolving a network of virtual campuses — universities literally without walls. There's more about this at the end of this chapter, in the section

▼▼▼
OWLS

    Purdue University
    <http://owl.trc.purdue.edu/writing-labs.html>

    Purdue has a page with links to many OWLs, including the following:

    Bowling Green State University OWL (Writime)
    <http://www.bgsu.edu/departments/writing-lab/Homepage.html>

    Oregon University's Writing Online Resource Directory (WORD)
    <http://darkwing.uoregon.edu/~uocomp/word.html>

    Syracuse University's Plethora Writing Consultant Page
    <http://plethora.syr.edu/PLETHORA/WC/wchomepage.html>

    University of Florida Writing Environment
    <http://www.ucet.ufl.edu/writing/nwe.html>

    University of Illinois Writer's Workshop Online Handbook
    <gopher://gopher.uiuc.edu/11/Libraries/writers/>

    University of Michigan OWL
    <http://www.umich.edu/~nesta/OWL/owl.html>

    University of Texas at Austin's Writing Lab
    <http://www.utexas.edu/depts/uwc/.html/main.html>

on Distance Learning. Meanwhile, here's a place where you can enroll in writing classes no matter what your schedule:

Spectrum Virtual University
<http://www.horizons.org/register.html>

Take advantage of Spectrum's free writing courses online. Participate either through e-mail or their Web page. (They also offer tutorials in the Internet, the Web, and HTML.)

Online Workshops and Watering Holes

The Internet is also building its own virtual network of courses, labs, workshops, and just plain watering holes for writers. Here are a dozen or so:

The WritingLab
<http://www.hypercon.com/~jilla>

Writer J. R. Lankford launched the WritingLab in October, 1995, as part of the Internet Writing Workshop (highlighted next). It has since branched off as an independent list (a forum mediated via e-mail). Currently, it's a group of about 100 members who:

- flex their writing muscles for the fun of it and sometimes try new things
- discover or revisit fiction theories and techniques to see what they offer
- exercise their writing skills to keep fit

On alternate Fridays, a new exercise is posted to the WritingLab. Each exercise is devoted to a single aspect of fiction writing. Members then have two weeks to write and submit a response of 300 words or less, according to instructions in the exercise. Past exercises have focused on such subjects as: POV (point of view), sense impressions, dialogue, internalization, credible prose, flashbacks, opening hooks, action and suspense, the classic scene, the classic sequel, characterization, omniscient narration, creating atmosphere, the love scene, and similar topics. Occasionally, the WritingLab holds friendly competitions in which certificates are awarded based on member votes for the best submissions.

The lab is open to writers eighteen years of age or older. To retain membership, those on the list must meet a minimum participation requirement of at least

POV
by J. R. Lankford, founder of WritingLab

About three years ago I sat down to write my first novel, entitled *Home Fires Burning*, without having studied fiction theory and technique — though, like most aspiring writers, I was a voracious reader. I just dove in and started writing until, four months later, I typed "the end." My husband brought champagne home; I'd written a novel. Weeks later, I realized it was a mess. The agents I sent it to kept writing back to me and saying things which amounted to: you write beautifully here and there, but this is a mess! After the requisite period of dejection, these letters caused me to decide to find out what was wrong and fix it.

First I went online for help. My critiquer said my novel would give a reader POV whiplash. I wrote back and asked: what's POV? When I got an answer, I knew I had work to do, so I went to a bookstore and bought every book on the shelf about fiction writing. I studied them, did the exercises in them, made up new ones, and outlined each book's principles to make sure I understood. For months, I felt like I was back in college. Then I revised my novel well enough to land an agent, but the publishers she contacted said: we love this book but we don't want to buy it. Some said: send us the next one she writes. My agent looked at my second novel, a spy/thriller called *A Danger to the Peace*, and, in effect, said: this is a beautiful story, but I'm not going to send it out because I know they won't buy it; commercial publishers aren't interested in Bosnia! Now I'm writing a mystery entitled *Murder Without Motive*.

The first thing I learned from all this is that a writer needs an idea, something to write with, and twelve buckets of extra perseverance standing by to dip his/her head in at tough moments. The second thing I learned from all this is that agents and editors tend to notice if you don't have a handle on fiction technique.

All the while I stayed online, finding groups in which writers functioned in a self-help mode, giving and getting critiques. Again and again a new fiction writer would ask, "What's POV?"

I participated in GEnie's "Theme Park," run by Ed Williams, in which short pieces were written biweekly on a particular theme. All this gelled into the idea for WriteLab. Bet you can guess what its first exercise was about. It addressed the question, "What's POV?" And in WriteLab's primers, I tell others what I learned: if you want to bag a publisher the first time out, settle in and nail your fiction craft. No need to give up if you're rejected. So were Clancy, Grisham, Shakespeare, etc.

one submission and at least one critique of another's submission per month. Complete information on membership, as well as old exercises and links of interest to writers, can be found on the Web page.

The Internet Writing Workshop

The Internet Writing Workshop was founded by Chuq Von Rospach in 1986 as the Science Fiction Writers List. Since then, the list has broadened its focus, moved a few times, and every so often changed administrators — mainly writers themselves, with day jobs in various fields. Today, the original group has branched out into six mailing lists:

- Writing: general discussion of the craft and business of writing
- Fiction: submission and critiques of short fiction
- Nfiction: submission and critiques of nonfiction
- Novels-L: submission and critiques of novel chapters
- Poetry-W: submission and critiques of all forms of poetry
- Yawrite: submission and critiques of children's and young adults' writing

Members typically belong to Writing and one or more of the other lists. Except for Writing, active participation is required for all lists, with nonparticipants being dropped.

Total membership is about 550. Of the critiquing lists, Fiction is the largest with about 150 members, Novels-L has about 100, and NFiction and Poetry-W have about 70 each.

Some typical topics have been: viewpoint, advisability of simultaneous submissions, and the possibility of organizing some real-life get-togethers.

For writers interested in actively participating (as opposed to only reading), request a copy of the Writing Workshop Guidelines for Prospective Members. E-mail <listserv@psuvm.psu.edu> and in the message body put: "subscribe writing *YourFirstName YourLastName*".

Writers' Internet Exchange (WRITE)
<http://www.ilinks.net/~jkent/write/index.html>

The Writers' Internet Exchange is a place to share work-in-progress with other writers and receive constructive criticism from them. Members may post up to 30K each day and must commit to sending a minimum of three posts (messages) a month, consisting of original work or comments on the work of others. The moderator is Janet Kent.

To join, send e-mail to <jkent@camcat.com> with a request to be added to the list, including your e-mail address.

The Writer's Planet
<http://www.digiserve.com/connect/writers/writhome.shtml>

Publish your work, receive feedback, and talk with other aspiring writers.

Writers' Workshop

Work in progress is shared and critiqued, and members also discuss writing in general.

To subscribe, e-mail <listserv@mitvma.mit.edu> with the message: "subscribe writers *YourFirstName YourLastName*".

The Fiction Writers' Workshop

The Fiction Writers Workshop gives people who want to write fiction professionally a support group of peers, where information can be shared and the task of writing can be discussed. The workshop fosters an environment in which work-in-progress can be passed around and criticized so that authors can find the weak spots and polish their manuscripts into salable works.

To subscribe, e-mail <listserv@psuvm.psu.edu>, leaving the subject header blank, with the message: "subscribe fiction *YourFirstName YourLastName*".

Book Stacks Unlimited's Fiction Writers' Workshop
<http://www.books.com/scripts/ctopics.exe?/level~10/param~66>

Book Stacks Unlimited is an online bookstore — a phenomenon which we'll look at further in Chapter 16. In addition to selling books, they create community via their Cyberspace forum, where fiction writers present drafts of short stories or chapters of novels for comment and critique by other writers and interested readers. Writers at all levels of experience are welcome to present their work, and everyone is encouraged to provide constructive criticism. Participants also post and discuss any number of other topics.

DeVry's Online Writing Support Center
<http://www.devry-phx.edu/lrnresrc/dowsc/>

The emphasis here is on learning to use the Internet as a tool for writers — for "digital dialogue," "cyber-reference," making Web pages, teaching writing, etc.

ONLINE LEARNING, FOR A FEE

While the resources listed above are free, for a fee you can find assistance that's often more specialized. Many accredited colleges now offer distance learning, and online-only sites with professional staffs are springing up. Here's a sampling:

New School for Social Research
<http://dialnsa.edu/home.html>

The New School was one of the first accredited colleges to offer its classes over the Internet, including over a dozen writing programs. See their seasonal course listings for details.

Online Writing Workshop
<http://www.teleport.com/~bjscript/wclass.htm>

Bill Johnson has a virtual reality office at the University of Hawaii, via MOO, from which he teaches fiction writing.

Writers' Conference
<http://www.writersconf.com/>

The Writers' Conference is a virtual writers' conference without the hotel and transportation fees. Just as at a land-based writers' conference, you'll find guest speakers, Q&A sessions with writers on tour, script evaluation programs, access to agents, and books for sale, plus full-semester workshops taught by writers and editors in every genre and discipline.

Writers on the Net
<http://www.writers.com>

"Writing has always been a central preoccupation in my life," confesses Mark Dahlby, founder and administrator of Writers on the Net. When Mark first crossed the Internet threshold and went online, the first thing he explored were the resources available for writers. But he found that there were no classes offered online, other than a few OWLs. So he rolled up his sleeves, gathered together sixteen published writers with teaching experience who were interested in being mentors, and launched Writers on the Net in autumn of 1995.

It is normally a rarity for a writer to receive one-on-one tutoring. Indeed, for teacher as for student, the central problem of the classroom or workshop structure is that students must compete for recognition and attention.

Mentoring obviates that bind. "Mentoring or apprenticeship in the arts," Mark notes, "is a revered tradition but, for many reasons, generally less available in the literary arts than in some of the other media. There have been remarkable literary relationships that flourished through correspondence — and there are still — but it's often luck or happenstance that connects a writer to someone experienced enough and generous enough to serve as a mentor. We want to make the benefits of the mentoring relationship more available."

Tutoring or mentoring has no one set subject or method. At Writers on the Net, a mentor may be of use for a business proposal, a screenplay, or investigative journalism. Some students may need help with the fundamentals of the craft; some may want an experienced eye to help them see why a line is wrong, dialogue is dead, or plot is unengaging. Other students may have research questions for an article or a historical novel. Some may need writing exercises to bring a particular facet of writing to life, or feedback on a novel they've worked on for the last five years before they send it out for submission. Receiving support from someone who lives the writer's life can support and further their own identity as a writer.

Tutor and student communicate by e-mail. While there's no physical presence, the fact that the medium — the written word — is implicitly part of the work also makes the process rewarding.

The student is charged for the tutor's time at thirty-six dollars an hour, and students dictate the amount of time they wish to have tutors work with them. Similarly, editors are available to work with articles, business writing, stories, and entire books.

Following the successful launch of Writers on the Net's one-to-one mentoring services, Mark developed classes via e-mail. Says Mark:

> The medium is perfect for writing classes, and the convenience for the student is unparalleled. You can lie in a hammock in Costa Rica, just you and your laptop, and take a class with a writer who has published a handful of books and who has a decade of teaching experience. Or you can download your e-mail during a lunch

break, or after the kids have gone to bed, or at three in the morning on a Saturday night. If you can connect your modem, you can participate fully in class.

The first class we put on the Net was a scriptwriting class taught by Jeff Sweet. Jeff lives in New York, I live in San Francisco, and the eight students in the class lived in four different countries — quite remarkable. At the end of the class, six of the eight students signed up for another eight weeks, which I think is a validation of the use of the medium for teaching as well as of the quality of what we are offering.

Curricula and faculty are all top-notch. Classes include: "Introduction to Fiction" and "Get That Novel Started," taught by Donna Levin (author of two novels and two books for writers); "The Short Story: An Introductory Workshop," taught by Ann Packer (*Mendocino and Other Stories*); "Episodes & Voices: Short Short Story Writing," taught by cosmopolitan author-poet-editor John High; "Mystery Writing," taught by Shelley Singer (author of eleven published novels, nine of them mysteries); "Scriptwriting: Screen and Stage," taught by Jeffrey Sweet (who has extensive Hollywood and Broadway credits); and "Screenplay Structure" and "Hypertext 101," taught by Charles Deemer (whose online resources for screenwriters we spotlight in

PASSING IT ALONG

Writers on the Net founder Mark Dahlby disagrees with writers who insist writing can't be taught. To his way of seeing, it's about transmittable skills, or craft, but also about transmission itself. As he puts it (tentatively):

> It's about meeting someone who is a writer beyond all doubt; finding them human like you, resonating with them, and finding your own confidence transforms you. Mentoring can save people a lot of time in learning a craft, but even more, they can enter a relationship in which their ambition to write is respected and nurtured. In being taken seriously the student can take him or herself seriously. It doesn't mean they'll get rich and famous; what is the percentage of writers that do? But it does mean that they can invest their writing with the seriousness that it deserves.
>
> I think that if any art is taken seriously, it rewards the artist whether they become commercially successful or not. Rilke has a great poem in which he talks about growing by being defeated by successively greater beings; writing can be such a being, such an endeavor. A mentor can be a guide.

Chapter 8). The roster is ever-changing, and alumni who blossom today may one day become online tutors themselves.

TEACHING WRITING THROUGH DISTANCE LEARNING

Many writers support themselves by teaching. It's a rewarding activity in many ways besides the income, which is nice, too. Now the Internet expands the opportunities for teaching, through distance learning. For example, Spectrum University's writing classes are free, whereas the New School offers accredited courses and charges a fee, thus compensating their instructors.

Normally, academic institutions require a minimum class enrollment to justify reserving a classroom, not to mention paying a teacher's salary. Distance learning eliminates the need to support a certain amount of real estate; all that's needed is a certain amount of space on a computer. And a teacher with a specialized or esoteric subject, such as Urdu poetry or John Milton, need not be limited to the local community for students but can now drum up class enrollment from an international market.

This also offers new opportunities for the student. In fact, this medium is student-centered, with the teacher being a guide on the side rather than the sage on the stage. Because it's self-paced, some students are performing better with computer-based, rather than classroom-based, curriculum. At classes with a common Web site, where students can see what their peers are doing, the class works to stay at the level set by the smarter students.

Many universities are currently creating online curricula, and new universities are springing up that are online-only. In addition, online services such as America Online are getting involved in distance learning.

Alliance for Computers and Writing
<http://english.ttu.edu/acw/operations/news.html>

If you're interested in joining forces with other writing teachers online, you should consider joining the Alliance for Computers and Writing; membership is free. In addition to writing teachers, members include representatives of academic institutions and computer-related businesses.

The Alliance maintains a number of a forums and a megasource jumpstation of links listed by topic, spanning a wide range from distance learning to issues of the profession.

MEGASOURCE JUMPSTATIONS

OWLs

National Writing Centers Association
<http://www2.colgate.edu/diw/NWCAOWLS.html>
<http://www2.colgate.edu/diw/NWCA.html>

A megasource jumpstation with links to over 160 OWLs. They link to many relevant journals, tutorials, and other materials.

Colgate University
<http://www2.colgate.edu/diw/NWCA.html>
<http://www2.colgate.edu/diw/NWCAOWLS.html#Tutoring>

Maintains a list of national writing centers. Also lists writing centers offering online tutoring.

Inkspot
<http://www.inkspot.com/~ohi/inkspot/courses.html>

Has links to OWLs, distance learning courses, and workshops.

Distance Learning

Distance Learning Directory
<http://www.con-ed.howard.edu/Webpages/Husce/Dld.htm>

Distance Learning Laboratory
<http://199.125.205.20:80/webpages/dll>

Distance Learning Resource Network
<http://www.fwl.org/edtech/dlrn.html>

Links to Higher Online Higher Education
<http://www.cstudies.ubc.ca/genesis/g_ref.htm>

✳ ✳ ✳

The Internet is thus like a campus that goes wherever you go. As we'll see further in Chapter 2, it can also be like a big park, where writers come together at all hours, from all directions, to touch bases with each other, critique ideas, pick up writing assignments, share battle stories, and just hang out together. It's like a coffeehouse to repair to, after the course, workshop, or lab.

2
Networking — Reaching Out and Getting Ahead

We cannot live only for ourselves. A thousand fibers connect us with our fellow men.
—HERMAN MELVILLE

Coming together is a beginning; keeping together is progress; working together is success.
—HENRY FORD

This chapter focuses on the many collectives, workshops, and watering holes where writers gather with other writers to trade battle stories, give each other support twenty-four hours a day, post news about festivals, readings, and prizes, and also connect with editors and publishers, and land freelance jobs.

First, I'll introduce you to a number of writers' forums that operate on the Internet, where you can polish your craft and join in free-form discussion groups. Then we'll survey networking resources available through the major commercial online services. Next, I'll highlight a number of online magazines of interest to writers. The chapter concludes with a look at some valuable megasource jumpstations.

FORUMS

In Chapter 1, you discovered how the Internet provides new ways of learning, for example by making resource materials readily available. Now we'll look at group learning through forums (discussion groups for people with shared interests). While some of these might be less focused than the courses and mentoring opportunities discussed in Chapter 1, you will find that being part of a "group mind" of other writers, sharing their collective wisdom and support, is empowering in and of itself.

WritingChat

WritingChat is a discussion forum for writers, owned by Debi Shinder (and thus sometimes called "Shinder's List"). WritingChat is not a workshop, and the topics discussed are not limited to issues related to writing techniques. Rather, WritingChat was designed to be a friendly place where writers from more technically oriented lists could get together and become acquainted, "shoot the bull," share aspects of their lives outside their work, crow over triumphs and commiserate over tragedies, and lend one another support and friendship.

The diverse members of WritingChat represent many genres and forms: poets, novelists, nonfiction writers in every field from religious publications to technical journals, and fiction writers whose material covers everything from children's literature to erotica. The common bond they share is a love of language and words and the creation of something new and exciting out of what was once a blank page or computer screen.

To join the list, e-mail <majordomo@bel.avonibp.co.uk> and, in the body of the message, type: "subscribe WritingChat".

Writers

For both professional and aspiring writers, group discussions in the Writers forum center around the art, craft, and business of writing.

Topics of discussion include poetry, fiction, and a fictional locale the group has created, the Haven for Hopeful Romantics. The group also talks about "the Oscars, the lunch boxes we had as kids, buttered cats and gravity, Tori Amos, and whether *Picket Fences* and *Northern Exposure* are too similar." As its FAQ (Frequently Asked Questions) file states:

> This [range of topics], too, is part of our inspiration for writing, and it isn't something we intend to change; one of the constants of Writers is the freedom to

wander down conversational byways. While it can lead us very far afield, it has also given us some of the finest material that Writers has seen.

It also makes Writers something more than just an academic list; for many of us, it has become a true part of our lives, a place of friendship and mutual support. That friendship and support allows many people who always wished they could write to discover that they can."

Currently over 800 members strong, the Writers group asks members to identify their postings with prefixes in the subject header: "SUB" for a submission, "CRIT" for a detailed critique of someone else's submission, "COMMENT" for quick comments, "TECH" for a discussion of technical aspects of writing, "ROBIN" for round-robins (the equivalent of "a writers' relay race"), "FILLER" for things unrelated to writing,

WRITERS, IN THEIR OWN WORDS

Moderator Mike Barker (a.k.a. "Tink") asked Writers group members to describe the group to writers.net; he forwarded some of the replies:

- Catherine Berchtold: "I enjoy Writers because I've met a group of people I can relate to — people who believe that just about anyone can be published if they work hard enough. If I have a question, it's answered ten times over. Everyone is helpful, and I've not seen a cutthroat attitude. When someone gets published, the whole group is excited. . . . I learn from reading other writers' stories and from the criticism that comes afterward. I have also made special friends from all over the world. I'm having a blast being part of a group of people who are funny, creative, open, friendly and have the same fragile ultra-ego that I do."

- Alisha, Mistress o/t Catacombs of InSANiTy: "Writers is like a group of friends who base their opinions on my mind, rather than my looks, or what my personal life is. They are the family who gets along, who doesn't hate everyone else for things done in the past, who may fight, but who eventually have chocolate wrestling matches or hugfests and make up. Not to mention the fact that the members are damned good writers, and will help me improve my writings, and not ostracize me for it because they know how it feels to pour darkness out through words."

- Chris Vaughan: "Writers is like a creative writing class, but clothing is optional."

and so on. Besides round robins, other writing programs have included "story swaps" — in which each participant writes a story around a common theme and then the stories are exchanged and rewritten by their new recipients — and "title challenges," in which members propose a phrase as a possible title for a writing piece. Members who wish to share longer works can use a subgroup, Works-L.

To subscribe, e-mail <listserv@vm1.nodak.edu>, leaving the subject field blank and entering the message: "subscribe writers *YourFirstName YourLastName*".

TeleCafe

Liz Walentynski's TeleCafe is an informal, relaxed meeting of minds to critique work and discuss trials and tribulations of the trade. Group discussions take place on Tuesday nights from 8:00 p.m. to 10:00 p.m. Eastern Standard Time in the TeleCafe at <http://www.idirect.com/TeleCafe> on Rhiannon's private channel. Scan for "Rhiannon" and, unless she's expecting you, page her for permission to come onto the channel.

The group is restricted to fifteen people, so first come, first served. Anyone interested in writing, from the published to the unpublished, is welcome to join. To keep the conversation from jumping all over the place, guests are requested to submit a topic of conversation. Liz keeps track of all topics, and she makes every effort to cover them all and respond to everyone's interests. Usually, one individual submits a sample of his or her work to all members via e-mail, and they discuss it as a group the following Tuesday.

If interested, e-mail Liz at <rhiannon@idirect.com> to reserve a place. Her reply will include a copy of the Discussion Group Guidelines. To see samples of her own work, visit her Web site, <http://web.idirect.com/~rhiannon>, which is also studded with writers' links.

Misc.Writing
<http://vanbc.wimsey.com/~sdkwok/mwrit.html>

Misc.Writing is a "newsgroup" (a style of forum on an area of cyberspace parallel with the Internet called Usenet, whose "news" is about its particular users) that provides a forum for discussion of writing in all its forms: scholarly, technical, journalistic, artistic, and mere day-to-day communication. (The sidebar "Rediscovering the Joys of Writing," located later in this book, was taken from Misc.Writing.) It is a venue for professional writers, would-be professionals, and all those who write to communicate.

This is one of the few Usenet forums that also has a Web site, which offers a number of references. The Misc.Writing FAQ addresses the following questions:

- "What format should I use for a manuscript?"
- "I've written a picture book; how do I get it illustrated?"
- "Can I sell a manuscript I've posted online?"
- "What about copyrights?"
- "How do I find a market for my manuscript?"
- "How do I submit a manuscript?"
- "Do I need an agent?"
- "How do I get an agent?"
- "What do agents charge?"
- "What professional groups are useful for writers?"
- "Who do I contact about additions to this FAQ?"

The Web site also contains the Freelance Writing FAQ, the Misc.Writing Recommended Reading List, the Internet Writer's Resource Guide (online resources for the writer, including a list of magazines and other outlets that accept submissions by e-mail), and a list of Neat Places to Visit (other Web sites). Forthcoming are the Misc.Writing E-Mail Book — the equivalent of a telephone book for the group, with both white pages and yellow pages — and the Misc.Writing-Ville Chronicles, a compilation of biographies and narratives contributed over the years by the townsfolk of this virtual writers village.

Usenet newsgroups can be less focused than mailing lists, and this is a perfect example. The diversity of members means you'll receive much more e-mail than you'll care to read, but you'll also rub elbows with a greater cross-section of the community. For example, Lee Spratt, of the writing team of Lee and Steven Spratt, posted a congratulatory message in response to another writer's "yahoo" (a word signifying the sale of a work). "Next time I logged on," Lee relates, "I found a message from a book editor with a subject line of 'so what are you working on now?' I told her we'd proposed a second how-to book for writers to our wonderful editor at Wiley, but it was outside the parameters of the Wiley series, at least for now. She said she'd love to see it, we polished it up and sent it to her through our agents, and the rest is chewed fingernails and waiting by the phone."

Freelancers
<http://www.idirect.com/jasmine/freelancers>

The Freelancers mailing list (a forum via e-mail) is dedicated to discussion of freelance writing as a career choice for professional writers and serious students. The moderators intend to provide a serious networking platform for freelance writers. Via the Web, they archive articles, tips, and links to online resources that further the aspirations of members. They also welcome participation by freelance artists and consultants, as the list tends to focus on marketing and self-promotion — issues that are of universal concern among freelancers.

To subscribe, send a note to <freelancers-request@idirect.com>. Put only the word "subscribe" in the body of the message.

Reminder: Always differentiate between the two addresses of a list: one intended for instructions to the list server (the computer that acts as the robot host and responds only to commands like "subscribe" and "unsubscribe"), and the other for messages to the group. Here, for instance, <freelancers-request@idirect.com> is the address for automated instructions such as "subscribe" and "unsubscribe". Messages sent to <freelancers@idirect.com> go to every member of the list.

The Web site is the list's information sheet, so to speak. If you have any questions, e-mail <nitefall@idirect.com>.

Creative Freelancers Online
<http://www.freelancers/com/>

An organization for connecting freelancers in the arts to clients, this site offers free listings for freelancers.

OASYS Network
<http://www.oasysnet.com/index.html>

Free postings to freelance writers available for hire.

FREELANCE WRITING FAQ

Publicist Marcia Yudkin makes the latest version of the following FAQ available by e-mail. Just send e-mail to <fl@yudkin.com>, with subject line and message body blank, and you'll receive one automatically.

This FAQ addresses the following questions:

I: Making Contact with Editors
1. I've written an article: how do I find someplace to publish it?
2. What's a query?
3. Can I fax or e-mail a query?
4. Do I need to enclose an SASE?
5. Should I try to find an agent?

II: Rights and Other Legal Stuff
1. Do we need to bother with a contract?
2. What do "first serial rights," "all rights," "one-time rights," "electronic rights," and "work for hire" mean and why should I care?
3. What's a "kill fee"?
4. Can I deduct writing expenses for tax purposes, and if so, how?

III: Common Worries
1. How do I prevent people from stealing my ideas?
2. How long do I normally have to wait for a reply?
3. What if I've never published anything yet?
4. How do I get interviewees to talk to me?
5. Can I ask an editor for more money?
6. Are multiple submissions OK?
7. Why do I keep getting rejection letters?

IV: Freelance Writing as a Career
1. Can one make a living as a freelance writer?
2. What about publishing fiction?
3. How do I sell a regular or syndicated column?
4. How can I get those first clips?
5. How do I break in to big-time magazines?

V: For Further Information
1. How can I find out more about freelance writing?
2. Are there organizations for freelance writers?
3. How about freelancing resources on the Internet?

Authorlink!
<http://www.authorlink.com/>

Based in Dallas, Authorlink! acts as a clearinghouse for the traditional publishing industry. The hosts aren't agents, but they provide editors and agents with fast access to prescreened, professional-quality fiction and nonfiction manuscripts.

The Author Showcase section, for example, showcases ready-to-submit manuscripts by providing editors with quick synopses, excerpts, and author resumés. Currently, the fee is $10 a month for posting work, but there are also free areas, plus market data and industry directories.

In their first six months, Authorlink! has had sixty-five manuscripts requested, resulting in ten sales.

Send e-mail to <dbooth@authorlink.com> or phone 214-650-1986.

COMMERCIAL ONLINE SERVICES

An essential ingredient that distinguishes commercial online services (America Online, CompuServe, The WELL) from plain-vanilla Internet service providers (Earthlink, Mindspring, Netcom, Whole Earth Network) is the opportunity to join other members in special interest forums, as well as to access members-only resources such as proprietary databases. Here are some basic examples; you will find others in the topic-related chapters throughout this book.

America Online (AOL)

America Online, currently the largest online service (six million members, and growing), has a large selection of resources for writers. The Writers' Club there is now in its seventh year, with some 200,000 messages posted each month. Catering to all writers — from beginners to best-sellers, in any genre, medium, or professional capacity — they offer live, weekly conferences; twenty libraries to share works; message boards for daily postings inviting other writers to network, find jobs, and solicit work; a twenty-four-hour live chat room; regular workshops and events, such as mentoring and Meet the Writer; resumé postings; and hundreds of articles, from the "business" of writing to writing the best query letter. Within the Writers' Club, there is a Romance area and a Teen Writers' area, with message boards, libraries, and chat rooms of their own.

To find the Writers' Club, log on to AOL, pull down the menu called "Go To" and click on "keyword." When that dialog box comes up, type in WRITERS or WRITE (or WC to get right to the chat rooms). Then click on "Welcome Newcomers" or "Welcome." A box will pop up listing such topics as "About the Writers' Club," "Newbie Tips," "Info on Message Boards," and "Chat Schedule."

Another forum at AOL is Electric Word (keyword: ELECTRIC WORD), which hosts excerpts of new and unpublished works, live chat with authors, a message board, and original reviews. The proprietor is John Fall.

Since America Online allows members to search the membership directory using keywords, some writers have been able to find AOL members who identify themselves as editors or publishers, e-mail them a career summary and wish list, and score some work.

Most AOL chat groups have some sort of e-mail newsletter. And there is an AOL Writers mailing list: e-mail <listserv@listserv.aol.com>. In the subject field, put "subscribe", and in the body of the message, put "subscribe writers-club@listserv.aol.com *YourName*". To reach America Online, telephone 1-800-827-6364. To reach the Writers' Club directly, call 1-888-SCRIBES or go to <http://www.writersclub.com>.

And the Writer's Web is a megasource jumpstation with resources for all genres, including science fiction, as well as other writing organizations and other topics. Though mentioned here, it contains a whole spectrum of hyperlinks for writers: <http://members.aol.com/jinglefish/incoming/home1.htm>

CompuServe

CompuServe has long been a haven for writers, editors, journalists, and other such literary movers and shakers. When its Literary Forum was founded in 1982, it averaged thirty messages a day; now it gets several thousand a week, although thousands of members lurk — viewing content without participating. Now there's a Literary Forum (LITFORUM) broken into twenty-three areas, and a Writers' Forum (WRITERS) with another twenty-three. A separate Journalism Forum (JFORUM) for published journalists and freelancers will put your name into a database which assignment editors will search when they need writers. The Journalism Forum is also a good resource for research, as is the Showbiz Forum (SHOBIZ). There's also PR & Marketing Forum (PRSIG). Some CompuServe forums are invitation-only.

Rich with information, CompuServe has a number of exclusive resources, such as their "knowledge index" — a searchable database of articles from 200 newspapers.

Celebrities who've been online for conferences include Tom Clancy, Robin Cook, and Peter Straub. Phone 1-800-336-6823 to become a CompuServe member.

GEnie

Writers' groups ("roundtables") are easy to find at GEnie (a product of General Electric), one of the oldest online services. The original group was Writer's Ink. For genre writers, there is Romex, an exchange for romance and women's fiction, as well as four separate science fiction groups. Call 1-800-638-9636 to sign up for GEnie.

The Microsoft Network (MSN)

The Microsoft Network offers a journalism forum, bulletin boards for writers (chats, education, research, advertising, and self-publishing), a popular Style Guide BBS (Bulletin Board System), and subareas for student writers (ages thirteen through eighteen) and writing kids (ages six through twelve).

Prodigy

Prodigy offers writing workshops (story, novel, poetry); an "Arts Club" for discussion of writing techniques; a "Young Adult Fiction" section; a marketplace called Accumulation of Opportunities for calls for submissions, contests, and other such listings and announcements; a National Writers' Association section to check the professional reputations of editors, book doctors, publishers, and agents; and more. Phone 1-800-822-6922 to join.

The WELL

<http://www.well.com>

The WELL (Whole Earth 'Lectronic Link) is another granddaddy in the online service scene. Howard Rheingold has written about his experiences with the Well in a groundbreaking book, *Virtual Communities*. He states:

> Finding the WELL was like discovering a cozy little world that had been flourishing without me, hidden within the walls of my house; an entire cast of characters welcomed me to the troupe with great merriment as soon as I found the secret door.

As of 1996, the WELL turned over the business of getting people online (as an Internet service provider) to Whole Earth Networks, and now concentrates solely on its online conferencing available to WELL members over the Web.

Many members are writers. Conferences include Books, Literature, and Writers. The Writers group has discussed notebooks, the muse, narrative voice, editing and editors, self-publishing, the success of friends, and "What Do You Wish You Had Known When You Started To Write?" The Byline conference is a freelancers group (under the WELL's Media heading) which has discussed such topics as query letters, collaboration, reworking articles for other publications, procrastination, electronic rights, industry standards, what writers wear when they write, and so on.

Writer's Digest

Writer's Digest had a space at eWorld until Apple pulled the plug on that whole online service. *Writer's Digest* hosted weekly writers' conferences and online critique groups, and it may find a new home in cyberspace soon.

INTERNET RELAY CHAT (IRC)

<http://www.nauticom.net/www/drmforge/cafe.htm>

IRC is an Internet feature devoted to twenty-four-hour "live chat." Forum areas are called "channels."

Two popular IRC channels for writers are #Writers and #WritersCafe, where you can go if you have writer's block, if you have a question about writing, or if you just want to talk about your bunions. Many of the WritersCafe denizens post their pictures and short biographies.

ONLINE MAGAZINES

Here are a few online magazines for writers. As you'll discover in Chapter 15, "Net Magazines", some general magazines such as *Salon* and *Utne Reader* also host their own forums, many of which are very stimulating and literary.

@Writers
<http://www.geocities.com/Athens/6608>

@Writers is an e-mail magazine, produced by Allie Lim, which includes writers' markets, writers' Internet resources, writing know-how articles, book reviews, classifieds, and more.

For a free subscription, e-mail <majordomo@samurai.com> with "subscribe a-writers" in the body. Leave the subject line blank. Back issues can be obtained at <ftp://ftp.samurai.com/pub/lists/a-writers>.

Inklings
<http://www.inkspot.com/~ohi/ink/inklings.html>

This e-mail newsletter for writers includes market information, writers' resources on the Net, reviews, interviews, writers' tips, advice columns, and market information. *Inklings* is published every two to three weeks, and has over 3,500 subscribers. For back issues and more information, see the Web site. For more information, e-mail <majordomo@samurai.com> with "info inklings" in the message body.

Poets & Writers Online
<http://www.pw.org/webnew/html>

The esteemed magazine *Poets & Writers* is now on the Web, with news of contests, conferences, events, and more.

The Scrivenery
<http://www.scrivenery.com>

This free monthly online journal for fiction writers contains prose exercises, vignettes submitted in response to the exercises, essays on writing and the writing life, a calendar of literary birthdays with quotations from well-known authors, marketplace information, and other assorted tools of the author's trade. There's also an online bulletin board, the Locutory, for talking with other Scrivenery readers, discussing the exercises and the published vignettes, and meeting others with similar interests in writing fiction.

The Scrivenery has links for text-only browsers as well as tables and in-line graphics for those who wish them. (The graphic for the content map is by Rembrandt.) The editors are Ed Williams and Leila B. Joiner.

MEGASOURCE JUMPSTATIONS

There's no one central writers' Internet site. Instead, some sites have key focal points; others are jumpstations to various Net writers' resources; and some are a little bit of both. In this chapter, I've included some of the most general sites.

Bricolage
<http://bel.avonibp.co.uk/bricolage/bricolage.html>

Bricolage is an online-only magazine (that is, a Webzine) with one of the richer collections of Net writers' resources. Besides offering a lounge that provides marketing news and contact information, and a seminary for budding writers, it furnishes a breakdown of major Web sites for writers. And, as a megasource jumpstation, *Bricolage* is a home page well worth bookmarking.

Callie's WritePage
<http://www.writepage.com>

This jumpstation is very orderly, primarily aimed at genre writers, but of possible interest to all. The jumping-off points of Callie's WritePage are organized around such categories as:

- Tools of the Trade: books about writing, getting published, and managing a writing career
- Write Organizations: local and national writers' groups that meet in person
- Write Online: online groups for writers
- Conferences and Contests: entry and registration information, by event date or by deadline
- The Write Sites: pointers to sites of interest on the Internet (library listings, research archives, interesting information, etc.)

Readers can contribute items to any of these areas; there are also headings for research, products, public service efforts, and writers' rights.

Nebraska Center for Writers
<http://acm-www.creighton.edu/NCW>

This thorough, orderly megasource presents links about creative writing programs, writers' groups, writers' tools, and employment and publishing opportunities for writers, as well as festivals, prizes, readings, contests, retreats, literary centers, and online libraries. For example, their compilation of documents scattered across the Internet about literary agents includes how to translate rejection letters, how to research and get an agent, how agents charge, and other FAQs.

Poet Warrior Press: Writer's Resource Center
<http://www.azstarnet.com/~poewar/writer/writer.html>

John Hewitt maintains many resources and links at this site of interest to all writers: authors' home pages, book publishers, classics, editing, how-to articles, market information, research tips, and writing festivals.

The Writer's Market Board
<http://rain-crow-publishing.com/>

This is a free-for-all bulletin board for writers, editors, and publishers in all forms of printed or electronic media. Publishers use this bulletin board to post calls for submissions; writers find markets here for their work.

Specific areas include: periodicals and presses looking for fiction, poetry, creative nonfiction, and drama; journalism publications looking for reporting, columnists, and feature articles; companies looking for technical writers who can document complex products clearly; regional publications looking for material; presses looking for book proposals; screenwriting, audio books, comics, cartoon markets, music, and interactive media; poetry, fiction, and essay contests; writer's groups and events; services and tools — editors, writing instruction, periodicals for writers, software, and agents.

Writer's Resources
<http://www.vmedia.com/shannon/writing.html>

This site has hyperlinks to many online writing tutors and other sources of general writing help, as well as links to genre resources, reference materials, writers' associations, and related professions.

Writer's Resource Center
<http://www.comet.net/writersr/writers.htm>

Comet.Net specializes in creating Web pages for writers. As a service to the writing community, their site features links to authors' pages, professional associations and organizations, literary agents, reference resources, worshops, conferences and online courses, bookstores and booksellers, magazines and e-zines, market news, genres (mystery, science-fiction, romance, children's books, and poetry), literary resources, digital texts, copyright law, libraries, historical research, grant information, publishers, and book reviews.

WritersNet
<http://www.writers.net>

You can imagine my surprise when I discovered an Internet resource with a name so similar to this book. And I'm pleased to tell you that it's one of the better venues around. WritersNet[SM] is a free service that is home to a bulletin board of writing assignments and to two directories: one of published writers and one of literary agents, both Internet-accessible. WritersNet also hosts discussion groups over the Web.

The Internet Directory of Published Writers is a searchable directory of hundreds of published writers; it contains a listing of published works, biographical statements, and contact information. Writers often choose to list here in order to receive writing assignments.

The Internet Directory of Literary Agents includes a description of each agency listed, areas of specialization, and contact information — including a hyperlinked e-mail address. Agencies are broken down according to specialties: fiction, nonfiction, scripts, and children's books. The directories are free — quite a bargain.

HOW WRITERSNET CAME TO BE

by Stephen Spencer, founder and proprietor

As the husband of a writer, I can appreciate the difficulties that come with a career in writing — the difficulty breaking into the field, the difficulty making money from writing, the difficulty in making the connections.

One day, I saw the cover of the November 1994 issue of *Writer's Digest*: "Get Writing Assignments Online." That intrigued me, so I read the article. It was about how writers can make connections with publishers and editors in online forums on CompuServe and other online services. I was skeptical; how would an editor or publisher find the time to chat real-time with writers of unknown caliber on CompuServe? I figured there was a better way — specifically, to have a database that would help the publisher or editor qualify that writer quickly and easily before making the contact through the Net. So by the end of December 1994 WritersNet[SM] was online and announced on various writing-related discussion groups.

I have a server already on the Internet, so there is no additional cost for me to have this Directory residing on the server. The real cost for me is in my time: in upkeep and development of new features.

One of the pioneers in Web-based discussion groups, WritersNet topics of conversations include editors and editing, agents, and publishers and publishing.

WritersNet acts as a clearinghouse where writers, publishers, editors, and literary agents can build relationships. Not only can editors and publishers find writers, and writers find agents, but writers can form friendships and alliances with other like-minded writers.

Yahoo! — Writing
<http://www.yahoo.com/Social_Science/Communications/Writing>

This megasource jumpstation has links for such topics as: agents, conferences, contests, festivals, online forums, workshops, and writer directories.

Zuzu's Petals
<http://www.lehigh.net/zuzu>

Zuzu's Petals is not only a poetry magazine, but also a searchable megasource jumpstation. It includes over 1,700 links to resources, not only for writers (writers' conferences, literary magazines, genres, etc.), but also for artists, performers, researchers, and Webmasters — the online creative community as a whole.

* * *

Whether you're hoping to share your work with others, in need of assistance with gerunds, hungry for work, seeking a tutor in dialogue and character development, or scouting literary agents for manuscript or proposal, the Internet can put everything at your fingertips. Some writers, however, may aim to network within a special field of writing, such as science fiction or romance. Having just touched on one genre-based resource, Callie's WritePage, we turn next to chapters devoted to various genres and types of writing, as they, too, are well-represented on the bounteous Net.

3

Net Science Fiction/Fantasy Writers

Cyberspace is a metaphor that allows us to grasp this place where, since about the time of the second World War, we've increasingly done so many of the things that we think of as civilization. Cyberspace is where we do our banking . . . it's where the stock market actually takes place. . . . So I think that since so much of what we do is happening digitally and electronically, it's useful to have an expression that allows that all to be part of the territory. I think it makes it easier for us to visualize what we're doing with this stuff.

. . . Cyberspace is the place where a long-distance telephone call takes place. Actually, it's the place where any telephone call takes place, and we take that very much for granted. Otherwise I would say that when people use the Internet, that's when they're most obviously navigating in cyberspace. When you use the Internet, you enter a realm in which geography no longer exists.

—WILLIAM GIBSON (who coined the word "cyberspace")

In this chapter, you will see how science fiction and fantasy writers are using cyberspace to chat with readers and with other writers, to access magazines both paper and paperless, to hunt for and sell books, to contact and keep up with publishers, to play games and otherwise collaborate, to post home pages for authors (themselves or others), and to create megasource jumpstations from which to teleport to all these resources.

Science fiction explores the invisible interface between culture and science. Of all the genres, it may be the one most altered by the rapid pace and sweeping scope of scientific and technological change in our time.

"Isn't science fiction," we might ask, "by definition, immune to future shock?" Hardly. Science fiction was predicated on being ahead of its time, but by the late sixties — what with submarines, space satellites, robots, and computers having become facts of life — the sciences caught up with the fiction.

Far out has become far in. Such sci-fi themes as the alien "other," cyborgs, the mutability of identity, and technological "haves" versus "have-nots" are now staples of discourse in college humanities studies.

Thus, there's now the label "speculative fiction," embracing sociology and alternative realities, as well as fantasy, sword and sorcery, and horror. Here, we'll use plain old "sci-fi" (SF) interchangeably with all of that.

Sci-fi: technology + art. What better place for it than on the Internet?

FORUMS

Artificial intelligence (AI), genetic engineering, parallel worlds, and other exotic, cutting-edge topics are all being discussed in online forums, making them fertile trolling grounds for sci-fi writers seeking to develop their material.

Usenet hosts tens of thousands of conferences about science, many of which are extremely technical. More to the point, there are dozens of forum sites here for fantasy and science-fiction–related interest groups, many of which have FAQ files. Three of the best are: rec.arts.sf newsgroups, alt.fan.newsgroups. rec.arts.sf.written, and rec.arts.sf.misc. There are also a few dozen Usenet newsgroups for *Star Trek*. (There are so many *Star Trek* goodies on the Internet, in fact, that someone once even published a guidebook to them.) *X-Files* is another Net cult favorite. There are even clubs for people who still remember *Star Wars* and *Doctor Who*.

Järvinen's List
<http://joyds1.joensuu.fi/sf-newsgroups.txt>

Petteri Järvinen (Finland) has compiled a master list of over 200 science fiction/fantasy/horror newsgroups. There are groups for discussing authors, books, cult movies, cyberpunk, fandom, *Star Trek*, TV, and more. But there are also discussions that are more specific or more general: about mythology, animé (Japanese animation), and Croatian science fiction. The *writers.net* Christopher Columbus award for "Newsgroup That Sci-Fi Writers Won't Want To Miss" is: soc.history.what-if, where people discuss alternative histories — for instance, "What if Germany had won WW II?" and "What if Columbus never sailed to America?"

That same Finnish domain that archives Petteri's list of usenet groups has a master list of over 100 mailing lists, at <http://joyds1.joensuu.fi/sf-mailing-lists.txt>. Lists range from such magazines as *InterText* and *Gothic Tales* to discussions of fantasy costumes, fandom, highly imaginative technology, the Klingon language, and the writing submitted for critique.

Literary Science Fiction & Fantasy Discussion Forum

The Literary Science Fiction & Fantasy Discussion Forum (SF-Lit) is a moderated forum open to anyone interested in discussing issues related to the literary side of fantasy and science fiction in all its various media forms. Maintained and moderated by the Library of Congress, SF-Lit provides an opportunity for members of the international community to participate in discussions related to reference, research, analysis, and other library and information center activities in the field.

To subscribe, e-mail <listproc@loc.gov>, with the message "subscribe sf-lit *YourFullName*".

Science Fiction Fantasy Writers
<http://seidel.ncsa.uiuc.edu/SFnF-Writers>

One group you won't want to miss is Science Fiction Fantasy Writers. To subscribe, e-mail <macjordomo@seidel.ncsa.uiuc.edu> with the message: "subscribe SFNF-WRiters *YourName*". (Yes, that is "macjordomo.")

Critters
<http://www.cs.du.edu/users/critters>

Critters, moderated by Andrew Burt, is for serious fantasy and science fiction or horror fiction writers. Members commit to submit critiques if they want their own work reviewed. E-mail <critters@cs.du.edu> for information about joining.

Talk.Com
<http://www.hotwired.com/headspace/>

Members gather "to discuss and dispute books, film, television, and new media produced by the most important thinkers in SF today."

SFnF-WritersWorkshop

Moderated by Peter Leppik, SFnF-WritersWorkshop is for fantasy and science fiction writers. For information, e-mail <macjordomo@seidel.ncsa.uiuc.edu>, leaving the subject line blank, with the message: "subscribe SFnF-Writers *YourFirstName YourLastName*". (Yes, "ma**c**jordomo" is correct.)

Because it's a high-traffic group, you may want to set your subscription to digest mode; if so, e-mail the address above with the message: "set SFnF-Writers digest *YourFirstName YourLastName*".

Dueling Modems
<http://www.sfrt.com/sfrt2.htm>

Dueling Modems is an Internet BBS (bulletin board service) which evolved out of GEnie's Science-Fiction Round Tables (SFRT). Kate Daniels hosts a writers' workshop, and fans, professionals, and just plain folks discuss all aspects of sci-fi, including books, movies, television shows, conventions, artwork, and more. Membership is $6.95 a month and includes access to over seventy-five private forums as well as many other amenities. Nonmembers can visit via the Web, but not post.

ONLINE MAGAZINES AND NEWSLETTERS

The Internet furnishes access to all kinds of science-fiction zines (short for "magazines") — in Finnish, German, and Catalan as well as English — from Aberdeen University and Australia's Mensa, as well as Chicago and Manhattan. Here are a few:

Adventures of Sword & Sorcery
<http://www.erinet.com/dspress/>

Ansible
<http://www.dcs.gla.ac.uk/SF-Archives/Ansible/>

Ansible Fanzine provides the online archives for the paper version of this superb, erudite, witty, nine-time Hugo award-winner, which celebrated its 100th issue in 1996.

Century — The Magazine of Speculative Fiction for Adventurous Readers
<http://www.suprenet.com/century/>

Cheap Truth
<gopher://fir.cic.net/11/Zines/CheapTruth>

A 1980s cyberpunk fanzine.

InterText
<http://www.etext.org/Zines/InterText/>

MT Void
<http://sf.www.lysator.liu.se/sf_archive/sf-texts/MT_Void/>

Omni
<http://www.omnimag.com>

As of 1996, this magazine exists only online.

Quanta
<http://www.etext.org/Zines/Quanta/>

One of the Internet's oldest online magazines.

Redrum Coffeehouse Horror Zine
<http://www.oz.net/cornix/redrum>

Science Fiction Weekly
<http://www.scifi.com/sfw/index.html>

For more online outlets, see Chapter 15, "Net Magazines."

BOOKSTORES

Basement Full of Books
<www.randomhouse.com/delrey>

Sells books directly from authors, and there is no charge for listings.

House of Speculative Fiction, Ottawa
<http://www.cyberus.ca/specfic/>

Has many related links, as well as reading lists and staff favorites, in its superb online offerings.

Sentry Box, Alberta
<http://sentrybox.com>

A shop specializing in adventure, gaming, and fantasy and science fiction.

Future Fantasy
<http://futfan.com/home.html>

Future Fantasy bookstore wins the *writers.net* "Seven-Eyed Green Smoking Face in the Dark Window" award for Best Genre Bookstore Web site. The home page for this Palo Alto bookstore has both an excellent graphic presentation and a simple, text-only version. Future Fantasy offers a searchable online book catalog and notifies readers of current events at the store and in the field in general. It also provides a jumpstation of hyperlinks to other stores, publishers, online magazines, original fiction, and other sites with sets of links. Thus, it's a must-bookmark site for all writers and fans.

For more information, e-mail <futfan@netcom.com>.

PUBLISHERS

Baen Books
<http://www.baen.com>

Del Rey Books
<http://www.randomhouse.com/delrey/>
<gopher://gopher.panix.com/11/DRB>

Includes submission guidelines, and a very good megasource jumpstation of hyperlinks.

NESFA Press (New England Science Fiction)
<http://www.transarc.com/afs/transarc.com/public/jmann/html/nesfa.html>

Putnam Berkley (Ace)
<http://www.mca.com/putnam/>

Knopf Publishing Group
<http://www.randomhouse.com/knopf/index.html>

Steeldragon Press
<http://www.player.org/pub/flash/steeldcat.html>

Tor Books
<http://www.tor.com/>

Includes a few chapters, a monthly newsletter, submission guidelines, hot links, etc.

Voyager
<http://www.harpercollins.co.uk/voyager/>

HarperCollins' UK sci-fi imprint.

Warner Aspect
<http://www.jvj.com/gateway.html>

Requires registration.

GAMES AND ONLINE COLLABORATIONS

Orson Welles' infamous "panic broadcast" of *The War of the Worlds* brought sci-fi to national attention overnight. Since then, Hollywood has done its fair share to popularize the genre. (The Sci-Fi Channel now has thirty million subscribers.) Today, we must factor in the video/computer gaming industry, which currently surpasses Hollywood in profits. Often drawing from science fiction and fantasy for its locales and premises (*Doom*, *Myst*, and *Sim-City* being best-selling examples), the success of computer gaming cross-fertilizes the fantasy and science fiction industry as a whole.

Gaming provides a whole new field for writers to work in. Sci-fi writer Alan Dean Foster is now writing for the Web. Online users can log on to one of his futuristic settings and direct characters in his "online interactive novels," such as:

The Marexx
<http://www.magicmaker.com>

Story making, not just storytelling. Characters, game play, and plot developments can be rendered live via the Web, interacting with a "hybrid" CD-ROM.

The Internet is becoming a driving force in the gaming industry. The success of *Doom*, for example, has been attributed, in part, to the fact that the first level was distributed for free over the Internet — a ploy one critic compared to offering free samples of crack cocaine at school yards. The Internet now supports multi-user game-playing, and players often bring their own software enhancements. To get a taste of this growing industry, check out the glossy industry magazines, such as *PC Gamer* (at your bigger newsstands), and visit:

Cyber Park
<http://www.inngames.com>

Games Domain
<http://www.gamesdomain.com>

Utopia Technologies
<http://www.utopiatech.com>

The Internet provides a perfect environment for developing an actual product. Utopia Technologies (producers of *Montezuma's Return*), for example, recruited its team over Usenet. Team members work from home ("telework") and hold a weekly business meeting on IRC.

Red Alert Internet Strategy Guide
<http://www.netcomuk/co.uk/~cncfaq/raguide>

The computer gaming industry has spawned a whole new sub-industry: gaming strategies. Besides technical support, it also furnishes insider hints and tips for winning. (Prima Publishing, by the way, has become a leader in this field.) An example of an Internet gaming strategy guide is Roger Wong's *Red Alert*. Publishing one of his guides and asking for a two-dollar gratuity, Roger Wong estimates that his readership will eventually reach 100,000.

Spectrum
<http://www.geocities.com/area51/7188/spectrum.html>

Another Internet gaming angle is role-playing games, quite popular in the sci-fi fantasy genre. *Dungeons and Dragons* is the most famous, but *Spectrum* is a *Star Trek* role-playing game that takes excellent advantage of the Web.

The Dargon Project
<http://www.shore.net/~dargon>

The creation of fiction also takes on new dimensions, seen from a playful, collaborative perspective. The Dargon Project was the world's first reader-written interactive "novel." It opened with a single chapter introducing the protagonist and establishing a minimal setting. This chapter ended with a decision to be made by the protagonist. Each of the protagonist's options was a link allowing readers to submit continuations of the story based on that decision.

The project's manager selected the best continuation chapters submitted for each link. The links at the end of the initial chapter were then changed to point to the continuation chapters, each of which, in turn, ended with a decision to be made. Writers of such continuation chapters were then responsible for selecting the continuations from their chapters. This sort of project might result in hundreds of completely different stories, starting from a common point.

In this shared world, the diverse authors write in a common fantasy world, predominantly human, at a late medieval technology level.

See Chapter 18, "New Writing," for other collaborative writing projects.

AUTHORS' HOME PAGES

Many home pages are created and maintained by fans.

The J.R.R. Tolkien Information Page
<http://www.csclub.uwaterloo.ca/u/relipper/tolkien/rootpage.html>

Eric Lippert's megasource jumpstation of J.R.R. Tolkien pages, for example, links to about four dozen home pages by fans, twenty Tolkien games, a dozen Tolkien societies, a dozen Tolkien art galleries, a couple of Tolkien forums, plus a Tolkien timeline, Tolkien encyclopedia, Tolkien music, Tolkien fonts, etc.

Pat Cadigan
<http://www.wmin.ac.uk/~fowlerc/patcadigan.html>

A simple but efficient example of a home-grown home page.

Hatrack River
<http://www.hatrack.com/>

Orson Scott Card's home page is an example of a very high-powered author's site, and even includes his writers' workshop.

Yard Show
<http://www.idoru.com>

William Gibson's home page is graphic-intense eye candy, a highly poetic collaboration between the author and Web weaver Christopher Halcrow. It's named after those open-air exhibits you sometimes see on front lawns of homes in the South.

SFF Net
<http://www.sff.net/people>

Hosts home pages of hundreds of science fiction/fantasy writers and readers.

House of Speculative Fiction Bookstore
<http://www.cyberus.ca/specfic/lnkauth.htm>

Has about four dozen hyperlinks to authors' home pages.

MISCELLANEOUS

The Dominion
<http://www.scifi.com/>

The Sci-Fi Channel's Web site. In November of 1996, they hosted the world's first Internet sci-fi convention.

Given its origins in advanced research, the Internet abounds in research opportunities for sci-fi writers seeking scientific details or atmospheric background. For example:

The Exploratorium
<http://www.exploratorium.org>

Provides an excellent megasource jumpstation of links for scientific research, listed by topic.

For information on cyberpunk (the subgenre spawned by William Gibson's novel *Neuromancer*), the Internet provides:

- a FAQ document: <http://bush.cs.tamu.edu/~erich/alt.cp.faq.html>
- forums, such as alt.cyberpunk and alt.books.phil-k-dick as well as MSN's

Cyberpunk Forum, CompuServe's Cyber Forum, and the Well's Cyberpunk & PM Culture conference

- a jumpstation of links: <http://www.en.utexas.edu/~tonya/cyberpunk>

For more information on speculative fiction, the Internet provides:

Speculative Fiction Writing Resources
<http://thule.mt.cs.cmu.edu:8001/sf-clearing-house/writing/>

Speculative Fiction Clearinghouse at Carnegie-Mellon University
<http://thule.mt.cs.cmu.edu:8001/sf-clearing-house/>

Includes a page on resources for writers.

Writing Speculative Fiction
<http://www.clark.net:80/pub/ahasuer/www/writing.html>

Two megasource jumpstations for Trekkies are:

Star Trek Nexus Top Picks
<http://userwww.sfsu.edu/~kschang/trektopk.htm>

Star Trek: WWW
<http://www.stwww.com/index2.html#lcars>

And for X-philes:

The X-Files Official Web Site
<http://www.TheX-Files.com>

Terminal X
<http://www.neosoft.com/sbanks/xfiles/xfiles.html>

The X-Files
<http://bedlam.rutgers.edu/x-files/>

X-Files producer Chris Carter claims to read online critiques of the shows, incorporating their feedback into the series.

MEGASOURCE JUMPSTATIONS

In addition to hyperlinks at the Web sites of magazines, publishers, and bookstores, you can find leading sci-fi megasource jumpstations.

The Lysator Science Fiction & Fantasy Archive
<http://sf.www.lysator.liu.se/sf_archive/sf_main.html>

Maintained by Swedish fan Mats Ohrman, this major site features an archive of Usenet newsgroups, organized by authors, books, and movies, and a list of lists: the A–Z List (circa 1985), the Alternate Histories List, the Transformations List, and the Science and Magic List. For example, the Science Fiction Omnicon list, <http://www.iinet.com.au/~fanjet/sfomain.html>, is an index of characters, objects, places, and terminology in science fiction, very well laid out.

SFRT on the Web
<http://www.sfrt.com/sfrt2.htm>

SFRT on the Web is the Internet outgrowth of GEnie's Science-Fiction Round Tables, and host of the Dueling Modems BBS. It hyperlinks to events, conferences, conventions, publishers' news, TV and film, Mars exploration news, and specialty sites.

The Science Fiction Resource Guide
<ftp://sflovers.rutgers.edu/pub/sf-lovers/Web/sf-resource.guide.html>
<http://www.geocities.com/Area51/2801/sf-reference-guide.html>

Chaz Baden keeps this site up to date and covers all the bases: archives, art, authors, awards, bibliographies and lists, bookstores, fandom, games, movies, publishers, reviews, TV, Usenet, writers' resources, and zines. Of particular note are resources for role-playing and other fantasy and science-fiction–related games.

The Speculative Fiction Page
<http://www.cs.cmu.edu/afs/cs.cmu.edu/user/awm/mary-html/wr.html>

Mary Soon Lee created this Web site for science fiction writers, focusing on marketing. Here the links are embedded in a narrative flow that guides the writer through the chutes and ladders of researching magazines, querying, making submissions, waiting, and the other phases of selling one's work. For example, she leads you to magazines with information on markets, such as *Adventures of Sword & Sorcery Magazine*,

Scavenger's Newsletter, *Science Fiction Chronicle*, *SF and Fantasy Workshop*, *The SFFWA Bulletin* (Science Fiction and Fantasy Writers of America), and *Tangent*.

Wisely and patiently, she covers all the ins and outs, such as whether to join a workshop or not, how long to wait for a response, and how to learn if a magazine is dormant or defunct.

Her site is also an example of an author who, having paid her dues, gives back to the community. In her first year of publishing, Mary made 127 submissions of her short stories. Today, she publishes in such premiere magazines as *Fantasy & Science Fiction* and *Interzone*. Her "square one" advice is: write, research the market, submit, start writing your next story, and persevere.

WWW Virtual Library Resources for Fantasy and Science Fiction Writers
<http://www.interlog.com/~ohi/www/sf.html>

The WWW Virtual Library is an omnium-gatherum megasource of all megasources spanning the gamut of *writers.net* topics. The science fiction section emphasizes marketing (like Mary Soon Lee's Web site). It offers links, for example, to the new magazine *Speculations*, for writers who wish to break into or increase their presence within the speculative fiction genres. *Speculations* maintains a list of markets it calls Market Maven. It also pays three to ten cents a word for original articles of up to 2,000 words; reprints are considered at a lower rate.

The Virtual Library also offers links to the Market List, <http://www.greyware.com/marketlist>, a list of over 100 fantasy and sci-fi or horror short-story markets, plus articles, tips, and hints, updated bimonthly. Categories are Pro, Semi-Pro, and 'Zine, with Anthology, Contest, and E-Zine sections forthcoming. Other areas of particular note at the Virtual Library are news of workshops and conventions, and essays about writing.

※ ※ ※

Within science fiction, the subgenres of ghost story, Gothic, and time travel lead to the next genre. From outer space we boldly venture to inner space and romance, mapping the still uncharted regions of the human heart.

4

Net Romance Writers

Monsieur de Nemours threw himself at her feet and broke down completely. By his words and tears he bared the most sincere and tender passion which a heart has ever sustained. Madame de Clèves was by no means insensitive . . .
—Madame de LaFayette, The Princess of Clèves (1677)

The romance genre reveals interesting parallels with the Internet: they're both successful, despite the scorn of established players, and they're populist to the core. On the Internet, as we've noted, consumers are producers, and vice-versa.

Once you've traded in the trusty Underwood for a personal computer, you'll find that the Internet contains a cornucopia of resources for romance writers, including: forums (for exchanging correspondence with others in the field), magazines and newsletters (for sharing business news), Web sites of book publishers (some with submission guidelines), reviews (always a good place to get some exposure), authors' home pages (perhaps yours, too, one day), and megasource jumpstations. And there are numerous waystations, from medieval to old West.

FORUMS

Isn't It Romantic
<http://www.bdd.com/bbs/conv1.html>

Discusses questions of romance fiction (brought to you by Bantam/Doubleday/Dell Online).

Romance Forum
<http://comet.net/writers/romance/html/confer.htm>

A Web-based forum for readers and writers of romance and women's fiction.

Romance & Women's Fiction/Readers' Groups
<http://www.geocities.com/SoHo/6666/readersgroups.html>

A megasource jumpstation of forums.

Romance Readers Anonymous
Usenet: bit.listserv.rra-l

Discusses love and sex, manners, religious romance, and much more.

Romance Writer's Mailing List (RW-L)
Provides writers with an open, unmoderated, and helpful forum for discussing all aspects of the craft and business. Established in 1994 at Cornell University with about forty charter members, the list currently has a roster of about 400 subscribers, including more than fifty published authors. Topics are tagged for easy reference: Bstorm, Crit, Exer, Intro (for new members), Promo, Social, and Tech. Suzanne Barrett, author of *Late Harvest*, quips, "We discuss one another's triumphs and woes, film stars' attributes, publishers, editors and agents, and, occasionally, writing." Archived are such practical, general resource files as Robin Nobles's workshops in "Grammar Hints" and "Using the Five Senses."

E-mail <listserv@sjuvm.stjohns.edu>, leaving the subject line blank, with the message "subscribe rw-l *YourFirstName YourLastName*".

E-mail contact: Bev Morgan, <morganb@ddi.digital.net>

RomANTICS
<http://www.uc.edu/~smitsp/index.html>

Produced by the Romance Writers and Readers Group from America Online; features a bookshelf and research library, tips on the business of writing, contests, a list of publishers, writing workshops, critiquing, and networks.

RomEx (the Romance & Women's Fiction Exchange)
<http://www.romex.dm.net>

Pat Ocain and Jenn Kettell run RomEx. Begun on GEnie's online service in 1990, RomEx hosts newsgroups covering all aspects of reading, writing, and promoting romance and women's fiction: workshops, writing basics, technique, lifestyle, and so on. To participate, you'll need a Web browser with newsgroup capabilities (such as Netscape Navigator or Internet Explorer).

Painted Rock Readers and Writers Colony
<http://www.paintedrock.com>

Offers chat rooms, bulletin boards, writing classes, and author home pages for fee.

▼▼▼

FROM: SCOTT KERLIN
SUBJECT: WRITER'S BLOCK—GREAT SUGGESTIONS!

Hello!
I am just overjoyed to awaken this morning and find so many great suggestions from list members on how to deal with writer's block. Thank you! :-) You have helped me to realize how many different ways there are to make peace with my "inner critic," who at times is my worst enemy. I know for some people, writing is a very solitary activity, but for me the role of others has always made a difference in my motivation to write and express myself. I know that's one major reason I've found the Internet so fabulous, because it enables me to feel connected to others through writing in a way I seldom was able to experience in all my years of "formal" education. Being highly introspective by nature has often set me to "quiet brooding," but being a part of these forums helps me to come out of it and see what a joy it can be to come up for air and give my critic the day off... I'm going to spend some time thinking about your various ideas (and others should still feel free to share yours, too), and I know they will help me to get back to creating. It seems accurate that, as one respondent to my question wrote, I may not truly be blocked — that the ideas have just been "stewing" in my brain for a while. But I'm sure everybody has that time when they feel that things have stewed long enough and it's time to just get it out and to heck with the inner critic. Well, I'm just about there... Many thanks again — I'm truly grateful for your responses. I promise to stay in touch! Best wishes,
Scott Kerlin
From Romance Writers List (RWL).

MAGAZINES AND NEWSLETTERS

GEnie Romance Writers' Newsletter
<gopher://gopher.genie.com/11/magazines/romex>

GEnie Romance Writers' Newsletter is flat-out fabulous. The first issue of Volume 4 (January 1996), for example, includes Michele Wyan's "Self-Inventory and Writing Goals Worksheet" — a thoughtful, useful checklist from which all writers can profit. The issue also offers the transcript of a really fascinating talk, "Covers, Blurbs, Shoutlines: the Editorial Process," by two representatives from Harlequin on how they work with authors to create their covers. The September 1996 issue features a 500-word confession about dropping a novel to accept a publisher's invitation to write a series that reads like some sinister horror story. The site also offers reviews of romance writing, and archives of software applications, such as schedulers and word processing programs for teleplays.

The Literary Times
<http://www.tlt.com>

The Web version is a good companion to this romance periodical, begun ten years ago as the newsletter for the writer's support group, The Literary Connection. It furnishes manuscript critiquing, how-to articles from authors and editors, industry gossip ("Embracing the News"), readers' letters, and a rich jumpstation of links to such resources as research, promotional aids, booksellers and distributors, and women's issues.

For more online outlets, see Chapter 15, "Net Magazines."

PUBLISHERS

Bantam/Dell/Doubleday, Isn't It Romantic
<http://www.bdd.com/romance>

Genesis Press
<http://www.colom.com/genesis/index.shtml>

Harlequin/Silhouette Publishers
<http://www.romance.net/>

Includes guidelines.

Red Sage Publishers
<http://www.freenet.mb.ca/iphome/r/reidpage/redsage.html>

Includes guidelines.

Soda Creek Press
<http://www.sodacreekpress.com/>

Publishes *Manderley*, a catalog of 800 titles for readers, plus *Romance Reader's and Writer's Guides*.

REVIEWS

Romance writing accounts for forty-nine percent of all pocketbook sales (about 175 million books a year). Yet daily newspapers, Sunday book review supplements, and other major outlets for discussion of books still treat the romance genre as a second-class citizen — much the way mystery and science-fiction were treated twenty years ago — and review it only rarely.

Now readers can turn to the Internet to find the latest in unbiased, professionally written news and reviews. Here are some outlets where your review might get published, or your book might be reviewed (pre- or post-publication).

CompuServe Romance Reviews (CRR)

A new program started in the Romance Forum. You don't have to be a member of CompuServe, however, to have your writing reviewed. Not only is the author free to use quotes from the review in promotional material and on book jackets, but the review is posted in the libraries of both the Romance Forum and Book Preview Forum on CompuServe.

Contact Katt Bragg, <KBragg@aol,com> or <75150.1665@compuserve.com>.

The Romance Reader
<http://www.dallas.net/~rreader>

An online magazine of unbiased reviews.

Romance Readers' Corner
<http://www.quake.net/~autopen/Romance.html>

Has a generous selection of excerpts from books, articles by writers, and reviews, with navigation by subgenre.

Romantic Notions
<http://wwide.com/rnotions.html>.

Reviews books and interviews authors, with emphasis on time travel or other fantasy romance.

SLAKE
<http://www.slake.com>

Quotes, reviews, and information about books and authors, for "obsessed romance novel readers."

Under the Covers
<http://www.silcom/com/~manatee/utc.html>

AUTHORS' HOME PAGES

Romance Authors Page
<http://www.nettrends.com/romanceauthors>

Romance Novelists Author's pages
<http://www.comet.chv.va.us/writerhp.htm>

Designed by Comet.Net.

The Write Page
<http://www.writepage.com/romance.htm>

MISCELLANEOUS

Here are some signposts in the meadow which the romance writer or reader will encounter while roaming the Net.

Castle Aphrodesia
<http://lcopt.physics.fsu.edu/Local/thad/conroy/aphrodesia.html>

Medieval romance.

From the Heart
<http://www.wbm.ca/users/kgreggai/html/heart.html/>

Love poems and love letters from real people.

Gothic Journal
<http://www.visi.com/romance>

Historical Library
<http://www.idbsu.edu/courses/hy101/library.htm>

Europe from ancient Greece through the seventeenth century.

Market Guidelines
<http://pooh.freenet.mb.ca/iphome/r/reidpage/guides.html>

Mako's Angel
<http://ourworld.compuserve.com/homepages/smako/makoangl.htm>

Suzette L. Mako bestows a monthly Angel award for excellence in presenting romance on the Web.

The Official Page of the Hopelessly Romantic
<http://www.primenet.com/~ejones/hrhome.html>

Rawhide & Lace
<http://www.writepage.com/lace1.htm>

The newsletter about women of the wild west. (Reviewers are usually needed for historical romance, historical fiction, westerns, American romance, nonfiction regarding the West, and contemporaries with a rural or ranch setting.)

The Romance Novelist's Home Page
Resources for Romance Writers
<http://www.comet.chv.va.us/writerhp.htm>
<http://www.comet.net/writersr/romance.htm>

MEGASOURCE JUMPSTATIONS

A Reader's Guide to Romance & Women's Fiction
<http://www.netforward.com/poboxes/?ReadersGuide>

A Reader's Guide to Romance & Women's Fiction has hyperlinks to authors, reviews, and groups.

Reid's Page for Writers
<http://www.freenet.mb.ca/iphome/r/reidpage/romance.html>

Joanne Reid has organized an extensive array of valuable information on romance writing, including writing guidelines (by Alicia Rasley and Pat Collinge), writers' markets, newletters, and research, as well as other megasources.

The Romance Pages
<http://comet.net/writers>

The strength of The Romance Pages is in providing resources that romance writers (and other writers) will find helpful in researching their novels: history sources, libraries, museums, genealogy, and other reference topics. Links are also offered to author home pages, books, and other Web resources.

Romance Writers of America (RWA)
<http://www.rwanational.com/>

Romance Writers of America (RWA) currently has eight affiliates with Web sites, each bringing something different to the table. The parent site also hosts authors' home pages, a guide for booksellers, and other links.

Romancing the Web
<http://www.romanceweb.com/>

Romancing the Web (RTW) specializes in creating Web pages for romance authors. Whether or not that's your bag, you might be interested in the free services they offer for both authors and readers: online publications, industry contacts, services for writers, online romance readers' forums, a bookstore, and more. They're also building a library of links to writing materials (how-to) and research resources (historical, contemporary, fantasy, paranormal, futuristic). They publish a newsletter; contributors are welcome.

Resources for Romance Writers
<http://www.interlog.com/~ohi/www/romance.html>

Resources for Romance Writers is part of the WWW Virtual Library megadirectory of links. Especially helpful are the market guidelines, forums, and newsletters.

The Write Page
<http://www.writepage.com/romance.htm>

The Write Page covers every genre, including romance.

* * *

In short, the range of romance writers' resources on the Internet is as far-reaching as are the subcategories of the romance genre itself — American and Canadian west, British, countryside, Georgian, Gothic, pirates and swashbucklers, Victorian, and so on. Given such genre crossovers as romantic suspense, it's a mere stone's throw from the romance of a foggy night . . . to its mystery.

5

Net Mystery Writers

To many writers, the Internet itself is a complete mystery. But Net writers will learn the terrain the way James M. Cain and Raymond Chandler learned old Los Angeles. The Internet abounds with cafés where you can puzzle over clues with other mystery writers, and dark alleys down which to pursue your suspect.

Perhaps no other genre requires as much research as does mystery — from the intricacies of lock-picking to the minutiae of historical accuracy and the convolutions of the legal system. And research is one of the most fruitful uses of the Net. (See also Chapter 14, "Net Research.")

In this chapter, you'll learn about forums (for exchanging correspondence with others in the field), magazines and newsletters (sharing business news), bookstores (for your reading pleasure or to promote your book), book publishers (some you might never have heard of before), authors' home pages (perhaps yours one day), and megasource jumpstations.

You'll also find miscellaneous way stations for specialty items. As the mystery field shades out into many subgenres — cozy, hard-boiled, procedural, senior sleuth, suspense/thriller, true crime, Victorian, and female detective — the Internet zeroes in on any interest level. The closer we look, the greater the variety we find. Now you'll never be clueless.

FORUMS

Usenet has such groups as rec.arts.mystery, alt.pulp, and alt.fan.holmes. Mailing lists include DorothyL, Gaslight, Mystery, Shortmystery-L, and the Convention Connection.

DorothyL

A large mailing list about all aspects of mysteries, leaning, however, toward the cozy end of the mystery spectrum. For more information, e-mail <listserv@kentvm.kent.edu> with the message "get dorothyl welcome f=mail". A list of home pages created by members is also available.

The Convention Connection

Brings together fans, writers, editors, literary agents, and convention planners. To subscribe, e-mail <majordomo@teleport.com> with the message "subscribe con-con-l-digest".

Gaslight

A mailing list devoted to early crime fiction. A list of home pages created by members is also available. For more information, e-mail <mailserv@mtroyal.ab.ca> with the message "help".

Mystery

A mailing list focused on reviews. To subscribe, e-mail <mystery-request@lunch.engr.sgi.com> with the message "subscribe mystery" — or "subscribe mystery-digest" if you prefer the digest version.

Shortmystery-L

For readers and writers of short mystery fiction. To subscribe, e-mail <majordomo@teleport.com> with the message "subscribe shortmystery-l-digest".

The Internet Crimewriting Network
<http://Crimewriters.com/Crime/>

An expanding, semicommercial site that has kept five of its areas free: the Bullet-In Board, the Squad Room Chat Lounge, the Crimewriter's Directory, the Consultants and Reference Center, and the Little Shop of Crime boutique. The rest is now available as a members-only inner sanctum, for $39.95 per year. The site offers a $29.95/year rate for members of the Writers Guild of America (East, West, and all associated Guilds), Mystery Writers of America, Sisters in Crime, the Writer's Connection, and Women in Film.

These member-only areas include: a Q&A desk, the Interrogation Room, regarding crime, law, crisis intervention, private investigation, screenwriting, and more, all staffed by informed specialists; Courtroom, with new laws, courtroom techniques, and articles by trial attorneys; extensive law enforcement contacts; Facts on File; Crimespeak Glossary; a Literary Marketplace; and a classified section called Wanted!

MAGAZINES AND NEWSLETTERS

The Armchair Detective
<http://www.booksellers.com/armchair_detective>

Dead Write
<http://www.iceonline.net/home/whidwarf/webpage.html>

Friends of Mystery Newsletter
<http://www.teleport.com/~cedarbay/fom.html>

Includes interviews with authors and how-to tips.

Magnifying Glass Mystery Newsletter
<http://emporium.turnpike.net/~mystery/tmg.html>

Monthly news about awards, bookstores, catalogs, conventions, writers' conferences, special events, and more.

Murderous Intent
<http://www.teleport.com/~madison/>

Mystery/suspense fiction and nonfiction.

Mysterious Bytes
<http://www.db.dk/dbaa/jbs/mystbyte.htm>

Studies of mysteries and related subjects.

Mystery Readers Journal
<http://www.slip.net/~whodunit/MRJ.html>

A fine quarterly, with thematic issues — British regional mysteries, San Francisco, gay and lesbian detectives, art mysteries, senior sleuths.

The Mystery Zone
<http://www.mindspring.com/~walter/mystzone.html>

A venerable newsletter/magazine of mystery, suspense, and crime fiction, featuring interviews, reviews, and links to other resources.

Over My Dead Body
<http://emporium.turnpike.net/~mystery/omdb.htm>

A magazine and BBS.

Scandinavian Mystery News
<http://www.db.dk/dbaa/jbs/scannews.htm>

For more online outlets, see Chapter 15, "Net Magazines."

BOOKSTORES

If you're looking for a special mystery, or are marketing your own, you can find dozens of mystery bookshops online.

Book Links
<http://freenet.vcu.edu/education/literature/mystbkstores.html>

Book Links can take you to many bookstores, including Black Bird Mysteries, Bloody Dagger, Booked for Murder, Dead Write Books, It's A Mystery, Janus Books, Murder By The Book, Mystery One Snoop Sisters, Partners in Crime, Poisoned Pen, Secret Staircase, The Space-Crime Continuum, and Tangled Web Online Book Shop.

PUBLISHERS

Intrigue Press
<http://www.intriguepress.com/mystery>

Mysterious Press
<http://pathfinder.com/@@igfFiAYAeUqGLXOr/twep/mysterious_press/>

The Pocket Crime Series (Australia)
<http://users.hunterlink.net.au/~ddslp>

St. Martin's Press
<http://freenet.vcu.edu/education/literature/stmartins.html>

AUTHORS' HOME PAGES

Classic Mystery Authors
<http://members.gnn.com/MGrost/alphlist.htm>

Lists over 350 names old and new.

The Mysterious Page
<http://users.aol.com/bchrcon97/mysteris.htm>

A megasite with one of the best indexes around for author's pages, including detectives too.

Personal Mystery Home Pages
<http://www.db.dk/dbaa/jbs/pershome.htm>

Indexes pages of about fifty contemporary authors and their books.

MISCELLANEOUS

The Case
<http://www.thecase.com/>

Three challenging and fun weekly mysteries: A "Twist" surprise ending, a "Solve-it" mini-mystery, and a "Mysterious Photo" inviting a caption.

The Gumshoe Site
<http://www.nsknet.or.jp/~jkimura/>

A Guide to Classic Mystery and Detection
<http://members.gnn.com/MGrost/classics.htm>

With more than 300 reviews.

Investigative Database
<http://world.std.com/~mmoore>

Organized crime, white-collar crime, corruption, fraud, finance, politics, and government; free search, $25 fee if name is found.

Mayhem
<http://www.sound.net/~fiskem3/index.html>

A mystery fiction guide.

Mystery Corner
<http://www.quake.net/~autopen/Mystery.html>

Includes investigators throughout history.

The Mystery Page
<http://freenet.vcu.edu/education/literature/mystpage.html>

Features organizations, awards, publications, and bookstores.

The Softer Side of Murder
<http://www.quake.net/~autopen/Mystery.html>

Accent on female detectives, historical mysteries, "softboiled," and so on.

Tangled Web
<http://www.thenet.co.uk/~hickafric/tangled-web.html>

British site providing Tools of the Crime Fiction Trade section, links to authors' home pages and other sites devoted to authors and their alter egos, bibliographies, and more.

MEGASOURCE JUMPSTATIONS

The Internet Crimewriting Network, mentioned earlier in this chapter under "Forums," is a jumpstation of resources. Here are four more:

ClueLass
<http://www.slip.net/~cluelass/>

"ClueLass" is the online pseudonym for Kate Derie, a writer who lives in Berkeley with her husband and Bernese mountain dog. When not surfing the Net or writing a monthly column for the Mystery Writers of America national newsletter, *The Third Degree*, she's hard at work on her first novel, *Deathstyles of the Rich and Famous*.

While using the Net to do research for her own projects, Kate picks up clues for her own Web site. ClueLass touches on many pertinent areas, including awards; a BookNet for booksellers, publishers, and electronic texts; a Café for prepublished writers, who discuss such topics as agents, rewrites, marketing, and characterization; events listings (conferences, conventions, classes); links to groups, of both writers and fans; obituaries; opportunities for unlocking the doors to success as a mystery writer; a pulpit for published writers to engage in blatant self-promotion; new releases for the mystery shelf; and much, much more. Browsing ClueLass text-only really doesn't do it justice, given the ingenuity of the graphic layout. To view forensics links, click on a computer being stabbed. To shoot to the bottom of the page, click on a gun.

The Mysterious Page
<http://www.db.dk/dbaa/jbs/homepage.htm> or
<http://users.aol.com/bchrcon97/mysteris.htm>

ClueLass is a definite "keeper," but the Mysterious Page wins the *writers.net* "Gold Dustbuster Award for Exhaustive Detail in a Genre Fan Site." It's the labor of love of Jan B. Steffensen, Associate Professor at the Royal Librarian School, Aalborg, Denmark, as a supreme tribute. Since following Sherlock and Moriarty across the moors in *The Hound of the Baskervilles*, the first book in English he ever read, he's collected over five thousand mysteries, plus a large reference collection. Thanks to his fascination, other mystery lovers will now know where to find mystery materials on the Internet; the Mysterious Page currently provides twenty-three screenfuls of links.

Jan begins with links to forums and then moves on to links to other Web sites. Then the site delves deeper, linking to a dozen or so authors (bibliographies, reviews, short stories, quotes, or official/unofficial home pages), from Ernest Bramah to Kinky Friedman, and a half-dozen characters (for example, Nancy Drew, Rumpole, 007, Nero Wolfe, Spenser). Then come publishers; booksellers (fifteen), both real and virtual; magazines, both paper (seven) and electronic (seven); film and TV links,

MYSTERY WRITERS' TOOLS

Links to topics like forensics, security systems, even mortuaries are an important asset for mystery writers. Perhaps far more than in other genres, the mystery writer must rely on a wealth of background research, usually secondhand unless he or she has also worked in the field. While the Internet may not bring a bail bondsman or a mortician to your studio for a live interview, it will put a wide array of sources at your fingertips.

TOOLCHEST

by Kate Derie, a.k.a. ClueLass (from the Mystery Writer's Internet Toollchest)

CopNet
<http://police.sas.ab.ca/>

Links to police departments and law enforcement agencies.

Zeno's Forensics Page
<http://www.bart.nl/~geradts/forensic.html>

Dozens of sources of forensic and criminalist information.

U.S. Fish & Wildlife Service Forensics Lab
<http://ash.lab.r1.fws.gov/labweb/for-lab.htm>

A fascinating look at the world's only crime lab dedicated to the animal kingdom.

Internet Crimewriting Network
<http://Crimewriters.com/Crime/>

Answers to crimewriting questions from an advisory panel of experts.

Twists, Slugs, and Roscoes — a Glossary of Hardboiled Slang
<http://www.io.org/~buff/slang.html>

Argot from the Golden Age of Pulp Fiction, compiled by William Denton.

Rec.Guns FAQ
<http://www.teleport.com/~dputzolu/RecGuns.html>

Leads to technical and consumer information about firearms; high political noise-to-information ratio.

Yahoo's index to security companies
<http://www.yahoo.com/Business_and_Economy/Companies/Security/>

Offers links to all kinds of security-related gizmos and gadgets, as well as private investigators.

Guide to Lock Picking, by Ted the Tool
<http://www.lysator.liu.se/mit-guide/mit-guide.html>

Includes a thought-provoking ethical discussion from the MIT hacking community.

alt.law-enforcement

LEOs chat about traffic stops, drug busts, and cops in the news; polite procedural questions generally get polite answers at this Usenet newsgroup.

---

including Hitchcock and an *X-Files* page, as well as BBC and PBS; Sherlockiana (twenty-two entries); electronic books and texts (including Sherlock, Poe, and Bierce); and even interactive mystery games (ten), including *Night*, a murder mystery told and solved entirely through pictures with hypertext visual links; plus practically everything else, from vintage postcards to a FAQ file on *The Maltese Falcon*.

Mystery Connection
<http://emporium.turnpike.net/~mystery/index.html>

This mini-megasource is largely event-driven, with news of book signings, conventions, writers' conferences, and other murder mystery activities. It is also the site for the *Magnifying Glass Mystery Newsletter* and *Over My Dead Body!*, the magazine and the forum.

WWW Virtual Library — Mysteries
<http://www.interlog.com/~ohi/www/mystery.html>

Besides general links and links to other jumpstations, the WWW Virtual Library has links to mystery periodicals, associations, and bookstores, as well as to groups, workshops, and conventions.

Meanwhile — mystery, itself, still remains.

* * *

Yet another breed of writer is taking to the networks. Just as poets these days use word processors and phones and faxes, they're taking to the Internet, making the Voice of the Bard heard . . . online.

6

Net Poets

If you think about Winesburg, Ohio, *with people literally running naked down the streets for want of a way to express an inner life, you realize that people today can find a way to such expression. There are over 1,000 books of poetry published a year now; that's three a day. And there are hundreds of magazines on the Internet.*

—Robert Hass

America is taking notice of poetry, from open-mike readings in church basements, to Bill Moyers' *Language of Life* TV-series featuring thirty-four diverse poets, to the surprise-hit Italian film *Il Postino* (The Postman). Many people on the Internet are turning to poetry as a way of finding their balance after plugging away in the oft-giddy realm of computers.

For working poets, the Internet multiplies the available options. From the Nebraska Center for Writers to the Naropa Institute's Poetics Program; from contemporary Sufi poetry to interactive stream-of-consciousness poetry; from aviation poets to telepoetics video conferencing; and from haiku to slams, the voices of the muse and the bard are now online. If poets are, indeed, the antennae of the species, then it's no surprise to find them right at home on the front lines of the Internet.

In this chapter you'll learn how poets are using the Net to critique writing, publish work, find keypals, and keep up-to-date. You'll also learn about some new formats and venues for poetry that arise from the unique nature of the Internet.

FORUMS AND ONLINE CRITIQUES

The Usenet site for poetry is rec.arts.poems, known as RAP, and people who post there often call themselves "rappers." People post poems, critique each other's work, call for submissions, and just chitchat. In early 1996, RAP, led by poet Tim Patterson, created a highly informative FAQ; it explains both the rules of the group and the rules of poetry. For example, in its growing dictionary of poetic terms, the definitions of limerick and haiku are hyperlinked to Internet sites specializing in those forms. You can also find a directory of poems that are quoted in movies, consult a small bibliography of books about poetry, learn how to search for poems and poets via the Net as well as in traditional library references, and locate previous posts and members' works on the Web. In progress is a list of e-zines that publish poetry.

The Web, too, abounds in poetry. Here are some representative sites:

Albany Poetry Workshop
<http://condor.lpl.arizona.edu/~tim/rapfaq.html>

An educational, inspirational poetry workshop that accepts submissions for review and critique.

Byron Poetry Server
<http://www.sonic.net:80/web/albany/workshop/>

A showcase for original poetry. Submit original works or read and comment on others' poems. Favorite poems by known authors are also accepted.

The Poems Gallery
<http://rama.poly.edu:1800/poem/index.html>

Encourages you to publish your poems in any language and criticize others.

The Poet's Workshop
<http://cac.psu.edu/~dmp137/makar.html>

An interactive complex where poets and lovers of poetry can congregate, share their poetry with one another, have their work critiqued by others, and critique others' work. It is also a warehouse of information for poets wanting to publish on the Internet. Any day is "Poet's Workshop Day." Membership is free.

The site is laid out with an architectural metaphor: The Front Desk explains the setup, poems on the workbench are at the Shop, finished work is displayed at the Showroom, Internet publication opportunities are listed at the Library, and poets gather and network at the Café.

Wr-Eye-Tings

This is a mailing list for discussion of concrete/visual, sound, and performance poetry. To subscribe, e-mail <majordomo@sfu.ca> with the message "subscribe wr-eye-tings@sfu.ca".

Yahoo! — Poetry Forums
<///www.yahoo.com/Arts/Humanities/Literature/Genres/Poetry/Writing/Online_Forums/>

Links to about twenty other online forums for critiquing poetry.

MAGAZINES

When you publish your work on the Net, it can reach a larger audience because of extensive distribution and the archiving of back issues. So what are you waiting for? Check out these magazines and when you find any you like, drop them an "e." (Additional sites are described in Chapter 15, "Net Magazines.")

Adam's Poetry Page
<http://www.primenet.com/~ebola/poetpage/poetry.html>

A facility where authors can exchange their poetry without giving away the rights to their work.

Asian Poets' Page
<http://pantheon.cis.yale.edu/~skyjuice/poempg.html>

Avec
<http://www.crl.com/~creiner/syntax/avec.html>

A magazine of innovative and language-oriented poetry, prose, and translations; *Avec* also publishes books. Samples are online, as are a few pages of some cool links.

Best-Quality Audio Web Poems (BAWP)
<http://www.cs.brown.edu/fun/bawp/>

Breakfast Surreal
<http://www.indirect.com/user/warren/surreal.html>

This site pushed the definition of "magazine" a bit farther; a magazine collection of links to poetry on other people's home pages: sonnets and dissonnets, lyrics, electronic chapbooks in progress, haiku under the influence of UNIX, poems with imbedded multi-user commands, and links to other poetry magazines. Though editor/publisher/Webmaster Warren S. Apel pulled the plug on it, the links are still there.

Grist
<http://www.thing.net/~grist>

Having edited one of the best poetry magazines of the sixties, John Fowler made the leap to the electronic realm in 1993. His site now has a treasure chest of books (e.g., *Light & Dust*, *Linguablanca Electronic Chapbooks*), and magazines (e.g., *Glossolalia Electronic Journal for Experimental Arts*, *Room Temperature*), and his list of cool links is *nonpareil*.

Hootenanny
<http://wweb.syr.edu/~drkeith/hootenanny.html>

A hootenanny is a gathering at which folksingers entertain, and the audience joins in. Born of a running dialogue between the editors — a painter and a writer — this forum is an open invitation to anyone who might offer some contribution regarding art, writing, life, and the construction of meaning. By 1999, the publishing venture will have produced ten books, which will mark the conclusion of their ongoing discussion. *Hootenanny* — a magazine printed twice a year in New York City in limited editions and sold at places like art museum bookstores — may seem an unlikely candidate for an online adjunct. Yet the online version nicely carries on the dialogue of the magazine's editors, authors, and artists, after its own fashion. They accept unpublished fiction, poetry, and essays via e-mail.

isibongo
<http://www.uct.ac.za/projects/poetry/isibongo/isibongo.htm>

A gorgeous poetry Webzine from South Africa.

Lingo
<http://hardpress.com/newhp/lingo/lingo.html>

A leading-edge collaborative, multimedia magazine, publishing established and emerging literary, visual, musical, and theatrical artists. Poetry Editor is Susan Levin.

The Occasional Screenful

An edited daily magazine featuring one original, short, rhymed, metered poem every few days. Readership is currently 1,550 or so. To subscribe, e-mail <listserv@netcom.com> with only the message "subscribe occasional-screenful".

OZ Poetry Page
<http://www.wavenet.com/~infinite/>

Focuses on technique and structure in an effort to push the limits of what is considered poetry.

The Poetry Exchange
<http://poetryx.guinet.com/>

The exchange lets you set up your own poetry home page. It accepts non-English poetry, and now supports forms to get your poems online faster. There are also links to other poetry sites (Children Churches & Daddies, Oyster Boy Review, Albany Poetry Workshop, and others).

Real Poetik
<http://www.wln.com/~salasin/rp.html>

This is a magazine via mailing list (1,200 subscribers), plus a Web site, publishing since 1993. (Print out only the poems you like — in the typeface of your choice.) Their editorial staff is helmed by poets and writers, and they accept submissions in hard copy, or online to <rpoetic@listserv.win.com>. To subscribe, e-mail <listserv@listserv.win.com> with the message: "subscribe rpoetik *Your Full Name*".

SomePIG
<http://virtu.sar.usf.edu/~zazuetaa/SomePig.html>

This "poezine" is an interesting and varied source of poetry. You never know where the next link may lead you. Submissions are accepted.

JStarr's Poetry Forum
<http://www.wolfenet.com/~jstarr/poetry>

Open to poetry from all walks of life and levels of accomplishment. There is a featured poet each week. Poets published can get their own poetry page on the Web (with a choice of several backgrounds).

Stars in the Night
<http://www.travel-net.com/~cygnus/others.html>

Almost a hundred poets are published here and new work is always welcome. A place for quiet reflection.

Sudden
<http://eng.hss.cmu.edu/sudden/>

A triennial online publication of Carnegie Mellon University (CMU). "We want poetry that moves us, language that speaks to personal experience. The poems we publish have to affect us in a way that makes us and our readers think in our own writing and lives. No children's, nature, religious, or sentimental poetry."

THUNDER (THe UNstoppable DreamERs)
<http://www.uni.edu/pirill44/th/>

A new poetry place on the WEB. It accepts either e-mail or hypertext forms.

Web Poetry Corner
<http://www.dreamagic.com/poetry/poetry.html>

The place where poets of all types meet and display their stuff. All submissions are considered for inclusion.

PUBLISHERS

Thanks to advances in desktop and Webtop publishing, small poetry publishers are now augmenting their handset, crab, or proof presses with digital tools. As described in Chapter 17, digital printing now makes short runs — a staple of poetry publishing — more affordable.

Here are several electronic catalogues and small publishers with e-mail addresses and a Web presence.

Above Ground Press
<http://www.undergrad.math.uwaterloo.ca/~nhenness/aboveground.html>

Chapped Lips
<http://www.undergrad.math.uwaterloo.ca/~nhenness/chaplips.html>

HardPress
<http://www.hardpress.com>

Poetic Immolation Press
<http://www.undergrad.math.uwaterloo.ca/~nhenness/pip.html>

A Small Garlic Press
<http://www.enteract.com/~marek/asgp/chaptext.html>

Publishes short-run chapbooks and an online magazine, *Agnieszka's Dowry*.

TapRoot's Electronic Edition (TREE)
<http://wings.buffalo.edu/epc/ezines/treehome/chapdir.html>

Reviews chapbooks.

Yoohoo Inc.
<http://www.virtualforum.com/yoohoo/>

Fine Press Bookshop Online
<http://www.tdigital.com/finepress/>

Truepenny Books maintains a megasource jumpstation that guides you to publishers of fine, letterpress edition books, from Abbattoir to Yolla Bolly. They also include information on how you can list your press.

POETS' HOME PAGES

The Academy of American Poets
<http://www.artswire.org/poets/page.html>

Provides a jumpstation of links to the pages of Maya Angelou, Joseph Brodsky, e.e. cummings, Emily Dickinson, T.S. Eliot, Robert Frost, Audre Lorde, Sylvia Plath, Anne Sexton, and Walt Whitman.

Bengali Poetry
<http://gl.umbc.edu/~achatt1/poem.html>

Rabindranath Tagore, Sankha Ghosh, Jibanananda Das, and others.

British Poetry, 1780–1910
<http://etext.lib.virginia.edu/britpo.html/>

A substantial collection of Romantics, plus ancient English poems such as *Beowulf*.

The English Server at Carnegie Mellon University
<http://english-server.hss.cmu.edu/poetry.html/>

A large collection of poetry, including work by Maya Angelou, W.S. Auden, e.e. cummings, Henry Rollins, and S.T. Coleridge.

Incognito Cafe
<http://www.jaffe-soeder.com/poets.htm/>

Links from classical (Burns, Chaucer) to contemporary (Bromige, Rollins).

Internet Poetry Archive (IPA)
<http://sunsite.unc.edu/dykki/poetry/home.html>

A trailblazer in multimedia poetry, this site added the nuanced working-class lilt of Philip Levine's speaking voice, Seamus Heaney's brogue, and the indomitable humanist exhortations of Czeslaw Milosz to their work, via online audio. The project has been on hold following this initial, groundbreaking unit.

Poets of South Africa's Western Cape
<http://www.uct.ac.za/projects/poetry>

A collection of about four dozen poets, one of the many must-see features of the University of Cape Town Poetry Web.

MISCELLANEOUS

20 Consonant Poetry
<http://www.au.com/ammx/20cp.html/>

Simple rules create beautiful confusion. Use all twenty consonants (bcdfghjklmnpqrstvwxz) at least once in each sentence. Do not repeat consonants except when repeating one consonant uninterrupted by other consonants (for instance, the fragment "bunnies suck Kool-Aide dope"). Use vowels freely.

National Poetry Month (April)
<http://www.poetry.books.com/>

A year-round home page, thanks to Book Stacks Unlimited.

The Poetry Reading Room
<http://www.coolsite.com/poetry.html/>

A compilation of poems from the Net. You view them, one at a time, according to their order, not your choice.

Poets' Corner
<http://www.lexmark.com/data/poem/poem.html/>

An anthology of poetry, alphabetical by author, from Conrad Aiken, Matthew Arnold, Margaret Atwood, and W.H. Auden to Richard Wilbur, William Carlos Williams, William Wordsworth, and W.B. Yeats. (Note: this is one of about a half-dozen different sites called "Poetry Corner.")

Slams
<http://www.primenet.com/~mychele/slams.html/>

In case you haven't heard, slams are sweeping the nation. Slam poetry is a style that emerges out of poetry slams — competitions of original performance poetry with judges picked from the audience. After three rounds, the poet with the highest score (Olympic-style) wins. One megasource jumpstation is Poetry Slams!, with archives of annual national slams. Official slam news, monthly online slam contests, and links to slam scenes around the continent.

Voice of the Prisoner
<http://clickshop.com/prisoner/prisoner.tam>

Art, poetry, and letters created by people behind bars.

The Web Poetry Kit
<http://www.best.com/~jnc/cd>

Lets you build your own computer-generated poetry with twenty pull-down menus containing 100 words and parts of words. You can read what others have composed with them, or compose and post your own.

MEGASOURCE JUMPSTATIONS

The Academy of American Poets
<http://www.artswire.org/poets/page.html>

This home page furnishes a fine jumpstation of links to awards and prizes, readings and residencies, bookstores, poets, and the like.

Electronic Poetry Center (EPC)
<http://wings.buffalo.edu/epc>

The Internet's hub for new poetry is based geographically in Buffalo, New York. Besides its own activities in poetics and poetry, its searchable home page links to a vast array of poetry sites.

The Haiku Server
<http://cc.matsuyama-u.ac.jp/~shiki/>

Located in Japan, this is Internet central for the shortest form of literature (one-breath long), with many links to haiku sites, such as the superfine online haiku magazine, *Dogwood Blossoms*.

The National Poetry Association
<http://www.slip.net/~gamuse>

The oldest all-volunteer literary arts association in Northern America remains a font of vitality. Their jazzy Web site links to their various projects — Poetry Film Workshop, Café Arts, *Poetry USA*, *Mother Earth International*, and The Living Word — and to a poetry Disneyland of links for Websurfers.

Poems-Poetry-Poets
<http://www.execpc.com/~jon/index.html/>

Following an in-depth study of one poet, you'll find a wealth of poetry links here.

Poetry Web Spotlight
<www.uct.ac.za/projects/poetry/wwwtous.htm>

A megasource jumpstation of fine resources — about half of them from South Africa, owing to the site's origin at the University of Cape Town.

San Francisco State University (SFSU) Poetry Center
<http://www.sfsu.edu/~newlit/links.htm>

One of the best poetry megasource jumpstations around.

Writers Resource
<http://www.azstarnet.com/~poewar/writer/writer.html/>

John Hewitt has posted a number of excellent articles, such as "Poetry Writing Tips" and "Son of Poetry Tips."

WWW Virtual Library Resources for Poets
<http://www.interlog.com/~ohi/www/poetry.html/>

Yahoo! — Poetry
<http://www.yahoo.com/Arts/Humanities/Literature/Genres/Poetry/>

Zero City
<http://gate.cruzio.com/~zerocity/zcpoetry.html>

"Ground zero for explosive poetry" has a Small Press Bulletin Board profiling a few dozen worthy magazines and chapbooks with hyperlinked e-mail addresses. They also have a long list of links to all kinds of poetry and poets. (And Zero City also publishes original, gritty, Web poetry broadsides and a print.)

* * *

If poetry is tested by its truth, sincerity, grace, beauty, and naïveté, then the best poets around may well be kids.

Many of them are unbeatable poets, themselves. Perhaps it's because they imagine in their own mind's eye every word, ringing clear and true as a bell.

In the next chapter, then, are some resources for those who work in this grandest of genres.

7

Net Children's Writers

You have to write the book that wants to be written. And if that book will be too difficult for grown-ups, then you write it for children.
—Madeleine L'Engle

Since the mid-eighties, children's literature has been one of the few thriving areas of the publishing industry. Some of the projects on the Internet with the most "sizzle" are those in K-12 (kindergarten through twelfth grade). Here the guiding principle is not to use the Internet to do old things differently, but to do new things. Teachers and students around the world are networking and teaching each other about just-in-time, self-paced, peer-based learning. ("Just-in-time" means it's there when you want it; "self-paced" means the students go as fast or as slow, and as often, as they like; "peer-based" means students learn from each other — the teacher goes from being "the sage on the stage to the guide on the side.")

In this chapter you'll learn about Internet resources for children's writers, including: forums (for exchanging correspondence with others in the field), personalized literature, books and magazines (for your reading pleasure or to promote your work), resources for kids by kids (where you can learn more about, and from, your audience), book publishers, authors' home pages, and megasource jumpstations.

FORUMS

The main Usenet newsgroup for children's writing is rec.arts.books.childrens, where people discuss current books, awards, and writing.

The Children's Writing Mailing List

An unmoderated exchange for writers, illustrators, and publishing professionals. To join, e-mail <majordomo@lists.mindspring.com> with "subscribe childrens-writing" or "subscribe childrens-writing-digest" in the message.

PERSONALIZED LITERATURE

The Internet adds special magic to the children's genre through the medium of personalized literature — stories with the young reader written into them. Like a personalized greeting card, a personalized story names the reader by name and makes them a main character.

Yahoo! — Personalized Children's Literature
<http://www.yahoo.com/Business_and_Economy/Companies/Books/Childrens/Personalized>

Has links to about two dozen sites that specialize in personalized children's literature.

BOOKS AND MAGAZINES

The Children's Book Council
<http://www.cbcbooks.org>

Provides a page of links to children's book publishers.

Children's Publishers & Booksellers on the Net
<http://www.ucalgary.ca/~dkbrown/publish.html>

Furnishes catalogs and news direct from the publishers.

Stone Soup Magazine
<http://www.stonesoup.com>

Yahoo's Guide to Children's Books
<http://www.yahoo.com/Business/Products_and_Services/Books/Children>

FOR KIDS BY KIDS

Children's literature is traditionally thought of as "by adults, for children." *Stone Soup* magazine shifted that paradigm in 1973 by publishing writing by children. No longer are kids' writings and art reserved for display only on their parents' refrigerators. Here are some of the resources that carry this new kind of kids' lit.

Banyan Tree Friends
<http://sashimi.wwa.com/~uschwarz/poetry/btf000.html>

Dozens of fine poems written by elementary school students.

Center for Talented Youth at Johns Hopkins University
<http://jhunix.hcf.jhu.edu/~ewt2/>

CyberTeens
<http://www.mtlake.com/cyberteens/>

Art, writings, puzzles, games, and links for teenagers by teenagers.

KidPub
<http://escrime-engarde.com/kidpub>

Accepts kids' work via e-mail directly from the Web site.

Kidworld
<http://www.bconnex.net/~kidworld/>

A meeting place where kids under sixteen can share their artwork and writing (stories, jokes, ideas, and letters) with other kids, for education and global understanding; underwritten by Tandem House.

The Little Planet Times
<http://www.littleplanet.com>

An interactive online newspaper for kids, by kids, that promotes reading, writing, and communication skills for Kindergarten through fifth grade.

Scriptito's Place
<http://cl.k12.md.us/RES/Text/WRITING.HTML>
<http://members.aol.com/vangarnews/scriptito.html>

A creative writing resource center to inspire creative writers age seven through fifteen, and to provide a place to publish their creative work.

Teen Writers
<http://www.teenwriters.org>

Publishes stories and poems; provides resources and discussion for teen writers.

Urchin Reefs
<http://www.geocities.com/athens/4770>

A modest-sized literary endeavor devoted to stories and poems of young writers.

WebKids
<http://www.hoofbeats.com>

Invites kids to join others in writing adventure stories.

ADULT AUTHORS' HOME PAGES

Silly Billy Page
<http://www.sillybilly.com>

Author/illustrator/teacher Bill Dallas Lewis maintains this site, where you can read (and buy) Bill's work and find out about his tour schedule. He adds value with links for teaching, a tutorial on computer art, and a killer writing project, "How To Write a Real Book," for students and teachers.

Bruce Balan
<http://www.hooked.net/users/balan/">

Kids' writer Bruce Balan makes the most of the Web by putting his office online. You'll find his file cabinet, books he's written, his calendar (in case you want to invite him to your school), and some poems.

MISCELLANEOUS

Harold D. Underdown
<http://www.users.interport.net/~hdu/l>

This children's literature editor publishes over a dozen articles for children's writers and artists, by himself and others. Topics include writer's guidelines, frequently asked questions, agents, multiculturalism, and publishing trends.

Unknown Children's Book Writers
<http://www.writepage.com/unknown2.htm>

The time has long passed for the children's book writers of our forefathers, but they are not forgotten on the Web.

Children's Theatre Resource
<http://pubweb.acns.nwu.edu/~vjs291/children.html>

This site provides information on the growing art form of children's theater.

MEGASOURCE JUMPSTATIONS

Children's Literature Web Guide
<http://www.ucalgary.ca/~dkbrown/rwriter.html>

Geared for parents and librarians, this site breaks the field down into dozens of topics, including authors, publishers, and bookstores.

The Children's Writing Resource Center
<http://www.mindspring.com/~cbi>

Presented by *Children's Book Insider* magazine, this is a veritable cornucopia of resources and links.

Inkspot
<http://www.interlog.com/~ohi/inkspot/>

Excellent links for children's writers, including directories of authors and illustrators. A must-see.

Yahooligans
<http://www.yahooligans.com/>

In 1996, the famous Yahoo! directory started this separate guide for kids. Like Yahoo!, the site is searchable. Literature and writing are found under Art Soup.

* * *

The secret of eternal youth still hasn't been discovered yet. But don't tell showpeople that. (Who was it who said, "Broadway and Hollywood are like high school, only with more money"?)

In the next chapter comes some prime Net spots for writers of stage and screen. Grown-up kids trade in their lunch pails for modems and share toys and tips.

8

Net Screenwriters

Most people have never heard of screenwriters. They think the actors just make up their lines as they go along.
—Charles Brackett and Billy Wilder, *Sunset Boulevard*

Cinema has always been a wedding of technology and art. Now update that image by adding the computer. On the Internet there are sites for every niche imaginable in the megagalaxies of the entertainment industry: Native Americans in silent films, *Star Trek* costumes, classic movie theaters, Eastman House, vintage posters, and Urdu/Hindi soundtracks. They're all online.

Computers are also revolutionizing the film industry as aids to creativity. Recently, the first Oscar was given to a computer software application, Scriptor. The Internet is now beginning to play a part in what we see on the silver screen, as digital pre- and post-production are clicking in, and Internet delivery of video (PC-TV) and film (digitally projected screenings and downloadable movies from Blockbuster) lurk in the wings.

Meanwhile, screenwriters have been taking advantage of every aspect of the Net. Says screenwriter Tracie Hines, "I landed my first option from a contact made on the Internet, where I also found out about a contest in which I ended up placing in the finals — a definite career booster."

In this chapter, you'll see how screenwriters use the Internet to share tips, market work, and generally keep current; to learn and teach the nuts and bolts of screenwriting; and to study scripts and film reviews.

FORUMS

An important part of screenwriting is hanging out with other screenwriters for leads, advice, and mentoring (or, as they say in Hollywood, "to schmooze").

Jack Stanley maintains the Scrnwriters mailing list. Here, working professionals rub elbows with newcomers and discuss a variety of topics. Traffic averages about 100 messages per day, and a weekly digest is available. To subscribe, e-mail the command "subscribe scrnwrit *YourFirstName YourLastName*" to <listserv@tamvm1.tamu.edu>.

There are also mailing lists for filmmakers and video producers; lists for other film people, ranging from buffs to projectionists; and specialized lists, such as one for members of the Wisconsin Screenwriters' Forum and another for black screenwriters.

Usenet has such newsgroups as misc.writing.screenplays and rec.arts.movies.production.

CompuServe has a Screenwriting section in its Showbiz Forum, where working writers share their experience and expertise. Script consultant Lou Grantt notes that their Bizfile resource gets him "the current address and phone info on all production companies in a specific region, to tide me over until the next *Hollywood Creative Directory* arrives."

CYBERMENTORING

Tips from the pros are essential to the apprenticeship of the scriptwriter, who, in addition to mastering pictorial, dramatic, montage storytelling, must master the arts of pitching, deal-making, threading through labyrinthine movie studio food chains, fitting the property to the budget, keeping up with the Flavor of the Month and the merger of the week, and so on — all the while, perhaps, keeping a day job. The pros know that their first big hit didn't change them as a screenwriter, nor as a person, and thus many are glad to pass along what they've learned climbing up the ladder.

The screenwriter Internaut will find interviews in such online magazines as *The Biz* <http://www.bizmag.com> and in archives of such Net night spots as the Celebrity Lounge at Mr. Showbiz <http://www.mrshowbiz.com> — with the likes of writers Christopher McQuarrie (*The Usual Suspects*) and producer David Permut (*Dragnet*).

CROW (Capsule Reviews of Original Work)
<http://www.ReadersNdex.com/crow>

This organization helps writers market story ideas to other writers, agents, and producers.

The Internet Entertainment Network
<http://www.hollywoodnetwork.com/hn/writing/>

Here you'll find an electronic screenplay database, access to Hollywood players, chat lounges, and more. Founded by Carlos de Abreu, originator of the Christopher Columbus Screenplay Discovery Awards. For more information, send an e-mail inquiry to <writing@hollywoodnetwork.com>.

The Internet Screenwriters' Network (ISN)
<http://Screenwriters.com/hn/writing/screennet.html>

Provides tips and articles by industry professionals, contest tips, career strategies, message boards, columns, legal advice, and professionally hosted chat lounges (Hosts have included Greg Beal, Rhonda Bloom, Steven de Souza, Dan Gordon, Brad Mirman, Donie Nelson, Dr. Linda Seger, John Truby, and John Vorhaus); a commercial clearinghouse for products and services.

Screenwriters' Homepage
<http://www.earthlink.net/~scribbler>

Created by screenwriter Brad Mirman, this is a place where working writers tell their stories. You'll also find columns and interviews, plus articles by directors, producers, and studio executives detailing exactly what they look for in a script.

Screenwriters Online: The Insider Report
<http://www.screenwriter.com/insider/news.html>

A hot electronic magazine of professional tips, published by ISN (see above).

The Screenwriter's Nebula Drive
<http://users.aol.com/blcklab666/home.html>

Offers "ailing, failing, and otherwise wailing" *unrepresented* screenwriters a vehicle for networking and sharing battle stories.

NUTS AND BOLTS OF SCREENWRITING

Common Movie Clichés
<http://www.like.it/vertigo/cliches.html>

Avoid or emulate these clichés, depending on your goal.

Essays on the Craft of Dramatic Writing
<http://www.teleport.com/~bjscript/index.htm>

Hollywood Scriptwriter
<http://www.ids.net/picpal/script.html>

Interviews.

"Making the Hollywood Film"
<http://www.hyperweb.com/linklater/dazedays.html>

An essay by Richard Linklater, auteur of *Slacker* and *Before Sunrise*.

Screenwriter's Master Chart
<http://members.aol.com/maryjs/scrnrite.htm>

Mary Shomon's map of fifteen basic plot points.

Screenwriters FAQ
<http://emsplum.eecs.uic.edu/ScrnFAQ>

Jack Stanley's essential FAQ offers an excellent overview of the field, mixing humor with common sense. It covers art versus commercialism, agents, books, brads, contests and fellowships, copyright/registration, legal matters, magazines, options, script sources, script format (1 page = 1 minute), seminars and workshops, software, e-mail, BBSs, the Writers Guild of America (WGA), and writing tips.

Writers' Guild of America
<http://www.wga.org>

In addition to Guild business and news, this site has informative sections on Research, Craft, Tools of the Trade, and Interactive Media. The Craft section, for example, includes advice on how to start and finish a script, quotes from the pros

("Overheard at the Commissary"), over a dozen articles about "the biz" (salaries, script doctors, surviving meetings with executives, development hell), and interviews with and profiles of a dozen or so screenwriters.

SCREENPLAYS AND SHOOTING SCRIPTS

Whether for your edification or your reading pleasure, you as a screenwriter can profit from reading many scripts by others. However, since scripts are usually a producer's or a studio's property, they're not freely distributed. Nevertheless, just as there are specialty bookstores dealing in scripts, so too are there small Internet niches archiving dozens of scripts.

Drew's Scripts-O-Rama
<http://home.cdsnet.net/~nikko11/scripts.htm>

Posting scripts can constitute copyright infringement, of course. However, this site doesn't house any actual scripts, but merely provides links to other Web sites that link to FTP sites that do. Hardly anything available dates from before 1980, but you'll find the likes of *Star Trek*, *Blade Runner*, *Jurassic Park*, *The Lion King*, and *Silence of the Lambs*, as well as different drafts of the same film.

Yahoo! — Screenplays
<http://www.yahoo.com/Entertainment/Movies_and_Films/Screenplays>

Links to produced and unproduced scripts and script-related resources.

FILM REVIEWS

While online scripts may be in relatively short supply, there's no dearth of film reviews. On the democratic Net, every filmgoer is a critic. Here's your chance to sound off.

The Movie Review Query Engine
<http://www.cinema.pgh.pa.us/movie/reviews>

A search engine for the films reviewed in various places on the Internet. (My search for *Casablanca* yielded six reviews.)

(Note: If you see the word "spoiler" in the subject line of a review, that's to alert you that the review reveals significant portions of the plot and could thus "spoil" it for you if you haven't already seen it yourself. Neat.)

AUTHORS' HOME PAGES

Lou Grantt's home page
<http://ourworld.compuserve.com/homepages/lgrantt/>

This well-known script consultant proffers articles on topics such as "style in action sequences" and "doing research." You'll also find assorted news and links and a flyer about his services.

CyberMad
<http://www.cybermad.com/index.html>

Christopher Parr published his screenplay, *Shadow Underground*, online as a serial — an act a week — at his awesome pop-culture Webzine.
And the Yahoo! entry <http://www.yahoo.com/Entertainment/Movies_and_Films/Screenplays> has a dozen more self-published scripts.

MEGASOURCE JUMPSTATIONS

CineMedia
<http://www.afionline.org/CineMedia>

The American Film Institute's megasource jumpstation links to over 6,000 film and media sites.

Screenwriters & Playwrights Home Page
<http://www.teleport.com/~cdeemer/scrwriter.html>

Charles Deemer should win an Oscar for best screenwriters' Web site, but the Academy hasn't come to grips with the Internet yet. This site has an index that breaks resources down according to the phases of screenwriting. His main categories are: the nuts and bolts of the craft of screenwriting (format, structural paradigms, marketing, getting an agent, and so on); screenplays online; film reviews; opportunities for networking with other screenwriters and wannabes; tips from the pros and voices of experience on business as well as craft; festivals, seminars, and special events; and archives and directories of information about films and filmmaking, video, and multimedia. The reference shelf includes a dictionary, a thesaurus, world maps, ZIP and Area Code directories, and more.

There are also links to film resources at the Library of Congress, PBS, and the BBC, plus Mike Vidal's Independent Filmmaker's Internet Resource Guide, Enzian Theater's Filmmaker's Resources, Mandy's Film and TV Production Directory, MEDIANet, and The Moviemaker's Home Page, and hypertext links to the archives of the Usenet group rec.arts.movies.

Writing for Stage & Screen
<http://www.azstarnet.com/~poewar/writer/pg/script.html>

John Hewitt's Web site includes a list a of production companies on the Net.

9

Net Playwrights

Most playwrights go wrong on the fifth word. When you start a play and you type "Act One, Scene One," your writing is every bit as good as Arthur Miller or Eugene O'Neill or anyone. It's that fifth word where amateurs start to go wrong.
—MEREDITH WILLSON

You won't smell greasepaint on the Internet, but you will sense the excitement of live theater. As with screenwriting, the Internet provides a vital hub of viable information, helping to keep theater alive.

In this chapter you'll see how playwrights use the Internet to network with peers; to learn and teach the basic nuts and bolts; to read and write for trade magazines; to study scripts; and to find resources of all kinds.

FORUMS

Primary Usenet newsgroups include rec.arts.theatre.plays, rec.arts.theatre.musicals, rec.arts.theatre.misc, and alt.arts.storytelling.

The Clearinghouse Guide to Theatre Resources on the Net
<gopher://una.hh.lib.umich.edu:70/00/inetdirsstacks/theater:torresm>

This is a rich megasite for forums by or about the American Society for Theater Research, Canadian theater, Hispanic theater, Asian performing arts, historical costumes, and more.

The Dramatic Exchange
<http://www.dramex.org>

A place for playwrights to publish and distribute their plays, for producers to find new work, and for anyone interested in drama to browse.

Theatre People
<http://www.iquest.net/bizcardz/theatrepeople.html>

Networks showfolk with each other.

NUTS AND BOLTS OF PLAYWRITING

Richard Toscan's Playwriting Seminars
<http://www.vcu.edu/artweb/playwriting>

A professional manual of the playwright's craft, with an inevitable excursion into film. This 196-page site is an exemplary use of the Web.

McCoy's Guide to Theatre and Performance Studies
<http://www.stetson.edu/~kmccoy/index.html>.

Provides academic resources.

MAGAZINES

Akropolis Magazine
<http://www.iquest.net/akropolis/>

A high-powered monthly Webzine focusing on theater, as well as music, literature, and art.

The Journal
<http://www.theatre-central.com/fea/jou>

An original publication of Theatre Central (see the end of this chapter for more details).

Playbill Online
<http://www.iquest.net/akropolis>

Theatre Insight
<http://www.utexas.edu/students/ti/>

A scholarly journal of theater and performance arts.

Theatre Network Magazine
<http://www.interlog.com/~artbiz/home.html>

SCRIPTS

The Internet is a library of scripts, from the classics to new plays.

Classics
<http://english.hss.cmu.edu/Drama.html>

Aristophanes, Goethe, Molière, Ibsen, et al.

Hypertext Shakespeare
<http://the-tech.mit.edu/Shakespeare/works.html>

ELAC (East Los Angeles College) Play and Monologue Collection
<http://websites.earthlink.net/~omniverse/elactheatre/workshop/collect.htm>

MEGASOURCE JUMPSTATIONS

ELAC Theatre Arts
<http://home.earthlink.net/~omniverse/elactheatre>

Kudos to East Los Angeles College Theatre Arts' hot home page, where you can post monologues and playlets and collaborate online with other playwrights. It also has a great jumpstation of links, including theater Webzines, the history of theater, Ken McCoy's Brief Guide to Internet Resources in Theatre and Performance Studies, Headquarters Entertainment, and Joe Geigel's Directory of Theatre Resources.

Scott's Theatre Links
<http://www.monmouth.com/user_pages/snaef/theatre.html#contents>

This is a fairly thorough site for everything: shows, casting, goods and services, theatre groups, FAQs, magazines, etc.

Screenwriters & Playwrights Home Page
<http://www.teleport.com/~cdeemer/scrwriter.html>

Charles Deemer's jumpstation, mentioned in Chapter 8, applies here, too.

Stage & Screen Writing Resources
<http://www.azstarnet.com/~poewar/writer/pg/script.html>

John Hewitt's jumpstation, mentioned in Chapter 8, applies here, too.

Theatre Central
<http://www.theatre-central.com/>

The *writers.net* judges hereby announce that the "Sarah Siddons' Greaseless Greasepaint Award for Best One-Stop Home Page of Theater Resources on the Net" goes to Theatre Central. Here you'll find the largest collection of theatrical links on the Internet; a searchable database of names and contact information of "wired theater professionals"; a monthly journal of articles, editorials, and columns; a callboard of jobs, auditions, and other openings; and shows and performance listings.

WWW Virtual Library: Theatre and Drama
<http://www.brookes.ac.uk/VL/theatre/index.htm>

The emphasis here is academic, but not exclusively so: academic institutions; events and festivals; plays online (in English, French, German, Greek, Italian, and Spanish); about a dozen mailing lists; syllabus bank; theater studies.

* * *

Of course, to write for stage and screen requires mastery of the *technical* rigors of proper script construction as well as the art of dramatic conflict — such as to convey instructions to crafts people as well as to deliver emotional payload to the audience.

The next chapter covers technical writing in general.

Then we'll cap our tour of genres with a unique and recently emergent dramatic genre, which stage/screen writers won't want to miss: cybersoaps and Web serials (a.k.a. webisodics).

10

Net Technical Writers

user-friendly: *adj. Programmer-hostile. Generally used by hackers in a critical tone, to describe systems that hold the user's hand so obsessively that they make it painful for the more experienced and knowledgeable to get any work done.*

—The Jargon Lexicon

Technical writing is the broadest of the genres covered in *writers.net*. It's a natural for technical writers to network on the Internet. In this chapter, you'll learn how technical writers are using the Internet to share industry news, polish up on skills, scout out jobs, and so forth.

Computer writing is the big, new, lucrative branch of technical writing, where a writer can pull down an annual $70,000 net (with the help of an agent). This covers a range of activities, but consider computer books: since company product user's manuals are notoriously from hell, publishers are making a living off of creating books that are essentially third-party documentation.

For specific topics related to technical writing, such as business, government, computers, etc., please refer to Chapter 14, "Net Research."

FORUMS

The Usenet newsgroup for technical writings is alt.books.technical. There are also several lists and a wide array of Web offerings.

Computer Book Publishing
<http://www.studiob.com>

A lively, high-powered discussion group of computer book authors, both seasoned and raw, plus agents, lawyers, editors, and salespeople. The discussions are archived at their Web site, which also features interviews and essays. To subscribe, e-mail <list@studiob.com>, and in the subject line write "Subscribe". As this is a fairly high-volume list, you might wish to write "subscribe digest" instead.

Copyediting
<http://www.c2.org/~srm/samples/net/celfaq.htm>

Carol Roberts maintains this mailing list for copy editors and other defenders of the King's English who wish to discuss editorial problems, client relations, Internet resources, dictionaries, or whatever. E-mail <listserv@cornell.edu> with the message "Subscribe COPYEDITING-L *YourEmailAddress YourName*". Copyediting-L has also produced a FAQ, available at the Web site.

The Technical Writers List

A heavily trafficked list based at Oklahoma State University. To subscribe, e-mail just the command "Subscribe Techwr-L *YourFirstName YourLastName*" to <listserv@vm1.ucc.okstate.edu>.

The National Writers Union

A more lightly trafficked forum for technical writers. To subscribe, e-mail the message "subscribe newu3-tw" to <andreas@netcom.com>.

Internet Resources for Technical Communicators
<http://www.rpi.edu/~perezc2/tc/email.html>

An index of other mailing lists and Usenet newsgroups for the technical communicator; also links to journals and dictionaries.

PERIODICALS

Technical Communication Quarterly
<http://beauty.agoff.umn.edu/~tcq/>

Posts announcements, abstracts, books available for review, submission guidelines, and so on.

Writer's Block
<http://www.niva.com/writblok/index.html>

A quarterly newsletter of NIVA (a Canadian technical documentation and communications firm) with resources of interest to communications specialists, including writers, editors, graphic designers, and desktop publishing operators.

BOOKSTORES

Cody's Books
<http://www.codysbooks.com>

Computer Literacy Books
<http://www.clbooks.com>

Digital Guru
<http://www.digitalguru.com>

Quantum Books
<http://www.quantumbooks.com>

Roswell Electronic Computer Bookstore
<roswell@fox.nstn.ns.ca>

San Diego Technical Bookstore
<http://www.sdtb.com>

Stacey's Bookstore
<http://www.staceys.com>

AUTHORS' HOME PAGES

Larry Aaronson
<http://www.users.interport.net/~laronson/>

Larry writes about HTML and has a very simple Web site, beginning with his resumé, biography, and work history, and moving into his writings and seminars. He also adds valuable tools and links, as well as numerous links about his personal interest, world music.

Prof. Randolph Bentson
<http://www.ssc.com/ssc/insidelinux/>

Professor Bentson writes and publishes about Linux and UNIX.

James Bryce
<http://www.bryce.com>

James writes, consults, and speaks about communications and computer technology, and has a very professional-looking, high-powered Web site.

Steve Heller
<http://ourworld.compuserve.com/homepages/steve_heller>

Includes sections from Steve's book *Who's Afraid of C++?*, plus personal information, author e-mail, and links to more information on C++ and Java.

David Rand
<http://www.cwcinc.com/davidr/>

This technical writer builds community via links to shareware archives and other technical communication resources online, including information on how to search the archives of the Techwr-List.

Technical Authors on the Web
<http://user.itl.net/~gazza/authors.htm>

An alphabetical collection of Web sites of over three dozen technical writers; you can hyperlink your home page to it, too.

MISCELLANEOUS

The PRC Home Page
<http://pip.dknet.dk/~pip323/index.htm>

Tips and links dedicated to the creation of user-friendly manuals and the measurement of their quality.

Professional Communication Society
<http://www.ieee.org/pcs/pcsindex.html>

A leading scholarly and professional organization in technical writing and allied fields.

The Slot
<http://www.theslot.com>

The Web spot for copy editors, containing *The Curmudgeons' Stylebook*, word choices, capitalization, quotations, and the like.

The Society for Technical Communication (STC)
<http://stc.org/>

A job board with weekly list of employment openings, by region.

Technical Writer Salaries
<http://www.clark.net/pub/stc/www/salary.html>

An index of industry standards.

Working Writers, Inc.
<http://www.working-writers.com/>

Registers technical writers for no fee; companies pay a referral fee to get information about registered writers from the database. The site also offers workshops and other support resources for writers.

See also Chapter 18, "New Writing," for leads on writing for multimedia.

MEGASOURCE JUMPSTATIONS

Gary Conroy's Technical Writing Resources
<http://user.itl.net/~gazza/techwr.htm>

Links and information galore.

John December
<http://www.december.com/john/study/techcomm/info.html>

A list of technical communication organizations, resource collections, topics, programs, and related information.

John Hewitt
<http://www.azstarnet.com/~poewar/writer/pg/tech.html>

Articles, dictionaries, job leads, and other links.

Internet Links for Technical Communications
<http://www.muohio.edu/~mtsccwis/techcommlinks.html>

A top-level guide to resources, organizations, academic pages, and indexes, maintained by Anne Munson.

Keith Soltys' Internet Resources for Technical Communicators
<http://www.io.org/~ksoltys/techcomm.html>

A fine top-level guide with hyperlinks to a bibliography, copyright information, desktop publishing, HTML, language, mailing lists, newsgroups, online help and documentation, SGML, and more.

Purdue University's OWL
<http://owl.trc.purdue.edu/resources.html#business>

Interesting pointers for business and technical writing.

Stephen Schiller's Technical Communications Resources
<http://www.in.net/~smschill/techcomm.html>

An impressive site that includes writing resources, job opportunities, competitions, books, academic programs, useful software, and related links.

* * *

We cap our tour of genres with the latest craze, a unique writing realm that draws a little from all that have come before: cybersoaps and Webisodic sites.

11

Cybersoaps and Webisodic Sites

... the most effective metaphor for soap opera is to regard it as a form of collective game in which viewers themselves are the major participants.

—D. Buckingham

One reason writers use the Internet is to work in new forms. If you've been writing nothing but sonnets, then haiku is a welcome change. In this chapter, I will introduce you to a cutting-edge Internet genre that needs good writers: serials (a.k.a. cybersoaps and Webisodic sites).

Once second-class citizens, TV soap opera writers now play golf at the most exclusive Bel Air country clubs. Perhaps one day soon cybersoaps, too, will blossom into a thriving industry. Meanwhile, Webisodic sites offer a writer the freedom of the early days of TV. Maybe what this crazy world needs right now is a good literary, interactive, hypertext, collaborative soap opera.

HOW THE GENRE BEGAN

In 1836, the modern serial began when Charles Dickens's *The Pickwick Papers* went on sale for one shilling an installment. The narrow audience for books widened, and soon people lined up to await the latest installment of a Dickens novel, while other publishers reached out even farther to the masses, producing utter trash called "penny dreadfuls."

A century later, radio discovered serials. At first, advertisers were reluctant to underwrite "wireless" broadcasts for fear that no one was listening. However, serials guaranteed a repeated, if not growing, audience. Originally, they featured single actors, often reading multiple parts, but they evolved into elaborate productions, with sound effects and musical accompaniment. Eventually, the serials format was adopted by television.

Think, too, of the enormous popularity of the serialization of cartoons. And, in 1996, Stephen King revived the serialized novel with his *Green Mile*, which locked up four of the top fifteen slots for paperbacks on *The New York Times* bestseller list for six weeks running. Serialization is, in a word, hot-hot-hot. Online, it gives a temporal dimension to cyberspace, and opens new possibilities for interactivity.

The Spot
<http://www.thespot.com>

In the summer of '95, "an episodic Web site" called *The Spot* appeared on the Web with relatively little explanation. It featured the "secret" daily, multimedia diaries of eight roommates (seven dudes, one gal, and a dog) living in a big, ramshackle beach house — "the Spot."

(Further demonstrating the responsiveness of this new medium, just weeks after *The Spot* debuted, someone else introduced *The Squat*, <http://www.thesquat.com>, featuring some trashy kids in a ramshackle Southern trailer park.)

The Spot is purely fictional, but you wouldn't know that from looking at it. There are no credits for director, actors, writers, or the like. And although *The Spot* is staged at a studio, where the roles are scripted and portrayed by actors, viewers send mail to the characters as if they're real. The characters reply, acknowledging the letters in subsequent episodes, even striking requested poses (such as eating a strawberry, wearing a bikini, by the refrigerator).

The craze for Webisodic sites on the Net had begun! Aimed at the college/youth market, *The Spot* attracted multitudes to come and come again — Web heaven — thus attracting, in turn, big advertisers and major investors. It has since spun off into a book and may also spawn a TV soap or movie.

Flush with success, its creators launched a cyberserial production company, American Cybercast, budgeting three future Web series at $1.2 million each: <http://www.amcy.com>. The three Webisodics (*Eon-4*, *Pyramid*, and *Quick-Fix*) are at their Web site, but went into limbo when the company hit financing woes shortly thereafter.

SAMPLING THE WEB SERIALS

You will find Web serials to be a dramatic art form untainted by the maddening bureaucracy typical of Hollywood. Just as interesting, many of them pay their writers real money.

East Village
<http://www.eastvillage.com>

This serial changes twice a week. Its seventeen characters are seen from the point of view of Eve Ramsay, a twenty-four-year-old neo-bohemian writer. The site features an archive, character profiles, a map of the character's relationships, a history of the Lower East Side, bulletin boards and live chat rooms, and an East Village products boutique. (Backer Time-Warner has scripted the neighbors to make a film called *The Wedding*, to publicize a similar film made by the company's new film production company spun off of the site's popularity.)

The Family Jewels
<http://www.iontheprize.com>

A word puzzle game, with prizes, set in an episodic online mystery.

Ferndale
<http://www.ferndale.com>

With all its characters in Net therapy, *Ferndale* was intended as a satire on soaps. Twins, mysterious comas, forbidden romances, and multiple personalities — so what else is new? It failed to generate sufficient advertising revenue, and *Ferndale* died on the vine, but the site remains.

Crime Scene Evidence File
<http://www.quest.net/crime>

Ferndale director Tim Arriola continues to direct this policier serial, which began several months before *The Spot*. The Crime Scene is a repository of investigative information regarding the murder of Valerie Wilson. Web surfers can view evidence photos, coroner's reports, witness interviews, and more. Updated weekly.

Caffeine Destiny
<http://www.teleport.com/~denning/caffdestiny.html>

A text-only cybersoap, named after a fictitious coffee house. Each week, the audience is solicited to determine the outcome of the latest installment. ("Is Jake Really Holly's Baby?")

The Lurker Files
<http://www.randomhouse.com/lurkerfiles>

This joint production of Random House and the Yahooligans is set in a chat room at Wintervale University. In a prototypical depiction of the Technothriller Bad Guy — a faceless terrorist who hacks secret information, plants computer viruses, launches missiles by remote log-in, and so on — the "lurker" weaves an electronic web of deceit around all who log on.

Media Search and Techno3
<http://bluepearl.com/>

Two Latino/Hispanic-based serials, featuring a recent addition to the genre: chat rooms where readers can interact with the characters, "live."

Gay Daze
<http://www.gaydaze.com>

A gay/lesbian cybersoap.

Two Tickets to Rio and Product Placement
<http://www.laslett.com/soap.htm>

A self-published Webisodic site, boldly put together with no more than bubble-gum, paper clips, and sheer moxie.

Eon 4
<http://www.eon4.com>

One of the latest serials of note, as of this writing. Skillfully mocked up as documentation of recent close encounters of the third kind, the site seems to induce some readers to take it perfectly seriously.

Also of interest:

101 Hollywood Blvd.
<http://home.navisoft.com/brewpubclub/101.htm>

MelrosEast
<http://www.inx.net/~mvo/melroseast.html>

T@P Virtual Dorm
<http://www.taponline.com/tap/voyeur/vdorm/>

Union2
<http://www.totalny.com/city/union/>

12

Net Money

Neither information nor money is in short supply on the Net; it's attention that is in keen demand.

—Esther Dyson, Computer Guru

Whether or not you agree with the above epigraph, you'll probably be wondering, who *is* paying for all this stuff on the Net? That is, canny writers always keep in mind the Golden Rule: the one who controls the gold, rules.

Whether you plan on going into self-publishing or are considering working for an online venture, you'll want to understand what the current revenue options are. For example, if you write for an Internet site where readers pay a small amount (via a "micropayment," such as a fraction of a penny) to access an article of yours, then you're not beholden to any corporate policy but rather to what the market demands, and that financial method could generate a whole new kind of demand for what you write.

As you see how the Net is transforming not only publishing but also its means of support, you'll also learn new ways of selling work to publishers and to readers.

There are four distinct ways people make money, directly or indirectly, via the Internet:

1. unpaid self-promotion
2. subscriptions, sales, and fees

3. sponsorship and advertisers
4. micropayment

We'll also look at online currency (digital money and virtual cash).

FOR FREE OR FOR FEE?

Right now the Net is in a dynamic equilibrium between its origins in the academic research community, where information is freely shared, and its more recent commercial subsidization and absorption of enormous globs of venture capital (attracting one of the largest concentrations of wealth in human history).

This tension between the ideals of "the greatest good" and "the greatest goods" is of consequence to all writers, because it measures our freedom to write and get published. Today, a writer can publish a daily essay about anything and, if it's good, attract a following of about ten thousand readers. A subsistence revenue could be generated by this — enough to keep the project alive, but hardly a living wage. If the big polyglomerates were to take over the Net, on the other hand, and use it as a broadcasting medium, writing for the Net could pay big bucks — but only for a few. Ideally, both modes will survive, reinforcing each other symbiotically.

Meanwhile, the writer needs to understand the economics of the Net. Until recently, writers have donated their work to improve the Net (a "gift culture" of free exchange) and to gain exposure for themselves. This is all well and good, considering that many online publications have vast readerships, and that their archives may stay "in print" in perpetuity. But what are the alternatives?

UNPAID SELF-PROMOTION

The writer who gives away work on the Net is generating public awareness that can be parlayed into such paying gigs as speaking engagements, writing jobs from editors, and book sales to an admiring public. The traditional model for this is the free sample.

The guiding principle here, as with shareware, is usually: try it before you buy it. The Electric Newsstand, for example, lets you browse tables of contents and sample articles from hundreds of magazines. If you like what you see, they sell subscriptions, with patrons now in over forty-five countries. You'll find them at <http://www.enews.com>, <gopher://enews.com>, or <telnet://enews.com> (log on as "enews"). They started with just eight magazines in June, 1993, and now have over 275. For more information, e-mail <info@enews.com> or call Lisa Losito at 202-466-8688.

Branding. An important trade term for "buyer awareness" is "branding" — making the public aware of your "brand name." Via the Net, an author can create personal "brand" awareness among both a community of readers and a community of publishers and editors.

Consider twenty-something Justin Hall, who created Links from the Underground, <http://www.justin.org/>, his ongoing annotated collection of Web links begun a bit before Yahoo! Soon he was getting ten thousand readers per day and receiving an average of $400 a month in donations from strangers around the world, at random, which he in turn gave to his Internet service provider. Then Justin began taking ads from authors who were getting fewer "hits" than he and seeking increased exposure (when a viewer clicks on a file, that is called a "hit"). In time, he was asked to speak at the Rand Corporation, the Newspaper Association of America, and Lollapalooza.

Before launching Links from the Underground, Justin Hall had applied for work at *WiReD*. But, lacking a track record, he was turned down. When *WiReD* started its online sister, *HotWired*, Justin knocked on their door again. They asked for his e-mail address, he gave them his Web URL, they visited his Web site, and he was in. Having an online presence paid off.

SUBSCRIPTIONS, SALES, AND FEES

Making money on the Internet can also involve the familiar models of pure economic transaction: paid subscriptions, sales of merchandise (such as books), and services (database searches, Web page design, etc.) for a fee.

There are also hybrid arrangements, in which for-free publicity can be combined with fee-based services, such as with Electric Newsstand. Another such hybrid is Ken Jenks' online magazine of genre fiction, *Mind's Eye* <http://tale.com>; it offers the beginnings of contributors' work for free, but charges $.18 to $.50 for the endings.

Sometimes a publication is initially provided at no charge, to promote awareness, then subsequent editions are available only for a fee. For example, the *Wall Street Journal Interactive Edition* launched for free in April, 1996, but in August of that year became subscription-only.

There can also be simultaneous free and for fee information — for example, ESPN's *SportsZone*, where the news is free but columnist Charlie Vincent's commentary costs $4.95/month or $39.95/year.

Not all Net publishers give something away; many are strictly for paying subscribers. Usually, subscribers are given a log-in I.D. and password, necessary to access the site. Some newsletters and specialty magazines began as subscription-only/paper-only and then migrated to subscription-only/online-only to save printing and distribution costs.

Online Currency. Online sales of goods and services are not yet commonplace. The main reason is the state of online currency.

Online currency was born in 1994, when First Virtual Holdings, <http://www.fv.com>, introduced a viable transaction medium for online commerce. If you send them money, you can open a First Virtual account, and you can shop with participating online merchants 'til you drop. If you're an online self-publisher, you can even be such a merchant. Within a year, First Virtual had competition from CheckFree, DigiCash, and OpenMarket, to name a few virtual banks and credit companies. One relative newcomer, CyberCash, at <http://www.cybercash.com>, has created a CyberCoin system that will be bundled with the Navigator Web browser.

Credit cards can be used online, but since the Internet isn't a secure medium, this application hasn't taken off. Credit card companies are currently exploring various forms of "e-credit."

Whatever evolves in the way of digital currency, the impact will be tremendous. It's not only a topic worth writing about, but it will affect your very pocketbook.

SPONSORS AND ADVERTISERS

If you want to create a Web site or Webzine, one way to get paid is to attract sponsors or advertisers. Microsoft benefits by being an initial sponsor of *Slate* magazine, just as Ford does by advertising there. Adobe and Borders get attention by sponsoring *Salon* magazine. Sponsorship is a low-key form of advertisement.

Online magazines don't carry full-page ads, like print magazines do. An online ad is more like a bumpersticker or a billboard — a company logo, with a few lines of type. But, unlike the print media, here the advertiser has its own Web site linked to its online "banner," where there can be pages and pages of information, games, forums, and other fun stuff, as well as the inevitable purchase form.

The pricing structure of Internet advertising is still in flux. Ad revenue can be keyed to traffic, running in the neighborhood of $25 to $35 per thousand visitors. At a site like Yahoo!, getting six million viewers per day, ad space can thus be sold at a premium.

MICROPAYMENT

This payment model depends on a new form of currency. Imagine that you publish an online newspaper, magazine, or book that makes a substantial portion available for free, but then affixes a small fee (say a couple of cents) for either viewing more or downloading the material. Given the Internet's ability to reach readers around the globe, twenty-four hours a day, this could create a substantial revenue stream.

One viable mechanism for micropayment has been developed by the Clickshare Corporation, founded by veteran journalist Bill Densmore, <http://www.clickshare.com> or <info@clickshare.com>. Clickshare has been utilized by the *Christian Science Monitor*, <http://www.csmonitor.com>, as well as the entertainment industry intelligencer *Studio Briefing* and the Internet's first original daily "newspaperless," *American Reporter* (spotlighted in Chapter 13). Clickshare users have a single ID and password, enabling access to multiple Web sites. Clickshare tracks usage and bills charges to the user's credit card.

Another micropayment system is DigiCoin, whose clients include the online archives of the *Los Angeles Times*, <http://www.latimes.com/HOME/ARCHIVES>. Here, transactions are charged to users' banks. And Visa and Digital, among other players, are also working on micropayment systems.

Yet another micropayment possibility is electronic tagging: though an online property has been purchased, it can't be freely distributed. One way to do this is to put work in a digital "envelope" (a.k.a. CyberLope or DigiBox) that follows the work and tracks each time it's viewed, downloaded, and forwarded — charging an appropriate, pre-set fee each time. And Ted Nelson's Xanadu Project <http://www.xanadu.com.au/xanadu> is perfecting a radical new approach to give writers fuller freedom.

For the Net writer, micropayment possibilities can be very tantalizing. A fifty-fifty split with a publisher of revenues from a mass-market feature at ten cents a click might pay far more than $1 a word. And it reintroduces readership as "the bottom line" back into the publishing equation.

Whatever the model, creativity is key, because the divisions I've made aren't hard and fast. And there are other factors, as well — for example, community.

Communities are traditionally a valuable resource, as a target audience ("niche marketing"). The community of yachtspeople, say, may be very small, but relatively wealthy. If you published a newsletter for this community, they'd probably keep coming back each month. Now, if you set up an online forum for yachtspeople to exchange information and chat, and charged $25 a month — then you wouldn't have to produce any original content whatsoever, just the space. The community would be producing and consuming their own content. And you might be making some extra spending money, easy.

Self-publishing is explored in Chapter 17, but, here, consider that such online services as America Online and Lexis-Nexis might be thought of as magazines, with very successful subscription models. And much of America Online's original content in its highly popular chat rooms is created by its community of consumers themselves.

So webzines and online adjuncts of magazines are adding forums to their online pages, building community, to create value. A quantum leap on the Letters to the Editor section, these forums of online magazines now enable readers' words to

▼▼▼

BYLINES

Bylines magazine is the brainchild of Pulitzer laureate Jon Franklin and his former editor at the *Baltimore Evening Sun*, George Rodgers. As a gallery of literary journalism that will be financed through micropayment, it is but one example of how that revenue model provides the basis for an independence of vision.

Bylines welcomes literary journalists, editors, and even a few columnists who are interested in writing for general readers of the Internet on a micropayment basis, with payment based on the number of times their work is downloaded. Previously published work is also welcome if the author retains electronic rights; however, previously published work might need to be rewritten for the medium — or, if cut for print publication, restored to original length. The average length of *Bylines* stories will be four to ten thousand words.

Bylines is an outgrowth of WritersL (discussed in Chapter 13, "Net Journalism"). The prospectus states that it will have the literary qualities of the old, general-interest *Saturday Evening Post* and the pencil/press flavor of a newspaper, but that neither metaphor exactly fits. "Perhaps a gallery . . . a place where readers can browse and buy or reject as they please. Or a pay-per-read library."

> . . . Having been buffeted by shrinking news holes, assailed by bean-counters, readership surveyors and corporate downsizing, we believe that journalism can only be good if it is profitable. Our long-term goal is to prove that such profitability can be achieved, and achieved on the basis of superb journalism. . . .
>
> . . . The price per read has to be kept very low, so that we can deal in volume — which is to say a mass readership. . . . We believe that a good read shouldn't cost any more than society's most standard measures of value: the price of a cup of coffee. . . .

> At least for starters, *Bylines* will do what I think traditional media (including the alternative press) do the poorest job of, which is reflecting how everyday life is lived here at the bitter end of the Twentieth Century. Real life, not ideal life, and not ideological life. . . .
>
> . . . As I watch the first posts shape up, I see within them the kernel of what may be an interesting literary philosophy. That is, most if not all of the stories focus on what people do (build pianos, try to get to Prague, shoe horses, etc.) as a way to illuminate what and who we are and the nature of the culture we live in. . . .
>
> . . . The literary mainstay of *Bylines* will be the genre that is variously called literary journalism, creative nonfiction, and even (once upon a time) the new journalism. By whatever name, it is as old as journalism itself. Lest we tend to forget: It is Gannett-think, and not storytelling, that's experimental.
>
> . . . As I go through the submissions I'm getting . . . I am repeatedly struck by how the business of journalism has, over the generations, crammed the art into a smaller and smaller box, until now some of our work is so compacted and telescoped it's grotesque. But from what I'm seeing, and what people are saying, the same thing has not happened to our souls.
>
> Thus, mode of remuneration can help shape the content of online publishing. Readers will be able to visit the site free, with a micropayment system for whatever they select to read/capture/download. Writers and editors interested in guidelines and the full prospectus can contact *Bylines* at: <jonfrank@bylines.org>.

become part of a magazine's content. (Conversely, webzines are taking on the characteristics of online services.)

This also means readers help shape editorial direction (in keeping with the "bottom-up" model of the Internet). Editors now pay more serious attention to their readers' feedback through these forums, which points to a fresh avenue for writers to capture the attention of magazine editors, besides the traditional route of mailing samples (tearsheets or clips). Instead, you can start a thread in a magazine's online forum. If the thread takes off and other readers join, the editor will notice, and then might solicit an article about that topic from you, or at least be well-primed for your proposal. So, in that sense, Esther Dyson's epigraph (at the beginning of this chapter) is correct.

In any event, this is just the beginning. So hold on to your keyboards! Everything that isn't nailed down is bustin' loose.

❖ ❖ ❖

Having grounded yourself in the Internet's financial possibilities, you have the opportunity to apply what you've learned by exploring how New Media are affecting the news media and journalists. As you'll see, the following chapter has many elements of interest for all writers.

13

Net Journalism

It used to be publishing was all formatted packages. We're quickly getting to the point where publishing consists of constructing useful interfaces to databases.
—Robert Ingle, Vice President of New Media, Knight-Ridder

"Computer-assisted reporting" is the currently accepted phrase for Net journalism that uses the Net to gather and disseminate information, but one day it may sound as out of date as "telephone-assisted reporting." Meanwhile, not only is it a craft that's transforming news, but it also offers exciting opportunities to *all* writers; journalists or not, we all find, filter, and put facts in formation from a number of sources.

This chapter is juicy with information that will reward Net writers regardless of speciality or metier. Likewise, Chapter 14 is entirely reserved for the topic of research — an essential for journalists, but also of use to all writers.

In this chapter, you'll learn about:

- making the transition from print to digital journalism
- the first daily "news(un)papering" and the first daily "newspaperless"
- forums and associations where journalists network
- research resources for journalists (and all writers)
- feeds and leads, where you can gather or contribute the latest news
- trends to watch, including information farming, information agents, civic journalism, nonmainstream press, "New Journalism," and local/global news

- online newsstands
- where to find jobs
- self-publishers of news

MAKING THE TRANSITION TO DIGITAL NEWS

Research isn't the only aspect of journalism being revolutionized by the Internet. Online, the concept of the newspaper is being augmented by such new features as:

- video and sound
- searchable archives
- interactivity through forums
- customized news on personally selected topics
- in-depth links to background, sources, and further information

NET JOURNALISTS

Here is some anecdotal wisdom from two journalists who've successfully made the transition to digital news.

Television investigative reporter Mike Wendland (WDIV, Detroit, <http://www.wdiv.com/htt.html>) has reported for numerous nationally syndicated TV specials. He's been involved in computer-assisted reporting since 1982. He averages two hours a day online, and "every day," he attests, "I discover something new and practical online that makes me a better journalist."

For example, Wendland was surfing the Web one day for any leads on workers' compensation fraud, a topic his news director had penciled as "a strong possible." First, he found a report from the President's National Economic Advisor, Laura D'Andrea Tyson, noting that workers' compensation costs have been rising at an annual rate of 200 percent. Writing that down in his notebook, he moved on, coming up with several private detective agencies that do "activity checks" (documenting allegedly handicapped people who may prove, in fact, to be active and healthy). Surfing onward, he discovered an organization called the National Insurance Crime Bureau and downloaded several of its reports and statistics.

Within half an hour, Mike had background and sources that would soon turn into a break: e-mail from an insurance company investigator with specific case names and a phone number. Mike called the number that morning, and by 3:00 P.M. he had raw video footage, taken by a hidden camera, of nondisabled people receiving permanent disability pay. His subsequent two-part exposé had the highest ratings during its time period on the nights when the stories aired.

* * *

Patrick Lee, a business reporter for the *Los Angeles Times*, attests:

> I use the Internet frequently, but only for things I can't get more easily on the telephone (such as a live comment from a human being) or on a fax machine (such as a brief document).
>
> I have found the Internet quite useful as a business reporter. Most government economic, employment, census and other kinds of data are readily available. So are a lot of financial documents, both from the SEC and from private companies that choose to post them (annual reports, etc.). Pulling them off the Internet can save a lot of time. E-mail is also very useful, particularly if I can persuade a source to send me a compressed data file (DataQuick, an information service, will send us Excel files of recent real estate sales and prices, for example, over e-mail, which we can then decompress and sort).
>
> In writing about the U.S.-China trade dispute this week, I was able to download U.S.-China export and import information from the International Trade Administration site. In writing about electric utility restructuring, I pull briefs and data off the California Public Utilities Commission site. In writing about Boeing's trade with China, I was able to access Boeing's recent financial report to shareholders, which had some detailed information about Boeing's operations. In writing about gasoline prices and their recent surge, I was able to access both the daily emergency situation reports, with updated price data, from the California Energy Commission site, as well as U.S. data from the American Petroleum Institute and the Monthly and Weekly Petroleum status reports from the Energy Information Administration of the U.S. Department of Energy. I have downloaded U.S. Census county business patterns data for reference on stories having to do with employment and industry breakdowns. And on and on and on.
>
> I have found the Internet so convenient that I routinely check it for any story I happen to be working on, to see if there are relevant documents or data that will enhance the story. (I spend no more than an hour on any story doing so).
>
> My advice is to familiarize yourself with search techniques, know what you're looking for and where you're getting your information, and rely on primary sources of data from reputable sites: government, trade associations, academic institutions.

For journalists, the transition to the Internet is becoming career-critical. Editors and publishers now want digital copy, not hard copy. In a 1995 survey of 800 newspaper and magazine editors, eighty-one percent said that they want manuscripts from their freelancers and correspondents in computer-readable form, as opposed to paper or fax — up from fifty-four percent in 1994. More than two-thirds of the journalists use the online world to track breaking news or do other forms of research. And (publicists, take note!) more than half of the respondents prefer online press releases to paper ones. (You can see the complete survey results at <http://www.mediasource.com/study/index.html>.)

Other surveys reveal a push for adoption of computers for external as well as internal communication. The Newspaper Association of America estimated that the number of American newspapers online has tripled in 1995; it is expected to double in 1996, bringing the total to 350. There are about 600 foreign newspapers online. With increased competition in the business of purveying news, an Internet presence may be the crucial link to market share.

TWO CASE STUDIES

The price of paper pulp is rising steeply. The depth and variety of copy supported by traditional advertising revenue models is shrinking. And, as ownership concentrates into fewer and fewer hands, competition for readers gets tougher. Here are examples of digital news pioneers from two ends of the spectrum.

Mercury Center — News(un)papering

<http://www.sjmercury.com>

A major metropolitan daily, based in California's Silicon Valley, the *San Jose Mercury News* is owned by the Knight-Ridder chain, America's biggest news service.

In 1993, AOL offered to pay the *Mercury News* for an exclusive on making their news content available to AOL subscribers. AOL could bring in subscribers by providing local news, and the *Mercury News* would have a new revenue stream for copy it was already generating.

The resulting publication, *Mercury Center,* was the first full-text version of a newspaper online — complete with ads and classifieds, plus a ten-year archive, totaling over a million stories, with a search function.

A code at the end of a story enables readers to access more information in various forms: background, text of speeches, reporters' notes, full wire feeds, interviews, additional articles, and more. *Mercury Center* also carries online-only material. Special articles have pointers to related online forums. Readers can send messages to specific editors, writers, and columnists.

Another new feature of online news is the "intelligent agent." *The Mercury News* calls its agent "NewsHound," the *L.A. Times'* is "Hunter," and other papers follow the metaphor: a faithful retriever dog that fetches information on command. The subscriber selects subjects, and the personalized news service searches not only the newspaper's database but other news databases as well and brings back relevant articles, usually by e-mail.

The promotional literature spells out some of the uses, asking:

> What's your competition up to? What's going on in your home town? How is the out-of-town press treating a recent announcement by your company? What's the latest news in your hobby? Is your neighborhood in the news? Did anyone pick up your press release? Have you or anyone you know been mentioned in the press? How are the companies in your investment portfolio performing?

In late 1996, *Mercury Center* left its AOL home. The day after amicably severing ties with AOL, the *San Jose Mercury News* made a bold stroke: it broke a major story with simultaneous appearance on its *Mercury Center*. Authored by *Mercury News* drug war correspondent Gary Webb, and fourteen months in the making, "Dark Alliance" attempted to document a covert effort to arm a Latin American guerrilla army, resulting in one of the first major pipelines between Columbia's cocaine cartel and a Californian inner city, which, in turn, helped touch off a drug epidemic that still ravages urban America.

It's well beyond the scope of *writers.net* to debate whether "Dark Alliance" advances any significantly new material or how circumstantial it may prove to be. The story *is* pertinent, however, in terms of its formal use of the Internet for presentation and dissemination. The Net adjunct here wasn't an afterthought, but was an integral part of the piece (see sidebar on following page), taking three months to design and one month to produce.

"Alliance" is a non-mainstream tale with an enormous unbelievability quotient, and the Web enables the reader to see the material evidence on which the story is based. Using *frames* (simultaneous windows), the Web version opens the reportage out with a chronology, the cast of players, diagrams, documents, and maps. Items are hyperlinked to resources elsewhere on the Net. And the reader can not only inspect relevant documents and peruse court motions, but hear key testimony exactly as the reporter heard it. Plus, the site is updated and hosts readers' comment. Since "Dark Alliance" was published, daily "hits" at *Mercury Center* rose from 600,000 to 800,000. (*The Mercury News* circulation, on the other hand, is under 300,000.)

The San Jose Mercury News has pioneered adoption of and adaptation to the online news medium. They emphasize content rather than techno-flash. They use such Web resources as graphics and hyperlinks to great advantage, while maintaining the feel of traditional newspaper layout, with headlines, feature articles, beat sections, and such. They have created an exemplar for other papers, applying the Internet's rare blend of durability, accessibility, and flexibility.

THE LOWDOWN ON THE WEB VERSION OF "DARK ALLIANCE"
by Gary Webb

<http://sjmercury.com/drugs>

When I began to realize where this story was going to lead, I spoke to my editor, Dawn Garcia, about doing a Web page version for *Merc Center*. She agreed that it was something we should think about and I called Bob Ryan, *Merc Center*'s director, with an idea to link the source documents somehow to the text, so a reader could click on a quote or a word and get the actual document. Ryan said that was technologically possible and expressed a great deal of enthusiasm for the idea. From that point on, I began thinking not only of how to document the series in the paper, but how to augment it for the Web. As a result, every document I could get was copied and forwarded to *Merc Center* for scanning.

My main reason for doing a Web page was that I had seen the press reaction to the contra-CIA revelations of the mid-1980s, which were dismissed as the ravings of drug dealers. I knew from my own research how much hard evidence of this ring existed and wanted to be able to put the documents into the hands of the readers, so they could judge for themselves. Another reason was that this was a national and international story and I wanted people everywhere to be able to read it, which they could not do if it stayed on the printed page.

Finally, I have been an investigative reporter for eighteen years and I know the kind of shit that passes for journalism these days. As I told Dawn in my project memo, playing show-and-tell on this story not only would give the readers the very same information I had, but would also raise the standards of investigative reporting for the future. Now, it's not going to be good enough to say, "Records show . . ." or "Sources said . . .." You got something big?. . . Let's see it. Let's hear it. Prove it. Put it out there.

Plus, I now had unlimited space to tell my story. Don't want to use it for the paper? Fine, let's put it on the Web. No longer did I have to be constrained by the edge of the page. I had all the headroom in the world.

The Web version is the one I really wanted to do, but we didn't have the space in the paper for it. So there were a lot of selfish reasons as well.

Fortunately, the people at *Merc Center* also wanted to advance the craft and blaze some new trails themselves, and this was the perfect vehicle for that. They designed and laid out a Web page that not only incorporated everything I wanted to see, but went so far beyond it, it blew me away. I was literally speechless the first time they fired up the internal server and showed me what they had come up with.

And while it was a lot of extra work, it bulletproofed the story and made a better version available to journalists and readers worldwide. People from Germany, Japan and South America have written to me about it.

So that's the story. To me, the Web page was the most exciting thing about this whole project.

American Reporter — The News, Paperless

<http://www.newshare.com/Reporter/today.html>
<http://www.uvol.com>

In the Society of Professional Journalists' online forum, a group of journalists were discussing the closing of the *Milwaukee Journal*, one of two newspapers to bite the dust in the first quarter of 1995. Dozens of good reporters and editors were being fired, some having worked there for many years. At other papers, cost-cutting and revenue maximizing was affecting the content.

One of the discussants, Joe Shea, recalls the direction the discussion then took: "Why not start a paper run by reporters? A newspaper we would own ourselves, that could therefore never fire us, and which would reward us in proportion to our work."

Joe had been a daily reporter for two New York papers, a research editor at *Esquire*, and a long-time contributor to such alternative papers as the *L.A. Weekly* and the *Village Voice*, for a total of about two dozen years. He had only $63 in the bank, but he owned a 386 SX/25 PC and an account with Netcom, and he found 210 other journalists across the country somewhat like himself. So he started the world's first online-only, daily, general-interest, commercial newspaper with original content: the *American Reporter*, a paperless newspaper.

The first issue hit the "stands" on April 10, 1995. Competing with the media giants made for a striking image at first, but it wouldn't necessarily keep bread on the table. Then, a week later, the Oklahoma bombing tragedy rocked the nation, and one of the *Reporter*'s correspondents was on the scene. Forty-two-year-old newsroom vet Bill Johnson had been at AP's Oklahoma City bureau, and drew on his savvy to scoop the other news reporters by as much as a full day, landing interviews with the head of the day-care center in the destroyed building and with local scientists. Soon thereafter, a Washington correspondent for the *Reporter* filed reports about related hearings.

After that, many took notice of the *American Reporter*. At 35,000 bytes each issue, it continues to feature articles with depth or scope not found elsewhere: investigative and analytic reporting, book reviews, science, entertainment, and humor. The paper often reports both sides of controversial issues, such as the crisis in Cuba in March, 1996. Its coverage of the Rabin assassination, the Kurdish civil war, unrest in Indonesia, the road to peace in Ireland, and the 1996 Presidential campaign have been outstanding. It also runs Pinkerton's daily briefing on the urgent, violent news of the world; daily Asian business news; film reviews; plus many columnists.

The *Reporter* also captured notice on two other fronts: its economic structure and its ideological stance. Actually, the two are intertwined. Economically, the paper is a reporter-owned cooperative. Correspondents have equity in the company and receive premiums when their stories are picked up. Besides selling subscriptions to readers ($10 a month or $100 a year), the paper acts as an alternative national news wire for dailies and weeklies. News media can obtain a feed and the right to buy with an ordinary subscription, plus they must pay the author a premium of one cent per word for articles they reprint. For small papers unable to afford wire services or extra reporters, an alternative fee of $125 a week buys blanket reprint rights; the latter system has also proven successful for small Internet start-up companies that wish to offer a daily news feed.

Syndication is growing slowly. Wyoming's only statewide newspaper (the daily *Casper Star-Tribune*) recently subscribed. In all, there are a few hundred paid subscribers, including the Unlimited Vision Online Network, with 113 Web sites in sixteen states and Canada. "We get sixty- to ninety-thousand hits through them," Shea states, "and ten thousand of our own at the Web site (all 'pure' hits, in that there's just one button and it gets the whole paper). We can legitimately lay claim to a readership of 100,000 a month, plus whatever we get from the various BBSs that distribute us. We have readers and correspondents all over the world."

Since the paper is reporter-owned, its journalists can write what and when they want, in depth, and without having to worry about the Journalists' Golden Rule ("Never argue with a man who buys his ink by the barrelful"). As Shea describes the paper's unique perspective:

> [Our stories] tend to be more personal, more capricious, more direct, more heartfelt, more from the grass roots than from the top down. There's a lot of expression in our paper that you don't read anywhere else, and it's certainly not because many Americans aren't feeling that way. It's because it's not part of the predigested mix.

At *American Reporter*, as on the Internet, we invent as we go along.

> For more information: <http://oz.net/~susanh/arbook.html>
> Submissions: <JoeShea@netcom.com>, Editor-in-Chief

For More Information

"Inventing an Online Newspaper"
<http://www.sentex.net/~mmcadams/invent/invent2.html>

For further materials on the transition from newspaper to newspaperless, I recommend media Web designer Melinda McAdams' twenty-six-page hypertext essay, which chronicles the design of *Digital Ink*, the online version of the *Washington Post*. Beginning with the newspaper paradigm, she shows:

- how the "digital ink" paradigm led to abandoning the Style section and eliminating Page One, yet expanding local coverage and still providing a mirror of the print product
- how original content not only led to archives and linked articles but also opened out of the newspaper's traditional one-way model into two-way dialogue with readers
- how the interface was designed as "an information space" that could be logical, navigable, and searchable, and
- how the requirements of the newsroom and advertising were accommodated

Mindy also maintains the Online News forum, for those involved in cutting-edge technology of newspapers online. E-mail <majordomo@marketplace.com> with the message: "subscribe online-news *YourEmailAddress*".

Editor & Publisher Interactive
<http://www.mediainfo.com/ephome/research/researchhtm/research.htm>

This site has a megasource jumpstation of articles, papers, and publications about online news, as well as Jodi Cohen's weekly column and Steve Outing's thrice-weekly column. *Writers.net* awards them the coveted "Hildy Johnson Locked Desk Award" for best news about online news.

Mike Erlindson
<http://ourworld.compuserve.com/homepages/MErlindson/paper1.htm>

Mike has written an award-winning paper, *Online Newspapers: The Newspaper Industry's Dive into Cyberspace*.

"Online: Will It Hurt or Help Newspapers?"
<http://www.facsnet.org/top_issues/state/main.html>

This Hearst survey finds newspaper executives evenly divided as to the Net Effect on traditional newspapers.

Dom's Domain: Media Sites and Strategies
<http://www.arcfile.com/dom/coltimes.html>

Dominique Paul Noth has made the transition from paper to digital, from traditional media coverage (drama/film, arts/entertainment, *Milwaukee Journal Sentinel*) to new media. His online column is available by Web or e-mail. Topics include: abuse of the word "interactivity"; diversity in international newspapers (a guided tour); niche products; an "evaluation of the political news sites created from heavyweight alliances of newspaper, TV, and magazine bigwigs on the Internet"; a comparison of major online newspapers; and reader discussion. For more information, contact Dominique Paul Noth, <milwnews@aol.com>.

Steve Outings' FAQ
<http://www.mediainfo.com/ephome/research/researchhtm/faq.htm>

This cybercolumnist provides many links regarding online news, here and abroad.

Way New Journalism
<http://www.journalism.sfsu.edu/www/spj/digital.html>

The Journalism Department at San Francisco State University posts a few dozen reports from their major conference on the digital revolution.

FORUMS

Some journalist's forums are like a twenty-four-hour green room, where journalists can discuss anything — from office politics to national political trends — with peers at various news media and academic journalism departments. Topics are initiated by students, teachers, and reporters on an ad hoc basis. Journalist-oriented lists are also excellent places for keeping up to date with the Internet, as journalists keep up to speed with the latest and greatest.

In addition to journalist-oriented forums, there are thousands of others organized around a locale, an event, an issue, a population group — anything with a dozen or more adherents. Some journalists have posted a question to a conference and found experts doing valuable research/legwork for them. These areas are often a few days ahead of mainstream media, and are excellent sources for eyewitness accounts or person-on-the-street quotes.

Lists

Here are some watering holes where online journalists play town-crier, network together, or just hang out and gab.

Communet
The discussion group of the Community and Civic Network, for engaging citizen participation. To subscribe, e-mail the message "subscribe Communet *YourName*" to <listserv@uvmvm.uvm.edu>.

The Computer-Assisted Research & Reporting List (CARR-L)
Largely a one-way filter of news on how to find data and software programs and how to use data in stories, plus relevant journalism topics for all beats. To subscribe, e-mail <listserv@ulkyvm.louisville.edu> and in the message body type "subscribe carr-l *YourName*".

Copyediting-L

A copyeditors' discussion group for those brave souls defending the King's English against sports columnists, Internet pundits, and other manglers and maligners of the language. To subscribe, e-mail the message "subscribe copyediting-l *YourName*" to <listerv@cornell.edu>.

Dawn-l
<http://www.ualberta.ca/usaul/DAWN>

An unmoderated list for news junkies. It solicits commentary, opinions, and statistical and anecdotal evidence from members about what is happening in the world of news, whether it be neighborhood, town, state, region, or world (along with other topics of interest). Members are urged to submit noncopyrighted news stories for discussion and debate. To subscribe, e-mail <majordomo@majordomo.srv.ualberta.ca>, and in the message body state "subscribe dawn-l *YourEmailAddress*". This is a high-volume list with as many as 100 messages each day. For the digest version, in the message body state instead "subscribe dawn-l-digest *YourEmailAddress*".

Edupage

A news digest on media issues and information technology, delivered three times weekly. Translated into Chinese, French, German, Hebrew, Hungarian, Italian, Lithuanian, Portuguese, Romanian, Slovak, and Spanish, it's one of the Internet's real bright spots, and it's indispensable for staying up to date. E-mail <listproc@educom.edu>, and in the message body put "sub edupage *YourName*". (You'll also find information about their new project, Innovations, at <http://www.educom.edu/>.)

FOI-L

This list is for persons interested in freedom of information issues, the first amendment, and the public's right to know. It's a project of the National Freedom of Information Coalition, located at Syracuse University and managed by Barbara Fought. E-mail <listserv@suvm.syr.edu>, and in the body type "subscribe FOI-L *YourFirstName YourLastName*".

HOTT

A new list designed to include the latest advances in computer, communications, and electronics technology, culled from the trade press. E-mail <listserv@ucsd.edu>, and in the message body type "subscribe hott-list".

INTCAR-L

An internationally oriented computer-assisted reporting list, particularly helpful to students interested in global communication. To subscribe, e-mail <listserv@american.edu> and write the following in the message area: "subscribe intcar-l *YourName*".

IRE-L

The forum for the professional organization Investigative Reporters and Editors (IRE). E-mail <listproc@lists.missouri.edu>, and in the body type "subscribe IRE-L *YourName*".

JourNet

A discussion list for journalism educators with helpful information on courses, resources, new teaching strategies, and more. E-mail <listserv@listserv.net>, and in the body type "subscribe journet".

Media

An investigative journalism list. E-mail <listserv@listserv.net>, with the message "subscribe media". For more information, contact <media@sokrates.mip.ki.se>.

News Research

A forum for news librarians, cybrarians, online researchers, media archivists, mass media bibliographers, reporters, and journalism educators. Topics have included online databases, sites for breaking news, CD-ROM networks, twenty-four-hour news library staffing, and photo reprint sales. To join, e-mail <listserv@gibbs.oit.unc.edu> with the command "subscribe NewsLib *YourFirstName YourLastName*".

NICAR-L

The forum for the National Institute For Computer Assisted Reporting. E-mail <listserv@mizzou1.missour.edu> and, in the body of the message, type "subscribe NICAR-L *YourFirstName YourLastName*".

NIT

Run by the *Houston Chronicle* as a service of the New Information Technology Committee of the Society of Professional Journalists (SPJ). Most subscribers are professional journalists and subscribers. The list discusses information technology and general journalism issues. This is a private, professional list for which you must get permission to join (not difficult). Send an e-mail message to <nit-approval @chron.com>.

Online-News

For those involved or interested in the cutting-edge technologies of online newspapers. To subscribe, e-mail <online-news-request@marketplace.com>, and in the message body type "subscribe online-news *YourName*".

SPJ-L (formerly known as SPJ-Online)

The online forum of the Society for Professional Journalists (SPJ), begun in 1994 under the administration of Jack Lail, chair of the SPJ's New Information Technologies Committee. It's an unmoderated forum for any journalism-related issue, and many journalists find it indispensable. To subscribe, e-mail <listserv@psuvm.psu.edu>. Leave the subject line blank, and in the body of the message type "subscribe SPJ-L *YourName*".

WritersL

Last, but not least, I must point out one list that charges a nominal fee ($17 annually, and a one-time-only $5 sign-up fee) that's well worth paying. Carefully moderated, WritersL is ever-stimulating, convivial but highly focused, intensive, and capable of heavy lifting, unlike many of the free free-for-alls. Writers-L deals with "feature-writing, explanatory journalism, literary journalism, book journalism, and the high-level reportage that is generally associated with such writing." Its moderator is the Pulitzer-Prize–winning author Jon Franklin, coordinator of the University of Oregon's creative nonfiction program, who adroitly collects members' repartee and organizes it, along with his own commentary, into one daily posting. Currently there are about five hundred members.

> Open subjects include techniques, markets, jobs, privacy law, criticisms of stories and media, agents, sales, contracts, and, eternally, the pedigree of editors. Though the medium is the Net, the discussion is not about the Net, except as it applies to the future of nonfiction writing.

Recent topics have included interviewing techniques, voice, the "fly on the wall," filtering, and an example of literary journalism about a woman whose husband was diagnosed with AIDS, which ran as a twenty-eight-part serial.

To subscribe, e-mail <writer@pioneer.net>, requesting an autobiographical template and send a check for $22 to:

WriterL
P.O. Box 929
Philomath, Oregon 97370

Usenet Newsgroups

As explained in Chapter 2, conferences are a variant of mailing lists; they are potentially larger electronic forums wherein conferees post their views, as on a bulletin board, by subject. The primary site for this is Usenet (where conferences are called "newsgroups" — even if they're about recipes, gardening, or gay parenting).

There are a dozen and a half Usenet newsgroups for journalists, including: alt.freedom.of.information.act, alt.internet.media-coverage, alt.journalism (shoptalk), alt.journalism.criticism ("I write, therefore I'm biased"), alt.journalism.freelance, alt.journalism.gay-press, alt.journalism.gonzo (the school of Hunter S. Thompson), alt.journalism-objective (showcasing minimally-biased, high-quality, grassroots news and feature reporting by anyone on the Net), alt.journalism.photo, alt.journalism.print (newspaper, magazine, and online reporters), alt.journalism.students, alt.news-media, alt.politics, alt.politics.media, alt.tv.news-shows (tabloid journalism on the tube), and rec.radio.broadcasting.

Online Services

Lexis-Nexis is the premiere online service for information professionals; but just because it's online (available on a computer via modem) doesn't mean it's on the Internet. Nor is it free. Similar proprietary, non-Internet online database services are Data Star, Dialog, and H.W. Wilson.

CompuServe. Of the major commercial Internet online services, CompuServe is traditionally known as the best one for research. After more than a decade, it's attracted over 40,000 media professionals and ordinary people interested in media, who exchange commentary, story ideas, and professional career tips. The Journalism Forum (JFORUM), founded in 1985 by former NBC News director Jim Cameron, consists of: a message board, divided into topics; conference rooms, where members can gather either to chat in real time or participate in prearranged press conferences or online discussions; data libraries, with programs, how-to's, job listings, and online newsletters; and an archive of press releases, an AP Technical Committee, an online Master's Degree, and more. Assistant sysop (system operator, or human host) is Dan Hamilton, <76701.13@compuserve.com>. Other areas include the News Grid searchable wire service compilation (GO NEWSGRID); CompuServe News Forum, providing journalists with timely events, files, conversations, and other news areas at CompuServe (GO CSNEWS); media newsletters (MEDIANEWS); and numerous databases.

Magazines predominate at the News Source USA, which is searchable by keyword. Executive News Service performs electronic article clipping from such wires as AP, UPI, Dow Jones, Business Wire, and Comtex. Some CompuServe features have independent fees, such as IQuest InfoCenter, a gateway to hundreds of databases (Dialog, NewsNet, Data Star, and many more).

But CompuServe features can add up to more than $100/month if used more than now and then for more than one or two articles.

Prodigy. On the other hand, some online services, such as Prodigy, have been giving away free accounts or at least substantial discounts to full-time reporters from TV and radio, newspapers, and magazines. Prodigy features a nonstop newsroom, and its News Search allows keyword searches on AP stories and Dow Jones business reports. In addition to its newsstand, it has online material from many cable TV companies. For more on that free account offer, contact Publicity: (914) 448-2125.

America Online. Researchers using America Online will find the following tip extremely time-saving: in the "Keyword" dialogue box, enter the word "keyword" to see all the options (5,000). The resulting list is printable, too, for future reference.

JOURNALISTS' RESEARCH RESOURCES

Chapter 14 explores research in general, but here are a few resources of particular interest to journalists.

> **The Canadian Broadcasting Company's Journalists' & Broadcasters' Resources**
> <http://www.synapse.net/~radio/welcome.html>

An extensive series of links designed for journalists and broadcasters in Ottawa, but of use to others interested in information. Areas covered include news, current events, government, politics, music, film, and other arts and culture areas, as well as education, science, and technology. The site also includes links to professional information for journalists and broadcasters, plus a large selection of Internet search tools.

Documents in the News
<http://www.lib.umich.edu/libhome/Documents.center/docnews.html>

Furnishes primary texts pertinent to current events.

The John F. Kennedy School of Government
<http://ksgwww.harvard.edu/ksgpress/~journpg.htm>

An online news office — a group of online resources for reporters, which includes connections to online news services, reference and academic centers, trade publications, international sources, and articles on using the Internet for reporting.

John Makulowich
<http://www.clark.net/pub/journalism/jexercises.html>

A series of free, not-for-profit, step-by-step online tutorials in Internet research.

The Launchpad for Journalists
<http://www.tribnet.com./journ.htm>

A megasource jumpstation to 18,000 Web sites, arranged by subject.

The Reporters Internet Guide (RIG)
<http://www.crl.com/~jshenry/rig.html>

Truly great shareware resource (free download, $25 if you decide to keep it). It's divided into topical beats and updated about twice a month. Resources are described, links are checked, and dead ends are repaired. Topics include arts and entertainment; business and labor; computers, crime, and law; education; environment; health and medicine; the Internet and the World Wide Web; international sources; the U.S. government; and others, as well as journalism and searching the Internet.

Reporter's Internet Survival Guide
<http://www.qns.com/~casey>

Patrick Casey, with AP's Oklahoma City bureau, maintains this Guide at his Web site.

Internet Newsroom
<http://www.dgsys.com/~editors/index.html>

The Journalist's Toolbox
<http://www.ccnet.com/CSNE/toolbox.html>

Launchpad for Journalists
<http://www.tribnet.com/journ.htm>

FEEDS AND LEADS

Competition is heating up for news sources. Comparing the international and national news of most dailies, you see news coming from similar sources, with local news becoming a prime asset. Let's look at how the Internet is a conduit for both traditional and new news sources.

Associated Press (AP)

Associated Press is available at least three ways:

AP Online
<http://www.latimes.com/HOME/NEWS/APONLINE/>

Requires free registration with the *Los Angeles Times*. News briefs, international, national, Washington, entertainment, business/finance, Wall Street, sports, and science/health.

AP Breaking National News
<http://www.globe.com/globe/cgi-bin/globe.cgi?ap/apnat.htm>

Available from the *Boston Globe*.

Christian Science Monitor
<http://www.csmonitor.com/headlines/apfeed/apfeed.html>

The *Christian Science Monitor* offers a straight feed of raw "tear sheets."

ClariNet

<http://www.clari.net>

Begun in 1989, ClariNet was the first electronic newspaper service on the Internet, (thus, arguably, one of its first commercial content providers). ClariNet e.news has over 500 categories to choose from, and culls news from various wire services, feature syndicates, and other professional news organizations (such as Reuters, AP, Newsbytes, Sports-Ticker, Business Wire, and Commerce Business Daily) — including columns, cartoons, and stock quotes — delivering it all via Usenet and the World Wide Web. General categories are Business, Finance, and Markets; Technology; Lifestyle; General; Sports; and Local, U.S., and World. At least 2,000 stories are published a day, with 150 daily updates and 900 story revisions. Foreign news exceeds CNN and the *New York Times* combined.

Founder Brad Templeton once created and moderated a conference on Usenet for the latest jokes, with eventual daily readership estimated at half a million. As of late 1995, his current company, ClariNet, surpassed that figure by chalking up one million paid subscribers. Subscriptions fees are $1.00 per user per month.

In Usenet, the groups are prefaced "clari" (clari.biz.media.releases, clari.news.issues.poverty, clari.living.books, and so on). Clari.tw is the TechWire, technology news (with fifty-two subtopics, from aerospace to telecommunications).

IT Informer

<http://www.keyway.net/mmp/>

IT Informer carries four news services related to the business world: banking, finance, retail, and manufacturing/public sector specialists. Any bona fide professional journalist is welcome to subscribe indefinitely, free of charge. The wires are all updated daily and mainly comprise subbed releases. They are listed chronologically, by buyer, by supplier, by sector, and by product or service. International in scope, the service also functions as an archive for background information. Registration is required for free subscription. For more information, contact Charles Newman, <mmp@pavilion.co.uk>.

Other News Services

The Foundation For American Communications (FACS)
<http://www.facsnet.org/>

FACS is well known for its numerous issue-oriented seminars and workshops across the U.S. Its Web presence, FacsNet, is free but requires registration. It consists of: background on the key issues; reporting tools "to help slice through complex issues"; highly selective, annotated links to Internet resources; and sources online —

"names, phone numbers, and e-mail connections to people who can answer your questions." The editor is Randy Reddick.

American News Service (ANS)
<http://www.americannews.com>

News media may be unaware that they can reprint up to eight articles a month for free from ANS, the largest nonprofit service of its kind in the world. ANS Stories are also a challenge to all working journalists, covering topical subjects in the context of society's search for solutions to problems affecting people's lives — in education, race relations, media, environment, community development, workplace, and government — rather than for exploitive sensationalism. Edited by Frances Moore Lappé (author of *Diet for a Small Planet* and co-founder of the Center for Living Democracy), ANS' focus on innovations in public problem-solving is a welcome relief from shock-oriented reportage, and represents a significant trend that's highlighted further a few pages ahead.

Pacific News Service (PNS)
<http://www.pacificnews.org>

The Internet provides both writers and publishers with ideal access to PNS, the venerable California wire service, established circa 1970 and maintained by MacArthur Fellow Sandy Close. PNS syndicates its writers, scholars, journalists, and young people — all new voices and perspectives — through original newspaper and magazine articles, essays for TV (in particular, *News Hour with Jim Lehrer* on PBS) and radio (*All Things Considered*), and a youth publication, *YO!*

Since 1975, they've immersed themselves in the changes transforming America — from immigration, deindustrialization, and the globalization of the economy to the turn to religion by the dispossessed, the growing gap between poor and rich, and the opening up of cyberspace.

A selection of their feed is available online at their Web site, via selections from two magazines. For more information about how to write to individual PNS contributors, or how to contribute your writing to PNS, e-mail <pacificnews@pacificnews.org>.

YO! (Youth Outlook)
<http://www.pacificnews.org/yo/>

YO! is a bimonthly news journal of youth culture produced by young people in the San Francisco Bay Area — a unique model for integrating writers, journalists, and scholars with young people, sponsored and syndicated through PNS.

Jinn
<http://www.pacificnews.org/jinn/>

Jinn is the PNS's biweekly, online-only, global media magazine. Featuring personal essays, investigative reports, and commentaries, it carries stories typified by a welcome, self-styled "chicken's-eye view of the world — from two feet off the ground, through the lens of culture rather than of politics."

MSNBC
<http://www.msnbc.com>

The formation of strategic alliances is an important trend in major media. The Microsoft Network (MSN), for example, formed an alliance with the NFL and NBC during the 1996 Olympics. Following that rehearsal, MSNBC (MSN + NBC) officially launched in July of that year with a Web site to augment Microsoft's new twenty-four-hour news cable.

Presslink
<http://corpweb.krmediastream.com>

Launched May 1995 by Knight-Ridder's Media Stream, this is an online service providing access to Knight-Ridder/Tribune, Agence France Press, and Reuters.

Reuters
<http://www.reuters.com>

As news provider for the major online services as well as for CNN, IBM infoSage, and Yahoo!, Reuters is developing new products for the Web.

Sternberg's Daily News
<http://www.helsinki.fi/%7Elsaarine/news.html>

Provides a number of daily public-domain news services.

Touch Today
<http://www.clickit.com/touch/news/news.htm>

Maps sources for online news.

World Media Link
<http://www.dds.ul/~kidon/media.html>

World Media Link provides a couple hundred links to international magazines, newspapers, broadcast media, film and news agencies, and related Web sites, maintained by a political science student at the University of Amsterdam, who goes by the handle "Kidon."

Voice of America
<gopher://gopher.voa.gov>

Another interesting Net source for news. Voice of America has not only kept up with the Internet (for one thing, having pioneered delivery of audio online), but has adopted a new, refreshing, post-Cold-War editorial stance. Text of all articles is available, arranged by date, on a weekly basis.

TRENDS TO WATCH

News in the Future
<http://nif.www.media.mit.edu>

No one can say for sure what journalism will look like ten or twenty years from now, though there's at least one Web site devoted to the topic.

Ego Interactive
<http://www.thespectator.com/ego/>

For a peek around the corner and into the future, consider *Ego Interactive*, an ongoing experiment of the *Spectator*, a daily paper in Hamilton, Ontario, Canada. *Ego*, released weekly since November, 1995, is a music and entertainment section of the paper for the Web. In conjunction with the R&D department of the paper's owners, *Ego* has developed tools and processes enabling its journalists to create stories from the outset that can be used in both print and multimedia.

All too often, online versions of print stories are merely "repurposed," as if the text were shoveled up and dumped into another hole — now illustrated, but essentially the same as before. *Ego*'s editor and writers plan a story that has a multimedia version from the outset. So *Ego*'s writers are capturing audio, doing voice-overs and stand-ups, and making decisions that affect both print and Net versions of the stories.

Special features of *Ego Interactive* include:

- digital archives of more than 100 local bands, including sound (both Real Audio and Aiff formats) and video clips, pictures, bios, and past stories about the groups
- direct e-mail to *Ego* writers and editors
- an opportunity to submit CD reviews and other feedback via e-mail
- a narrated version of the Job's Palace comic strip
- local poetry read by the poets themselves
- a weekly audio overview of the local music scene
- an updated guide to hundreds of local restaurants and clubs
- a guide to the history, communities, and culture of Hamilton

For more information, contact Dean Tudor <dtudor@acs.ryerson.ca>.

New Skills

For training in the newsroom and classroom, HTML is becoming a staple skill, though no one is sure yet where to slot it or how much emphasis to give it. Many a good journalist is being outdistanced by editors and designers less talented than they but who know how to format a Web page.

Does this mean that reporters will become superfluous? No. Ask yourself: can you keep up with all the newsprint to which you subscribe? Hence the journalist is still needed to research, sift through, focus, filter, and organize information for us in bite-sized bits, which are the journalist's traditional stock in trade — albeit with new skills, and in new ways, for a changing information environment.

Information Farming

Along with multimedia, electronic journalists (Net writers) are handling larger and larger amounts of information. To use an analogy drawn by Paul Peter Evans, it's like the invention of stone tools. Instead of going out into the Paleolithic wilds to hunt, the Mesolithic farmer grew his food locally. Similarly, in the Mesoelectronic, wherever you happen to be you can grow information locally, whether your beat be statewide, national, or international.

Project Crayon (CReAte Your Own Newspaper)
<http://www.crayon.net>

Crayon offers over a hundred news sources for free via the Web and lets you bookmark any links as files on your hard disk so that you can view them again via your Web browser. Sources include AP, *Money*, *Time*, and *PC Week*, as well as Internet-only, off-the-beaten-track items such as Adam Curry's *Cybersleaze Report*. Jeffrey Boulter, one of the two computer science students who created Crayon, confessed that he dreamed it up because he was too lazy to walk to the store for a newspaper. Apparently it's a popular dream, as evidenced by the fact that more than 22,000 people have created their own Crayon papers in the first two months since the service went online.

Information Agents

I mentioned information agents (a.k.a. intelligent agents and personal agents) in the case study of *Mercury Center*, earlier in this chapter. These agents affect journalism on the user end (readers), and they can also be used by journalists.

PointCast Network (PCN)
<http://www.pointcast.com>

The PointCast Network (PCN) was the Net's first demonstration of a personal agent, providing users with customized news. Launched February, 1996, it gathered 1.7 million "viewers" before year's end. What makes it so popular? PointCast lets you select from news sources (a.k.a. "channels") — national, international, financial, entertainment, and so on — from Business Wire, PR Newswire, Reuters, S&P Comstock, Sports Ticker, TimeWarner Pathfinder, the *Los Angeles Times*, the *San Jose Mercury News*, and the *New York Times*, and have the latest information delivered directly to a screensaver interfacer on your computer, via your Internet connection. The software is downloadable for free from the network's Web site.

If you have access to a dedicated twenty-four-hour-a-day Internet connection, it can be set to continually update information; otherwise, replacing old information with new takes a few minutes. And as the PCN software changes, it will automatically update itself.

Like the software, PointCast's service is free, being advertising-supported. Ads appear as brief animations in a corner of the screen. There are currently fifty national advertisers, targeting specific audiences.

For more information about PointCast, call 1-800-586-4733. For your information, there are several dozen other push software programs currently available (BackWeb, for example, <http://www.backweb.com>) that don't require a "network" such as PointCast.

PPS Online
<http://www2.pps.ca/pps.html>

Another example of information agent technology is PPS Online, of definite interest to science and health reporters. It began as an ordering service for medical professionals. Now it will keep you up to date on medical subjects of your selection, such as new drugs for specific conditions, data on various diseases, or the URLs (an URL, or Uniform Resource Locator, is simply an Internet address) of new medical sites. Selections include geographical criteria.

Civic Journalism

At the forefront of the nineties media movements has been the trend toward what's variously called civic journalism, public journalism, and public interest journalism — within which the Internet figures prominently.

Civic journalism can be seen in the "solutions" segment on *Peter Jennings' World News Tonight*, and in metropolitan newspapers that add coverage of their cities' search for solutions. Civic journalism challenges journalists to find newsmakers who are working from the bottom up as well as from the top down, and to see their work in the context of a changing society. As such, it's parallel and congruent with the bottom-up, open network model of the Internet, which is playing a big part in its adoption.

Harvard's prestigious Nieman Foundation held a symposium in 1996, entitled "Public Interest Journalism: Winner or Loser in the Online Era?" Transcripts are available at <http://www.Nieman.harvard.edu/Nieman/CAgenda.html>.

James Fallows is a torch-bearer of this movement. A member of the Eastern media establishment (Harvard-educated, Rhodes Scholar, former chief White House speech writer), in 1995 he broke ranks and wrote *Breaking the News: How the Media Undermine American Democracy*. With David Rothman, he created a Web site called Fallows Central, <http://www.clark.net/pub/rothman/fallows.htm>, to go with the book, with links to such entities as the Pew Center for Civic Journalism, <http://democracyplace.org/pew.html>, and the Civic Projects Network, <http://www.cpn.org>.

Progressive Media

When the *Village Voice* launched in 1955, its journalists were given free reign. By the seventies, there were hundreds of such papers across the land (the epithet "underground" having been replaced with the more marketable "alternative"). Today, there are many more options.

The Institute for Alternative Journalism's Media and Democracy Congress
<http://www.igc.org/an/congress/index.html>

Non-mainstream media publishes such cogent papers as "The Internet & the Future of Democracy," "http://www.journalism.now: A Tour of Our Uncertain Future," "Talking Back: What Journalists Can Learn from the 1930s Reporter Ernie Pyle," and "Will the Internet Become the Next Mass Medium?" These can all be found in the archives of The Institute for Alternative Journalism's first Media and Democracy Congress, February 1996, which brought together thirty-two organizations and over 650 attendees — now an annual event. And it would be an appropriate hack to visit the alternative network, AlterNet, who hosted the proceedings, <http://www.alternet.org/>.

The Institute for Global Communications (IGC)
<http://www.igc.apc.org>

For another non-mainstream venue, IGC is an online service that builds viable, progressive community. Their stated purpose is "to expand and inspire movements for environmental sustainability, human and workers' rights, nonviolent conflict resolution, social and economic justice, and women's equality by providing and developing accessible computer networking tools." In the thousands of conferences they host, member journalists will find a wealth of sources.

World Free Press
<http://www.wwfreepress.com/>

Making a case for the nineties being the sixties all over again, only upside down, this site has included Congressman Bernard Sanders (Vermont) on the viability of a third party, Deena Metzger on whales, Michael Ventura on revolution, Robert Scheer on the CIA, and a directory of activist organizations. Editor-publisher Art Kunkin welcomes information from already extant regional free presses, and posts information on how to access free Web servers and set up a free newspaper thereon.

Fat City News
<http://www.fatcitynews.com>

Beyond non-mainstream outlooks, this site is a repository of outlandish and gonzo journalism.

Mother Jones
<http://www.motherjones.com/coinop_congress/coinop_congress.html>

Progressive news resources can do some clever things online. In early spring of 1996, for example, *Mother Jones* (named after the feisty, dedicated labor organizer Mary Harris Jones, 1830–1930) took a feature article — "Taking Stock in Congress" by Professor Gregory Boller and his students at the University of Memphis — and gave it a new twist in cyberspace. The electronic adaptation took the voting records database of U.S. representatives and congresspeople, plus the database of their personal stock portfolios — both public information, though not immediately accessible to everyone — and interlinked them with a common search function. Click on the name of a representative or congressperson, and you may discover if that politician had conducted a trade that might benefit from his or her political influence. By being interactive, it brings the point home far more effectively than would a journalist reporting on the results.

New Journalism

Just as the Internet has inspired a new literary subgenre, cyberpunk, so too is it spawning a new reportorial style. It's an heir to the New Journalism of the sixties, and it's all over the Usenet.

It is copy submitted as e-mail. It isn't written in Yankee AP-neutral. The authors' "I" is very much in the piece, locating a living world, where explosions go <ka-BOOM!>; it isn't constrained when it comes to focusing and elaborating on details otherwise ignored. Often stream-of-consciousness, it invests in the world in all its variousness, remaining open to multiple points of view. It pushes people's buttons; even if it's wrong it gets readers involved. And it's so darned colloquial. Shucks, it's gonna qualify as a new dialect, I reckon, and, sheesh, you just gotta love it for that. It makes transcontinental paper planes out of the PMLA's rectilinear style template — unafraid to be elliptical rather than expository, mosaic instead of prosaic. It uses cyberjargon as metaphor, defaulting to common sense before the application crashes and the paragraph reboots for a fresh pass. It can cite sources with great care, even hyperlinking directly to them if need be. And it has a place in world culture that is postcolonialist, challenging the English language's centuries'-old resiliency to further evolve and adapt through still yet more foreign contact. Plus, not only can it think locally and act globally; it can think globally and act locally.

Global Journalism

Lastly, there's a unique relationship between local and global, online. Whether we write explicitly of foreign affairs or not, things just don't happen in one part of the world anymore. Take one step out on the Internet, and you're instantly communicating in a global environment. Capturing a global audience is one of the Net's primary attractions to media. And it's ideal for the open, market-oriented structure, necessary for a global economy.

Our global village is fast becoming a global apartment house — or housing project, the kind with thin walls. For example, in June, 1994, Indonesia banned *Tempo* magazine, but a year or so later it resumed publication — on the Net, <http://www.idola.net.id/tempo>.

In February, 1996, the government of Zambia banned both a print issue of the *Post* there and its appearance at the paper's Web site; it revealed government plans to hold a referendum on the adoption of a new constitution — information of great interest to the regime's opponents, but which the ruling regime deemed classified. A few days later, Net activist Declan McCullagh posted to a few mailing lists asking if anyone had seen a copy. Two days later, a copy went up on the Web (<http://www.cs.cmu.edu/~declan/zambia>).

> **Association of Progressive Communicators (APC)**
> <http://www.igc.apc.org>

Many regimes aren't comfortable about the presence of the Internet in their country. Others simply have difficulty being able to afford it. This organization, affiliated with the Institute for Global Communication (IGC), is dedicated to helping countries adopt and adapt to the Internet. Its Web site has a daily list of selected headlines from the thousands of conferences it hosts. IGC has also hosted UN summits online — on the environment, in Brazil; on human rights, in Vienna; and on women, in Beijing. These special projects are the next best thing to being there.

In addition to the IGC and the APC, there are other good gatherings of foreign affairs news sources.

International Affairs Net
<http://www.pitt.edu/~ian/ianres.html>

An excellent compilation.

One World News Services
<http://oneworld.org/news/index.html>

An alternative source for international news, produced by a British charity, linking the worlds of development and broadcasting.

Foreign Affairs
<http://www.foreignaffairs.org>

A jumpstation of fine links on a par with the magazine's sterling content.

Others' special projects have broken further ground. Throughout June, 1996, the *New York Times* with IBM launched "Bosnia: Uncertain Paths to Peace," with a narrative illustrated with 150 photos by journalist Gilles Peress and supplemented with maps, audio clips, archival *Times*' articles, and hyperlinks. Moreover, beyond this hypermagazine format, ten forums were hosted by leading intellectual and political figures specializing in different aspects of the Bosnia conflict, including preceding history, the war and its destruction, the religious dimension, and political ramifications. Terminals were installed at the International Criminal Tribunal for the former Yugoslavia in the Hague and at the UN, as well as in Sarajevo, so that Bosnians could take part. The site remained accessible for two months.

Local News

As we noted in our case study of *Mercury Center*, a very viable Net trend is local news. Shrinking sales figures for some metropolitan dailies can be attributed to the rising sales figures of newer, local weeklies. Some of these alternatives are going online as well, such as the thirty-year-old *San Francisco Bay Guardian*,

<http://www.sfbayguardian.com>, which is including its valuable classifieds (the Crown Jewels of local news) and building community by offering free e-mail accounts.

New players in the local news market include:

Microsoft's Sidewalk
<http://www.sidewalk.com>

AOL's Digital City
<http://www.digitalcity.com>

CitySearch
<http://www.citysearch.com>

AT&T's Hometown Network
(Not yet launched, as of this writing.)

Yahoo's regional pages
<http://www.sfbay.yahoo.com>

Case Study: 24-Hour +

<http://www.cyber24.com>

To wrap up, here's an example of a cyberspace news project that raised the bar for all net journalists. In the early morning of February 8, 1996, Rick Smolan crossed his fingers on his way to his company, Against All Odds Productions. On that pre-set, well-publicized date, four million Internauts "tuned in," as 150 photojournalists scattered around the globe covering Internet-related events, plus hundreds of amateur photographers, each filed their rough reports all on that same day to a common Web site, every half hour:

> . . . Cape Town students getting degrees via distance learning, the fourteen-acre twenty-seven-ton AIDS quilt being preserved digitally, Palestinian and Israeli kids designing Web sites together, rebuilding a Russian cathedral with online coordination, keeping tabs on elephants in Malaysia, exploring a fourth-century archeological dig in Egypt as students follow along from their computer screens in Michigan, a Kentucky couple finding a four-month-old Korean boy on the Web to adopt, Inuit villagers who hunt caribou and surf the Web, Disney studios con-

ducting auditions and doing dubbing over ISDN lines, Tom Reilly cutting a $3M deal for Planet Out, digital graffiti artists in Singapore, a murder convict clearing himself with evidence submitted to his Web page, monks in a fifteenth-century Buddhist temple awakening the world through their laptop ...

That day the hits just kept on coming. Two hundred thousand photos, plus text both written and spoken (including interviews with the photographers themselves), filled up 11,000 megabytes of RAM and nearly 300 gigabytes of hard disk storage back at "Mission Control," staffed with eighty human editors who were testing experimental gear such as NetObjects Fusion software, automating layout on the fly.

"It was like jumping out of an airplane with some cloth and rope," Smolan said, "and building your parachute while watching the ground come up real fast." Subtitled "Painting on the Walls of the Digital Cave," *24 Hours in Cyberspace* not only put a human face on cyberspace but also became the ultimate Web site, the largest event in the history of the Internet, and arguably the most elaborate news story in the history of journalism.

Now edited into final form, it's a book/CD-ROM/Internet site — with aspects of newspaper, radio, and TV as well. In the early eighties, when Smolan authored the very first *Day in the Life of . . .* book, photographers were assigned to document a pre-designed story or event; now they have not only more media with which to document, but also more power to discover events. Raising the bar for all Internet publishers and writers, it's an exemplar well worth experiencing.

SELF-PUBLISHING THE NEWS

There are a number of identifiable, self-proclaimed amateur journalists out there.

The American Amateur Press Association (AAPA)
<http://members.aol.com/aapa96/>

A nationwide nonprofit organization of currently about 350 members who enjoy writing, editing, printing, or publishing as a hobby.

Other amateur journalism groups' subsites include: <http://members.aol.com/aapa96/otheraj.html> and Reciprocal Links: <http://members.aol.com/aapa96/reciprocal.html>.

For more information, contact Dave Tribby, <tribby@cup.hp.com>.

The Columns
<http://www.the-columns.com/>

Features editorials sent in by readers from around the world. Each Monday, they print five.

The Net enables working journalists to become their own publishers. Here are some journalists who self-publish their own Web sites, concluding with a look at a journalist with his own mailing list broadsheet.

Farai Chidaya
<http://www.popandpolitics.com>

Pop&politics is the home page of Farai Chidaya, a reporter on CNN television. Online, she publishes her articles, "letting down her hair," as it were, about many of the same topics and events she covers on TV.

Andrian Kreye
<www.users.interport.net/~akreye>

Andrian Kreye is a German journalist based in New York, publishing an electronic e-zine, *@reportage*. *@Reportage* is in three sections. There are stories from such places as Gaza, Moscow, Haiti, L.A., Guatemala, and Bosnia. There is a gallery for photojournalism. And there is an international newsrack of hundreds of newspapers, magazines, and information sources.

Tom Mangan
<http://www.iaonline.com/users/tmangan/newsies.html>

Copy editor Tom Mangan, in Peoria, Illinois, maintains a megasource jumpstation called Newsies, hyperlinking to as many journalists' personal pages as he can find.

Keith Mays
<http://www.sightphoto.com>

Keith Mays hosts Sight, for photojournalists.

Mike Wendland
<http://www.wdiv.com/htt.html>

Mike Wendland's "High Tech Talk" and "Net Surfing" shows are syndicated to millions of TV viewers, but also available online at his home page, where he also provides FAQs about high tech from his shows, hotlinks for research, Internet search tools, etc.

Brock Meeks
<http://cyberwerks.com/cyberwire>

At the age of forty, Brock Meeks is a highly regarded, award-winning reporter. After a stint in San Francisco, including serving as foreign correspondent for the *San Francisco Chronicle* during the Afghanistan War, Meeks moved his base to Washington, D.C., covering the Beltway for *Communications Daily* by day. By night, he posted online his own hard-hitting, take-no-prisoners-style articles, letting other people distribute them across the Net. For example, one of his sources leaked a confidential FBI cost analysis of the controversial Digital Wiretap Plan. It showed that the White House signed off on the Plan based on incorrect figures furnished them by the FBI. "I wrote about the White House being essentially duped," Brock recollects. "I put it online on Friday. On Saturday it showed up in the *New York Times* — without attribution."

And so he decided to give his digital newsdesk/newsletter a name — *CyberWire Dispatch* — and to copyright his stories. As Elizabeth Weise of AP quipped, "A wire service of one was born." He's received no recompense other than exposure and recognition. "I like the fact that all the hard work and effort has created a brand and reputation that's respected. That's the payoff; it makes a difference. That's why I went into this business."

Among the stories he broke in 1994 were the Clinton administration's support for "front loading" the so-called Information Superhighway with eavesdropping technologies, the FBI plans to install "easy access" wiretap software on telephone networks, the National Security Agency's withholding information about known flaws in the Clipper Chip from the public, and the claims that cellular phones can cause cancer. By then, *CyberWire Dispatch* had a circulation of 800,000, including readers in high places, such as the FBI, the Pentagon, and the Department of Commerce.

In 1995, *CyberWire Dispatch* broke the story that not only was *Time* magazine's notoriously lurid "CyberPorn" cover article based on highly spurious information, but it had been sourced by someone who'd authored a book entitled *Pornographer's Handbook: How to Exploit Women, Dupe Men, & Make Lots of Money*. (Further independent Internet investigation alleged that this person had been turned away from the doors of a couple of Atlantic City casinos.) In a rare occurrence, the media giant knelt, ate crow, and publicly apologized for its incorrect information

— resembling, to many, a Goliath defeated by a David armed with only a modem for a slingshot.

Writing with an attitude hasn't been without cost. Meeks, along with countless other Netizens, received a flyer in his e-mail box one day, offering him full Internet access for agreeing to receive occasional commercial messages there. He called the 800 number, leaving his name and address as instructed. Instead of receiving information, he was hit with a mail solicitation for a plan that promised earnings of up to $1 million a year for an investment of a mere $159. His investigation revealed not only that the source of both solicitations was the same, but that the corporation had committed further questionable practices in the past. So he wrote it up. And for questioning the viability of their claims, the $100 million corporation attempted to silence him with a lawsuit — a case that Steven L. Baden, on page B1 of the April 22, 1994, *Wall Street Journal*, called "one of the first U.S. libel cases to arise out of the free-for-all on the Internet." It was finally settled out of court, with a payment of $64 to cover legal filing fees, but the *Dispatch* "issued no apology, no retraction, no correction, and there was no admission of liability."

And the reputation he has built up through *CyberWire Dispatch* has paid off. After two and a half years, Meeks moved to *Inter@ctive Week*, and then on to being Washington Correspondent for *Wired* magazine, chief correspondent for *HotWired*. Today he plies his cyberskills as chief Washington correspondent for MSNBC, writing for both the cable site and the Web site, and *CyberWire Dispatch*.

PROFESSIONAL ORGANIZATIONS

Freedom Forum
<http://www.freedomforum.org>

National Newspaper Association (community newspapers)
<http://www.oweb.com/naa/naahome.html>
<TheNNA@aol.com>

National Press Club
<http://www.townhall.org/places/npc>

Newspaper Association of America
<http://www.infi.net/naa>

Poynter Institute
<http://www.poynter.org/profpoynter/home.html>

Shorenstein Center
<http://ksgwww.harvard.edu/~presspol>

ONLINE NEWSSTANDS

As more and more newspapers go online here and abroad, the Net writer has access to them, whether to research a story or research new markets for selling a story. Of the twenty-four-hour newsstands where you can peruse the world's news, here's a representative sampling.

Ecola's Newsstand
<http://www.ecola.com>

A searchable megasource jumpstation for both newspapers and magazines.

Editor & Publisher
<http://www.mediainfo.com/edpub/>

Steve Outings maintains a comprehensive, active list of online newspapers.

IBM's News Rack
<http://www.ibm.net/news>

Links to various publications and other forms of major media, for world news, general interest, finance, technology, and weather, plus megasource jumpstations.

netMEDIA
<http://www.gopublic.co.at/gopublic/media/>

Provides access to hundreds of media outlets, print and broadcast. For more information, contact Thomas Schwabe, <public.relations@gopublic.co.at>.

Newslink
<http://www.newslink.org>

Run by consultant Eric Meyer, this site arguably has the vastest array of links to newspapers anywhere, plus magazines and TV/radio home pages. Winner of the *writers.net* Golden Coin Changer for Best Twenty-Four-Hour Newsstand.

Newspaper & Journalism Links
<http://www.spub.ksu.edu/other/journ.html>

A goodly array of daily newspapers on the Internet.

Online Newspapers on the Web
<http://www.intercom.com.au/intercom/newspapers/index.htm>

An excellent index with terse comments.

The Spring
<http://www.spring.com/~epub/>

Runs such a poll on the top ten Internet news periodicals. The site also serves as a newsstand jumpstation to the ever-growing selection, and maintains a media conference.

The Ultimate Collection of Newslinks
<http://pppp.net/links/news>

This site has a frames-based interface enabling browsing through over 3,700 newspapers around the world, organized geographically.

JOB BANKS

The Internet is a terrific medium for classified ads, including those for employment in journalism. There are regular postings of journalism job openings in many of the forums listed above. And journalists can post their resumé to online job banks such as:

Monsterboard
<http://www.monsterboard.com>

Online Career Center
<http://www.occ.com>

CareerPath
<http://www.careerpath.com>

Pools classifieds from sixteen major metropolitan newspapers.

Editor & Publisher
<http://www.mediainfo.com/edpub>

Posts classifieds for writing and editing jobs.

Freelance Online
<http://haven.ios.com/~freelans>

A directory and database for employment plus resources for freelance writers, artists, designers, illustrators, indexers, proofreaders, photographers, and providers of production, editorial, and creative services in publishing and advertising. For more information, contact <freelans@haven.ios.com>.

"How to Find an Online Journalism Job on the Web"
<http://www.careermag.com/newsarts/jobsearch/1042.html>

J-Jobs
<http://eb.journ.latech.edu/jobs/jobs_home.html>

A free digest of journalism jobs and internships that have been posted on the Internet.

National Diversity Journalism Job Bank
<http://www.newsjobs.com>

A comprehensive listing of journalism openings, hosted by the *Florida Times-Union* on the Internet. Openings include police reporters, copy editors, features designers, feature writers, associate editors, general assignment features writers, and a varied assortment of other opportunities.

News Mait Writers' Cooperative
<http://nwsmait.intermarket.com/nmfwc/>

A very thorough menu of work-related journalism listings and postings.

MISCELLANEOUS RESOURCES

"The Internet: A Goldmine for Editors & Reporters"
<http://www.ru.ac.za/departments/journ/gold.html>

A sixty-one-page discursive view by Guy Berger, head of the Journalism and Media Studies Department at Rhodes University, Grahamstown, South Africa, delivered in 1996 at the World Editors Forum.

Digital Edge
<http://www.naa.org/edge.html>

The online magazine of the Newspaper Association of America features: the latest and hottest in Web publishing software, tools, and techniques; cybercolumnists on copyright, Web advertising, and Web news coverage; hot links; and more. Membership, open to individuals whose newspapers or organizations belong to the Newspaper Association of America, costs $125 a year.

"The Effect of the Net on the Professional News Media: Will This Kill That?"
<http://www.cs.columbia.edu/~hauben/papers/net-and-newsmedia.txt>

An intriguing graduate paper by Michael Hauben, with special emphasis on Usenet. Bibliography.

"How Reporters Use the Net"
<http://www.ksg.harvard.edu/~ksgpress/umdcc.htm>

A general survey.

"Tabloids, Talk Radio, and the Future of News: Technology's Impact on Journalism"
<http://www.annenberg.nwu.edu/pubs/tabloids/>

By Ellen Hume.

News in the Next Century
<http://policy.net/rtndf/>

A project of the Radio and Television News Directors Foundation, with a number of monographs and companion videotapes from recent roundtable discussions on the future of news.

Investigative Reporters and Editors
<http://www.ire.org/pubs/>

Offers many print books about journalism at a discount.

See the Bibliography for further resources in print.

MEGASOURCE JUMPSTATIONS

Beat Page
<http://www.ire.org/~shawn/beat.html>

Put together by investigative reporter and editor spokesperson Shawn McIntosh (*Dallas Morning News*).

The Best News on the Net
<http://www.NovPapyrus.com/news>

A reader's collection of wire services, newspapers, magazines, etc. Not as thorough as some of these other sites, it has the excellent, unique feature of linking to the various departments within a single paper.

Charles Brumback
<http://www.naa.org/edge/charlie.html>

The former *Tribune* chairman shares his forty-seven pages of personal bookmarks at the server of the Newspaper Association of America (NAA), with such tempting topics as the Detroit newspaper strike, electronic publishers, and think tanks.

The CAR/CARR Links
<http://www.ryerson.ca/~dtudor/carcarr.htm>

Dean Tudor at Ryerson Polytechnic University has put together a stunningly useful and educational jumpstation that's an absolute must. ("CAR/R" stands for Computer-Assisted Reporting/Research.)

Emerson College's "New Media" students' page
<http://www.emerson.edu/acadepts/mc/cnme/cnme.html>

A number of finely tuned topics, including Censorship, Electronic Publishing, New Media Tools, and Stereotyping.

Finding Data on the Internet
<http://www.probe.net/~Niles>

A journalist's guide to basic reference sources, currencies, world population stats, census data, CDC, etc.

Internet Journalism Resources
<http://www.moorhead.msus.edu/~gunarat/ijr/>

A marvelous and extensive jumpstation of links, including a fine collection about civic journalism, curated by Professor Shelton Gunarat at Moorhead State University.

Journalism Bookmarks
<http://www.sjmercury.com/homepage/gillmoor/bkmk.htm>

A creation of online journalist mavens Randy Reddick and Dan Gillmoor.

Journalism Resources
<http://npc.press.org>

The National Press Club's home page, with links to dozens of journalism resources, as well as a newsrack.

Journalist's Toolbox
<http://www.ccnet.com/CSNE/toolbox.html>

Megasources Journalism Resources
<http://www.acs.ryerson.ca/~journal/megasources.html>

Courtesy of Dean Tudor, the Webmaster of the CAR/CARR Links site, and of Ryerson Polytechnical University, Toronto, and *Ego Interactive*, this site includes sources, beats, breaking news, search engines, and libraries.

News Place
<http://www.niu.edu/newsplace>

For current events and public policy issues, this site offers not only news media but also sources (government, activist, travel, and corporate) and tools (resource, search, reference, and locator). Available in Japanese.

Reference Information
<http://point.lycos.com/reviews/database/niri.html>

The bookmarks of the reference librarian at a news company. About thirty pages of listings in all, meticulously rated in terms of content, presentation, and experience, and each summarized on a separate page.

Resources for Journalists
<http://www.cio.com/WebMaster/journalism.html>

Includes not only in-depth Web links but also e-mail resources and newsgroups and mailing lists, as well as magazine articles and books, brought to you by *WebMaster Magazine.*

Scoop CyberSleuth's Internet Guide
<http://scoop.evansville.net/>

Reporter James Derk (*Evansville Courier*, Indiana) maintains this site, with files and links regarding current news, plus links to resources in over a dozen categories, including search sites, government sites, demographics, medicine, law/crime, business/technology, newspapers/magazines/entertainment, environment/weather, sports, kids, and journalism tools.

WebOvision
<http://www.webovision.com/cgibin/var/media/sd/index.html>

Boasts over 3,000 links in more than sixty countries. Besides the voluminous journalism links, there are also links to TV, radio, film, and more.

Wordbiz.Net
<http://www.wordbiz.net>

Debbie Weil's outpost, with her monthly column, "Online Wordbiz"; enriched by links to some very sharp online journalism resources.

WWW Virtual Library — Journalism
<http://www.cais.com/makulow/vlj.html>

John Makulowich maintains a great, searchable compilation of mailing lists, Gopher sites, and such.

WWW.Reporter.Org
<http://www.reporter.org/index.html>

A joint venture of Investigative Reporters and Editors (IRE) and the National Institute for Computer-Assisted Reporting (NICAR), this site expanded to serve as home for several other journalism organizations and journalism-related mailing lists (e.g., Asian-American Journalists Association, National Association of Black Journalists, New York Association of Black Journalists, Education Writer's Association, CompuServe Journalism Forum, and *Bylines*).

14

Net Research

Knowledge is of two kinds. We know a subject ourselves, or we know where we can find information upon it.
—Dr. Samuel Johnson

We are just beginning to raise the vital question, "What information do I need and in what form and when?" I am not suggesting that we ignore developments in hardware and software. But I am saying that, increasingly, hardware and software are going to be less important than the use we make of them in defining and exploiting information.
—Peter Drucker

In the Age of Information, Man the Food Gatherer returns as Man the Fact Finder.
—Marshall McLuhan

Quick, what was the Iroquois Confederacy?

If the answer wasn't on the tip of your tongue, where would you turn?

Knowing how and where to find information — research — is crucial to the work of most writers, whether it's the historical research of a romance novelist, the legal research of a mystery writer, or the scientific research of a technical writer. In this Information Era, finding your path between lack of knowledge and infoglut is a survival art.

In this chapter, you'll learn about:

- Locating people as information sources
- Doing research via forums, FTP, gopher, WAIS, and the Web
- Advanced research strategies and skills
- Searching, surfing, and scouting
- Using information agents
- Finding online reference shelves

Infoglut may be a cause for alarm for some people, but I celebrate the variety and amplitude of information options that are out there. So I learn to hone my efficiency and productivity, keeping abreast of information about the information, to stay on top of the game. This chapter will show you how to do likewise.

LOCATING PEOPLE

Where's the first place writers go for information? More often than not, to other people. As you've seen, the Internet not only adds other computers to your computer, but it also adds other people: tutors, fellow writers, experts, editors, publishers, readers, and so on.

John Seabrook, author of *Deeper: My Two-Year Odyssey in Cyberspace* (1997), says:

> To me, the Net is most useful as a kind of fact-checking service. You can cut and paste whatever you need checked into an e-mail window, ship it off to the authority on the matter, and get back an annotated copy. Better than using the phone or fax to check facts.

Other writers conduct e-mail interviews from the convenience of their home offices.

Phone Numbers and Addresses

People are just a few keystrokes away. Here are some options for finding them.

Switchboard
<http://www3.switchboard.com>

The national phone directory is now available on the Web; a database of more than ninety million names and ten million businesses.

Telephonebook
<http://www.telephonebook.com>

A database of the Yellow Pages phone book of over ten million listings. Searchable by company name, category, and location. Finds Web pages, too.

Yellow Pages Online
<http://www.ypo.com>

A business directory with over eighteen million listings in the U.S.

AT&T 800 Numbers
<http://www.tollfree.att.net/din800>

Central Source
<http://www.telephonebok.com/index.html>

GTE, NYNEX, Yellow Pages, and so on.

E-mail Addresses

Deja News
<http://www.dejanews.com>

Will search e-mail addresses from messages posted to Usenet since March 1995.

Finding an E-Mail Address
<http://sunsite.oit.unc.edu/~masha>

This jumpstation brings together search engines by various criteria — country, university, domain name, submissions to mailing lists or newsgroups, home page, and others.

Four-One-One White Page Directory
<http://www.four11.com/>

This directory claims over six million e-mail addresses, and lets you e-mail the person you've found. The Sleeper Search will continue the search "while you sleep" and update you with new or updated entries.

Infoseek
<http://www.infoseek.com>

Offers an option for searching for e-mail addresses.

Internet Address Finder (IAF)
<http://www.iaf.net>

Claims nearly four million addresses, using mailing lists as at least part of its database. It includes a reverse directory (getting the name from the e-mail address).

WhoWhere? PeopleSearch
<http://www.whowhere.com>

This jumpstation brings together phone numbers, e-mail addresses, yellow pages, Web home pages, and more.

World E-mail Directory
<http://www.worldemail.com>

Boasts more than nine million entries, searchable by continent.

There's a FAQ, How To Find E-Mail Addresses
<http://www.cis.ohio-state.edu/hypertext/faq/usenet/finding-addresses.faq.html>

Focuses on methodology more than resources.

The Ultimate White Pages
<http://www.anglfire.com/pages0/ultimates>

Will search white pages directories and then map the address located. It includes a reverse directory (getting the name from the phone number).

E-Mail Sources. E-mail can be a gold mine for writers. Besides extending your access to, and ability to interview, people, it's a way of getting story ideas, leads, and sources. E-mail can be a good way of bypassing the various administrative lions that guard office doors, allowing you to contact a person directly. Even if a CEO doesn't read his or her own e-mail, it's still a likely bet that execs getting more unsolicited phone calls and letters than e-mail, position it better for priority handling.

When it comes to conducting an interview, perhaps the person you have contacted will find it convenient to be interviewed via e-mail. This is not only at the convenience of each party, but some shy people feel more emboldened about communicating over the Internet due to the seeming anonymity and distance. (Internet interviews have disadvantages, however, such as the lack of the cues of vocal nuance and the absence of those spontaneous asides that can develop into gold mines.)

Investigative reporter Robin Rowland's chapter on "The E-mail Interview" in *Researching the Internet* (Prima, 1995) covers pre-interview screening, formulating and posing questions, and post-interview follow-up, so I won't duplicate them here. Suffice it to say that, despite the speed and seeming intimacy, e-mail never replaces other media, especially human contact. So cultivate your sources, but remember that they're human, too. The quality of what you can get from them will be in direct proportion to what you give.

Miscellaneous People-Finders

Ask An Expert
<http://www.askanexpert.com/askanexpert/ask.html>

Hyperlinks to Web sites of over 200 experts, in fields ranging from the Amish to zoology.

N.E.W. BASE Internet Directory Service
<http://www.theniche.com/niche>

Offers keyword-searchable databases of information on individuals and companies or organizations on the Internet. Search results include hypertext links for e-mail, WWW, and/or FTP addresses, as well as other information. Requires forms-capable browser (such as Netscape, Explorer).

People Finder
<http://www.stokesworld.com/peoplefinder.index.html>

Lets you post a message for the person you're looking for, with your name and address; someone may know how to contact them. (Usenet has a similar newsgroup: soc.net-people.)

Public Information Officer Databases.   As many writers already know, Public Information Officers (PIOs) are often the best liaisons for contacting experts at an academic institute, federal entity, corporation, or medical center.

ProfNet
<http://www.vyne.com/profnet/ped>

In 1992, the University at Stony Brook set out on a two-pronged mission to facilitate the process of connecting with PIOs. One goal was to use the Internet to link together PIOs at the world's major educational, scientific, and cultural institutions. The other goal was to use the Internet to increase the frequency, immediacy, and quality of communication between writers and such a community.

The result, ProfNet, today sends out a writer's query to its extended Rolodex of over 2,200 public information officers at 550 academic institutions and 200 corporate, nonprofit, and government affiliates in seventeen countries. If the query is urgent, it can be answered the same day. The service is free, but it is appreciated that informants be made aware of the finished product. (Note: Sources have been known to reflect their company line, naturally.)

Address your query to: <profnet@vyne.com>

The success of ProfNet has led to other, competitive expert-finders.

Big Ten Plus NewsNet
<http://www.purdue.edu/uns/bigten>

Represents Indiana, Michigan, Michigan State, Northwestern, Penn State, Purdue, Chicago, Illinois, Illinois at Chicago, Iowa, Minnesota, Ohio State, Notre Dame, and Wisconsin. Address your query to <beth_forbes@uns.purdue.edu>.

Public Affairs Web
<http://www.publicaffairsweb.com>

Tracks spokespersons in over a dozen categories.

ExperNet
<http://www.cvcp.ac.uk/expertnet.html>

Links you to experts in universities in the United Kingdom. Contact: <paul.clarke@cvcp.ac.uk>.

MediaNet
<http://www.infinet/ncew/medianet.html>

A journalist-owned-and-operated, computer-assisted reporting tool that helps journalists quickly find experts to interview via e-mail from corporations, consultants, associations, and nonprofit groups. Contact <uslifeline@aol.com> or <71344.2761@compuserve.com>.

Stumpers

A mailing list fielded by reference librarians. Members who are stumped by a difficult question pose it to the group. To join, e-mail the command "subscribe Stumpers-L *your e-mail address*" to <mailserv@crf.cuis.edu>. The list moderator is <roslibrefrc@crf.cuis.cdu>.

CONDUCTING RESEARCH VIA FORUMS

You can also pursue your subject of interest in special interest groups such as mailing lists and Usenet newsgroups. One-way bulletin boards (such as online newsletters) promise more diversity and depth than the mainstream media. Two-way forums (where members both read and post) afford a researcher the opportunity to pose a question to a group of people involved in a particular topic. How you should go about doing this depends on the particular group, the question, and Netiquette. A successful technique in certain instances is posing a question for members to respond to personally at the inquirer's e-mail address, to keep the forum from getting bogged down with your personal matter, with the promise of summarizing the results later to the group in a single post.

Finding Forums

Usenet and commercial online services offer a number of useful forums that you can scout out online.

Most online mailing lists use Listserv software. To obtain a list of all Listserv mailing lists, e-mail <listserv@vm.temple.edu> and, in the body of the message, type "list global". You'll be e-mailed a list that's at least 750K in size, which you can save and search for key words. To narrow your search, for a list of all lists on a particular topic, change the message to "list global/*topic*" (for example, "list global/Africa").

To search archives of a list, send a message to the server (not to the list): "get database search". To receive a copy of frequently-used mailing list commands, with explanations, e-mail <listserv@ubvm.cc.buffalo.edu>, leaving the subject line blank, and in the message body type "get mailser cmd nettrain f=mail".

E-Mail Discussion Groups
<http://www.Webcom.com/impulse/list.html>

Describes the three most commonly used software tools for managing electronic mailing lists: Listserv, Majordomo, and Listproc. The site provides the basic commands for each, as well as links to more detailed guides for these list managers. Pointers to several search engines for locating discussion lists by topic are also provided.

As of about 1996, the riches of online forums (mailing lists and Usenet) became even more valuable with the advent of sophisticated tools for finding and searching them. Here are eight of the best:

Alta Vista
<http://www.altavista.digital.com>

Can search Usenet as well as the Web.

CataList
<http://www.lsoft.com/lists/listref.html>

A great catalogue of over 8,500 Listserv lists.

CyberTeddy-OnLine
<http://www.CyberTeddy-OnLine.com/teddy/>

A jumpstation for searching mailing lists and Usenet newsgroups, with such important links as DejaNews and the Usenet Info Center Launch Pad.

Liszt
<http://www.liszt.com/>

At last count, this incredible engine searched 40,738 mailing lists and 15,264 newsgroups. (An exhaustive search, however, will still employ other search tools.) It also offers LisztSelect, organizing lists into a subject-oriented directory by 100 categories.

Publicly Accessible Mailing Lists
<http://www.NeoSoft.com:80/internet/paml/>

Vivian's Neou's searchable index
<http://catalog.com/vivian/interest-group-search.html>

The Reporter's Guide to Internet Mailing Lists
<http://www.daily.umn.edu/~broker/guide.html>

A step-by-step guide to finding and using Internet mailing lists, geared toward reporters and writers for their day-to-day work.

Searchable Index Newsgroups and Mailing Lists
<http://www.nova.edu/Inter-Links/cgi-bin/news-list.pl>

FAQs

A forum's list of answers to Frequently Asked Questions (FAQs) not only teaches good Netiquette but offers excellent briefings on a vast range of topics. The topics of FAQs

---

▼▼▼

HOWARD RHEINGOLD'S WORDS OF ADVICE FOR INTERNAUT WRITERS

I'd say that online (virtual communities like the WELL or larger forums like Usenet):

- Is good for gathering information. You can find out more than you'll ever want to know about any conceivable topic. But: nobody guarantees the veracity of the information. You still need to double-check, and you need to know which sources are often bogus and which ones are not.
- Is good for debugging: technical experts will come out of the woodwork to tell you the hidden dangers or the outright mistake in the way you describe something about their specialty. But: everybody has an opinion and you have to have enough experience judging the quality of feedback to know when your piece is being debugged and when somebody is trying to sell you their agenda.
- Is great for getting instant response. But: the writing-as-performing-art is a warm-up for the kind of writing you are going to allow trees to die for. If you write some great riffs online and download them, be sure to print them out and look at them with a critical eye tomorrow.
- Is like an ongoing online think tank that will actually go beyond giving you answers; people will go out and do research for you, gratis. But: nobody is going to go to any trouble for you over the long run unless you give at least as good as you get. You have to nourish the source. You better go out of your way to do research in response to someone else's query once in a while, or your responses will dry up.

are diverse, and the information is often written "from the field," rather than by seemingly anonymous observers. FAQs, written collectively and updated over time, are a unique form of literature, and one of my all-time favorite Internet resources.

One site, <http://www.cis.ohio-state.edu/hypertext/faq/usenet/FAQ-List.html>, archives FAQs alphabetically by subject, with limited search capability (by newsgroup name, archive name, subject, and keywords).

Another FAQ archive site, also searchable, is <http://www.cs.ruu.nl/cgi-bin/faqwais>.

FTP

FTP (file transfer protocol) is the Internet's original archiving system. (See the Appendix for basic information about FTP.) Using it can be like playing Blind Man's Bluff unless you have some extra software programs, such as Fetch for Mac or WS_FTP for Windows, for navigating its menus. Even then, it helps to know where the needles in the haystacks are, which is where the search tools like Archieplex come in.

Archieplex
<http://www.lanet.lv/services/archieplex/archieplex.html>
<http://www.amdahl.com/internet/archieplex>

A great search tool for combing FTP sites.

TELNET

This is the original application for the Internet, its original function, for operating other computers from a host computer (a.k.a. remote log-ins). (See the Appendix for general background about telnet.) There are many good resources available via telnet. For example, this is where you'll find most of the (land-based) library catalogues on the Internet.

Peter Scott trailblazed a program called Hytelnet for indexing and searching the various sites. I used it to do a cursory search for the word "writing," and turned up handouts on writing from Rensselaer Writing Center, a guide to writing HTML, resources for technical writing, and so on.

There are a number of different Hytelnet sites now, some via the Web and others via gopher. For a hyperlinked directory of Hytelnet sites: <http://www.ukans.

edu/hytelnet_html/START.TXT.html>. If you don't know where to begin to surf, try the WWW version, <http://library.usask.ca/hytelnet>, for starters.

GOPHER

When gopher debuted in 1992, it promised seamless Net navigation. (See the Appendix for basic information on gopher.) Hardly was that year out, however, when it was eclipsed by the popularity of the Web. While many want to remake the Net in the Web's image, there is still a good network of sites that support gopher, although, alas, some no longer keep their sites up to date and others have even abandoned them for the Web.

It is said that the difference between searching through gopher and the Web is like the difference between shopping at a general store and at a megamall. At one you find a good supply of hardware, dairy goods, clothing, and such, and at the other you can get lost for days. Text-only and menu-driven, gopher is rich with hearty fare, both basic and special. Once you get the hang of it, it's quick and easy, and full of nice information pathways.

There are navigational tools for gopher, such as WS Gopher and Turbogopher. And, best of all, you can save any item or menu with "bookmarks."

Gopher Search Engines

The leading gopher search engine is Veronica. The results of its search remains a hot list, the links active, until another search is initiated, and results can be bookmarked at any time. It is also capable of Boolean searching (described later in this section).

In my cursory search for "writing," Veronica turned up writing tips, a business writing reference book, computer writing, and a slew of writing-center-related materials. However, there was also the inevitable repetitious dross, in part due to a gopher site's ability to "mirror" or link to other sites, which happens on the Web as well.

The University of Nevada has an excellent collection of gopher search materials: <gopher://veronica.scs.unr.edu/Other Gophers & Information Servers>. At the head of its gopher menu is a document entitled "How to Compose Veronica Queries," which will bring you up to speed.

Gopher Subject Trees

A broader way to search gopher-space is by menu-surfing via "subject trees."

Gopher Jewels
<http://galaxy.einet.net/gopher/gopher.html>
<gopher://cwis.usc.edu>

The best of the subject trees.

Global Information Services
<gopher://genome-gopher.stanford.edu/11/global>

Library of Congress Global Electronic Library
<gopher://marvel.loc.gov>

Very rich.

Peripatetic Eclectic Gopher (PEG)
<gopher://peg.cwis.uci.edu:7000>

Eclectic and rich.

Rice Subject Gopher
<gopher://riceinfo.rice.edu/11/subject>

Texas A&M Subject Gopher
<gopher://tamuts.tamu.edu/11/dir/Subject.dir>

University of California, Santa Barbara
<gopher://summit.ece.ucsb.edu>

The WELL (Whole Earth 'Lectronic Link)
<gopher://gopher.well.com>

Eclectic.

WAIS

When Veronica searches gopher, it looks for words only in the titles of files. But what if you're searching for "Dr. Spock" and the file "Spock" is in a file entitled "Vulcans"? To find it, you could use a tool called WAIS (Wide Area Information Server), pronounced "wayce."

WAIS can also search multiple databases at once. It returns its findings ranked by relevance, according to such criteria as how often the word occurs, how close it appears to itself, and how close it occurs to the top of the document. Based on the results, you can further refine your search.

You can play around with WAIS and gophers via <http://www.geocities.com/Hollywood/3223>.

CONDUCTING RESEARCH ON THE WEB

Like the Internet, the Web started mushrooming exponentially with relatively little planning. But here, too, gifted computer wizards have been creating magical applications that enable us to bring personal order to the daunting chaos. Two main types of Web search tools — similar in approach to Veronica and Gopher Jewels, respectively — are *subject guides* and *search engines*, also known as directories and spiders, respectively.

Subject guides are a *broad* search tool, zeroing in with ever finer granularity, until you come to a Web site home page and can search further from there. Search engines are a narrow search tool, taking you directly to the document where your specific word, name, or phrase is found.

In addition to tens of millions of "pages" out there on the Web (fifty million at last count), there are also over five dozen different search engines, and another dozen separate subject guides.

Subject Guides

Subject guides are human-organized approaches to the Web. Here, Web data are pre-sifted and sorted in a directory, much as with gopher subject trees. We've seen an example of this strategy in Chapter 13 with the Reporters Internet Guide, which organizes the Net by subject, or newspaper "beats."

A subject guide usually displays a menu with a hierarchy of topics and subtopics. As you navigate further "into" the guide, and zero in on a site of interest, you can enter its home page and browse further from there.

Subject guides often have their own internal search engine onhand, to search the entire directory as a database.

Excite
<http://www.excite.com>

One of the largest collections of categorized Web sites with descriptive notes. You can search its directory (NetDirectory) and the rest of the Net (NetSearch). Searching includes excellent relevance ranking as well as a feature called concept-based indexing. (If you're researching *Star Trek*, for example, related concepts might be "movie," "science fiction," and "outer space.") Concept searching can sometimes be far more fruitful than searching specific words; one drawback is that the results can also vary from day to day. Also, Excite can search Usenet.

Galaxy
<http://galaxy.einet.net/>

As its name implies, Galaxy is vast. A unique feature is that topics are guest-edited by specialists in each field.

The Internet Public Library (IPL)
<http://ipl.sils.umich.edu:80/ref/RR/>

IPL is laid out like a library. There's even a desk, staffed by human beings, for leaving your reference questions. The directory is searchable by title and keywords as well as subject. ("Writing" here is listed under "Literature.") In other words, here is a subject guide using a library metaphor as its interface (a.k.a. "virtual library." See also the UC Berkeley Sunsite Virtual Library, on the following page.

Magellan
<http://www.mckinley.com/>

A searchable database of selected sites, rated one to four stars and given Magellan's own thumbnail reviews. (Many sites review themselves in hyperbolic or misleading terms.) "Adult" content can be blocked. As with Excite, there is also concept searching.

Magellan's descriptions are some of the best on the Net; as of 1995, the site has hired a larger working staff and can be expected to continue to be one of the Internet's greater treasures. ("Writing," by the way, is listed here under "Communications.")

The Mother Load
<http://www.cosmix.com/motherload>

A modest directory of search engines and directories that helps narrow your search results to a manageable number of links worth bookmarking. It is also home to Insane Search, a multi-threaded search (described later in this chapter).

NetGuide
<http://www.netguide.com>

Launched by *NetGuide* magazine in August, 1996, this online directory is maintained by a team of editors who review and annotate thousands of sites.

University of California Berkeley Virtual Library
<http://sunsite.berkeley.edu>

Fast becoming a central hub for many of the other main virtual libraries on the Internet.

WWW Virtual Library
<http://www.w3.org/hypertext/DataSources/bySubject/Overview.html>

An excellent, in-depth overview of the Web by subject, with dozens of top-level categories, including all the writing genres. This virtual library began at the European Center for Nuclear Research (CERN), originator of the World Wide Web itself; it is now maintained by the W3 Consortium.

Yahoo! (Yet Another Hierarchical Officious Oracle)
<http://www.yahoo.com>

The grandfather of heavy-duty Web subject guides. It was begun in 1994 by two Stanford students who wanted a better way to bookmark their favorite sites, and so created some software to locate, identify, and index Web resources. Today, Yahoo! is one of the Internet's most popular sites, tracking about six million hits . . . per day!

Besides being awesome in scope, this mammoth indexing project includes some human elements. A pair of shades beside a site means "cool." Conversely, Yahoo's maintainers have been known to turn away sites they felt were not "up to snuff."

And, they often publish the descriptions that sites give of themselves, which are often misleading. Plus there's always the risk of finding a site still listed in Yahoo! that has moved with no forwarding address (a dead URL).

Yahoo's initial home page includes merely a dozen categories, but from there branching gets deeper and wider. Mining Yahoo! can require patience and concentration. "Writing," for example, is reached by going into "Arts" and, from there, looking under "Humanities." There you'll find about twenty subcategories (Agents, Contests, Institutes, Organizations, Scriptwriting, Workshops, Writer Directories, and so on) with about 125 different listings in all; well worth it.

Search Engines — Introduction

Search engines are sometimes called spiders, Web crawlers, Web wanderers, or robots. They are usually programmed to do two things: go out on the Web to collect URLs, and furnish descriptions (abstracts) of their discoveries. An abstract might be the first 100 to 1,000 words from a site, and it usually starts out with the document title. Following the abstract is the URL.

Caveat: Spiders (search engines) do not necessarily search the whole Internet. They will refer to an FTP site, a Telnet site, a gopher site, or whatever *if* (and only if) the non-Web site has been linked, with HTML, to a particular Web site. Thus, there are whole layers of Internet information that they won't pick up if the layers haven't been linked to Web sites (unless the engine already knows about them, as with Usenet in some cases).

Furthermore, not all search engines work the same way. The March 1996 *NetGuide* posted the results of an interesting, even amusing, match between Inktomi and Alta Vista. They conducted separate searches for six words. While Alta Vista scored the majority of hits, the spread is unusual. For "Florida," Inktomi found 38,828 URLs, where Alta Vista found 300,000. On the other hand, for "primaries," Inktomi indexed 53,689 hits, but Alta Vista had only 3,000.

Advanced Strategies and Skills. Composing your search can be as important as knowing where to search. This means choosing the right words and knowing how to string them together. Old-timer information specialists are used to composing searches in advance to economize on fees for online time. Here are some advanced strategies and skills for composing Inter-net searches.

A general rule of thumb for simple searches is to put as many words in as possible, including any possible variants such as "Qadaffi" and "Khadaffy."

But a simple search for "robins," for example, might yield "Mrs. Robinson" and "Robinson Crusoe." An advanced search can specify "robins + birds" to limit our search. We can both expand and narrow our limits by hanging our key words together with "operators" (a.k.a. Boolean operators).

Basic operators are AND, OR, and NOT. AND and NOT *narrow* our search. A simple search for "birds" would turn up tens of thousands of hits; we could narrow this down by searching for "birds AND pets" or "birds NOT pets." OR, on the other hand, *widens* our search: "birds OR pets." For example, Jack Solock, Special Librarian, InterNIC Net Scout, suggests:

If you are searching for information on teenage alcoholism, make a worksheet with the concepts you want to use before you start:

```
teenage AND alcoholism
```

Then think about what other terms there might be for these concepts:

```
teenage                       AND alcoholism
OR adolescents                AND alcohol abuse
OR secondary school students  AND alcoholic beverages
OR youth                      AND drinking
```

Then create a query that combines the terms:

```
(teenage or adolescents or secondary school students or youth) AND
(alcoholism or alcohol abuse or alcoholic beverages or drinking)
```

Other possible parameters include truncated searching ("Buddh" for Buddha and Buddhism), also known as a wild card ("Buddh*"); case-sensitive searching (as for proper nouns and names); proximity (for instance, how close the word appears to the top of the document); relevance ranking (e.g., 100% = best results; 99% = less of a match — rather than all the results in no particular order); date restrictions (how recent the information is); and geographical source.

A Web page can be divided into fields, such as its name, the text, headings, and keywords. Field searching enables you to specify where to search for what (e.g., "AIDS" in the title, "treatment" in the text). Alta Vista, Open Text, and Ultra Seek have notable field search capabilities.

Cheat Sheet
<http://www.intersurf.com/~powerdan/duz/search/boolean.html>

Once you get the hang of using Boolean operators, the next hurdle is learning how different search engines might use different symbols for "+" or "and." Assistant System Librarian Dan Kissane at McNeese State University, Lake Charles, Louisiana, jumps in and fills that need with The Internet Search Engine "Cheat Sheet." It allows searchers proficient in one Internet search engine's terminology to quickly cross-reference search terminology on other major search engines.

Now I will introduce you to some basic search engines.

Alta Vista
<http://www.altavista.digital.com>
 <http://www.altavista.digital.com/cgi-bin/query?pg=ah&what=web>
(Advanced search help)

Alta Vista (Spanish for "view from on high") is a project of Digital Equipment Corporation. It began with five networked computers that scanned sixteen million Web pages (not including graphics, video, and audio) every week, indexing each word.

Within three weeks of unveiling this search engine in summer of 1995, it was handling two million queries per day. Now it handles about sixteen million queries a day. Of course, as with everything on the Net, by the time you read this, these numbers will be dwarfed by current figures. The main point is that Alta Vista has staked a claim to being fast and, more important, to having the horsepower to stay on top of the snowballing Web.

Advanced searching includes Boolean operators (AND, OR, NOT, and NEAR), quoted-strings ("Star Trek"), and case-sensitivity (Jane, neXt, and the like). And, as noted earlier, Alta Vista also searches Usenet.

Infoseek
<http://guide.infoseek.com/>
<http://ultraseek.com>
Search help: <http://ultra.infoseek.com/Help?pg=help.html&sv=US&lk=1>

Infoseek is capable of simple and advanced searches; it searches Usenet, Reuters news wires for that month, e-mail addresses, collections of FAQs, and, for a fee, selected sites.

Infoseek Guide returns both search hits and a list of conceptual topics related to search terms. It has added a subject guide (for example, Books & Writing, under Arts & Entertainment, links to some interesting resources). And it has a customizable news service, <http://personal.infoseek.com>.

In August of '96 it added Ultraseek, which strives to not only compile the largest collection of Web pages, but also to update or delete them weekly; it claims it searches 100 to 6,000 times faster than any other engine.

HotBot
<http://www.hotbot.com>
Search help: <http://www.hotbot.com/help.hotbot/f-help.html>

In the summer of 1996, *HotWired* magazine joined up with some computer wizards at the University of California who had developed Inktomi (pronounced "ink to me," named after the mythological trickster spider of the Plains Indians); the result was the creation of HotBot. Inktomi had harnessed four Sun workstations and thirty-two networked computers. Using "hive computing," each machine could work on a separate part of a search of all the pages now on the Web.

Complex, advanced searches in HotBot are available using pull-down menus and forms. The default button can be overridden. For example, try a combination of "modify" and "expert" along with a geoplace of North America and twenty-five results per page.

Lycos
<http://lycos.cs.cmu.edu>
Search help: <http://lycos.cs.cmu.edu/reference/search-help.html>

Developed at Carnegie Mellon University, Lycos is one of the original Web search engines, and is still many users' search tool of choice. (Microsoft has licensed the technology.) It claims to cover ninety-one percent of the Web, searching summaries of Web sites, not full text of the sites, plus FTP and gopher.

Lycos' search options include AND, OR, BUT, FOR, NOT, and use of the minus sign in front (as in "star trek -movie").

Lycos has now split into a search engine and a subject guide called A2Z (business, education, entertainment, news, sports, Web resources, and more).

Open Text
<http://www.opentext.com:8080/>
Search help: <http://index.opentext.net/main/help.html>

Open Text indexes every word of almost one million Web pages. You can use such search techniques as Boolean operators, phrases, proximities, weight, relevance feedback, and searching just parts of pages. *Online* magazine voted Open Text its search engine of choice in 1996, due to its excellent online documentation and the accuracy of its power search.

Webcrawler
<http://Webcrawler.com>
Search help: <http://Webcrawler.com/Htlp/Help.html>
Advanced searching: <http://Webcrawler.com/Help/Advanced.html>

Webcrawler is one of the fastest search engines, and thus many people start here. It provides a description of its results and allows for simple and complex searching (such as [diving swimming NOT (pool OR "hot tub")].) There is a separate subject guide as well (here, instead of being under Arts & Entertainment, Writing & Journalism are under Humanities).

Multisearches

There are a few more possibilities available for navigating the Web.

Here are five sites that can perform simultaneous searches (multisearches):

Inference Find
<http://www.inference.com> (select "InFind")

Inference Find simultaneously searches major search sites (such as Infoseek, Lycos, and Yahoo!), eliminates duplicate findings, clusters the information by content type, and organizes that information according to user preferences.

Insane Search
<http://www.cosmix.com/motherload/insane/>

Housed at the Mother Load (cited earlier on page 171), Insane Search performs simultaneous searches of a gargantuan number of Web and Internet directories and lists, plus single-source databases from various fields such as business, computers, entertainment, government, health, sports, and travel. It will search for keywords or concepts, substrings of words, and Boolean limits.

Metacrawler
<http://metacrawler.cs.washington.edu:8080/>

Metacrawler is a multi-threaded Web searcher that queries Open Text, Lycos, WebCrawler, Infoseek, Excite, Inktomi, Alta Vista, Yahoo!, and Galaxy. It then verifies that each URL is valid, consolidates duplicate pages, and presents the results in a consistent display for all engines, ranked by relevance. There's an option for either fast or comprehensive searches. Speed can also be adjusted by limiting the query (such as by country). Phrases take about three times longer to search than individual words, and phrase searches require a Web browser capable of displaying forms (tables and blocks of text). Highly recommended.

Savvy
<http://savvy.cs.colostate.edu:2000/>

Savvy, also an excellent tool, multisearches nineteen search engines at once (e-mail addresses, Usenet, FTP sites, gopher space, Alta Vista, Yahoo!, and more). Boolean and phrase searches are supported. Results are displayed as a search plan, and duplications are eliminated, offering the five best results first.

Super Search
<http://www.webtaxi.com/taxi/busib.htm>

Super Search can comb through over two dozen sites at once (which covers a great deal of data). You'll also find such new, useful search sites as Tribal Voice and USEIT.

Miscellaneous Web Tools

AliWeb
<http://Web.nexor.co.uk/public/aliWeb/aliWeb.html>

Searches a selected list of descriptions of resources on the Web.

The Niche Resource Directory
<http://www.tricky.com/lfm/niches.htm>

Searches directories in specific niche areas.

Rex (Resource EXchange)
<http://www.skyline.net/>

Another engine searching a database of Web site descriptions.

Hacking

Note that "cracking" is illegal entry; "hacking" is more like feeling your away around in the dark, scoping out what's out there.

For example: if you knew Bill Clinton's e-mail address was <president @whitehouse.gov>, then you could hack Al Gore's: <vice-president@whitehouse.gov>. Likewise, if you had just one address from a company — a secretary, say, <Jane_Doe@Computercraze.Com> — then you could try that pattern for the names of other people at that domain; if the CEO were Sally Fields, you'd try <Sally_Fields @Computercraze.Com>. That's hacking.

What if someone gave you a URL that, say, listed the launch codes for nuclear missile silos, <http://www.spy.org/cloak/dagger/launch.html>, but when you tried it an error message appeared, "Error 404 — not found"? The common hack would be to try the URL again with one less path until you got in: <http://www.spy.org/cloak/dagger/>, <http://www.spy.org/cloak/>, and so on. The reason: Webmasters often move things around in their system. Another hack in this case would be: <http://www.spy.org/cloak/dagger/index.html>. (A search engine might work, but wouldn't be a hack.)

Let's say that the initial URL works and you find the launch codes. Here's one more hack: rummage around in the domain itself, "spy.org," and see what else they might have there in the way of resources and links to other sites. Then, you might try "www.spy.net," "www.spy.com," "www.spynet.com"; or try substituting "spies" for "spy," etc. The permutations and combinations of hacking are endless.

Scouting

One way to stay up-to-date with a topic is through a related mailing list or Usenet newsgroup. You can also bookmark megasource jumpstations that mark additions with a "What's New" tag.

There are several other scouting aids that you may find useful. Here are five:

Scout Toolkit
<http://rs.internic.net/scout>

A service of InterNIC (Internet Network Information Center), here you can find Net.Happenings (daily) and the Scout Report (biweekly). I recommend Scout Toolkit for helping you stay up-to-date with the burgeoning Internet and Web, which are growing before your very eyes. (Note: this domain is sometimes "sleeping.")

NBNews Daily Electronic Journal
I highly recommend Liz Tompkins' and James Porteous' publication, available Monday through Friday. E-mail <nbnews@juno.com> and in the subject line, type: "subscribe".

Lynx of the Week
<http://Web-star.com/lotw/lotw.html>

Howard Barton's site represents a variant or hybrid of the topical subject guide approach to navigating the Web: he lists sites by date of appearance and quality.

Project Cool
<http://www.projectcool.com>

Glenn Davis is credited with launching the "Site of the Day" genre. With Teresa Martin, he's launched this site, with daily sightings.

Point
<http://www.point.com>

Selects "the best five percent" of the Web.

Agents

Another way of scouting is through use of "agents."

Offline Agents. Chapter 13 described the "push" services that newspapers are providing: e-mailing you news on topics of your selection. Such services are an example of agents. That kind is called an offline agent, because you don't have to be online; it works offline for you. Some of the search tools, such as Infoseek (see pages 174–175), provide this service. Here are three others:

IBM's infoSage
<http://www.infosage.ibm.com/>

Delivers an e-mail newsletter to you twice a day, reporting on information from your chosen areas of interest.

Webcatcher
<http://www.dev-com.com/~rfactory/Webcatcher.html>

Searches the Web for the latest sites that match a region or a topic you select, and notifies you regularly by e-mail (offline) of their appearance.

My Yahoo!
<http://my.yahoo.com>

A customized service similar to Infoseek; linking constantly to updated material (new Web sites, press releases, the day's news, and so forth) based on your personal likes and dislikes.

Intelligent Agents. Chapter 13 described the personal agents PointCast and PPS. They aren't interactive, in the purist's sense of the word. They act as conduits, but they do not interact with your choices to create meaning . . . the way, say, Firefly does.

Firefly
<http://www.ffly.com>

Visit Firefly and register some musical preferences from the checklist it provides. Then — bingo! — it will recommend other songs to you that it thinks you'll like. "Thinks" as in "artificial intelligence" — which, from a purist's point of view, is true interactivity. Thus it's called an "intelligent agent." Its database of previous users' choices enables it to make abstract choices; thus, the more people use it, the "smarter" it gets. A reporter who tried it said that it told her the name of the song whose melody had been running through her head all week.

The Movie Critic Rate O'matic
<http://www.moviecritic.com>

If you're more a movie buff than a music maven, this might be the site for you.

Rex Adaptive Newspaper Service
<http://www.daptyx.com/rex/rexinfo.html>

A journalistic example of this sort of interactivity. Rex adapts to your taste through daily feedback. Analyzing your habits, it tailors the newspaper for you. As your taste in news changes, so will your Rex custom newspaper.

The Angel
<http://www.netangels.com>

An intelligent agent that dynamically changes to offer each user a unique road map of personalized content throughout the Internet.

"Intelligent Software Agents on the Internet"
<http://www.hermans.org/agents/>

Bjorn Hermans has posted this essay, surveying the present and the future of intelligent agentware.

Other Agents. Fuzzy logic enables agents to further mimic thought. (An example of fuzzy logic: "Are you growing a beard, or just not shaving?") For instance:

Time Warner's Electronic Publishing Search Engine
<http://pathfinder.com/twep/search.html>

Includes a fuzzy search option to use when you know what you're looking for but can't spell it. Fuzzy logic identifies similarly spelled words.

Then there's the option of specifying commands that mimic speech ("natural language"). For example:

Autonomy Web Researcher and Autonomy Press Agent
<http://www.agentware.com>

Researcher searches the Web, and Agent searches online news publications; both can search in plain English, such as for "best books about Armenian folklore" or "comparative prices and features of reading lamps." The software, which costs $49.95, is available online on a trial basis.

Caveat: For an excellent case against agents, read virtual reality pioneer Jaron Lanier's essay:

"Agents of Alienation"
<http://www.voyager.com/misc/jaron.html>

AN ONLINE REFERENCE SHELF

Chapter 16 explores books and the Internet. To get a taste of what's ahead, consider how nice it would be to have a number of reference books right at your fingertips. Formerly *next* to your computer, these books can now be *in* your computer, as it were. You wouldn't have to have a shelf for the actual books, because they'd be virtual — and you could search them in an instant, rather than flipping through pages.

Several online services provide new opportunities. Microsoft Network, for example, has its multimedia *Encarta* encyclopedia online. And at the Writers conference at the WELL, there's a place where *Bartlett's Familiar Quotations*, *Webster's Dictionary*, newspapers, a searchable database of magazine articles, the Library of Congress, and more are all bookmarked at one menu for easy reference.

Independent of any particular online service, however, the Internet provides a number of such instant reference shelves, plus some online-only references such as the *Free Internet Encyclopedia*. Here are seven online reference resources:

Virtual Reference Desk
<http://www.refdesk.com/outline.html>

Provides literally dozens of links to dictionaries (English, English-to-foreign-languages, acronyms, dialects, and the like), a dozen encyclopedias, several thesauri (I like Project Gutenberg's hypertext version the best, ported here from Britain), books of quotations, plus news, sports, stock market information, Internet resources, and more. Bookmark the site, and bookmark the reference titles you wish to use frequently.

The Electric Library
<http://www.elibrary.com/info/about.html>

Provides a database of 150 full-text newspapers, 800 full-text magazines, two international newswires, 2,000 classic books, as well as maps, photos, etc. Searching is very precise and includes a bibliography. Subscriptions cost $9.95/month, with a two-week free trial membership.

Encyberpedia
<http://www.encyberpedia.com/ency.htm>

A very interesting subject catalogue of resources, from gardening to mysticism, museums to reference centers. It even links to a few encyclopedias, such as *Encyclopedia Mythica*, and updates to the fabulous *Jones Digital Century* hypertext encyclopedia.

The Encyclopedia Britannica
<http://www.eb.com>

This new online version may be to online research what their celebrated eleventh edition was to books. In addition to being digitized and hyperlinked, it draws from its Propaedia, the conceptual index to the encyclopedia's full contents, to enable the searcher to navigate by hyperlinking between specific terms and broad themes. There's a free seven-day trial. Subscription costs $14.95 per month or $150 per year.

The Free Internet Encyclopedia
<http://clever.net/cam/encyclopedia.html>

A Web subject guide arranged like an encyclopedia. The MacroReference contains references to large areas of knowledge, FAQs where available, and pointers to relevant areas of the MicroReference.

OneLook Dictionaries
<http://www.onelook.com>

Searches seventy-five dictionaries.

Casey's Reverse Dictionary
<http://www.c3.lanl.gov:8075/cgi/casey/revdict>

This oddity tells you the word for the general meaning you are trying to think of. Finally, the remedy for that tip-of-the-tongue feeling! Plus, for those days when you really need one, there's a guru — try asking it: "What is the meaning of life?"

FOR MORE INFORMATION

Infoglut, and the means to minimize it, is nothing new. The fabled Di Medici financial empire was built upon a solution to the glut of numbers being generated by the new world of Renaissance commerce: the double-entry bookkeeping system. Here are a few ways to prevent Internet infoglut, all available online for free.

First, CINET-TV has three online articles well worth reading:

"Where To Find Anything on the Internet"
<http://www.cnet.com/Content/Reviews/Compare/Search>

An excellent overview.

"Search the Web in Style: Seek Right & You Shall Find"
<http://www.cnet.com/Resources/Tech/Advisers/Search>

Includes eight very useful tips.

"Boolean Logic Defined"
<http://www.cnet.com/Resources/Tech/Advisers/Search/search3.html>

A good primer in the use of AND, OR, and NOT.

Second, here are two guides to framing an advanced search:

"Structuring Simple & Complex Keyword & Phrase Queries"
<http://www.surrey.ac.uk/Harvest/brokers/simplehelp.html>

"Searching/Boolean"
<http://www.electionline.com/cpl-bin/help/oltoc.cgi>

Includes relevance ranking.

Third, here are three useful resources by librarians (information specialists):

Resource Selection and Information Evaluation
<http://alexia.lis.uiuc.edu/~janicke/Evaluate.html>

Links to pages on search strategy and evaluation criteria. Created by librarian Lisa Janicke.

"How to Search the Web — A Guide to Search Tools"
<http://issfw.palomar.edu/Library/TGSEARCH.HTM>

Nicely describes and compares various search tools. Posted by librarian Terry A. Gray. Also provides links to the following two sites:

Webmaster's Guide to Search Engines and Directories
<http://califia.com/Webmasters/>

Yahoo! — Web searching
<http://www.yahoo.com/Computers_and_Internet/Internet/World_Wide_Web/Searching_the_Web/>

Exhaustive index to searching the Web.

INTERNET RESEARCH REFERENCES

by Ross Tyner

Birmingham, Judy. Internet Search Engines.
    <http://www.stark.k12.oh.us/Docs/search/>
Brownlee, Rowan. Search Engines – Reference List.
    <http://www.lib.berkeley.edu/Web4Lib/archive/9604/0103.html>
Basch, Reva. *Secrets of the Super Net Searchers.* Pemberton, 1996.
Campbell, Karen. "Understanding and Comparing Search Engines."
    <http://www.hamline.edu/library/links/comparisons.html>
Courtois, Martin P., William M. Baer, and Marcella Stark. "Evaluation of Selected Internet Search Tools."
    <http://www.library.nwu.edu/resources/internet/search/evaluate.html>
Liu, Jian. "Understanding WWW Search Tools."
    <http://www.indiana.edu/~librcsd/search/>
Rowland, Robin and Dave Kinnaman. *Researching on the Internet.* Prima, 1995.
Scoville, Richard. "Find It on the Net."
    <http://www.pcworld.com/reprints/lycos.htm>
Stanley, Tracey. "Alta Vista vs. Lycos."
    <http://ukoln.bath.ac.uk/ariadne/issue2/engines/>
Webster, Kathleen and Kathryn Paul. "Beyond Surfing: Tools and Techniques for Searching the Web."
    <http://magi.com/~mmelick/it96jan.htm>
Winship, Ian. "World Wide Web Searching Tools."
    <http://www.bubl.bath.ac.uk/BUBL/IWinship.html>

"Sink or Swim: Internet Search Tools & Techniques."
<http://www.okanagan.bc.ca/libr/connect96/search.htm>

Librarian Ross Tyner has posted a virtual version of his wonderful workshop. At the end are hyperlinked references to a dozen other online analyses of Internet and Web searching. (See the preceding sidebar.)

MEGASOURCE JUMPSTATIONS

All-in-One
<http://www.albany.net/allinone/>

Gathers over two hundred Internet search engines for the Internet and Web (including such special interest sites as the Discovery Channel Net), and provides a consistent search interface.

Beaucoup
<http://www.beaucoup.com>

Corrals over 440 search engines into one spot, and publishes a monthly e-mail magazine with news about searching and search engines.

The Clearinghouse for Subject-Oriented Internet Resource Guides
<gopher://uba.hh.kub.umich.edu/inetdirs>
<http://www.clearinghouse.net>

One of the first Internet subject guides (circa 1993), this began as a class project in the Library Sciences Department of the University of Michigan. Originally, it was a repository of files about Internet resources, listed by subject. It soon developed into an off-campus project and was revised into a hyperlinked version, with over 100 headings. Unlike later subject guides such as Yahoo! and Magellan, however, it also lists such non-Web resources as Usenet groups, mailing lists, and FTP sites. The subject directory is subdivided into second-level categories, and is searchable.

Eureka!
<http://www.best.com/~mentorms/eureka.htm>

Provides a consistent interface for over four dozen Internet search engines, with its own descriptive text about each.

Infomine
<http://lib-www.ucr.edu/Main.html>

A collection of high-level information databases, electronic journals, electronic books, bulletin boards, list servers, online library card catalogs, articles, and directories of researchers, among many other types of information. Searchable.

Internet Research Pointer
<http://csbh.mhv.net/~rproctor/IRP.html>

Roger Proctor has collected, organized, and annotated 250 search engines, magazines, books, and software by topic, plus such general items as links for research, help on writing research papers, etc.

The Internet Sleuth
<http://www.intbc.com/sleuth/>

Stakes out its own distinct corner of the Net, linking to over 750 searchable databases.

LibWeb
<http://sunsite.berkeley.edu/libweb>

One of the latest SunSites (courtesy of Sun Computers), this is one dedicated to serving as a virtual library, gathering 900 libraries in forty-five countries into one spot. The Library of Alexandria had nothing on LibWeb.

Purely Academic
<http://apollo.maths.tcd.ie/PA>

Trinity College's home page of links for people involved with academic research.

RES-Links (The All-in-One Resource Page)
<http://www.cam.org/~intsci/>

A categorized list of search engines and tools, catalogs, indexes, FAQs, databases, locators, resources, guides, and reference materials. A description is given for each tool.

The Scout Toolkit
<http://rs.internic.net/scout/toolkit/3b2.html>

A very useful, comprehensive, must-bookmark collection. Of particular interest, in its subject catalog, is CyberDewey, which accesses Internet resources by the Dewey Decimal Classification system. The same subject catalog also links to BUBL (Bulletin Board for Library Systems), which does the same using the Universal Decimal Classification system.

Search.Com
<http://www.search.com>

This adjunct of C|NET-TV gathers over 250 search engines, including Yahoo!, Excite, Infoseek, Alta Vista, and many single-topic databases about cars, movies, recipes, stocks, and more. The site is customizable, enabling you to set up a personal page with just your favorite search engines and research topics.

Search Tools and Master Sites
<http://www.ucalgary.ca/~mueller/search.html>

John Mueller's index, laid out by Internet application (Web, Telnet, mailing lists, etc.), plus "master sites" (jumpstations).

Virtual Reference Desk
<http://www.refdesk.com/outline.html>

Links to not only most of the Internet's online reference books, but seemingly nearly every other research tool as well.

The WWW Virtual Library
<http://www.w3.org/hypertext/DataSources/bySubject/Virtual_libraries/Overview.html>

Described earlier in this chapter, this service provides four hyperlinked pages linking to other virtual libraries or subject guides besides themselves, a few of which are highly underpublicized. A mega megasource.

Writers Free Reference Desk
<http://www.writers-free-reference.com>

An eclectic megasource jumpstation of reference and research links designed for writers.

Scott Yanoff's Internet Services List
<http://www.spectracom.com/islist/>

One of the Net's oldest collections of a wide variety of resources. A diverse index of topics, A to Z, updated regularly. E-mail: <inetlist@aug3.augsburg.edu>.

15

Net Magazines

We've touched on some magazines relevant to networking and to genres, and our tour of online newsstands took us to some sites that stock magazines. In this chapter, we'll focus on magazines as possible purchasers and publishers of your writing. First we'll spotlight five leading online magazines to give you an idea of the range of online publishing possibilities:

- *Atlantic Monthly on the Web*, an online adjunct to a paper magazine
- *Slate*, online only, with a paper adjunct
- *Salon*, online only, with a quarterly paper anthology
- *Word*, online only
- *Utne Lens*, an online adjunct to a paper magazine

Then we'll highlight a dozen or so leading magazine titles to give you a better idea of where your own writing might find a publishing outlet online.

We'll also offer a few top-level guides, such as a list of Webzines that are seeking submissions.

And we'll finish up with a look at the e-zine scene, where anyone can publish, or be published, as easily as they can speak or think.

Thus far, we've been dealing primarily with the Internet's capability to network readers with shared interests. Now, let's focus on the Net as a medium for publishing. As such, it cuts through the traditional publishing infrastructure of printing, paper, and distribution like a chainsaw through cedar. In this chapter, I will focus how the Internet opens up the traditional magazine format, animating and enriching it with new dimensions. In addition to cost savings, Internet publishing affords new possibilities of:

- a seemingly inexhaustible wealth of text
- hyperlinks, for cross-referencing
- multimedia (animation, video, sounds, and the like)
- presentation, and revision, within minutes rather than months
- reader input and interaction

The Information Revolution asks us to redefine what we mean when we say "magazine." The word "magazine" means "storehouse" or "depot." As you can see, the Internet is bringing the current meaning of the term "magazine" full circle to its roots.

FIVE CASE STUDIES

Let's begin by comparing the "Net effect" on five magazines — one on paper, the other four paperless. We'll start with the familiar, paper, and a venerable example at that.

The Atlantic Unbound

<http://www2.theAtlantic.com/atlantic/>

The oldest continuously running magazine in America, *The Atlantic Monthly* remains a lighthouse in the cultural landscape. In 1993 senior vice-president Kimberly Smith Jenson proposed an electronic edition. There had been overtures from America Online, seeking exclusive sources of material to add value to their services. *Atlantic* staff members in their twenties gladly spearheaded the online project. In November of that year *The Atlantic Monthly* crossed the cyberspace threshold.

Still evolving, the online version has been characterized by the thoroughness, fair-mindedness, and respect for the reader that typify the paper version. From the outset, the publishers put the contents of the entire magazine online. Transcripts of James Fallows' weekly NPR broadcasts have been available here, not at NPR's Web site. And the first chapters of books they review are available for browsing, with the books themselves available for order online. Over time, unique online features have developed — in what is now called, generically, *Atlantic Unbound* — such as online-only sidebars and whole articles.

From the beginning, too, the publishers have understood the importance of reader interaction, and so they set aside not only places for Letters to the Editor or to the Webmaster, but also an interactive message board — their "Agora" — where readers participate in round-table discussions with editors, lead authors, and other readers. But the first "killer application" they eventually hit upon was their Flashbacks section, capitalizing on the timely value of the magazine's venerable, rich archives. For the anniversary of the Hiroshima bombing, for instance, they revived articles by Albert Einstein and Harry Truman. The film *Dead Man Walking* prompted reprinting of earlier essays on capital punishment, by, for instance, George Bernard Shaw. The unexpected discovery of a Louisa May Alcott novel furnished an occasion to reprint a short story she'd written for *The Atlantic*. And when the University of California made a sudden reversal on its affirmative action policy, *The Atlantic* retrieved seminal articles from the sixties to add to the current debate.

In February of 1995, *The Atlantic*'s publishers began a redesign, during which it became evident that the Web was where the action was heading. The new version, launched in October of that year on the Web as well as on AOL, capitalized on the Web's interactive, multimedia potentials. A reading by Robert Pinsky — augmenting an online-only exclusive interview about poetry, computers, and translating Dante — inaugurated their venture into multimedia, which by now includes a very active audio poetry anthology: <http://www.theatlantic.com/atlantic/atlweb/poetry/antholog/aaindx.htm>.

During the 1996 Presidential campaign, *The Atlantic Monthly on the Web* featured one of the more interesting Net attractions of the entire online campaign trail. Basically a readers' poll, it took the form of a fictional monthly memo to the President from the Chief of Staff (penned by either James Fallows or James Beatty) — a position paper on one of the many important issues facing the White House. The reader (as President) was asked to reply, and the results were posted within two weeks along with a thorough analysis, complete with boxed tables. These results were then open for reader post and riposte.

While *The Atlantic* isn't yet experiencing a quantum shift in revenue or readership since going digital, it's still early in the game. But the publication has been ahead of the curve for some time and may remain so, drawing on a rich heritage of vision for a modern scene that wants to connect.

Slate

<http://www.slate.com>

On June 24, 1996, all eyes in cyberspace were upon the inauguration of a new magazine: *Slate*. *Slate* wasn't just the first major magazine to originate online and have a paper adjunct; it was also the first major Webzine to charge a subscription fee.

Slate is the brainchild of Michael Kinsley, former editor of *The New Republic* and co-host of CNN's "Crossfire." At forty-four, he turned down an offer to edit *New York* magazine, and grew a beard. A year passed, by which time, as he recalled to *The New Yorker*'s media critic Ken Auletta, "I was determined to be on the next train to pull out of the station no matter where it was going — provided that I was the engineer." By this time, anyone could see that the Web was that next train, so Kinsley got on board the Internet Express and headed west. Capitalized by Microsoft and backed by the corporation's campus of resident technowizardry, he launched his new media event: an online magazine, with subsequent paper versions available at Bill Clinton's favorite coffee house, Starbuck's.

Slate opens with a round-table discussion, called Committee of Correspondence, held via e-mail over a number of days. The launch topic, "Is Microsoft Evil?" started out rather tamely, but developed into a very serious and pointed debate. While a print medium might have pruned the false start and the veering drifts, the discussion could never have been generated via print in the first place. And the sense of unfolding polemic has its dramatic allure. But while this component goes on at great length, other features in the launch issue run under two thousand words. Articles, however, are all archived (as "Compost").

The Briefing section features "meta-news: the news about the news, a sense of how the week's big stories are being played and perceived." While emphasis on infra-digs, spin analyses, and meta-information isn't unique to the Net, applying such punditry to weekly magazines' coverage of current events does exploit the Internet's ability to deliver up-to-the-minute copy.

Slate's forums weren't ready as of inauguration. In this respect, *Slate* will be competing with America Online and other online services, charging money for members to be able to converse with other members within a proprietary community — and, as such, following a new magazine format paradigm. Comparing content with

The Atlantic, *Slate* comes off well. But if *Slate* continues on a par with *The New Republic*, *The Atlantic*, and *Harper's*, the question remains: aside from distribution over the Net, what sets it apart from such glossies which cater to the same audience? As of launch, the answer is "Not all that much." Which leads to the next question: why charge a subscription fee?

In addition to high-ticket advertising (for instance, from Ford) as well as sponsorship (by Microsoft), Kinsley says that he opted for a subscription basis in order to be editorially independent. "If the Web can make serious journalism more easily self-supporting," he proclaimed, "that is a great gift from technology to democracy." If you detect a tone of stridency, then listen to him defend himself in his statement of purpose:

> . . . we intend to take a fairly skeptical stance toward the romance and rapidly escalating vanity of cyberspace. We do not start out with the smug assumption that the Internet changes the nature of human thought, or that all the restraints that society imposes on individuals in real life must melt away in cyberia. There is a deadening conformity in the hipness of cyberspace culture in which we don't intend to participate. Part of our mission at *Slate* will be trying to bring cyberspace down to earth.

Ultimately, *Slate* debuted as essentially an eighteenth-century concept draped in a twenty-first-century medium. *Slate* bundled together the three most traditional finance models — sponsorship, ads, and subscription — but missed a good bet by not bringing Microsoft's capital in to back a pioneering micropayment system. Six months after launching, *Slate* waved a white flag and announced it was abandoning the online fee model, an idea whose time had not yet come.

(For an elaborate parody of *Slate*, see Daniel Radosh and Michael Tritter's *Stale*, <http://www.stale.com>.)

Salon

<http://www.salon1999.com>

The November 28, 1995, debut issue of *Salon* — dedicated to being "the most engaging, well-written, and colorful party of artists and thinkers ever assembled" — introduced a new level of excellence to Internet magazinedom. The result is something on the order of the *Esquire/Vanity Fair/Granta* of cyberspace. Finely designed and illustrated under the direction of Mignon Khargie, it launched with star authors like John Le Carré and Amy Tan, and up-and-comers like Cinatra Wilson and Gary Kamiya. Interviewees have included Richard Ford, Sharon Olds, Jay McInerney, Calvin Trillin, Tony Kushner, and Scott ("Dilbert") Adams. James Carville and Mary Matalin have a monthly column. Anne Rice holds court in her own salon. And Anne Lamott's online column about writing, "Word by Word," never fails to connect. There's an emphasis on West Coast rather than New York culture, and the quality shows no signs of letting up.

Salon's illustrious debut has had high-power sponsorship from Borders Books & Music, from whom the many books and CDs reviewed in the magazine are available. And desktop publishing pioneers Apple Computer and the Adobe Corporation attain a "brand image" by sponsoring this high-quality magazine.

One factor in *Salon*'s success has been the professionalism of the founders. Publisher David Zweig was formerly a marketing manager for Time, Inc. Editor David Talbot helmed the Entertainment section at the *San Francisco Examiner* and ferried with him a bunch of talented ex-Examinerites from what appeared to be a burning building. (*Salon* was conceived during the *San Francisco Examiner* strike. The ongoing deathwatch over San Francisco's future as a two-newspaper town — a national trend, these days — helped spark the exodus.) Plus, there's the "shrinking newshole" phenomenon, exemplified by the "Style & Ideas" section that Talbot had talked *The Examiner* into letting him create and edit: in about a year, it had steadily drindled down from four pages to a half! Newspapers aren't what they used to be!)

True to its name, *Salon* creates a social space for public interaction. "Table Talk" features online forums for readers on over a hundred topics at any given time. "Participation has been incredible," said Talbot. "With newspapers you get letters to the editor, and once in a while you might take a phone call from a reader. A lot of newspapers have become insulated from the public, and that's to the detriment of the publication. Now we're forced to read mail from our audience. We deal with their passions and opinions every day. It keeps us on our toes." Indeed, even more laudable than their consistently high-level content is their attention to the community of the readers, in a manner unique to the Internet.

In May, 1996, *Salon* went daily — with a less-deep table of contents plus stories behind the late-breaking news. Readership immediately tripled; it currently gets visits from 400,000 discrete hosts per week. As a daily, it looks forward to increasing its use of freelancers for more editorial reporting. A quarterly, paper "Best of Salon" edition is also in the works.

Word

<http://www.word.com>

In 1994, Tom Lavaccari and Dan Pelson conceived of a magazine with print and online versions, aimed at readers of their generation (eighteen to thirty-four). As they proceeded to shop it around at various New York publishers, it became evident that the cogs of that world moved far too slowly for them. Instead, they found their publisher in a high-tech company, Icon CMT (Communications Media Technology), that specializes in networking. Both parties found a match of interests: Icon could give them technological infrastructure and know-how, and they could bring to the table something Icon could use to show off the company's abilities online. That was the beginning of *Word*.

Officially launched in July of 1995, *Word* publishes fiction, poetry, and creative nonfiction in a multimedia environment, where submitted texts invite in-house designers to conceptualize additional media for further depth. Their best writers have thus been people familiar with screenwriting. The table of contents has section titles such as "Machine," "Work," "Desire," "Habit," and "Switchboard" — quirky, enigmatic, but inviting further exploration (especially when coupled with the imaginative graphics). Ace designer Yoshi Sodeoka manages to keep a balance between high-power stylization and technical simplicity. Their biggest feature thus far has been a dense, complex documentary about three artists trekking in the rain forests of Guyana. A text-only version of *Word* is also available.

Word supports a staff of twelve full-time employees writing, editing, designing and selling ads — plus a number of freelancers. Some months they break even, and they are currently about one ad away from turning a profit. They retain the services of a professional PR agency, and their site is linked to over one thousand others. Their conservative readership estimate is forty thousand per week. They pay contributors; contributors' guidelines can be found at their Web site.

Utne Lens

<http://www.utne.com>

The road to cyberspace can be rocky and tough. Consider *Utne Reader*, the venerable periodical collection of the best of the alternative press. With more than half its readers being e-mail users, it would seem a perfect candidate for online adaptation. But one year and half a million dollars into its first online publishing venture, *Utne* had to pull the plug on a twenty-five-person staff overseeing the creation of original online content. Web ad revenue just couldn't meet the overhead of payroll.

Utne retraced its steps. It had crossed the online threshold with an e-mail forum that grew exponentially, splitting off into fifteen smaller lists. Building on that popularity, *Utne Lens*, the new online magazine, features Web conferencing — a relatively new and terrifically viable possibility for using the Net to create community. And in August of 1996, it opened the doors to its Writers' Studio. The Writers' Studio lets readers buy an original essay or short story directly from its creator, keeping only twenty percent of the sales price for themselves. Initial contributors included Senator Alan Cranston, Joseph Epstein, Barbara Kingsolver, Barry Lopez, and Brenda Peterson. Another bold stroke.

Having flubbed once, *Utne* didn't curse the Net but instead figured out other ways for themselves to be online. From original words by authors they went to original words by readers, and experimented with new revenue models using a royalty-based system. In so doing, they blaze new trails for writers as well as publishers.

❋ ❋ ❋

The Atlantic took one of the first steps across the Internet threshold. *Salon* raised the bar for quality for everyone from its very first issue. *Slate* took two steps forward and one back. *Word* took radical aesthetic steps forward that have proven valid. And *Utne* put one foot forward, one back, then both forward again.

Clearly, Internet publishing (like everything else in this new medium) is taking its first baby steps. Even phrases in today's vocabulary, such as "paperless printing" and "electronic journals" may well eventually become as quaint as "horseless carriage" has become today. Meanwhile, we ourselves are creating this industry as we go along. We can learn from those blazing the trail.

MediaCentral
<http://www.mediacentral.com>

Worthy of perusal is MediaCentral's archives of the research of Cowles Business Media and the Medill School of Journalism, exploring the role of magazines in the New Media era.

ALTERNATE UNIVERSE: A COMPASS FOR BEGINNERS
by Pamela Weintraub

<http://www.cloud9.net/~pam>

Cyberspace is untamed, but not lawless — like any alternate universe, it follows a physics and dynamic of its own. Magazine journalists leaving the terra firma of print for the new cosmology of cyberspace will learn by doing. But if the work is too derivative of older technologies such as print or video — if it is based on the laws of the Universe left behind — it will be sluggish and second-rate. Writers and editors who can navigate to "true north" in this off-world, low-gravity zone, on the other hand, will thrive. Energized by the sense of freefall, they will reinvent the craft of journalism, creating something exciting and fresh and new. Because the terrain is unfamiliar, I offer a touchstone for pioneers, something simple — my list of basic differences between the old medium and the new.

1. In the old medium, the magazine was a book. In the new medium, the magazine is a place.

2. The old medium was one-to-many — one magazine, many readers. The new medium is many-to-many. Readers, writers, sources all interact after first publication, enabling the story to evolve online.

3. The old medium was static, a finished product. The new medium is ever-changing, a perpetual work in progress.

4. The old medium meant publishing once a month (or once a week), the new means publishing every nanosecond, again and again.

5. The old medium was linear. Lead, billboard, story line, kicker. . . . Dump that linear story online, and it's b-o-r-i-n-g. You can't take it on the train, can't take it to the breakfast table. You're glued to a screen. . . . The new medium . . . is anything but linear. Instead, it's associative, interconnected, a giant neural net — the Web.

6. In the old medium, the great editors were able to put their ears to the ground and hear the rumbling, faint and distant, of the train on the tracks. They could SENSE the movement of society's tectonic plates, and cover it before others knew it had occurred. . . . In the new medium, this sixth sense is amplified because editors can speak to the world directly, through the infinite connectivity of the Net.

OTHER WEBZINES

Some relatively new Webzines such as *Slate* and *Salon* are already major, widely-known, prestigious places for writers to be published. Let's continue our tour of the Internet's growing magazine stand by spotlighting some lesser-known titles. If you are content with seeing your work published by small ventures, online you can reach not just hundreds but thousands of readers. (Some of these Webzines even pay!)

The Blue Penny Quarterly
<http://ebbs.english.vt.edu/olp/bpq/front-page.html>

Publishes short fiction, poetry, and creative nonfiction (average story length: three thousand words). They publish both established writers and newcomers, and are strongly interested in a global perspective. Contributors have included Richard Cumyn, Ioana Ieronim, Deborah Eisenberg, Edward Falco, and Robert Sward.

Electronic submissions are preferred. A query letter is necessary only for nonfiction. Simultaneous submissions are accepted. The publishers estimate their readership at five to seven thousand. While there are cash prizes for some work, the review's primary purpose is as "a service to readers and writers and for the promotion of literature in an increasingly commercialized Internet."

Feed
<http://www.feedmag.com>

A literate, classy, sassy gadfly of culture, politics, and technology. The late *Virtual City* declared *Feed* the *Paris Review* of cyberspace. Since its beginning in May, 1995, it's built an advertising base while maintaining its alternative stance, making it as much an e-zine (independent, eclectic) as a Webzine (more mainstream).

The Mississippi Review Web
<http://sushi.st.usm.edu/mrw>

An online adjunct to the hard copy literary journal featuring original fiction, poetry, and prose by both established and emerging writers, edited by Frederick Barthelme and Rie Fortenberry. Winner of GNN's Best of the Net '95 Award for Best Professional Site, Literature.

Verbiage Magazine
<http://www.boutell.com/verbiage/>

A short fiction magazine on the World Wide Web that pays for stories and allows readers to comment publicly on each story. Editor: Thomas Boutell <boutell @boutell.com>.

The Web Inquirer
<http://www.gn.apc.org/inquirer/news.html>
<http://www.gn.apc.org/inquirer/>

A unique international investigative Webzine, publishing investigative stories from beyond the "stranglehold" of mainstream media. In addition to the articles, the site features an open library, with background documentation for breaking stories. Here, from five continents, are stories and elements of stories, interlinked, plus poetry, art, correspondence, and forums. Contributors are welcome. Editor Janine Roberts can be reached at <jan@gn.apc.org>.

There are also a number of online-only magazines based around computers and computer culture, for the digerati.

HotWired
<http://www.hotwired.com>

The granddaddy of all online-only magazines, with about 250,000 registered readers plus countless more who don't sign the guest list. One of its most popular areas has been NetSurf, its critical guide to other Web sites. As of August, 1995, *HotWired* made its archive available with a searchable interface.

Carl Steadman and Joey Anuff, independent comic buffs, were both working at *HotWired* when all the cyber-hype and Web boosterism got to them. In the summer of 1995 in San Francisco, you could cut the bombast in the air with a knife. So they started their own refreshingly iconoclastic, skeptical, cynical Webzine of daily rants, called *Suck*. Soon what began as a weekend exercise in personal sanity resonated with enough of the industry that *HotWired* gave them a corner of their own to work out of, editing other people's writings while refining their own unique *Suck* style and stance.

They have their work cut out for them. Interviewed by David Wall for *Navigate*, <http://www.netscape-press.com>, Steadman says, "I get the real feeling that we can suck all we want, they'll make more." However, "unfocused rants on obvious targets, such as marketing, capitalism, [and] Microsoft are out," he says. And though the editors are in their twenties, they've banned the term "GenX as hackneyed and basically meaningless." (Amen!)

HotWired calls itself a "network," rather than a magazine, with "channels" rather than sections. In 1996, it spun out whole new arms besides *Suck*: Talk.Com, for Web-based chat; Netizen, reporting on politics and the Washington beat; Packet, with a rotating daily column for the Web's business, technology, and cultural communities; POP, for TV, film, music, books, art, multimedia, etc.; Web Monkey, an "all-service tune-up station" for HTML, browsers, plug-ins, and tutorials; the HotBot search engine; and, last but not least, WiredSource, originally staff fact-checker Rod Simpson's in-house reference tool, which organically grew into an extraordinary, universal treasure trove.

C|NET
<http://www.cnet.com>

In another example of media synergy, the computer TV program C|NET has produced an online-only weekly Webzine with straight-ahead articles, plus software archives, reader forums, and search tools galore. In fact, the Web site now has more viewers than the TV show.

E-ZINES

There are scads of other kinds of magazines. Academic journals, for example, are finding the Internet a must; most subscribers have Internet accounts through their universities, and so the cost of paper, printing, and distribution is eliminated from the budget. Then, too, there are all those little niche magazines and newsletters, such as *The Journal of Buddhist Ethics*, that have gone online.

And there's a new element at magazine racks in major bookstores: the "zines" (rhymes with "scenes"). *Playboy* says that zines are "just below the surface of the mainstream media." *Details* calls them "soapbox samurai . . . invisible literature." *USA Today* calls them "wacky, obscene, gross, tender, funny." And major publishers are bringing out reprints and anthologies.

What's a zine? A zine can be about anything: underground music, literary genres, any cult, serial killers, your own life, alternative health, Christian fellowship, anti-Christian epistles, lifestyles, political rant, speculative fiction — anything goes.

Here's a definition from zine maven John Labovitz:

. . . "zine" is short for either "fanzine" or "magazine," depending on your point of view. Zines are generally produced by one person or a small group of people, done often for fun or personal reasons, and tend to be irreverent, bizarre, and/or esoteric. Zines are not "mainstream" publications — they generally do not contain advertisements (except, sometimes, advertisements for other zines), are not targeted toward a mass audience, and are generally not produced to make a profit.

One historic precedent cited by zine spokesperson Alex Swaine is Samuel Johnson's literary papers. Zinemeister Jerod Pore notes the roots of zines in a number of sources: the American pamphleteers of the 1760s and 1770s (whose clash with the British, in part, prompted the American Revolution); Davey Crockett fanzines in the 1830s; the family newsletter in the 1890s; and, in the 1930s, the new media of both mimeograph and pulp fiction.

In the last-named category, Swaine notes that the nickel pulp science-fiction mags printed a forum where readers could exchange letters and writing; soon many sci-fi fans started their own mimeo forums, called "fanzines," where now-notable writers — such as Robert Bloch, Robert Heinlein, and Ray Bradbury — got their start.

Since the early seventies, the decentralized, nonprofit, anarchistic Internet/BBS culture has influenced zine evolution. Many zine writers and publishers were also early adopters of BBSs and the Net. One of the first uses of Usenet, for example, was as an e-zine for *Star Trek* and *Star Wars* fans.

An "e-zine" is simply any zine that has a presence on an electronic network, such as a BBS or the Internet (mailing list, gopher, FTP, or Web). E-zines, too, cover the gamut as to special-interest audiences.

We've already seen a few examples of e-zines in the chapters on genres: *SomePIG, Ansible, Mysterious Bytes,* and *The Literary Times* all target special-interest groups — poetry fans, sci-fi fans, mystery fans, and romance fans.

The Atlantic on the Web, Slate, Salon, and *Word* could be called "Webzines" but not "e-zines." In a Webzine, you might find John Updike or Annie E. Proulx; in an e-zine, Stephen King or Dorothy Allison . . . or a complete unknown.

Zines are important here for three main reasons:

- a zine can be a no-sweat way to get published; less fuss, more freedom
- publishing in a zine captures the attention of a special interest group and builds a community of readers and writers
- if you really want to "make a name for yourself," then do it yourself; start your own zine

Today's computer permits a writer who so chooses to write, print, publish, publicize, and distribute all through a single computer, while creating community at the same time.

Insiders say that now's the time to get in before zines really hit — big. Jerod Pore estimates that there were over ten thousand print zines in 1990; by 1994 that figure quadrupled. (The number of print zines has now stabilized at forty to fifty thousand.) Likewise, as the Internet doubles and triples in size, today's mid-to-high-three-figure e-zine count could triple or quadruple fast . . . very fast.

A common pitfall, however, of the online zine scene besets any writer using computers: not knowing when to quit. Creating on a word processor rather than a legal pad, the writer tends to write more, especially with line wraps (no carriage return) and no paper to feed. Since the Internet is almost inexhaustible, some zines can run on and on and on and on. . . .

And if you do venture into e-zine publishing, keep in mind how accessible your zine will be. You will be open to feedback from readers you may never have intended as your audience. One e-zinester found out the hard way about how accessible information is on the Net: he whined in print about conditions at his workplace, then learned that his boss did a Web search for his name one day and found that rant.

Now I will introduce you to over twenty-five zines. They will give you an idea of the range of options that e-zines afford the writer — and self-publisher.

ArtCommotion
<http://www.artcommotion.com>

A great example of a local e-zine (Los Angeles) that is so well-presented and hyperlinked as to have relevance for the Internet community at large.

bOING bOING
<http://www.well.com/user/mark/index.html>

An e-zine that Mark Frauenfelder and Carla Sinclair founded in 1988, with Gareth Branwyn soon coming onboard as Senior Editor. The e-zine archives this popular mag, focusing on pranks, comics, subcultures, design, virtual reality, chaos theory, etc.

CTheory
<http://www.ctheory.com>

An international review of theory, technology, and culture getting about a million hits a year. Akin to *Suck*, it takes an oppositional stance toward technotopia, seeing in "the virtual class" the cruelty, as R.U. Sirius puts it, of "the love of novelty . . . married to the will to power in the context of a highly competitive social order."

Contributors have included Kathy Acker, Jean Baudrillard, Bruce Sterling, Deena and Michael Weinstein, and founding editors Mary Louise and Arthur (*Hacking the Future*) Kroker. On the cutting edge of the Scene, it makes its own events. A Baudrillard interview appeared here about eight months before it was published in French. And "30 Cyber-Days in San Francisco" was written and published on a daily basis, with immediate writer-reader interaction.

To subscribe, e-mail <listserv@vm1.mcgill.ca> with the message "subscribe CTheory *YourFullName*".

eSCENE
<http://www.etext.org/Zines/eScene/>

An annual compendium of fiction; an electronic anthology dedicated to providing "one-click access to the Internet's best short fiction and authors." For more information, e-mail <kepi@halcyon.com>.

Enterzone
<http://ezone.org:1080/ez>

Published by Christian Crumlish, *Enterzone* features top-notch cartoons, hyperstuff, poems, stories, polemics, and such, many linked from issue to issue. Entries include "Bigamy in the Desert, Confessions of a Closet Schizophrenic," and "Understanding Liberace." Contributors have included Frederick Barthelme and Robert Hunter. *Enterzone* invites browsing, with a "Path of Least Resistance" as a Table of Contents for the surfing-impaired. Hosted by American Arts and Letters Network (AALN).

Free Cuisinart
<http://www.on-net.net/wowzine/wowzine.html>

Publishes poetry, essays, and other work from around the world, plus maintains active resources: a poetry bulletin board, a message board for postings of magazines looking for writers or readers, and the latest information on the fight against censorship of artists on the Net.

Geek Girl
<http://www.next.com.au/spyfood/geekgirl/>

A high-powered Australian cyberfeminist e-zine.

George Jr.
<http://www.georgejr.com>

Edited by George Myers, Jr., books editor for the *Columbus Dispatch*, *George Jr.* is a literary e-zine with interviews, reviews, poetry, and comment. Contributors have included Wendell Berry, Joyce Carol Oates, and Belle Yang. Almost a Webzine, but not quite, and a tonic for not being one.

Athene
<gopher://gopher.etext.org>
   path: /Zines/Athene

The "online magazine of amateur creative writing" was one of the Net's first e-zines. It ended its run in 1989 (but read on).

InterText
<http://www.etext.org/Zines/InterText/>

The successor to *Athene*, *InterText* is a bimonthly fiction magazine printing stories in all genres, with a readership now in the thousands. Editors: Jason Snell, <jsnell@etext.org>; Geoff Duncan, <gaduncan@halcyon.com> (assistant editor); Susan Grossman c/o <intertext@etext.org> (assistant editor).

It's a Bunny
<http://www.iti.qc.ca/iti/bunny/>

This Montreal, Canada based e-zine for new English fiction, poetry, and art is a stylishly done endeavor, with the added value of hyperlinks to several other literary e-journals.

JetPack
<http://www.buzznet.com>

An ongoing adventure in Internet media featuring fiction, poetry, comics, alternative music, technology, science fiction, and international lifestyle. For more information, e-mail <info@buzznet.com>.

Jolly Roger
<http://jollyroger.com/beaconmag/jollyroger.html>

Armed with the Western Canon, *Jolly Roger* calls itself the flagship of the conservative literary revolution — proof that the Internet isn't entirely given over to progressive-minded anarcho-socialist liberals. Anyone attempting to deconstruct anything on board will be keelhauled.

Kyosaku
<http://www.cs.oberlin.edu/students/djacobs/kyo/kyomain.html>

Dedicated to endangered concepts: humor, art, philosophy, the quest for higher consciousness, uncalled-for-absurdity in the face of pessimism, and unpretentiousness. The name refers to the stick that Zen masters use to whup their students upside the head, sending them on the path to higher consciousness. Editors: David Jacobs, <djacobs@cs.oberlin.edu>; Michael Janssen, <janssmp3@wfu.edu>; Jim McNamee, <rg94900868@vax1.may.ie>; Sudama Rice, <sarF93@hamp.hampshire.edu>; Derek Kershaw, <dpkers@mail.wm.edu>.

Literary Kicks
<www.charm.net/!brooklyn/LitKicks.html>

Levi Asher's loving tribute to the Beats, and thriving like eucalyptus.

The Morpo Review
<gopher://morpo.creighton.edu>
   path: /The.Morpo.Review

"How about Sonnets to Captain Kangaroo, free-verse ruminations comparing plastic lawn ornaments to Love Boat or nearly anything with cows in it? No, not cute, Smurfy little 'ha ha' ditties — back reality into a corner and snarl! Some good examples are 'Oatmeal' by Galway Kinnell, 'A Supermarket In California' by Allen Ginsberg, or the sixth section of Wallace Stevens' 'Six Significant Landscapes.'" Editors: Robert Fulkerson, <rfulk@creighton.edu>, and Matthew Mason, <mtmason@morpo.creighton.edu>. E-mail <lists@morpo.creighton.edu> with the message "get morpo morpo.index" and you'll receive instructions on how to retrieve ASCII versions. To subscribe, e-mail <morpo-request@morpo.creighton.edu>.

Moscow Channel
<http://www.moscowchannel.com>

Published by two émigrés, Vladimir Druk and Alex Halberstadt, in English; swell poetry, reviews, satire, and art.

NWHQ
<http://www.knosso.com/NWHQ/index.html>

"A hypermedia magazine of art and literature. It is our intention that the artistic works in *NWHQ* can be ultimately 'grown' into a network of novel-length literature. As it is not a paper publication, we do not want to approach it as such; instead of a product, it is a process. It changes and shifts over time, a labyrinth in progress. Not everything is accessible from the front/homepage. Individual writers may grow their works, others may disappear." Editor: Elizabeth Fischer <NWHQ@wimsey.com>.

Obscure
<http://www.obscure.com>

Solicits quirky, unpublished, unapologetic creativity of all kinds: stories, poetry, essays, random thoughts, artwork, cartoons, and photographs for publication online and in hard copy.

Parallel
<http://www.va.com.au/parallel/x1/index.html>

A post-modern gallery of virtual artists and a journal of multidisciplinary articles, plus hyper-hip Web links.

Pen & Sword Hypersite
<http://www.rahulnet.jag/zine>

A post-beat e-zine, publishing diverse fiction, poetry, reviews, and photography.

Rapture
<http://theglobe.com/rapture>

Publishes poetry and fiction (in its "Ink" section) and book discussion and reviews ("Mocha") as well as art, international news analysis, music and film reviews.

The Silence
<http://www.altx.com>

An independent literary journal published as part of the Alt-X Web publishing project ("X" as in Generation-X). It's dedicated to providing a human voice on the

Internet and to publishing "new or emerging writers . . . who have found their voice but have yet to receive the recognition due them . . . work that can stand on its own as artifacts of the truth-telling imagination."

They seek poetry, fiction, and essays. Recently, they've been especially interested in essays on the writing life: "What jobs do writers take to support their craft?" "How does one approach a poem or story?" "Have there been important influences on your writing?"

The Silence reads entries year-round, and payment is made in the form of a sense of deep satisfaction. E-mail plain-ASCII entries to <silence@cs.widener.edu>.

Spanish Dagger
<http://www.kaiwan.com:80/~cortes/dagger.html>

Proudly leftist, *Spanish Dagger* stresses labor issues and the Americas. Editor Peter Rashkin states: "I like to think of it as a sharp instrument thrust at the heart of the greedy, imperialistic new world order. Essays, poetry, fiction, graphics. Here's how critics and fans describe it: 'A directionless zine with a wide variety of poignant essays' (Factsheet Five #58). 'I am a Christian, married with two children. My wife and I find this publication inappropriate' (Doug Lum). 'Thank God *The Dagger* keeps free thought alive when the mainstream media is bought and paid for by Disney Corporation and its few corporate clones' (An impassioned but anonymous fan)."

Sparks
<ftp://ftp.etext.org>
   path: /pub/Zines/Sparks/

"A quarterly literary zine for creative people. Fiction, poetry, essays, art, culture, rants, politics, pictures, and other meta-pseudo-stuff." Editors: Jim Esch, <jmesch@artsci.wustl.edu>, and Stacy Tartar, <Stacy.Tartar@launchpad.unc.edu>.

Spilled Ink
<gopher://gopher.etext.org>
   path: Zines/Spilled_Ink

A literary e-zine consisting of all sorts of works — poetry, prose, songs, short stories, and philosophy — tending to deal with the darker side of things, such as: betrayal, anguish, angst, darkness, doom, the question of existence. Editor: Twilight <twilight@mail.utexas.edu>.

Urban Desires: An Interactive Journal of Metropolitan Passions
<http://www.desires.com>

A high-powered Manhattan e-zine of art, books, sex, style, tech, and travel, published by Kyle Shannon, Gabrielle Shannon, and Chan Suh, and replete with an N-dimensional dataspace tunnel and a palace.

ZIPZAP
<http://zipzap.com/cover.html>

A hypertext e-zine featuring contemporary poetry, fiction, essays, interviews, and contemporary fine art. Editors: Evonne Fenn <evonne@zipzap.com> and Jeff Williams <jeffw@zipzap.com>.

Zine Forums

Alt.zines has been on Usenet since 1992, for discussion of zine culture, specific zines, tips on producing zines, which zines have been getting censored and why, and similar questions. Alt.ezines is for discussion of e-zines, where people actually post e-zines in ASCII (plain-code text, without any special programming). Alt.binaries.zines is for any non-ASCII zines and any other zine-related articles (it's been attracting non-zinesters, who make a bunch of noise). Also of interest are alt.etext, alt.pulp (Classic Era zines from the thirties), and rec.mag.

For those who speak AOLese, a big zine keyword at America Online is "PDA" (Palmtop Paperbacks -> EZines -> Fiction). Palmtop Paperbacks also branches into EZine Libraries -> Writing, and -> More Writing.

CompuServe carries the Electronic Frontier Foundation's "Zines from the Net" section, accessible by typing GO EFFSIG.

Electronic zine expert Jerod Pore hosts an online FactSheet Five conference at the WELL (go: f5): gopher."Authors, Books, Periodicals, Zines/Online Zines".

Under Publications, the WELL gopher, <gopher://well.com>, also links to over eighty zines, from *Ad Busters* and *Angst* to *Weekly_Weird_News* and *Zaginflatch*.

Webzine and E-Zine Stands

The Association of Research Libraries
<http://arl.cni.org/scomm/edir>

Publishes an online directory of over 1,700 electronic journals and newsletters.

Broken Pencil
<http://www.io.org/~halpen/bpencil.html>

The guide to alternative publications in Canada; reviews over 230 Canadian zines, chapbooks, newsletters, journals, and e-zines, also excerpts feature stories.

François Charoy's Home Page (Nancy, France)
<http://www.loria.fr/~charoy/zines.html>

A list of lists of zines: zines in the Netherlands, French zines, e-mail zines, Web-zines, scientific journals, and more.

Ecola's Newsstand
<http://www.ecola.com>

Stocks magazines as well as newspapers.

Etext
<http://www.etext.org/>
<gopher.etext.org>
   path: /Zines/
<gopher.locust.cic.net>
   path: /Zines

A central repository of e-zines, searchable by subject, maintained by Rita, <rita@etext.org>.

Electric Pencil
<http://www.execpc.com/~catrina/pen/ezine.html>

Maintains an in-depth listing of zines by genre or in alphabetical order.

The E-Mail Zines List
<http://www.propagandist.com/tkemzl>

Lists ASCII/text-only zines by category. (There are about a dozen topics for fiction and poetry.)

The E-Zines Database
<http://www.dominis.com/Zines>

Large, but searchable by multiple criteria. There are over thirty links under Fiction and Poetry, and another thirty under Literary. The database is dead-URLs-free, constantly updated and checked. To list your zine, e-mail <otis@dominis.com>.

Fact Sheet Five

The zine that's a guide to other zines. It has gone from small to an over 125-page magazine, reviewing over 1,000–1,500 different zines every three months. P.O. Box 170099, San Francisco, CA 94117-0099.

Factsheet Five — Electric
<http://www.well.com/conf/f5/f5index2.html>

The electric counterpart, of *Factsheet Five*, for e-zines. There are hyperlinks to the e-zines being reviewed, links to other e-zine lists, and archives of over 1,000 e-zines, e-journals and e-magazines, FAQs, tips, and more.

The Free Internet Encyclopedia
<http://www.cs.uh.edu/~clifton/macro.z.html#zines>

Has a category for zines and online magazines.

John Hewitt
<http://www.azstarnet.com/~poewar/writer/pg/lit.html>

Has an annotated list of dozens of literary Webzines, many taking submissions, some even paying (among them *15 Credibility Street, 256 Shades of Grey, Atmospherics, Caffeine, Circuit Traces, Coelacanth, Common Boundaries, Enterzone, Far Gone, Interbang, Kudzu, Lip Service, The Open Scroll, Recursive Angel*).

The Internet Writers' Guidelines
<http://www-wane-leon.scri.fsu.edu/~jtillman/DEV/ZDMS/>

A searchable directory of Webzines, created by James Tillman, editor of *In Vivo*.

John Labovitz
<http://www.meer.net/~johnl/e-zine-list/index.html>

John created his list of zines in 1993 because he was scouting places where he could publicize *Crash*, his print zine that he'd recently made into an e-zine. He didn't find enough outlets, so he started his own. This list now includes over 1,000 e-zines and is updated monthly. Zines are listed alphabetically, and he's experimenting with an area where people can search the list for keywords.

Web del Sol
<http://www.cais.net/aesir/fiction>

Based in Falls Church, Virginia, one of the oldest towns in America Web del Sol is one of the more sophisticated, high-bandwidth megasource jumpstations of literary Webzines on the Net. It recently added a Writer's Resourceplex with research tools and networking sources.

Writer's Page
<http://www.ccn.cs.dal.ca./Culture/WritersFed/Resources.html>

Courtesy of the Writers' Federation of Nova Scotia; maintained by Richard Cumyn, it highlights hundreds of online periodicals that publish poetry, fiction, and prose.

Zine News
<http://wild-turkey.acns.nwu.edu/~hrow/kl-e/z-news.html>

A compendium of hyperlinked news flashes from the zine scene.

Zine Online Newsstand
<http://kumo.swcp.com/xines>

Stocks over a thousand Webzines and e-zines, with short blurbs about each. Searchable by thirty-six subject areas, or alphabetically.

Zines Zines Everywhere
<http://thetransom.com/chip/zines/index.html>

The online supplement to "Going Digital: How to Take Your Zine Electric," which appeared in Issue 56 of *Factsheet Five*. You'll find it's a comprehensive, hyperlinked one-stop with links to e-zines, software, tutorials, archive sites, and other resources related to e-zine publishing, publicity, and distribution.

※ ※ ※

The following chapter continues the investigation into how the digital and paper worlds both diverge from and feed into each other. Some writers feel that the best outlet is magazines; others, books. Just as the two interpenetrate in the solid world of paper, so, too, do they overlap in the virtual world of cyberspace.

16

Net Books

Everything exists to be put into a book.

—Stephane Mallarmé

We live in a cultural continuum in which we are free to move back and forth through the centuries. Books are islands in the ocean of time. They are also oases in the deserts of time.

—Lawrence Clark Powell

The Internet is directly impacting the future of books — their publication, promotion, distribution, and sales. To orient you to this new paradigm, I'll begin this chapter with case studies of how the world's biggest publisher and a one-woman book packager each made a successful transition across the Internet threshold, from paper to electrons: Simon & Schuster and Online Book Services.

From there, I'll further acquaint you with:

- digitized books (already existing on paper), available online for your reading pleasure or writing research
- online-only books (again, for pleasure or research)
- bound books, for sale online (to help you locate books or sell your own)
- other resources for bibliophiles

(In Chapter 17, you'll also learn about self-publishing and promoting your own books via the Internet.)

You can also use the Internet to search for agents and publishers for your work. One success story in that realm is Skip Press. Skip searched AOL's member directory for the words "book publisher." He narrowed the results (fifty in all) down to about a dozen and e-mailed an informational letter, stating his track record and expressing interest in writing something new for somebody. Within weeks, he had a contract for *Writer's Guide to Hollywood Producers, Directors, and Screenwriter's Agents* for Prima's Writer's Guide Series.

BOOK PUBLISHING AND THE INTERNET: TWO CASE STUDIES

Let's begin our look at books with two related case studies that provide background on how even the traditionally conservative, tie-and-suspenders publishing world is taking to the digital road. The examples I've chosen come from two very different perspectives: one from Publisher's Row, and the other from a cottage industry that supplies publishers with "packaging."

Simon & Schuster — The View from the Top

Flash back to the mid-1990s. The world's third-largest publishing empire, Bantam Doubleday Dell, seemed to be barely budging from its pasture of paper print. Random House, the world's second-biggest house, had been proceeding relatively slowly into the burgeoning online arena. But Simon & Schuster, the world's largest publishing company, seemed to be taking the lead as the world's major digital publishing house.

How They Got Where They Are. Simon & Schuster (S&S) began in 1924 when Richard Simon and Max Schuster pooled their savings to publish a crossword puzzle book. An overnight bestseller, the book swept the nation in a crossword-puzzle craze. Soon their puzzle books were outdistanced by titles from "real authors," such as Will and Ariel Durant, Dale Carnegie, and Norman Vincent Peale. In the next decade they took advantage of mass production and mass distribution, selling hardcover books in paperbound pocketbook reprints for a quarter a book.

Now a quick recap of corporate history will show us how they came to the Digital Era. Fifty years after forming, the company was acquired by Gulf + Western Industries, which would, in turn, become Paramount Communications, Inc. Meanwhile, S&S had expanded from consumer publishing into the growing educational market with the acquisition of Prentice Hall. Today, education accounts for more than half of its total revenue — and the schools of tomorrow are digital and online.

Through 1990, S&S continued to make acquisitions and to expand into foreign markets, as well as to venture into new, electronic media, such as CD-ROMs. In 1995, one man redirected their growth strategy from acquisitions to the world of new media.

Jonathan Newcomb had left the helm of McGrawHill's financial information business in 1988 to become president of the S&S publishing group, under CEO Richard Snyder. At that time, electronic products were barely a blip on the corporate radar screen. But he'd already begun to see the power of delivering products electronically when he'd worked at Standard & Poor's debt-rating agency, which was beginning to make its financial information available online. He took the giant step of carrying the revolution in financial data over to text.

By 1995, Newcomb had become CEO of S&S, where electronic products had now come to represent almost a quarter of S&S's total revenues (which, as of this writing, now exceed $2 billion). In 1997 they expect their SuperSite to generate over $100 million through sale of books and software, books about the Internet, travel transactions, and advertising, with over 1 million hits each day.

Simon and Schuster SuperSite
<http://www.SimonandSchuster.com>

Within the S&S SuperSite.
The Information SuperLibrary
<http://www.mcp.com>

The Information SuperLibrary represents Macmillan, S&S Interactive, and Prentice Hall Direct. It contains information pertaining to over 6,000 book and CD-ROM titles, including more than 1,000 sample chapters — largely reference and computer, but also cooking, travel, health, fitness, and sports. The Information SuperLibrary has many unique features, such as the popular, free, interactive career and personal development quiz and evaluation, for individuals or corporations.

In addition, The SuperLibrary has subdivisions, such as: BradyGAMES and Jossey-Bass:

BradyGAMES
<http://www.mcp.com/brady>

Serves up news, games, contests, and free gaming goodies.

Jossey-Bass
<http://www.josseybass.com>

Has its own catalog of 1,200 educational and health-related titles online, plus a jumpstation of related Internet links.

These Web sites can be thought of as independent imprints — ones with a very good forecast. For example, in 1995 five college textbooks had online adjuncts; by 1997 the number grew to twenty-five, and will continue to snowball. And as colleges invest in distance learning, S&S can furnish original online curricula (a.k.a. "courseware") to be used in conjunction with their textbooks.

Thus, S&S is not only computerizing production (essentially an enhanced form of desktop publishing), but also using the Net to reach customers, connect with retailers, build relationships with authors, expand its range of titles, send out inspection chapters to instructors, create "brand" image, and so forth.

Viacom is, of course, pleased that it didn't sell off this publishing component when it bought the Paramount Group, contrary to industry expectation; it currently accounts for one-fifth of Viacom's revenues. And, as of this writing, S&S shows an overall thirteen percent growth rate — nearly double the industry average.

Says Newcomb:

> Books will always be our primary medium. But the Internet gives us a whole new way to make information public. We're pursuing online applications where we can deliver enhanced content and distribute information with greater immediacy and economy. Ultimately, technology is an instrument for pursuing our passion — leveraging our editorial and marketing judgment to educate, entertain, and inform.

A New Imprint: Simon & Schuster Online.
SimonSays
<http://www.SimonsandSchuster.com>

Rounding out the publishing group's online presence, in early 1996, Jack Romanos, president of S&S's consumer group, announced the launch of a new imprint: Simon & Schuster Online. Sleekly designed by the Razorfish Web studio, the purpose of the Web site, SimonSays, is to showcase new titles and authors online, as well as to publish original material and to electronically develop the most popular, provocative, and important titles.

For *The Choice,* for example — Robert Woodward's behind-the-scenes coverage of the 1996 Presidential campaign — they not only added some spiffy diagrams illustrating the book's survey of "spheres of influence" within each party; they also drew voters to a nonpartisan hyperlinked election guide throughout primary season. And, in addition to hosting reader forums, they hosted a live, real-time chat with Woodward from his home in Georgetown — the kind that authors have held at America Online or Prodigy, but here it was conducted Internet-wide, from their own domain.

S&S Online may also premiere a multimedia adaptation of Will and Ariel Durant's *Story of Civilization*, an interactive version of Brady's *Craft of the Screenwriter*, a hyperlinked cross-referencing of the works of Dale Carnegie, or an author's short stories interconnected into a forest of branching paths.

Here, too, you might submit an original online work, such as a nonlinear mystery in which the reader is cast in the role of the detective who must interact with the other characters in order to solve an offbeat plot winding through three-dimensional virtual reality worlds (VRML: Virtual Reality Markup Language), with a number of pre-scripted murders lurking within the twisty path. Or a romance fan might find a home here for her definitive compilation of online resources for romance writing, with a searchable database and weekly features; she might also want to host an online romance reading group here.(The readers' groups at SimonSays.com have been one of their biggest successes.)

S&S Online is also distinguished by its community-building interactivity via reader reviews, bulletin boards, chats, and monthly facilitated reading groups. The reading groups are watched over by Rachel Jacobsohn, president of the Association of Book Group Readers and Leaders.

Lisa Mandel of S&S Online. Lisa Mandel, the VP and Publisher of S&S Online, started out in magazine publishing, branched out into new media, and, in late 1994, joined Viacom's new Interactive Services as a Creative Director of Design and Development. In that role, she worked with Viacom's various corporate arms and legs, such as MTV, VH1, and S&S, helping them to "jump-start their efforts to develop online content."

Now she's back where she started: the word. And that raises an important point: the case cannot be made strongly enough that the Internet and other interactive media need "writerly" people. It's more than needing a writer to furnish content; S&S's Internet enterprises will always need an author's vision, an author's voice, an author's hand to shape and guide the online user's experience. Otherwise, it's a case of "the new clothes have no emperor" — storytelling taking the back seat to technology and special effects. Mandel also reflects another requisite for new media: the same innovative, creative entrepreneurial vision and drive that made

Richard Simon and Max Schuster's initial puzzle book venture into the empire that it is today.

Mandel likes to say that "the World Wide Web is more like the Wild Wild West," where whatever rules there may be are constantly changing. "You need to gain a foothold," she muses. "Build a town — and from it springs a big city. It's a question of being in the right place and putting up your homestead. Except," she adds, "'the right place' might mean 'as many places as you can.'"

Mandel is pleased to see the cable industry and telephone companies opening their doors to the Internet; their high-powered investment in an Internet infrastructure and an enormous audience can only enrich the medium. She sees cable, specifically, as capable of creating private, pay-to-play Webs, as on a toll route, offering first-class, guaranteed delivery, and including such broadband services as instant, seamless visuals and audio.

S&S Online's Frontiers. Of course, Mandel is well aware of the hurdles ahead, though many are obvious only to publishing insiders. For one example, consider what's known as "branding." Book publishers recognize that while most readers might have a bookstore of preference and pay attention to a book's author or the title of a series, they're oblivious to who the publisher might be. So how will people become aware of S&S Online's forthcoming digital releases?

For one thing, by linking to the many sites geared around the publishing industry, such as Book Page, BookWire, Readers' Index of Books, Amazon.com, and *Hungry Mind Review*. Mandel's analogy is that a shopper's destination might be a department store (such as Bloomingdale or Nordstrom), providing a context for Donna Karan and Armani, who might have outposts all around town. And S&S Online will do niche publishing. (Here's where the S&S marketing expertise comes in.) If there's enough of, say, the sophisticated, high-end audience for Annie E. Proulx that is sufficiently wired, S&S Online will reach out to them. (Primary target audiences are parenting, self-help, mystery, romance, politics, and current events.)

And then there's *Star Trek*. (Talk about narrowcasting or niche marketing: S&S currently sells fourteen *Star Trek* books a minute!) S&S Online has 130 Star Trek books and the two bestselling *Star Trek* CD-ROMs to draw from. Demand for a live Web-cast from the Paramount Studios set off "Star Trek: the Borg," a CD-ROM game that required users to sign up for a chat room seat in advance through InfoSeek — the first instance of "online ticketing."

When choosing a literary property to develop, S&S Online looks not only at the appropriateness of the work itself, but at the author's willingness to take an active part.

Mandel is on the lookout for authors who can make their presence available to readers online, dealing with frequently asked questions or participating in an online forum. Some writers will prefer to stick to a strictly ink-and-paper metier. But for the Internet-literate, the traditional lure of book publishers now enchants with interactivity's bold new spell. What that bodes for the future, only time can tell.

Open Book Systems

For a tour:
<http://www.obs-us.com/obs/english/about/tour.htm>

For a fine, hyperlinked speech:
<http://www.obs-us.com/obs/english/papers/gr1.htm>

Online Book Service (OBS) is a small operation, but it leaves a big footprint in the sands of publishing — one that also keeps moving boldly ahead.

Whereas Simon & Schuster stands as a beacon in the landscape of American corporate culture, OBS is essentially the handiwork of one person, Laura Fillmore.

ONLINE PUBLISHING

by Laura Fillmore

Timeliness and cost reductions are not the main reason publishers should be interested in the online medium. The principal advantages have to do with the things you cannot do in print, or even on CD-ROM. . . .

Many publishers simply want to know the bottom line: "Is online publishing good or bad for the industry?" Many publishers will rue the day when people stop going to bookstores and instead just browse the network from the confines of their homes. But others say that online publishing will expand the industry, without replacing paper publishing. . . .

But one thing is for sure: book publishers need to be involved, if only to assure that the Information Superhighway is not just a vast video-on-demand shopping mall. As all forms of other media are zooming along the Superhighway, publishers are responsible for keeping alive the works upon which the past five centuries of Western civilization have been built. Publishers, as major content holders, need to get on the bus. The capability of not using words is right around the corner. If we as a culture don't preserve our words, then there goes our abstract thought.

Not especially a big computer person, she has a most writerly academic background. Fillmore received her B.A. in English from Barnard in 1975. Following postgraduate work at the Sorbonne, Columbia, and Harvard, she spent four years as an editor at Little, Brown and Company, then hung out her shingle as Editorial Inc. (EI). EI operated as a book packager, representing freelance publishing professionals to publishing and related industries. This was in 1982, when the phrase "desktop publishing" was new; computers were just starting to become influential players in the printing/publishing world, and she made them her specialty. Within ten years, she'd produced hundreds of books for publishers — everything from Tom Robbins novels to MIT's *System Dynamics Review*.

In 1989, EI produced *The Matrix* by John S. Quarterman for Digital Press (meticulously mapping Internet usage — how many people had e-mail, how many had Web access, domestic versus foreign, and so on, and Laura was bitten by the Internet bug. She recalls today, "I was curious about the Internet and wrote a book proposal (*The Internet Companion*) which would explain to regular people in nontech language what the Net was and how to get to it." She found a perfect author, Tracey LaQuey, and Addison-Wesley bought the proposal. The timing was perfect for the first pocketbook guide. (*Dummies* guides to the Net had not yet appeared.)

The Internet's exponential growth was beginning to be noticed outside computer circles, and ordinary consumers were immigrating to cyberspace in significant numbers via America Online, CompuServe, and Prodigy. No less important, the book would tap a crucial need. While the Internet may be the greatest thing since sliced bread, it could easily languish in the advanced research laboratories where it was born if people couldn't understand its benefits. So Addison-Wesley made the leap to publishing the first trade book about the Net, *The Internet Companion: a Beginner's Guide to Global Networking* by Tracy LaQuey (with Jeanne Ryer).

The Presence of OBS in Cyberspace. While waiting for the finished work to arrive from Addison-Wesley's printers, EI did a little advance publicity posting Chapter 1 for free, via FTP. Thousands of people responded. And many asked, "What's your next book?" That's when OBS was born. (Originally "Online Bookstore", it later was renamed "Online Book Systems").

In putting her distinctive stamp on this new paradigm, Fillmore's contributions are best typified by continual innovation. In 1993, the first serialization rights to *Nightmares and Dreamscapes* by Stephen King were sold not to a magazine but to OBS. The 1993 publication by OBS of King's short story, "Umney's Last Case," was a turning point in the Internet as an alternative channel for commercial publishers to find readers. Way back in pre-Netscape 1994, Fillmore adapted *Bless this Food*, Adrian Butash's collection of table prayers from the world's religions, linking it to other resources and sites all across the Net.

Today, OBS still hasn't developed a "niche." Rather than specialize, it handles publishers and authors big and small, working with them to customize each title, finding a medium for its particular content and its readers' needs through the kinetic potentials of the Net. (This is contrary to the dominant trend in multimedia, where, once one title has been made, the basic programming work that goes into it and makes it work (a.k.a. the "engine") becomes a cookie-cutter template for future titles.) Pushing the Net's envelope, Fillmore is driven to, as she puts it, "continually explore our new medium and discover new ways to offer new breath and life — the capability to change — to the ideas and information contained in each book. Success comes when we collaborate and create something that can only happen on the Internet."

The list of OBS "distributive editions" ranges from fiction to travel, poetry to kids', and, of course, books about cyberspace. For instance, OBS launched Time Warner's Quick Read program for sale on the Internet with fourteen downloadable hypertext titles, interlinked with Internet resources. The free sampler allows readers to browse selections offline, and the external link sets allow readers to add context to the selections online. These "link sets" for each title in the TimeWarner Quick Read Library also laid the groundwork for an approach OBS would call Cyberdock, which it unveiled along with a number of other eye-openers at the 1995 American Bookseller's Association convention (the ABA).

Being Digital *Ushers in New Paradigms.*

For one thing, Penguin USA didn't have a booth on the floor that year; it relied, instead, on having Internet presence provided by the ABA Web site, Bookwire, and by OBS. At the same time, OBS unveiled their online "distributive" version of the bestseller, *Being Digital*, <http://www.randomhouse.com/knopf/index.html>, by the director of MIT's famed Media Lab, Nicholas Negroponte, with its new Cyberdock and Gumball Machine Billing paradigms. As the reader who visits the OBS version can discover, it goes beyond merely replaying (a.k.a. "repurposing") the book in another medium (a.k.a. "shovelware," shoveling a book's words, as it were, into an electronic format, clod by clod).

The online version of *Being Digital* redefines publishing text, using a maritime analogy — "a cyberdock" — for the new paradigm, with the book's text as "a stable casting-off point, from which the reader is invited to explore the Internet Sea on one of the many 'URL-Boats' tied to the Dock." Laura Fillmore elaborates:

Additionally, the *Being Digital* Cyberdock frees Negroponte's ideas from the words they are couched in and the paper they are printed on, into the media they describe, enabling the ideas to realize themselves, not only through the dynamic links tied to this Cyberdock, but also, and more importantly, through future inclusions and mediations of the ideas and inspirations linked to by . . . readers.

Thus, the links to the actual examples of Negroponte's observations "illuminate his work in a way that cannot be matched on paper," Fillmore observes. "And because these links are constantly changing, they successfully marry paper and online publishing. The electronic version offers readers an opportunity to add additional links. More than illustrate, they enable."

As an example, Fillmore cites Negroponte's discussion of intelligent agents. She explains:

> In a traditional paper book, these agents might be illustrated as a string of code or as an abstract drawing of a cybercreature roaming the Net for its master. On a CD of the book, this same "bot" might be illustrated in a finite and contained prototype form. But on the Net, the "intelligent agent" idea described in the book can evolve into itself in real time, by virtue of linking to existing intelligent-agent programs and resources on the Internet now and in the future. Delightfully, the idea of "intelligent agent" or "bookbot" may even take on an incarnation unanticipated by either the author or the readers, for example, by itself being linked to and perhaps manipulated by an intelligent agent.
>
> Thus, readers can become part of the book and include their own creative ideas about how to program a "knowbot" or "bookbot," which would then achieve one of the ends outlined in the book and validate the success of the Cyberdock.
>
> . . . Throughout, then, the *Being Digital* Cyberdock maintains its original integrity as a printed document, while proving protean enough to allow for others to affect and even determine its meaning. This is a new kind of book, to be sure, if it is a book at all!
>
> . . . The *Being Digital* Cyberdock is meant to provide a structure from which the book can evolve digitally as the ideas it advances are explored, realized, altered, or discarded.

The external links can be either of two kinds, editorial or commercial. Adding an editorial link is free. Adding a commercial link, on the other hand, involves what Fillmore calls Gumball Machine Billing.

In this model, the sponsor isn't charged one lump sum up front, but incrementally, according to usage. "The idea is that it's a no-risk billing model," she explains. "If nobody comes, it doesn't cost the company anything. But say thousands of people come. What we're delivering to them are qualified buyers who voluntarily put their pointer on the word." In the *Being Digital* Cyberdock, a distinction is made between noncommercial and commercial links, so readers are aware of their choices.

Among other innovations OBS has premiered, noteworthy too is their collaboration with Catbird Press on Floyd Kemske's latest novel, *Human Resources*. One of the runners-up in the unofficial race to post the first original novel on the Net, *Human Resources* was originally posted as an untitled, work-in-progress draft. The site later contained his editor's comments, and their ensuing correspondence. Then a later draft was posted. Thus, Catbird wasn't using the Web so much to publish the book as to put the editorial process online as it was taking place, for anyone to see. Readers could thus tap in to the editorial process in action by clicking on a paragraph or a scene and calling up what the author and editor were discussing about it. Such visitors could both observe the process and add their own input.

This pioneering use of the Web not only holds tremendous potential for anyone interested in the creative process, but also represents a new model of how editors and authors can collaborate; they can always be "on the same page" at a common Web site, which holds the latest draft, all their correspondence and notes, and any relevant links, available for easy reference at any time (the Web as literary "groupware," a.k.a. "intranet").

In addition to being a multipurpose packager and a teacher, OBS also acts as a literary agency, with emphasis on titles that have a cyberspace dimension. And Fillmore has ventured into publishing, her first title being a cooperative venture under the aegis of Protean Press, producing Joseph E. Garland's *The Gloucester Guide*, a coffee-table album of the history and people of what was once a fisherman's village, where Fillmore lives. Far from the hustle and bustle of New York's Publisher's Row, she also works in a classic old sea captain's house in Whistlestop Mall, Rockport, a three-hundred-year-year-old picture-postcard harbor town. It's an interesting juxtaposition: the seventeenth and twenty-first centuries.

The OBS Web site is available in English, German, French, and Romanian.

PAPERLESS BOOKS

Why would anyone want to read a book at the beach from a laptop on one's tummy, under an umbrella? What does it mean that the complete works of the Bard of Avon are now online (<http://the-tech.mit.edu/Shakespeare/works.html>)? Well, for one thing, carrying around *The Complete Works, Annotated* on a palmtop digital accessory (a shirt-pocket-size computer), can be much more convenient than carting around a

2,000-page volume. Some folks report that they prefer an online book because they can increase the text size (to, say, 18- or 24-point) and view the work in the font of their choice. Many readers, not to mention actors, would enjoy being able to designate different colors for the texts of different characters.

Moreover, there's unlimited instant indexing. Just as one can search for a word or phrase with a word processor, so can one search a digitized book for key words, by phrase, name, or concept.

Or if you want to refer, in your own writing, to a particular passage from your favorite writer, you can do a search for it then cut and paste it into your work, rather than retype word for word. Michael Hart of Project Gutenberg (which is digitizing vast amounts of literature; described later in this chapter), hopes that by minimizing researchers' trips to the library, they will have more time for original thought. He states:

> Your everyday research paper is ninety percent research and ten percent writing. With e-texts, it will be ten percent research and ninety percent writing the paper. . . . The term "exhaustive research" will disappear, because it won't exhaust you anymore. Painstaking research will be as far in the past as painstaking hardcopying in the monasteries.

Your personal annotations of *The Complete Works* (or a carpentry manual, novel, or poetry) can now be so much richer. The Bard's plays on the page don't leave much room in the margins, but with the digital version, you can create hypertext links from words or phrases, and even add multimedia. And, as noted in regard to Dante, you can collate various commentators to a common site, line by line.

Furthermore, an FTP site or Web site can make a fragile, rare manuscript (such as the first quarto edition of Shakespeare) available for unlimited perusal. We can compare various notable Dante facsimiles, 1472–1629, <http://www.nd.edu/~italnet/Dante>. Thus, the exhibition "Rome Reborn: Vatican Library and Renaissance Culture" is now a permanent fixture of the Net, <http://lcweb.loc.gov/exhibits/vatican/toc.html>. And I'm happy to see my tax dollars going to making Walt Whitman's notebooks available online, as part of the American Memory project of the Library of Congress, <http://lcweb2.loc.gov/ammem/ammemhome.html>

Finally, an electric book costs a fraction of the price of its paper counterpart.

Online digitization infuses the future of the book with new possibilities — and the paradigm shifts further when text originates online.

Where to Find Digitized Books Online

Here's a tour of books available online: digitized text, for your reading pleasure and your writerly research. As you take this tour, prepare yourself for the inevitable overlaps, redundancy, and lack of standardization. The Internet is often compared to a vast public library, with no central branch or head librarian — and no Dewey decimal system. At an online library, books might be grouped with magazines, journals, and audio-videos, as well as transcripts of speeches and even archives of forums.

The Electric Library
<gopher://wiretap.spies.com>

The main menu offers the following selection: Articles, Assorted Documents, Civic & Historical, Classics, Cyberspace, Fringes of Reason, Humor, Mass Media, Miscellaneous, Music, Questionables, Religion, and Technical Information. Under the entry Classics, we find over two hundred book titles online. A partial sample includes Aesop, Aladdin, Artephius, Austen, Bierce, Edgar Rice Burroughs, Chaucer, Conrad, Dickens, Hardy, Hugo, Melville, Paine, *Roget's Thesaurus*, a biography of George Sand, Carl Sandburg, *The Secret Book*, Sophocles, Robert Louis Stevenson, Sun Tzu, Tagore, Twain, Virgil (in Latin and in translation), Virginia Woolf, and Booker T. Washington. The only hitch: it's mostly alphabetized by first name ("Washington," see "George").

Project Gutenberg
<http://promo.net/pg>
<http://www.prairienet.org/pg>

Currently celebrating the twenty-fifth anniversary of its conception, Project Gutenberg is one of the first Net sites to release texts of books online. Its goal is to act as a clearinghouse and support center for "machine-readable texts," acting as an Internet public library with a collection that will total 10,000 of the most-used books by the year 2001. Director Michael Hart, one of the original Internauts and now a Professor of Electronic Text at Illinois Benedictine College, began his quest for digital texts by keyboarding the Declaration of Independence and e-mailing it to his friends. He sees future libraries as "computer searchable collections which can be transmitted via disks, phone lines, or other media at a fraction of the cost in money, time, and paper as in present-day paper media."

Public-domain titles are being digitized as a labor of love by about 500 volunteers around the world — contemporary equivalents of medieval monks, keyboarding or scanning in text, eliminating hyphens and page numbers from scanned text, checking copyright clearance, coordinating co-workers, and so on. Since each book becomes available to all the computers on the Internet, "they will not have to be reserved and restricted to use by one patron at a time," Hart observes. "All materials will be available to all patrons from all locations at all times." And "they do not have to be rebound, reprinted, reshelved, etc."

Project Gutenberg's collection falls into about half a dozen categories: Light Literature, for the whole family (e.g., *Peter Pan*, *Alice in Wonderland*, *Anne of Green Gables*); Heavy Literature, for more serious readers (e.g., *Paradise Lost* and *Paradise Regained*, *Moby Dick*, Descartes, and Caesar and Cicero in Latin); Reference (e.g., *Roget's Thesaurus*, world factbooks, census figures, NAFTA, the consumer price index, math constants); Computers (including Internet guides such as *E-mail 101*, *Zen and the Art of the Internet*, *Surfing the Internet*); Science Fiction (H.G. Wells, Jules Verne, *Flatland*); and Timely Releases (such as *A Christmas Carol* and *The Night before Christmas* in the winter and *The Bible* and the *Apocrypha* in the spring). They are also planning a library of texts in French, German, and Latin as well as other languages.

The Eris Project
<gopher://gopher.vt.edu:10010/10/33>

The Eris Project is the electronic book section at Virginia Tech online. Here, too, the alphabetization by author is haphazard: in the Bs we find Baroness Orczy, Benjamin Franklin, the *Bible*, Blaise Pascal, Giovanni Boccaccio, Bram Stoker, and the Buddha. (*The Cid* is listed under T, but Tacitus is under P, for P. Cornelius Tacitus. Go figure.) Nevertheless, they list 126 authors, with multiple titles for each, thus representing a larger virtual library than The Electric Library, with such notables as Alcott, Bacon, Baum, Bronte, Bullfinch, Cervantes, Confucius, Darwin, Dostoevsky, Frederic Douglass, Egyptian papyri (*The Book of the Dead*, of Ani), Firdausi, José Ortega y Gassett, Goethe, Hammurabi, Hindu literature (laws of Mani, the *Bhagavad-Gita*), Homer, Keats, Martin Luther King Jr., Kipling, Lincoln, Machiavelli, Montaigne, Nietzsche, Ovid, FDR, Sheikh Muslih-uddin Sa'di Shirazi, Montague Summers, and Yeats, to name a few.

The Online Book Initiative (OBI)
<gopher://gopher.std.com:70/111/obi/>

The Online Book Initiative at <world.std.com> is a repository of freely redistributable texts, a large number of which are nonbooks but of possible interest, such as testimonies of Hiroshima survivors, canticles, quotations, recipes, *Star Trek* stories and parodies, hate rants, fairy tales, the Unabomber Manifesto, and (one of my personal, all-time Internet favorites), selected documents from the files of the KGB.

Project Bartleby
<http://www.columbia.edu/acis/bartleby>

Steven van Leeuwen curates a select, growing collection called Project Bartleby, including appropriate facsimiles and period images, honoring the works and lives of George Chapman, Agatha Christie, John Keats, Herman Melville, Eugene O'Neill, Percy Bysshe Shelley, Walt Whitman, Oscar Wilde, William Wordsworth, as well as William Strunk's 1918 *Manual of Style* and the inaugural addresses of the Presidents of the United States.

The English Server at Carnegie Mellon University (CMU)
<gopher://english.hss.cmu.edu/>
<http://english-www.hss.cmu.edu/>

Like the Internet Wiretap Library and the Eris Project, the online books at the English Server at Carnegie Mellon University (CMU) share shelf space with other media, including academic cultural/critical theory (quite an industry these days), electronic journals (*Bad Subjects*, *CTheory*, *Cultronix*), currents in feminism, and media studies, plus a definitive collection of eighteenth-century studies and sources (novels, plays, memoirs, treatises, and poems, as well as modern criticism). Books include drama as well as fiction, and the collections feature many modern works, such as *Ulysses* and *Finnegan's Wake* as well as *Temporary Autonomous Zone* by Hakim Bey, Joseph Squire's *Urban Diary*, the Walking Man Project, and *Agrippa: Book of the Dead*, by the progenitor of cyberpunk, William Gibson. (The last of these was originally published in a limited, computer-only edition — programmed to self-erase upon the first reading. Someone cracked the software, and now it's been freely distributed across the Net.)

The English Server is cooperatively managed by the graduate students, faculty, and staff of CMU's English Department; they also maintain a mailing list and a telnet conference line.

Bibliomania
<http://www.bibliomania.com>

Bibliomania has three dozen fiction classics, from Alcott to *Ulysses*, with shelves built for nonfiction, news, and various reference works. The staff is creating cross-referenced hypertext databases for *Roget's Thesaurus*, *Bartlett's Quotations*, and *Brewer's Dictionary of Phrase and Fable*.

Realist Wonder Society
<http://www.wondersociety.com>

Amid the discoveries in this delightful realm of fable and art, treat yourself to Lyn Ward's wordless novels in woodcuts. Note: the plates here superimpose onto each other cinematically, rather than back-and-forth and across left-hand and right-hand pages, as in the bound book; another fertile feature of the Web worth exploring further.

Original Online-Only Books

Original works abound online. These are books that are published online and nowhere else. A visit to these book Web sites will give you a feel for how colleagues are purveying their creative efforts in this new medium. Most online books are available at no charge, but software systems such as SoftLock enable online publishers to give sample chapters away and charge for the rest (see Chapter 12 for more on the money angle).

Most big-time publishers are giving the Internet serious scrutiny, although the corporate tendency is to hang back and learn from others' mistakes or profits.

Delirium
<http://pathfinder.com/twep/Features/Delirium/DelTitle.html>

On December 23, 1995, Time-Warner staked its claim in cyberspace by being the first publisher to serialize an original novel on the Net, Dennis Cooper's *Delirium*. Juggling four simultaneous story lines — truly work-in-progress — *Delirium* was illustrated, soundtracked, hyperlinked, and serialized as Cooper wrote it, like Dickens hammering out serialized installments of his novels on deadline.

Quiet Americans
<http://www.hotwired.com/Ren2.0/Serial/>

Delirium made it online just under the wire: two hours before *HotWired Webzine* serialized Sonia Simone and Robert Rossney's *Quiet Americans*.

Other close competitors to being first were HarperCollins/HotWired's serialization of Alexander Besher's *Rim: a Novel of Virtual Reality*, and Catbird's publication of *Human Resources* (a.k.a. The *Lidsky Files*), as described earlier in this chapter.

Pulpless.Com
<http://www.pulpless.com>

J. Neil Schulman's Pulpless.Com is one of the first of what will soon become many publishers of online-only fiction and nonfiction.

Le Grand Secret
<http://www.dm.net.lb/le-secre.htm>

A new addition to the roster is *Le Grand Secret*, an online exclusive by default. In 1995, the world grieved upon hearing that François Mitterand had cancer. But prior to that announcement, his physician, Dr. Claude Gubler, announced in a book called *Le Grand Secret* the fact that Mitterand knew he had cancer years before he ran for reelection in 1988. Mitterand's family intervened and persuaded the French government to have the book suppressed as an invasion of privacy. But information appears to be harder to ban with the Internet on hand. Pascal Barbraud, owner of a cybercafé called Le Web, in Besançon, France, defied Paris and posted the book online.

This also raises questions of censorship and copyright. On the one hand, the book's ban was quixotic, given the nature of the Net. On the other hand, had the book not been banned, its posting online would have constituted piracy. (More on these matters in Chapter 19.)

Truth Machine
<http://www.truthmachine.com/>

Jim Halperin put his *Truth Machine* — "part novel, part forecast, part philosophical treatise" — online in its entirety before publication, like a sneak preview, for feedback and advance publicity.

Alix of Dreams
<http://www.primenet.com/~ciaran/>

B. Clifford Shockey considered it too daunting to submit his manuscript for publication. As technical support specialist for a digital film effects house, he's computer literate, so he posted his complete illustrated novel on the Web.

Gaia's Lover
<http://www.webcom.com/gaia000/> ("gaia" with three zeroes)

Caleb Wistar's novel is online only. Rocket into the Siberian future.

Understanding Internet: the Democratization of Mass Media and the Emerging Paradigm of Cyberspace
<http://strangelove.com/publish/paradigm/contents.html>

Web/Internet guru Michael Strangelove has been making his third Internet-related book freely available, either by installments sent by e-mail or on the Web. *Understanding Internet* is "an encyclopedia of changes . . . as the result of the emergence of the first democratic form of mass media."

City of Bits
<http://www-mitpress.mit.edu/City_of_Bits>

William Mitchell, Dean of Architecture and Urban Planning at MIT, published *City of Bits* simultaneously in paper and on the Web. The latter version has gradually been sedimented with hyperlinks and reader commentary. Mitchell has written of the process, "It has succeeded in provoking, capturing, and making visible a discourse in a way that is impossible with print. And, in the process, the seed provided by the original text has grown into a considerably larger and richer textual structure."

Release 2.0

Computer guru Esther Dyson promised that, upon publication of her book *Release 2.0* (for which she received a hefty million-dollar advance), she would host an online forum regarding its issues and themes and then incorporate material generated therefrom in the subsequent paperback, *Release 2.1*. As with *City of Bits*, the readers' comments will constitute original online content of the book. (The site has not yet been activated as of this writing. Check your local search engine.)

No Martyrs
<http://www.netcom.com/~ejgdude/NOVEL.html>

Eric James Geddes has Webtop self-published this novel — "an environmental action adventure, a love story, a heroic adventure. It has radical environmental activism, Big OIL as an enemy, the future of a continent as the goal." Geddes testifies, "The Web and the Net offer an opportunity for creativity unparalleled in human history. I may be a great storyteller, I may be horrible. But I no longer have to appease some third party, with a commercial interest, to present my efforts to the public. It's one-on-one now, and I, for one, love it."

ONLINE BOOKSTORES FOR BOUND BOOKS

One of the Web's most tantalizing possibilities has been for home shopping: the ultimate Sears catalog. In September, 1994, total monthly sales from Web sites was estimated at about $1 million; one year later, $23 million. According to software producer Steve Potash, books are the number two product sold on the Web, software being number one.

As authors, we stand to benefit from virtual bookstores on the Web. Stewart Brand is an author who uses a virtual bookstore to increase the sales of his books. His home page on the Web, <http://www.well.com/user/sbb/>, tells you that his books are available from an online bookstore called Amazon.com, and he gives them an extra plug, saying that he buys most of his books from them. Nobody can release exact figures, but a link like that can definitely be significant. Online bookstores are a force for writers to reckon with, and Amazon.com is the current leader of the pack.

Amazon.com
<http://www.amazon.com>
1-800-201-7575

Theoretically, Amazon.com is currently the world's biggest bookshop. Amazon was founded in 1994 by Jeff Bezos, a graduate of Princeton's computer science department, who'd worked on Wall Street before a light bulb lit up above his head. He picked up his tent and headed west to Seattle, close to many book wholesalers. Now Jeff's virtual bookstore boasts a catalogue of a million titles. Of course, he doesn't have to warehouse that many titles himself. Were he to print out a catalog it would take up the size of about seven New York phone books.

Browsing a million titles would be impossible in a real bookstore, but a reader can search online. Amazon.com's search facility is one of the best, allowing readers to cherry-pick to their heart's content.

Because Amazon doesn't pay real estate fees for stock, and because sales are largely automated, it can afford to offer discounts — thirty percent off bestsellers, ten percent off hardcovers and paperbacks, and frequent special sales. This can help to offset shipping fees.

It's truly one-stop shopping because once you've ordered, you don't have to return to pick up your book; Amazon ships anywhere in the world. Because they don't batch special orders, Amazon also claims to be at least a couple of days faster than paper bookstores.

Another special feature at Amazon.com is how it notifies readers about new titles. A feature called Eyes will announce the release of the latest book by a reader-specified author, or availability of a certain title in paperback. And the Editors feature is run by a group of real humans — departmental editors who preview galleys and read reviews to notify you about new titles in selected genres and subject areas. Plus there are lists of award winners, staff favorites, and even reviews by other readers.

Published authors with books in print can fill out a self-interview questionnaire, and can also attach readers' reviews, comments, links to their Web address, and such. (For more information on this, send a blank e-mail message to <listing-books@amazon.com>.)

Authors can also pick up extra change from sales of their books at Amazon: if someone buys your book because they followed a link you provided to Amazon.com from your own home page, they'll pay you an eight percent commission for the referral, as an associate.

Bibliobytes
<http://www.bb.com/BB.html>

One of the largest and most comprehensive online book shopping malls. Categorized into topical headings, this site is easy to use and contains a host of other book- and writing-related information as well.

Bookstacks Unlimited
<telnet://books.com>
<http://www.books.com>

Based in Cleveland, and established in 1991 by Charles Stack, Bookstacks Unlimited is one of the most venerable online bookstores. Its motto: "Your local bookstore — no matter where you live!" Its stock totals about 400,000 titles (about twice that of your average chain bookstore — and more than the fabled Library of Alexandria). Its search engine works by author, title, or ISBN, and you can browse through a well-structured subject hierarchy. The Web site also has reams of resources for book lovers. *Book of Days*, its literary journal, is updated daily. Fresh Ink highlights new releases. The Rack carries a number of high-quality magazines and journals. The Book Café hosts moderated Web chats and author interviews. There's even a place where fiction writers can post short stories for critique.

Electronic Book Aisle
<http://www.bookaisle.com>

The Electronic Book Aisle, born in Cleveland, July, 1996, is a Web site with a growing inventory of books on cooking, hobbies, self-help, how-to, reference, computing, and business, from publishers both big and small. They post a table of contents, index, or sample chapter for free. The entire book is available for download for a fee. Compared to a sticker price of $25 to $50 for hardbound books these days, Book Aisle's prices are very competitive at $8 to $15.

They also sell diskette or CD-ROM editions. And if you want to publish an electronic version of your book, they can handle that too.

The Internet Bookshop
<http://www.bookshop.co.uk/>

Before Amazon, the largest online bookstore was The Internet Bookshop, a catalog of over 783,000 titles. Detailed information is often given: description, contents page, reviews, jacket covers, and sample chapters. In addition to information on publishers and titles, the site offers Book of the Month and Featured Author sections. Its fine Good Reading Guide provides reading lists for ninety genres, with essays about 350 popular authors and their works.

Genre and Miscellaneous

Genre bookstores are starting to use the Internet to level the playing field and narrowcast to their special-interest audiences.

Future Fantasy Bookstore
<http://futfan.com/home.html>

Future Fantasy Bookstore in Palo Alto, California, is an excellent example of a genre bookstore using the Internet to advantage. Besides hosting readings and events, the store has increased its sales by marketing domestically and abroad over the Net, and it has a great jumpstation of links to other sci-fi/fantasy Internet sites.

Blackwell's
<Blackwells.extra@blackwell.co.uk> <http://www.blackwell.co.uk/bookshops/>

An excellent point of purchase for foreign books.

Bookserve
<http://www.bookserve.com>

Books in German, Spanish, and Dutch.

Antiquarian Booksellers Association of America
<http://antiquarian.com>

For out-of-print books, the Antiquarian Booksellers Association of America represents 450 book dealers, more than 175 of whom can be contacted via e-mail from the ABAA Web page. Some offer online searches of their inventories, and others offer online catalogs. The entire site is searchable by about 300 subject areas.

Biblio
<http://www.smartlink.net/~biblio/>

For used and out-of-print books, an easy Internet solution is Biblio, a mix of people who buy and sell old books. There's a mailing list: e-mail <biblio-request @smartlink.net> with "INFO" in the body of the message. Because daily traffic is heavy — over sixty messages a day — you are advised to try modifying your subscription with the Digest feature. (Instead of "subscribe" say "subscribe digest".)

Once you e-mail Biblio with your want list (WTB, wanted to buy) or books you're getting rid of (FS, for sale), you'll probably receive some response within a day or two.

Pacific Book Auction
<http://www.bridge.com/pba/index.html>

Some of the finer auction companies, such as this one, not only post catalogs but accept absentee bids online.

University Books
<http://www.universitybooks.com>

Here, college students can use the Web to sell their old textbooks and shop for used ones.

A Caveat about Local Booksellers

Online sales can fill a need for people who cannot find our books in their local community. And if online bookstores provide more community among book buyers and booksellers — such as the kind of knowledgeable hand-selling that local independents do so well — then the competition will prove healthy for both the chains and the independents. But, bear in mind that online book stores take money out of the local community: not only taxes, but also patronage of local office suppliers, printers, and similar businesses. Thus, online bookstores add fuel to the ongoing debate between independent bookstores and chains. And 1997 will mark the entry of book clubs and chain stores such as Barnes & Noble and Borders into the Internet mall.

Some local booksellers have increased their revenue by using their public Internet presence to make available to their customers features like Electronic Book Aisle. And distributors Ingram and Baker & Taylor are rolling out software programs enabling any bookseller with Internet presence to link to their book database. Customers then order through a bookseller's Web page, and the distributor ships directly to the purchaser.

Nevertheless, beginning authors usually remain loyal to their local independent booksellers, whose support can sometimes provide the crucial handhold up into national recognition. Rich and famous authors often maintain that loyalty as well.

RESOURCES FOR BOOK LOVERS

Much as e-mail is reviving the art of letter writing, the Internet is revitalizing the love of books. The Net provides unique opportunities for the free exchange of ideas and for building community among book lovers (also of use for author self-promotion, a subject of the following chapter).

Book Discussion Lists

Blister

Blister (a "books list-er") is a place to send lists of books, not to discuss them. It represents about 350 members, and an average of six times a month someone will create and share a list of books, with as much commentary as they like, as a way for members to gauge other members' personal taste and find out about new books they might not have heard of otherwise. Categories can include anything: favorite books, serious literature, books good for browsing, light reading/trash, scholarly books a lay person can enjoy, famous books a member despises, or even Books Only an Out-of-Work Paralegal Could Enjoy. To subscribe, e-mail <majordomo@world.std.com>, leaving the subject field blank, with just two words in the body: "subscribe blister".

Paul Phillips' One Book List
<http://www.internic.net/~paulp/one-book.txt>

Reader-writer-reviewers are invited to post the one book they'd like everyone to read: "the book that, for you, was the most influential, or thought-provoking, or enjoyable, or moving, or philosophically powerful, or deep in some sense you cannot properly define, or any other criteria you wish to set." Your entry will appear along with your name and e-mail address plus any commentary on your selection.

For two-way discussion, Usenet newsgroups such as rec.arts.books and rec.arts.books.reviews, and forums and chat rooms of online services, create tapestries of diverse strands out of the single subject of books. And book lists are a frequent topic of forums. Some lists exchanged and discussed in the Book conference at the WELL, for example, include: Books Bought Today, Books I Got/Gave for Xmas, The Book I'm Riveted By, New Books by Dead Authors, The Book That Changed Me, The Waiting List/Books I'm "Going To Read," and What Do You Read When You're Inbetween Books — each with contributions by both published authors, prepublished authors, and just-plain readers. In the democracy of the Net, reader and reviewer can be interchangeable terms. And readers interested in an eclectic author or topic can now form affinity groups beyond their limited geographic locale, as we shall see next.

Authors' Home Pages

In addition to publishing work online, authors now have their own home pages, a fairly fascinating phenomenon. Your fans may not have created a Web site for you as yet, but don't wait for that to visit other authors' home pages. You'll find sacred saints and leading lights from your own literary pantheon — be they of your generation, eighteenth-century authors, genre writers, Beats, postmodernists, or Biblical. Some may be "official" sites, such as from the author or publisher, whereas others may be created by fans. Some authors thus have more than one Web site. (Margaret Atwood: 5; Jane Austen: 11; Edgar Rice Burroughs: 12; William S. Burroughs: 6.)

And it makes no difference whether they're living or dead. "All authors are in eternity," declared William Blake (himself having nine home pages).

The depth and breadth of these pages is not be taken lightly. For example:

Work in Progress (WIP)
<http://www.2street.com/joyce/>

The James Joyce home page, conceived and maintained by R.L. Callahan of Temple University, is a stellar example of the power of the Web's hypertext mixed media. On site at WIP is a biographical time-line, maps of Dublin, digitized audio recordings of Joyce reading from *Finnegan's Wake*, a gallery of Joycean images, and *Hypermedia Joyce Studies*, a refereed hypertext journal edited by distinguished Joyce scholars.

WIP hyperlinks, in turn, to off-site discussion groups, reading groups, digitized Joyce texts (some with hypertext), online articles, and, of course, other Joyce Web sites.

Jane Austen's Writings
<http://uts.cc.utexas.edu/~churchh/janewrit.html>

A thirty-seven-page Web bonanza.

Yahoo! — Author's Pages
<http://www.yahoo.com/arts/humanities/literature/authors>

Lists a dozen megasource jumpstations of authors' pages, by genre and type.

Book Reviews

Having your book reviewed is an important part of being published. From a different angle, writing book reviews can be good for both published and prepublished writers. In addition to gaining exposure ("clips"), and receiving a bit of pay (comp copies, plus maybe $25 to $100), the practice of bringing in polished copy of a certain length (500 words, 750 words, 900 words) on deadline can be stimulating and self-clarifying to an author. Virginia Woolf, for example, practiced the craft of book reviewing regularly for years; James Updike still does.

With 50,000 books published a year, there never seem to be enough outlets for book reviews, despite such special-purpose magazines as *The American Book Review*, *San Francisco Review*, and *Select Fiction*. But the online world abounds in book-review outlets via magazines, forums, and reading groups (such as the one at SimonSays.com, described early in this chapter). Book reviews are a regular feature of online editions of such magazines as *Atlantic Monthly*, *BookPage*, *the Boston Book Review*, *Fiction Addiction*, *Hungry Mind*, *Laguna Life*, and *Children's Literature Newsletter*, to name some of the more distinguished examples. And *Salon* is largely book-review-driven, being of the philosophy that any topic can be covered by reviewing a related book. Other book review outlets include:

Booklist
<http://www.ala.org/booklist.html>

From the American Library Association.

The Washington Post Online — Chapter One
<http://www.washingtonpost.com/wp-srv/style/longterm/books/books.htm>

Features the first chapter of the books they review

American Reporter weekend edition
<http://www.uvol.com/>

Sports a hearty book review supplement

Book Stacks' Rants-N-Raves
<http://www.books.com/scripts/rants.exe>

A megasource jumpstation of links to over three dozen book review sites on the Net.

Miscellaneous

Usenet has a forum, alt.publish.books, where authors and publishers can discuss the vagaries of book proposals.

MEGASOURCE JUMPSTATIONS
Digitized Books

There are a number of master directories of bound books available online as digitized texts.

Alex
<gopher://gopher.lib.ncsu.edu:70/11/library/stacks/Alex>
<gopher://rsl.ox.ac.uk> (In Europe)

One top-level online book resource is Alex, based at Oxford, offering shorter texts as well as 700 full-length books. (As of this writing, it was in need of an update. Sometimes sites hyperlinked here have since changed their address or are now dormant or defunct. This is a common Internet problem.) Its menu allows searching by author, date, language, subject, or host (for instance, Project Gutenberg, Wiretap, the Online Book Initiative, Eris, the English Server, the Oxford Text Archive).

The Electronic Text Center
<http://extext.lib.virginia.edu/uvaonline.html>

The Electronic Text Center includes the following categories for public use (as opposed to some items such as the *Oxford English Dictionary*, for internal use only): 876 titles in modern English (A.D. 1500–present), including 1,796 manuscript and book illustrations; a hypertext archive of British poetry, 1780–1910; African American sources, the Michigan Early Modern English Materials collection, holy writ, and more.

The Online Books Page
<http://www.cs.cmu.edu/Web/books.html>

The Online Books Page is maintained by John Mark Ockerbloom at Carnegie Mellon University. It not only links to the English Server and to CMU's own library repository, for a total of 1,200 books, but it also links to other similar resources, many of which have already been mentioned, such as the Internet Wiretap Library, the Electronic Text Center at UVA, the Eris Project at Vermont Tech, Project Gutenberg, Project Bartleby, and the Online Book Initiative, as well as the Oxford Text Archive, the Humanities Text Initiative at University of Michigan, Britain's Data Text Library, Book Stacks Library, and Samizdat Express.

The Online Books Page also links to specialty or foreign-language repositories, including Willamette's Human Languages Page; University of Chicago's French ARTFL Project; Association des Bibliophiles Universels; Camelot Project (Arthurian texts); CURIA Irish Manuscript Project (from Cork, Ireland); Calgary's Children's Literature WWW Page; Smith's Contemporary American Poetry Archives; a Fourth World (indigenous peoples) documentation project; Freethought Web; NYU's Literature and Medicine Database; the Online Medieval and Classical Library (at Sunsite); Tufts' Perseus Project (200 classical Greek texts in translation); MIT's Tech Classics Archive; and Indiana's Victorian Women Writers Project; as well as non-English literature collections, including Italian, Dutch, Scandinavian, and Russian.

The site also links to book catalogs and retailers, online publishers, and companies that sell online editions, as well as libraries, journals and magazines, and exhibits. And, of course, there are links to other top-level directories.

Online Literary Resources
<http://www.english.upenn.edu/~jlynch>

Provides hyperlinks spanning from Homer to hypertext.

Booksellers Online

The American Bookseller's Association (ABA) BookWeb
<http://www.BookWeb.org>

Represents thousands of booksellers across America; and their online outpost, BookWeb, hosts member booksellers' home pages. Every June, the site posts daily news from the floor of the annual ABA trade show.

The Last Word in Book Megasource Jumpstations

The Internet Book Information Center (IBIC)
<http://sunsite.unc.edu/ibic/Commonplace-Book.html>
<http://sunsite.unc.edu/ibic/CPB/>

The other sources described in this section rely on the model of Laundry List of Hyperlinked Lists, or what I call a jumpstation. The Internet Book Information Center (IBIC) began as such but then changed, adding a guide (more on the model of, say, *writers.net*). The success of the transformation is borne out by statistics from the host (Sun): a thousand hits a day.

The guide is broken down into authors, publishers, booksellers, libraries, readers, rare books, online books and magazines, poetry, Web review databases, and a commonplace book (see sidebar).

ReadersNdex
<http://www.ReadersNdex.com>

Provides a centralized site for several dozen publishers, big and small, searchable by author, title, or subject, or by publisher's catalog; used by a number of

---

THE COMMONPLACE BOOK @ IBIC

Commonplace book (n.): an edited collection of striking passages noted in a single place for future reference.

There was a time when commonplace books were a popular way for civilized men and women to record striking passages they found in their reading. Who can forget the electrifying effect that some thoughts have on us when we encounter them for the first time? The commonplace book is a way of memorializing those striking passages so that one can return to them for renewed inspiration.

The experimental Commonplace Book uses e-mail, hypertext, and FTP archives to provide an edited Internet Commonplace Book built by and available to all Netizens, including such texts as:

H.P. Lovecraft on the nature of reality and on man's best friend; Percy on possibilities; Gandhi on culture; LeGuin on writing; a Pirsig sampler; Blake on the world in a grain of sand; Lincoln on bigotry; Pirsig on hurrying, meaning, romanticism, and institutions; Rand on achievement and why we have laws; Robbins on marriage; Hunter S. Thompson on deadlines and on drugs; Winterson on the scapula; Gene Wolfe on sanity; Hasek on strong language; O'Brien on vulgarity; Delany on (un)sanity; Vallee on artificial intelligence (or, what the Commonplace Book means . . .); Wittgenstein on novelty; Confucius on clarity of expression; Grass on knowing; Hart and Sachs on the function of a lawyer; Borges on the moment of dying; Sandburg on happiness; Machiavelli on innovation; Robert Fulghum on life's ups and downs; Milosz on meaning; Dillard on why we read; Jack London on the searching soul; Wilde on Balzac; Michener on how a writer must protect himself; Roscoe Pound on professionalism; Brooks on programming; Edison on genius; Edmund Burke on change; Steinbeck on discontent; Thoreau on the artist of Kouroo; and Thucydides on change, heroism, openness, and strength.

booksellers as well as individuals. They also maintain over 2,000 targeted electronic mailing lists.

Bookwire
<http://www.bookwire.com>

A service of *Publishers Weekly*, BookWire links to booksellers alphabetically or by category, and to bookseller indexes at other sites. At the Reading Room, you can download several hundred books for free. BookWire's bestseller information is about three days ahead of printed versions. And they maintain an archive of past bestseller charts — very useful when researching trends. Extensive book commentary resources, ratings, author tour calendars, links to professional associations, daily literary cartoons, and more. *Entertainment Weekly* calls BookWire "the motherlode of cyberspace-based book info" (quite rightly!).

Internet Book Fair
<http://www.bookfair.com>

A searchable, top-level index to both the publishing and bookselling communities that's absolutely indispensable.

Book Links on the Internet
<http://colab.net/books>

An eclectic set of links, including used books, newly published books, independently published books, and book review sites.

Book Lovers: Fine Books and Literature
<http://www.wxs4all.nl/~pwessel>

A splendid megasource.

* * *

The next chapter explores digital self-publishing and self-promotion, obviating the publisher/distributor infrastructure entirely, often with new results, and creating new opportunities for the Net writer.

17

Net Self-Publishing and Self-Promotion

I finished my first book seventy-six years ago. I offered it to every publisher on the English-speaking earth I had ever heard of. Their refusals were unanimous, and it did not get into print until, fifty years later, publishers would publish anything that had my name on it. . . .

I object to publishers; the one service they have done me is to teach me to do without them. They combine commercial rascality with artistic touchiness and pettishness, without being either good business men or fine judges of literature. All that is necessary in the production of a book is an author and a bookseller, without the intermediate parasite.

—George Bernard Shaw

The Internet's liberation of publishing has been compared to the way Gutenberg's movable type freed writers from Church control. The Net releases the word from Shaw's nemeses. Writers no longer need to elbow their way into checkout-stand book racks to be a success.

The Net makes self-publishing, once viewed as dicey at best, into a viable means of expression and livelihood — a medium with barely explored possibilities, both creatively and financially.

In this chapter, you'll learn:

- why Internet self-publishing is unique
- how to digitally publish your work on paper with the Net
- how to digitally publish your work online with the Net
- how to use the Net to publicize your services and your works
- how to create your own Web site for self-publishing and self-promotion

NET SELF-PUBLISHING

This section describes two different approaches to self-publishing via the Net: paper and paperless. Chapter 16 touched on the future of books. Now let's look at the future of the efficient production of books, augmenting the printer's platen with a modem and a floppy disk. To appreciate the impending changes, let's quickly recap what's gone before. From the outset, publishers were often printers. Their distributors were often stationery stores, who'd take up a subscription campaign; when enough pledges were collected, they'd print Erasmus' latest book, or suchlike.

Gradually, publishing evolved into an enterprise independent of printing. More recently, publishing began bundling with the entertainment and media industries. Now the publishing world disseminates text much like TV and radio do — broadcasting mass-market (often to "the lowest common denominator"). Until now.

Digital Self-Publishing On Paper

Enter the Digital Era, with its narrow-casting and niche marketing. We're just beginning to understand the potential of this new medium.

Printing on Demand.   Imagine readers ordering books over the Internet from publishers who only print a copy each time there's an order. Books on demand.

Something along these lines, often called "coursepacks," is actually already taking hold on college campuses (Stanford, Southern Cal, and Cornell, for example). Coursepacks are customized for one semester's course, and sometimes even for each student. ("You want this in 12-point Garamond, 5" by 8", tan paper, plain binding? With the French texts for extra credit? Come back in six minutes.") It's not too dissimilar to the music industry, where you can download the digital file of a CD and have a copy pressed for you while you wait. Wouldn't it be revolutionary if the number of available copies of a book matched the demand? Well, now they can.

An on-demand book industry would save a publisher the costs, not only of printing, but also of warehousing and shipping. With such a savings — distribution being a book's biggest cost — mass-market publishers could offer books at even lower prices. And for independent, smaller publishers, who traditionally lack the distributive reach of the bigger houses, on-demand publishing could level the playing field. All writers stand to be affected — including self-publishers, an increasingly visible avenue given the success of *The Macintosh Bible*, *The Celestine Prophecy*, and *The Christmas Box*, to name but a few. (Other self-published notables include Mark Twain, Carl Sandburg, D. H. Lawrence, Virginia Woolf, Henry David Thoreau, and Kathy Acker.)

Short Printing Runs. Let's say you have an exquisite manuscript that you want to self-publish — that you're certain will eventually be bought by about 750 people. Ordinarily, 1,000 copies would be the bare minimum you could print. Just to get the presses running would cost you $5,000. The breaks in printing costs ordinarily come only with much bigger print runs (the industry motto traditionally being "the longer the run, the cheaper the per-unit cost"). Thus, you might find yourself ordering a ten-year supply, which you'd have to warehouse.

But digital printing allows you to order a short run, enough for a one-year supply, and see how that goes. Essentially, it's the same principle as using your printer that's connected to your computer: you don't have to paste up copy, shoot it, burn a printing plate, etc.; and you can specify the number of copies, from one to one-hundred. It's just a more sophisticated model. And this capability now extends to full, four-color digital printing, which is finally making the quantum leap from looking like three-color Xerox to looking like offset printing. If you're creating an educational title, this will save you headaches over creating an adoption version (sample chapters for advance inspection). Moreover, now your book will never go out of print and need never be in short supply. Since revising your digital master doesn't entail making a new printing plate each time, you can always make changes and add updates or timely notices any time you order a new run.

This is a striking example of narrow-casting — the niche marketing characteristic of the Information Age. Marcia Lerner, <marlern@aol.com>, head of the On-Demand Printing Division of R.R. Donnelly (America's oldest and largest printer) says "[printing] is constantly growing faster and cheaper, with larger sizes and more choice of printing materials. It will be the entrepreneurs and the creative people, like writers, who discover the new uses for this technology."

If you are that sort of creative entrepreneur, there are several operations prepared to help you out.

Trafford Publishing
<http://www.trafford.com>

Trafford Publishing specializes in on-demand printing and combines that with Internet distribution/fulfillment. Their Web bookstore offers the works they publish, and a new copy is printed after an order is made (not before).

Print's Appeal
<http://www.prap.com>

Located in North Central Ohio; modem the text to them, and they'll do the rest.

Online Distribution. Once you have your book ready, there are online-only places for distributing it (such as the online bookstores of the previous chapter), as well as land-based distributors and bookstores you can contact online. One online-only book outlet is:

Author's Showcase
<http://light-communications.com/author/index.html>

An online bookstore of self-published authors who showcase their books with pictures, sample text, and ordering information. Their site also displays unpublished manuscripts for agents and publishers to peruse.

Printing on Location. Let's say you're going on a book signing tour, with a self-published book in your repertoire. Now you can have copies printed at each location on your itinerary, rather than lug around all the copies everywhere you go or have copies shipped from a central warehouse. Thus, you can now "ship" digital text to multiple locations (via the Internet) and then print, rather than the traditional model of printing and then shipping (to a central location).

A digital printer will usually collate, cut, fold, saddle-stitch, and bind. While they can laser print color soft-cover, hardback covers still have to be farmed out to a traditional binder. Turnaround can take from a few days to a couple of weeks, depending on the complexity of the job.

Kinko's
<http://www.kinkosdigital.com/prints.html>

Kinko's has a national digital printing network, for shipping-then-printing.

Digital Self-Publishing (Online-Only)

Paperless publishing cannot replace the familiar qualities of the traditional bound book, but neither is the paper book inherently superior to its online counterpart. I own two editions of Shakespeare's plays and I am glad to have CD-ROM, hypercard, and Web editions as well. Books made of paper will always have their place in our lives, but paper costs are rising steeply. And, more important, online publishing is a whole new animal; it allows us opportunities unimaginable with paper.

In the non-Internet world, self-publishing is often looked upon as a sign of desperation, with scant hope of success. On the Net, self-publishing is the norm and can lead to recognition, paid writing assignments, sales, and other valuables.

Why is self-publishing a plus in one medium, and a minus in another? A phrase frequently used by Net self-publishers is "leveling the playing field." Traditionally, the route of self-publishing has required an intermediary packager who would coordinate design, typesetting, paste-up/mechanicals, and printing. Then there would remain the issues of warehousing, distribution, promotion, marketing, and sales. Traditionally, large publishing houses had a monopoly on these services.

Desktop publishing came along in the early eighties and enabled self-publishers to become their own packagers. Marketing remained a major hurdle. With fifty thousand books published every year (the size of the entire stock of some small bookstores) capturing buyer awareness — to say nothing of shelf space — is quite tough in the print world.

Webtop Publishing. But now desktop has gone Webtop, allowing authors to carry their creative spark through to the finished product, on their own terms. Digital self-publishing can slay all the dragons in the path with one sword: the computer.

Webtop publishing is far less expensive than printing; it uses digitized electrons rather than the scarcer commodities of metal, paper, ink, hot wax, rubber cement, and human labor. And it enables the self-publisher to compete with corporate publishers in advertising and distribution. Now a self-publisher can target and reach its audience directly, without costly overhead for advertising and marketing. If your brochure is on the Net, as with a Web page, you don't have to pay a printer to make more copies to reach a bigger "market share." The digital "master" is unaffected by whether 200 visitors copy it or 200,000.

Achieving visibility is much easier on the Net than ever before. The Internet is easily divided into affinity groups, and searching by key words means that pet-lovers can easily find a new book about Dalmatians. And not only can your readers and buyers find you, but more and more acquisition editors are keeping an eye out on the Internet for new talent.

Creating a home page for yourself could be an excellent move (to learn the mechanics, see Authoring Your Own Web Site, later in this chapter). As self-published author Nan McCarthy attests:

> "Once you make the initial investment in a Web site, you'll feel more connected with the people who buy your books, and they'll feel more connected to you. The payoff of this could be higher book sales, a higher degree of loyalty from your readers, ideas and suggestions for future books, and better and more frequent feedback on your current books."

As a niche self-publisher, you can maintain a viable business, reaching a small audience, with a staff of one or two people, a PowerBook, and an account with an Internet service provider.

If you're going to be published in the small presses, the Net gives you an audience in the thousands, rather than the hundreds. And if you're going to be a small press yourself, the Web allows you to reach those numbers and be a viable business — a self-publishing success story.

Self-Publishing via E-mail and E-mail Lists. The Web has received the lion's share of attention in the realm of Internet self-publishing. But the Web isn't the only game in town. Remember, when you speak your mind in a Usenet newsgroup, you may have an audience of tens of thousands, so that's a form of publishing. There's also FTP, telnet, and, perhaps best of all, e-mail. One self-publishing option is an e-mail autoresponder (a.k.a. infobot). Anyone who sends a message to your infobot address (such as <info@author.net>) will automatically receive a text (such as a short story, poem, essay). The text could be an Index of all the texts available from the bot.

One-way mailing lists are an economical format for distributing text, as we've seen with the e-magazine *Real Poetik*, and with the daily *American Reporter*. Hosting a two-way mailing list is a form of publishing, too — a public space, much like a coffee house or town plaza — as we've seen with *Electric Minds*, *Salon*, and *Utne Lens*.

This Is True
<http://www.freecom.com/>

E-mail and mailing lists are the cornerstone of Randy Cassingham's success at self-publishing. First, he found what he thought might be his wedge into the highly competitive syndicated humor features market. He takes true stories from the news, concentrates them (400 words into 40, say), and frames them with telling headlines and apt, wry comments below. At first, he posted them on a cork bulletin board for his

▼▼▼

PAYMENT FOR WRITERS
by T. L. Kelly, Net writer-publisher

<http://www.teleport.com/~room101/wench.htm>

(from an ongoing discussion of publishing, the Internet, and payment, from the Digerati forum moderated by Rich Lethin)

First, my experience has been that creating a Web site for my own literary works, as a sort of open archive, [has] resulted in publishers and editors (print and cyber) soliciting me (for money!) for my work. It's a helluva lot less stressful to take care of the business of schmoozing over e-mail than it is to wait months and months for some publisher or editor to respond to snail mail. And so far, the time span between "we want your work" and receiving the check in the mail has not yet exceeded a few weeks. Not to mention that [never] in all the years that I have been a published writer has my work been read by so many people in so many places as it has been on the Net. More people read my work in one day than read my work in one year in some small literary zines, and even some slicks.

Second, my experience . . . as an e-zine editor [has been] that those same publishers are scouting the Net for anthologies. I have received offers [from] two major publishers to publish (in print) a "Best Of" version of my e-zine, on a yearly basis, for big bucks. So, although I haven't the resources to pay the writers for their contributions [to] the e-zine, I will have the resources to pay them handsome honorariums for the work chosen for the "Best Of" version in print.

friends to see. Then, as more of his friends moved away, he tried the postal system. But he began to hit his stride with e-mail and mailing lists. They were his initial means of taking the plunge, and they remain his primary channel of distribution.

Randy recalls:

> Like a lot of writers, I've always wanted to do it full-time, but it's a tough business to break into. I figured that making it 'professional' from the outset, and making it available on the Internet, would very quickly let me know if it would create a demand — a following. It did; at the end of the first year, I had an estimated 100 thousand readers per week, in eighty countries. Currently, it's in the 150 thousand range, and 88 countries that I know of.

Gradually, Randy is home-growing syndication of his material. Starting from $15, he charges on a fee-based structure depending on the size of the publication, the circulation, and how often and how much they use his material. He's collected 600 of the best entries from his *This Is True* newsletter into a self-published book, *Deputy Kills Man With Hammer* (commenting, "Didn't want to waste a bullet").

Randy uses a simple autoresponder as a home base. A blank e-mail message to <TrueInfo@freecom.com> will yield a list of available files. He also coordinates this with his Web site.

One-way or two-way, moderated or unmoderated, for free or for a fee, a mailing list can be read by the maximum number of Netizens; e-mail, not the Web, is the most ubiquitous feature of the Internet. If your Internet provider doesn't offer the necessary software for maintaining a list as part of their service, you might invest in it yourself.

Listserv
<http://www.lsoft.com/>

The most fully featured mailing list software is Listserv, created and sold by Eric Thomas. For more information, e-mail <listserv@listserv.net> with the message "help" or visit the Web site.

There are also Mailbase, Mailserv, Listproc, and Majordomo software. For a FAQ describing all the types of mailing list management, e-mail <mail-server@rtfm.mit.edu> with the message "send usenet/news.answers/mail/list-admin/software-faq".

"How to Set Up and Run Your Own Internet Mailing List"
<http://www.cnet.com/Content/Features/Howto/Mailing/index.html>

In December, 1996, c|net published this essay by Asha Dornfest.

NET SELF-PROMOTION

You've seen how self-publishing on the Net can be an indirect self-promotional strategy, as well as a possible direct revenue stream. Now we'll explore more ways of publicizing yourself and your writing over the Net. First, let's answer the question as to why an author needs to do publicity at all.

Why Promote Yourself?

The bottom line is that even the most capable publisher's publicist has several titles to promote at once but only so much time in a day to do so. Whether you self-publish or are published by someone else, self-promotion will always be an important element in your success.

Nowadays getting publicity is much more refined than sitting on a flag pole. Some authors have been known to hire outside publicists. If you want to explore that route, there are able publicists online, such as Barbara Baughen, Susannah Greenberg, Steve O'Keefe, and Phenix & Phenix, <http://www.bookfair.com>. Also available is Fauzia Burke <fburke@fsbassociates.com>.

Other authors prefer guerrilla marketing, and the Net is essentially a do-it-yourself publicity medium with world-class features. On the Net, not only can you send a press release around the world in an hour, but you can send it to targeted sources. Newsgroups, mailing lists, and e-zines, as well as online bookstores, are the gateways to thousands of readers — and customers.

If you're after the media, you can e-mail a fast-facts press release, stating the what, who, why, where, when, and how of your news. One release can be tailored for book reviewers, and another for radio/TV spot/interviewers. When possible, telephone first to get a green light to e-mail your release or ask permission online. In a forum of electronic journalists, one publicist recently invited anyone interested to sign up for her automated mailing list of periodic news releases about titles. Close to a hundred signed up. Had she sent her news releases uninvited, she would have run the risk of "spamming."

Promotion without Spamming

The Internet is a perfect publicity tool because it enables you to narrowcast to focused special interest groups. But it's important that you respect the rules of the Net.

Members of a forum, especially the moderator or owner, are well aware that they're sitting on the equivalent of a direct-marketing mailing list that certain advertisers would dearly love to use. But posting or e-mailing an unsolicited advertisement is called "spamming."

Spamming only abuses the privilege of access to a free "direct-mail" list. Worse, unlike junk mail, your unsolicited ad requires that the recipient pay to read it (they must pay their Internet service provider).

A better approach is to hang out in the forums you're targeting for a while; get to know the culture of the group and the potential future clientele. Then, when you see a thread to which you could make an intelligent contribution, do so — with your signature line containing relevant information about you. If you're an author, you might list your book (name, ISBN, and so on), along with your e-mail address, e-mail autoresponder, or Web site URL.

In summary, resist the temptation to use the sledgehammer approach, and instead spread your word indirectly. If you take unfair advantage of Net culture, the postmaster at your Internet service provider might cancel your account without warning. Use Net culture well, and you may find dozens, hundreds, even thousands of new allies — and readers.

Being Your Own Linkmaster

The Webmaster/Webmistress is responsible for maintaining a site. The Linkmaster is the one who makes the site's existence known, by having other sites link to it. The process can be both routine and innovative. The routine part is linking your URL to various places, such as NCSA (home of the Mosaic Web browser), the various search engines, and so forth. Fortunately, some Netizens have made the routine semi-automated. Here are some Linkmaster aids:

Submit-It
<http://www.submit-it.com>

Provides a single form (requiring a forms-capable browser) for having your URL linked to a plethora of search engines and subject guides, ranging from Alta Vista to Yahoo!

wURLd Presence
<http://www.ogi.com/wurld/>

Has a different interface and some links that Submit-It doesn't have.

And, to give you an extra boost, here are a few sites with thousands of places where you can promote your URL:

iDirect
<http://web.idirect.com/~tormall/links.html>

Links to thousands of pages for self-promotion.

Yahoo! Announcement Services Page
<http://www.yahoo.com/Computers_and_Internet/Internet/World_Wide_Web/Announcement_Services/>

A1 Index of over 200 Free Web Page Promotion Sites
<http://www.a1co.com/index.html>

The innovative part of the process comes after you've established those basic links. It's the mutual sharing aspect of the Web: you link to my page, I'll link to yours. First, your site needs a section (usually at the end) for links to related topics or people, such as "Cool Things on the Net" or "My Favorite Hot Links." Theoretically, you don't need to ask permission of the Webmasters of those sites to link to them. But you can e-mail them a letter anyway, expressing your interest in their site and, at some point, requesting that they reciprocate by linking to your site. You'll want to ask that they notify you when they've done so. The process requires good people skills: sensing whether to send a short or a long letter, knowing when to follow up, and so on.

If you spend an hour a day as Linkmaster, after a few months you should reach the hoped-for critical mass of people coming to your site. This happens in part because the people who link to your Web site are in turn linked to other people's sites. Once you've reached critical mass, you need spend only an hour a week, or a month, as Linkmaster.

For a good megasource jumpstation of links and tips, check out "How to Widely Publicize your Site":
<http://www.webcom.com/~webcom/html/publicize.html>

CREATING YOUR OWN WEB SITE

Here's a guide to creating your own Web pages, with places on the Internet to go for more information, including design resources. You'll also see samples of what other writers have done for themselves on the Web.

One day, creating Web pages will be a no-brainer. Meanwhile, writers may feel a bit of vain pride to hear that the Internet term for creating Web pages (formatting

HyperText Markup Language, or HTML) is "authoring." They may also be pleased to hear that there are software programs that can do the authoring for you.

There are now dozens of point-and-click HTML "authoring tools" (PageMill, FrontPage, HoTMetaL, Transit, BBEdit). Here, highlighted text can be manipulated using pull-down menus and dialogue boxes. And word processing programs now have HTML programming built in. Windows now comes with a Web browser, an authoring tool, and software enabling a computer to act as a server to host Web sites.

The latest trend is away from HTML and toward a Web site that can "dynamically generate Web pages," using such software programs as NetObjects' Fusion. The project *24 Hours in Cyberspace* (see Chapter 12), for example, used NetObjects' Fusion to generate its pages from the diverse data continually being piped into pre-set templates.

The server here stores data rather than pre-set HTML files, and mixes, matches, arranges, and displays from that data according to the user's own preferences, "on-the-fly." Thus 300 separate files can result in thirty different curriculum bundles being made up into Web pages, depending on the profile input by the individual student. (The product is personalized, "pulled" through a set of options by the user's preferences, rather than being a preset package "pushed" at them.) But this may not be within the reach of most writers, as yet.

Some packages feature templates and style sheets (Deltapoint QuickSite and HTML Transit). But what if the template you want isn't included in a template package? You could copy one you like right off the Web, but if you want to modify it you'll probably need to understand HTML. And what do you do if you've "authored" your text in HTML by using pull-down menus (without ever having to write any code), but you still need to edit out a bug or make a major coding revision? And then there's the question of hypertext style.

So no matter how you approach it, I think it helps to know HTML. You need to "look under the hood," as it were, serving an apprenticeship and learning how to code by hand.

Authoring

Writing hypertext involves two kinds of authoring. It means:

1. writing the substantive text (in which decisions about illustrations, branching paths, user interface, and suchlike are embedded), and
2. writing programming code ("formatting") for those embedded choices.

HTML

Whether you have a PC or a Mac, you will use a program called a Web browser to create a file for users to view. Microsoft Explorer, Spyglass Mosaic, and Netscape Navigator are common browsers.

HTML is the abbreviation for HyperText Markup Language. HTML is the most commonly used programming that enables Web browsers to read our Web pages. It is readable by both Macs and PCs, and can even be rendered in Braille and by speech synthesis systems.

Authoring HTML, we embed text with commands ("tags") for the browser to carry out: render type in boldface, insert a picture, follow a hyperlink, and so on. The browser does not display the tags unless they're specifically requested. Instead, the browser conceals the tags and performs their commands.

Sometimes, however, you want to see the commands. The HTML coding of any Web page is an open book to anyone. In Netscape, you can select "View" from the pull-down menu and click on Document Source ("source" being another word for coding or programming). Or in Lynx, the command is backslash ("\"). You can even save the coding thus revealed to your hard disk, to study or to use as a template.

Tags

HTML commands, called "tags," are bracketed within the "greater-than" and "less-than" sign, found on all ASCII keyboards as the shifted period and comma, like <this>. Tags often surround the subject text, on either side of it, toggling a command on and off. So, to say "Prince Hamlet is a character in *Hamlet*" we'd author it like this: "Prince Hamlet is a character in <I>Hamlet</I>."

HTML tags aren't case-sensitive, so <i> is the same as <I>. However, uppercase makes tags easier to pick out.

HTML doesn't recognize either hard line-returns or the paragraph indents we normally use in word processing. It would read this chapter's textstream as one run-on block of text.
 (for "break") adds a hard return (as in a new line in an address), and <P> (for "paragraph") adds two hard returns (a blank space and a new line).

As with uppercase tags, it's a good idea to use your word processor's hard returns, anyway, along with the tags <BR> or <P>, so that when you're reading offline (in your word processor rather than your Web browser), you'll get a better sense that what you see is what you'll get.

WYSIWYG. Authoring HTML requires WYSIWYG (What You See Is What You Get, often pronounced "wizzywig"), or being able to preview your work as it will look on the Web. For example, if you preview it in Netscape (opening it as a file) then make changes and save them, there's a button at the top of the Netscape interface called "Reload." Hit that, and the latest version will appear.

Authoring manually, be prepared to spend as much time correcting and reloading as authoring.

Links (Anchoring). Commands that make a word or words into hyperlinks perform what is called "anchoring." Two kinds of anchor are: (1) outside and (2) within the text body.

For example, to link to somewhere *outside* the text body:

<A HREF="URL">Text Anchor</A>

makes a link to the URL, selected by clicking on the phrase "Text Anchor."

For instance, if you've mentioned Dante and want readers to be able to click on his name to jump to a Web site at Dartmouth that contains a wealth of information about him, then you'll code it like this:

Italy is famous for pizza, the poet<A HREF="http://www.darmouth.edu/dante.html"> Dante Alighieri</A>, and the canals of Venice, not necessarily in that order.

Viewed on the Web, it would look like this:

Italy is famous for pizza, the poet **Dante Alighieri**, and the canals of Venice, not necessarily in that order.

And you can link to somewhere *within* your own Web site. The text might be something you keep at the host Web server, in which case the reference would be simple. Let's say you've entitled your own file about Dante "dante.html." Then the link would be coded like this:

Italy is famous for pizza, the poet<A HREF="dante.html"> Dante Alighieri</A>, and the canals of Venice . . . etc.

Navigation. There are some digerati who liken the Web to a world seen through a moving car window — a world experienced with a limited attention span while taking in sights as well as words plus choosing from branching paths.

Thus *Suck*, for example, uses large-size text type and doesn't publish anything longer than 1,200 words.

For a text that is longer than a few screenfuls, or for a bunch of texts, the savvy Webmaster will create navigation "buttons" (anchors). This is a prime example of how to keep the reader's attention. They can appear at the end of sections and/or at the bottom of a page.

Let's imagine you have a text that's more than a couple of screenfuls. You break it up into sections, so the reader can hop and skip. In between the sections you can offer the reader some navigation links, like this:

[**Forward**] [**Backward**] [**Return to Home Page**]

This process requires two kinds of anchor tags. One tag sets up an anchoring point to jump to. The other creates the jumping-off point to the anchor. The code for the first — the point to jump to — might go like this (let's say, for example, at the top of the page):

<A NAME="TOP"></A>

The second, the jumping-off point, would be:

<A HREF="#top">**Return to the top of the page**</A>.

The screen would show Return to the top of the page, which would be a hot link: click on it and you go back to the top.

Let's say you have a text about genres: science fiction, romance, mystery, Westerns, children's. At the end of each section, sandwiched in between rules, navigation options appear, like this:

Go to [Science fiction] [Romance]
[Mystery][Westerns] [Children's]

If we "View Source" to see the HTML code for this, it looks like this:

```
<HR>
<CENTER>Go to <A HREF="#sci-fi">[ Science fiction ]</A>
<A HREF="#rom">[ Romance ]</A> <A HREF="#myst">[ Mystery ]</A>
<A HREF="#west">[ Westerns ]</A> <A HREF="#child">[ Children's ]</A></CENTER>
<HR>.
```

And at the start of each section, an anchor tag is inbedded:

<A NAME="sci-fi"></A>.

Enhancements. In addition to graphics, there are other features that jazz up a Web site.

Tables create text/graphics in boxes, columns, and grids.

Frames allow simultaneous viewing of multiples pages, (or dividing one page into several, at once).

Java enables a software program to be embedded within it. All the user needs is to have Java plugged in to their Web browser in order to use applications on other sites written in Java, such as animation and interactivity. (Another "plug-in" is Shockwave, enabling Macromind animations to be applied to the Web.)

VRML (Virtual Reality Markup Language), just now coming into view, is sometimes referred to as 3-D. This doesn't imply that objects pop out at you, nor does it necessarily require special glasses (though some sites are trying that). What it can create, instead, are environments potentially endowed with three dimensions, through which the user can navigate. (*Myst* is a basic example.) Thus, a VRML home page might be a lobby, from which its viewers can use their mouse or arrow keys to go down hallways, open doors, return to the lobby, and so on.

VRML revolutionizes maps, of course, but also other things, such as tables of contents and search engines. While we must wait to see what ideas will look like in 3-D, we can already experience a new way of embodying them — through hypertext.

The Art of Hypertext. There's an art to HTML beyond authoring the programming language correctly. It's a matter of design, of writing decisions for the reader, as we've already seen with navigation buttons.

A gross example is the command that will make text blink on and off (<blink></blink>): the consensus is that it's cheesy — unless used intentionally so, as for satire. More subtly, and more important, style conventions have emerged for how and where to imbed a link. The following is gauche: "For more information about *writers.net*, click **here**." Better is "Click here for more information **about *writers.net***." Perhaps better still is just "More information about ***writers.net***" perhaps on a line all its own.

How many links occur on each screenful of text is another factor. Too few, and the text may seem too flat in the kinetic realm of hypertext. Given too many options, the reader's interest in your primary text might get lost. And how techie can you be?

Decide whether your audience is primarily high-tech power-users, or by-your-bootstraps low-bandwidth folk. The two extremes represent different philosophies of the Web: presentation-driven and content-driven. *Zyzzyva* editor Howard Junker kids that there's now a distinction between the Web-sters — wordsmiths for whom a Web page's content is more important — and the techie programmers, whom he dubs "http:sters."

Compare a high-end site with a low-end one and see for yourself. Designer David Siegel's Web pages are meticulously elegant, right down to the type: <http://www.siegel.com>. Writer James Fallows' Web pages are low-graphics, hypertext-intensive, easily navigable: <http://www.clark.net/pub/rothman/fallows.htm>.

The only way to preserve your design right down to the type is to save it as a picture file (such as a ".gif" or ".jpg" file format) rather than as a text file, or by using a document reader software application such as Adobe Acrobat. Otherwise, just allow for the fact that different readers have different preference settings for type and point size.

Even if you don't create a high-end site, it's nice to make sure it's readable by a text-only browser such as Lynx. Many sites offer the user an initial choice between a text-only version and a high-end one (with graphics, tables, frames, the works).

Do not presume that your readers will have the same level of equipment that you do. (Remember: some filks will be surfing the Net with only a TV.)

Self-Publishing. If you're posting samples of your work online, don't forget to make an autobiographical page for yourself. In it, you may want to include your picture, publications, organizational affiliations, personal interests, and contact addresses. And you can say a great deal about yourself by a "Cool Links" or "Favorite Sites" section. Even if you're creating only one page, put a signature/copyright line at the bottom, stating your name and the year. There's a tag for this too:

<ADDRESS>Created by Emily Bronte, January 25, 1999</ADDRESS>

You can embed your e-mail address here, for comments, with the <A HREF="mailto:> tag, such as: <A HREF="mailto:emily@emilynet.com"></A>.

Online HTML Resources

Beginning to Intermediate Resources.

Make Your Own Home Page
<http://www.goliath.org/makepage/>

David Hwang created this to help people at his church and school. He provides a form to fill out, which then generates a home page for you. You can download the final product or have it e-mailed to you. (Other Web tutorial sites use this template strategy, as well.)

Beginner's Guide to HTML
<http://www.ncsa.uiuc.edu/General/Internet/WWW/HTMLPrimer.Html>
<www.ncsa.uiuc.edu/demoweb/html-primer.htm>

Created at NCSA (the National Center for Supercomputer Applications, University of Illinois at Urbana-Champaign), home of Mosaic, the first breakthrough, popular Web browser and the prototype for Netscape Navigator and Internet Explorer. An excellent guide.

Creating HTML in 11 Easy Stages
<http://www.shef.ac.uk/training/web/crnotes.html>

The University of Sheffield posts this course along with notes, exercises, and Powerpoint presentation.

Bare Bones Guide to HTML
<http://werbach.com/barebones>

Kevin Werbach makes his guide available online in ten different languages.

HTML Demonstration of Basic HTML Tags
<http://spot.colorado.edu/~rossk/tutorial/htmldemo.html>

Index of HTML tags
<http://www.willcam.com/cmat/html/>

Berkana Productions
<http://berkana.com/train/resources.html>

Berkana Productions makes their course materials and Web-building resources available, including a jumpstation of links to image maps, CGI scripts, Web commerce, VRML, 3-D, icons, and graphics.

Tools for Aspiring Web Weavers
<http://www.nas.nasa.gov/NAS/WebWeavers/index.html>

This has the sophistication and thoroughness one would expect from NASA.

Dr. Klopfenstein's Help for HTML Tools
<http://www.bgsu.edu/departments/tcom/html.html>

A random jumpstation of tutorials and guides, with emphasis on images.

Joe Burns' HTML Goodies
<http://www.htmlgoodies.com>

A 400-item gif library, plus tutorials on image maps, counters, forms, link buttons, tables, background colors, and wallpaper.

Writing for the Web: a Primer for Librarians
<http://bones.med.ohio-state.edu/eric/papers/primer/webdocs.html>

Webmasters Reference Library
<http://webreference.com>

Has a searchable subject guide.

Creating a Successful Web Page
<http://www.hooked.net/~larrylin/web.htm>

Has far more than HTML guidelines — content, organization, style, finding a server, self-promotion, updating your site.

Advanced Resources.

Adv-HTML
<http://risc.ua.edu/adv-html>

A free, moderated, e-mail discussion list for the discussion of advanced HTML and other advanced Web topics, archived at a Web site. Posts with "Summary" in the subject line summarize several responses to the topic.

Advanced Usage
<http://www.ucc.ie/info/net/htmladv.html>

Design Resources

Crystal Waters' Web Concept & Design
<http://www.typo.com>

(See the Bibliography for hardcover versions.)

The Essential World-Wide Web Site Design Guide 1.1
<http://ad1440.com/class/design.html>

The David Siegel Project (author, Creating Killer Web Sites)
<http://ww2.best.com/~dsiegel/home.html>

Web Builders and Multimedia Resources
<http://www.arcade.uiowa.edu/proj/webbuilder/>

Home Pages by Writers

The Web has untapped potential still. There is so much opportunity for people to craft their Web-wide vision. Get out there, play around, and contribute your personal effort. Take someone you know with an interesting story, and help them tell it over the Web. Good telling of human stories is the best way to keep the Internet and the World Wide Web from becoming a vast wasteland. With enough perseverance and personality, you could create a seminal site.

— JUSTIN HALL

Surveying the Internet, we've already encountered a variety of Webtop self-publishers — *bOING bOING, CyberMad, CyberWire Dispatch*, James Fallows, Hatrack River, pop&politics, Silly Billy, Yard Show — from e-zines to genre writers to journalists. Here are a few more, mostly in it just for the exposure — and sheer pleasure. (They are arranged in a progression from simple to complex.)

Xander Mellish
<http://www.users.interport.net/~xmel>

After Xander Mellish took years to write and polish her short stories, she faced the inevitable question of how to distribute them. So she printed the first page of a story on a poster, with her phone number on the bottom, and tacked up thousands of posters in Manhattan — on telephone poles, on laundromat walls, in pizza parlors, and so forth. She received hundreds of calls, until Mayor Giuliani's "quality of life" campaign meant that she could be arrested along with graffiti artists and others. So she taught herself HTML and posted her work on the Web.

Syndicated technology columnist Jesse Kornbluth accepted her invitation to read her work (submitted to him via e-mail, of course), was captivated, and wrote her up in his column, which led to her being discovered by a high-powered New York literary agent. Meanwhile, you can still read her work for free.

Evolution's Voyage
<http://www.evoyage.com>

William A. Spriggs posts his entertaining, informative essays on evolutionary psychology to a site just so that they may enter public consciousness. He sees the power of the Net as its ability to proliferate.

Rainwater Press
<http://www.rainwater.com>

Nan McCarthy's business began as a book packaging and editorial service, but now she spends most of her time writing and producing her own books — currently a fictional trilogy, *Chat*, *Connect*, and *Crash*, told entirely through e-mail. Her site announces: "We love to write, we love to read, we love to create books, and we love talking to other people who love books and publishing." Besides promoting and selling her own books, she provides a very useful glossary of terms for electronic publishing, graphic arts, and conventional printing.

Neal Weiner
<http://www.marlboro.edu/~nweiner>

Having published seven travel books and one on moral psychology, Neal Weiner relates that he was "surprised to find myself called back to that adolescent poet who hung around in coffee shops and dimly sensed through smoke and fuss that somehow there was more." At the resultant Web outpost he's entitled "The Virtue of What Is: Philosophical Poetry and Fiction about God, Growth, Truth, and the Meetingplace of Good and Evil at the Heart of Creation," he's created a hypermedia world of sound, image, and poems with lines which link to further poems (the poetry thus being in between the poems as well as within them), plus short stories, and the makings of a novel.

Gary Kline
<www.eskimo.com/~kline/novel/>

Gary Kline has posted the first fourteen chapters of his romantic adventure novel, *Journey to the Dawn*; all seventy chapters are available for download for $2.

Karen Hall
<http://ourworld.compuserve.com/homepages/karen_hall/>

Karen Hall is a screenwriter, journalist, and novelist. Her very simple home page has a brief bio, an interview, a tour schedule, a link to her publisher, and an e-mail link to her.

Dale Furutani
<http://members.aol.com/dfurutani>

Dale Furutani, author of *Death in Little Tokyo*, has a very simple Web site for that book, his next book, his tour schedule, and e-mail, plus a section for other writers telling how he created the site.

Dale is member of America Online, who offered to host a Web page for him. He downloaded Microsoft's Internet Assistant for free and created a site using Word for Windows. He also recommends reading AOL's files about creating a Web site, but warns that some are in technical-ese.

Rosanna Madrid Gatti
<http://www.cco.caltech.edu/~gatti/gabaldon/gabaldon.html>

Rosanna Madrid Gatti is a romance writer whose home page offers not only selections from her work, interviews, tour information, and autographed books and bookplates, but also a newsletter, a FAQ, and a map of Scotland showing clan territories.

Fawn Fitter
<http://www.well.com/user/fsquared/>

Fawn Fitter is a freelance journalist whose simple but highly sophisticated home page is designed around the metaphor of a virtual diner. As such, it is an exemplary demonstration of the powers of conceptual design. The menu ranges from Today's Specials to Dessert. The Main Course is sample writings, with a mailbox where assignment editors can drop her a note.

James Gleick
<http://www.around.com>

James Gleick is author of *Chaos* and *Genius*. At his Web site, he has a mailbox for suggestions about the next book he's working on, plus articles by other authors he finds of interest.

Michael Berry's Cheap Ironies
<http://www.sff.net/people/mberry/index.htp>

Michael Berry has a selection of his own published work, book reviews, an online journal, and eclectic favorite links, plus an author home page he hosts: his homage to Tom Stoppard.

William H. Calvin
<http://weber.u.washington.edu/~wcalvin>

William H. Calvin is author of eleven books on evolution and brains. His Web site features not only his books, but his Webzine, a list of what he's reading, recent lectures, and so on.

Mason West
<http://www.pobox.com/~mason>

Mason West clearly didn't start his outpost on the Web yesterday. His menu has such diverse options as: Poetry, Fiction, Journalism, "From Homer to Hypertext: The WWW as a Literary Medium"; Thoughts; I-Ching; Parallel Gospels; Prufrock, a literary mailing-list discussion group; *Discretions* (a weekly polemic newsletter); Masterworks of Western Civilization; Movie Literacy; 50 Great WWW Hikes; and much more.

Brainstorms
<http://www.well.com/user/hlr/>

Brainstorms is what Howard Rheingold calls his home pages at the WELL but it's more like a glorious virtual cornfield. He's posted: the full text of his out-of-print *Tools for Thought* (1984), a classic book about the evolution of computers; his interviews with leading-edge luminaries; his DayGlo doodles; and his Tomorrow column, syndicated to a few million readers on paper, weekly, and read by a couple thousand more online, daily. (King Features reserves syndication rights; Rheingold reserves electronic distribution rights.)

KidsWeb
<http://www.hooked.net/%7Eleroyc/kidsweb>

While browsing for Web ideas, be sure to visit KidsWeb, maintained by Brian, Mark, and Amanda, who host pages by dozens of younger Webmasters — quite a few with a literary bent.

.i.n.t.e.r.b.e.i.n.g.
<http://www.geocities.com/Athens/Acropolis/2730 >

Speaking of beginners, this is my own home-page in-progress.

Free Web Pages

Many online services and Internet service providers include hosting Web pages as a benefit of basic membership; some charge a minimal additional amount to do so.

Starving Artists' Tip: Many sites host individual Web pages for free.

Angelfire
<http://www.angelfire.com>

Offers up to 35K of free storage space.

InfoChase
<http://www.infochase.com>

Offers 100K of free space.

GeoCities
<http://www.geocities.com>

Will let you homestead up to two megabytes of disk space. Check out current GeoCities writers in their Athens, Soho, and Paris sections, for example.

AlphaPoint
<http://www.alphapoint.com>

AlphaPoint actively seeks authors. They have a review board and are particularly interested in ongoing works-in-progress and creative interactivity.

ArrowWeb
<http://www.arrowweb.com>

Not free, ArrowWeb has a minimal charge, at $25 per year.

MISCELLANEOUS RESOURCES FOR SELF-PUBLISHERS

The Arachnoid Writer's Alliance
<http://www.vena.com/arachnoid>

This group, based in Santa Cruz, California, presents books for sale by independent and self-published authors, offering works ranging from *Presidential Sanction* to Jeremy Reynalds public policy tract, *Homeless in America — The Solution*. They also link to other promotional sites for small publishers and authors, publishing services, and so on. Searchable by genre, key word, author, and title. Highly recommended.

BookZen
<http://www.bookzen.com>

Jo Grant maintains this nonprofit site where academic and small-press publishers can freely publicize their works. BookZen is conceived of as a free library of information about books for browsing or purchase, for acquisition librarians and readers from around the world. For more information: <info@bookzen.com>.

Digerati
<http://www.ai.mit.edu/digerati/digerati.html>

Digerati is a mailing list forum for the intersection of the digital and the literary arts, for both writers and technical people interested in Net publishing. Digerati provides a safe place for each to find connections and get advice — for writers who've missed out on science and technology and techies who missed out on English and art history — as well as where the fortunate who've kept feet in both worlds can find others who've also done so. Sample discussion topics: tips on HTML coding, emerging payment methods, increasing readership, copyright, print/online symbiosis. Not yet heavily trafficked, it has been known to go dark for months at a time and then pick up out of the blue again; it currently has 350 members.

To subscribe, e-mail <digerati-request@ai.mit.edu> with one word in the body of the message: "subscribe".

Digerati's Web site is a semi-megasource of interesting links, such as to many self-published writers and to Alan Eyzaquirre's interactive index of HTML publishing resources. The site will eventually become a test bed for experimenting with various editing and distribution functions.

Guide to Web Publishing
<http://members.tripod.com/~jpsp1/freeweb.html>

Guide to Web Publishing is a megasource jumpstation for everything we've been dealing with: how to use HTML, where to find free Web space, how to publicize your site, and so on.

Publish Yo'self
<http://www.links.net/webpub/>

Justin Hall's hyperlinked online tutorial covers almost all aspects of Web self-publishing; it is absolutely worth seeing just for the art of it.

The Small Business Publicity FAQ

Marcia Yudkin, who makes her Misc.Writing Freelance Writers FAQ available by e-mail, also furnishes the excellent Small Business Publicity FAQ, with valuable information for authors trying to publicize books: angles, press releases, pitch letters, media kits, outlets, etc.

Send any e-mail to <prinfo@yudkin.com> (it's an autoresponder).

TuLiP Project
<http://www.ctnet.com/drew/tulip>

Ivan Drew has adapted his master's thesis, a general survey on Web design, in a useful, hypertext fashion. Good as either an introduction or a "reality check" for Webmasters or self-publishers.

Public Relations on the Web
<http://impulse-research.com/prlist.html>

Useful PR Links
<http://www.profilepr.co.uk/html/lnks>

MEGASOURCE JUMPSTATIONS
Self-Publishing

Books AtoZ
<http://www.booksatoz.com>

Here you can access everything you need to publish your own books. They hyperlink to photographers, typographers, printers and binders, CD-ROM producers, fulfillment software, publishing organizations, and distributors, as well as essays on self-publishing and self-published books. Elegantly designed and laid out, too.

Dan Poynter's Book Publishing Resources
<http://www.parapublishing.com/Welcome/para/pindex>

This publisher has resources online geared for self-publishing writers — from suppliers to publicity to speaking engagements. There's also a mail list.

Creating Web Pages

Guides to Writing HTML Documents
<http://union.ncsa.uiuc.edu/HyperNews/get/www/Html/guides.html>

Virtual Library HTML Style
<http://WWW.Stars.com/Vlib/Providers/Style.html>

Yet another jumpstation of online resources.

Writing Your Own Web Page
<http://users.ox.ac.uk/~shil0124/serious/web-writing.html>

A well-arranged jumpstation by Peter King.

Yahoo! — HTML Guides and Tutorials
<http://www.yahoo.com/text/Computers_and_Internet/Software/Data_Formats/HTML/Guides_and_Tutorials/>

Yahoo! has a jumpstation to dozens of tutorials and guides. For Webmasters, they have a slew of links:

<http://www.yahoo.com/Computers/World_Wide_Web/HTML/>

18

New Writing

The Internet may in fact be the manifestation of a vision from the South American writer Jorge Luis Borges: an infinite garden of forking paths, an infinitely expanding library, a world-sized map of the world, a labyrinth that becomes a book, an encyclopedia that is, in fact, the universe.

—David Hipschman

The structure of ideas is never sequential. . . . As you consider a thing, your thoughts crisscross it, constantly revisiting first one connection, then another.

—Ted Nelson

The Internet isn't just a typewriter. Nor just a phone. Nor just a computer nor a TV. Its whole is greater than the sum of its parts. As such, it affords viable possibilities for new ways to publish, market, and distribute, as we've seen — and also new ways to write.

In this chapter, we'll explore two important aspects of the Net's creative possibility:

- collaboration, including the many new career possibilities opened up by multimedia
- interaction, whereby co-creation in cyberspace overcomes the traditionally lonely craft of the writer

COLLABORATION

The Net is commonly seen as a conduit to information, as if it were a book or a library. But it also invites collaboration. (Some call it a "collaboratory.") The Net offers two kinds of collaboration:

1. multimedia, with diverse skill-sets
2. literary, with other writers

Multimedia Collaboration

Have you considered a career in multimedia? (Also known as New Media, interactive media, and hypermedia.) Now that you're Net-literate, you might give it a few moments' thought. If, for example, you enjoy networking with other people in online forums, you might love working in multimedia. Unlike your average writing assignment, which is fairly solitary, multimedia is highly collaborative. True, multimedia can be made by multi-talented individuals, as with some exceptional movies, but multimedia is usually multi-headed. A multimedia team usually consists of three roles:

1. writers
2. programmers
3. designers

Chapter 17 furnished some resources to help writers become more design-savvy. But the most important skill to master for hypermedia may be the collaborative ability, which writers, being good communicators, usually possess. A writer grounded in communications — a journalist, screenwriter, or technical writer — stands a good chance of being at the apex of a multimedia pyramid, pulling together and coordinating the other services. Such a writer can conceptualize a project from the outset with an eye to what its audience would want, and can communicate that concept to the design and programming people. In the final analysis, it's not the programmer, engineer, or designer who best understands how to structure information for the end user; it's the writer. That's what writers traditionally do.

Having an eclectic background is also an asset. Writers who draw upon varied personal experiences and diverse skills, and have often had the albatross of "overqualified" slung around their neck by potential employers, will find multimedia an environment where their checkered background becomes an asset rather than a liability.

Multimedia, by definition, requires people who can develop the thread of a concept through multiple dimensions and skills: generalists, not specialists. (As Howard Gossage said of generalism, "We're not sure who it was who discovered water, but we're pretty sure it wasn't a fish.")

So if you like to communicate, to collaborate, and to stand outside as well as inside the box, New Media might be the place for you. And the time is right; you have your choice of job descriptions: Webmaster, content provider, or something even more eclectic, like "generalist."

A *Webmaster* creates and maintains Web pages for others. Your home page, as well as reflecting your own interests, would link to your clients, as an active portfolio demonstrating samples of your work — plus samples of your writing to interest editors and/or links to personal areas of interest or special expertise. Two leading markets for Webmasters are corporate and educational. Corporations are using a common Web site as an in-house network — an "intranet." It's like a combination of a Local Area Network (LAN) with groupware, providing such features as a mutually accessible calendar, schedule, statistics, documents, and forums. And in the educational arena, distance education is becoming a huge industry. Both need writers for their site creation, and for new content.

A *content provider*, on the other hand, can either create text (much like copywriting) or adapt material (much like screenwriting) for multimedia. Since a high-powered Web site wants viewers to keep coming back, new content is always as much in demand as is new technology. And if there exists literary property, yours or another's, highly suitable for online adaptation, your development of the electronic rights would also be content-related.

And a word on that CD-ROM on the cover of this book. Many of you are probably wondering what it's doing on a book addressing the Internet. Well, like everything else these days, CD-ROMs are incorporating the Internet. (See sidebar.)

The *content* of writing in the Electronic Era is changing as it embraces new *contexts*: real-time, on-demand, interactive. Any point in a text can become equidistant to any other text, without beginning, middle, or end. And content is no longer the province of a privileged few — private property, off in some Ivory Tower. Instead, authority becomes fluid, changing hands among a variety of authors — and readers. Indeed, writers can now position themselves as characters in their own stories. And readers are now co-creative collaborators.

But there's always a need, now more than ever, for traditional "writerly" content, as in a good anthology or a training manual. New Media breathes new life into such traditional "genres" as training materials (corporate, medical, computer-related, etc.), product documentation, and academic courseware, as well as the new genres of infotainment, simulations, guided tours, games, and Webisodic serials.

And, as more companies re-engineer for the Information Age, there are more opportunities for work across distance, telecommuting to work at a virtual corporation. Likewise, the Internet provides numerous places for you to hang your shingle out, without having to send out multiple resumés and clips. Pounding the pavement no longer has to wear down your soles; instead you have to pay more attention to your wrists.

To assist your networking through the new world of multimedia collaboration, here are four valuable organizations —

Networking.

The International Interactive Communications Society (IICS)
<http://www.iics.org/cover.html>

IICS is a 4,500-member group with branches in many cities, committed to professional development, fostering the growth of the interactive industry, and keeping members current on industry news. Their Web sites' hot links include other professional associations, Web development tutorials, and centers of multimedia education.

Multimedia Developers' Group (MDG)
<http://www.mdg.org>

MDG facilitates communication among developers, producers, technology firms, infrastructure providers, and government. Opportunities for members to

CD-ROMS: A NEW INTERNET ADJUNCT, AND A NEW MARKET FOR WRITERS

CD-ROMs (Compact Disc Read-Only Memory) create a new market for writers, one becoming even more viable thanks to the Internet. Here's a quick overview.

It was at the 1994 American Booksellers' Association Convention (ABA) that the industry became keenly aware that New Media were here to stay. The amount of floor space given over to CD-ROMs just couldn't be sidestepped. CD-ROMs are compact discs just like the ones used for recorded music, but they allow interactive and multimedia presentations on a computer. One of these flat, opalescent discs can store 600 megabytes (MB) or more of data, giving them a seemingly limitless horizon of applications: guided tours, training, tutorials, games, encyclopedias, art galleries, annotated music, annotated movies, and so on. (For a sample of what they can do, I recommend that you experience the CD-ROM adaptation of Art Spiegelman's illustrated novels, *The Complete Maus*, from Voyager, a leading publisher of literary CD-ROMs.) And, unlike film or books, once a master has been made, it costs practically nothing to make copies.

But a major problem has been distribution. Blockbuster and Borders carry CD-ROMs, for example, but most stores haven't added the extra shelf space, so there's been a bottleneck, with more product manufactured than the sales pipeline can channel. And since 1995, CD-ROMs have been faced with an unexpected competitor: the Web.

I'll give you a quick comparison of CD-ROMs and the Web. Basically, the first medium is limited and fixed; the second, unbounded and malleable.

- When a CD-ROM is made, it's done, whereas material at a Web site can always be deleted, added to, corrected, and revised.
- A CD-ROM has a fixed size and thus an editorial horizon (whether 600 or 1200 MB), whereas theoretically a Web site has no size constraints, given sufficiently large server storage capacity.
- A CD-ROM is a discrete, stand-alone unit with limited access and limited connectivity, whereas a Web site can link to a multitude of locations and devices: other Internet sites, videocams, and so forth.
- A CD-ROM is bound by gravity to one location in time and space, whereas a Web site can be accessed simultaneously from multiple time-space coordinates.

Nevertheless, more and more computers are entering the home and workplace with CD-ROM attachments. The market (the "installed base") is thus growing into the tens of millions of users.

Ultimately, the two media will find compatible synergies. There are "hybrid CD-ROMs," "enhanced" withthe Internet such as *The Marexx*. And, conversely, there are Web sites from which one can access CD-ROMs. The wise Net writer will keep an eye on developments in both fields. On the horizon still, as of this writing, are DVD-ROMs (Digital Versatile discs) capable of storing five to twenty gigabytes of information.

network with each other include showcasing work, sharing news of important issues and opportunities, and gaining greater access to available services.

The Online Word Biz
<http://www.wordbiz.com/directory/>

A forum for freelance content developers and New Media writers/editors who specialize in creating content for Web sites and in writing about Internet and New Media issues. The directory is both a networking resource and a marketplace for Web editors looking to hire writers.

The Writer's Guild of America (WGA)
<http://www.wga.org/ia/>

Hollywood's WGA maintains a robust Interactive section on its home page, reflecting their aggressive commitment to New Media. You'll find an Interactive Writer's Database with a broad spectrum of categories, links to industry organizations, a sample interactive script, and a number of highly informative essays and interviews, including "Writers or Designers?" Other sections are of interest too; their guide to writing CD-ROMs is under their Tools of the Trade section, for instance.

Literary Collaboration

The Internet allows writers and editors to collaborate intensively on a particular text, going back and forth across vast distances many times within a fixed period of time. Whether for drafting legal documents or position papers, feature articles or screenplays, this capability is bringing writers together like never before. (The first published (paper) novel written by Internet collaboration is *The Hate Parallax*, by a Russian and an American — who've yet to meet face-to-face!)

Collaborative literature is as old as stories handed down from generation to generation. The gospels of the Bible had four authors. T'ang Dynasty Chinese poets sometimes got together to write linked verse. What we know as haiku are but links in a Japanese group verse format called "renga." And John Ashbery edited a magazine in the fifties for collaborative writing, *Locus Solus*. The Internet, however, offers a unique renaissance in collaborative literature.

We've already seen some examples of collaborative writing among Net science-fiction writers. Here are some further experiments from the Internet collaboratory:

Anime Crash
<animecrash@aol.com>

An ongoing writing experiment; a kind of twist on narration, round-table story writing, and character development. E-mail based, it doesn't aim to be literary as much as lively.

InterNovel
<http://www.internovel.com/novel>

A unique, professional collaborative project being introduced to students and teachers at several major educational institutions in the U.S. as an independent exercise in composition, creative writing, and screenplay adaptation; contributors will also receive any royalties earned.

Interactive Media
<http://www.sirius.com/~future/Media/imedia/menu.html>

An interactive e-zine. All articles are incomplete or ongoing. Readers can direct the emphasis and depth of all reports.

Lenov
<http://geology.wisc.edu/~delitsin/hypertext/LENOV/>

A collaborative novel in Russian and English.

Mola
<http://iberia.vassar.edu/Mola>

This project at the University at Albany is an interesting approach to a total immersion into multimedia hypertext collaboration.

My Name is Scibe
<http://www.tmn.com/0h/Artswire/interactive/www/scibe/story.html>

By Judy Malloy, et al, this piece was written during Malloy's recovery from a serious bike/car crash. (Note: that's Zero-h in the address above)

No Dead Trees
<http://www.nodeadtrees.com>

An interactive collaborative novel supervised by David Benson. If enough people join in and put the novel's characters through new permutations and combinations, eventually it could include every conceivable beginning, middle, and end. (Includes a megasource jumpstation of links to writing resources and interactive pages.)

run on, run along
<http://www.pobox.com/~pamplona/run/run.html>

This collaboration shuttles the reader back and forth between the sites of co-authors Nancy Lin and Susan Schweitzer in a seamless text flow, like two books that interleave into one.

Stories from Downtown Anywhere
<http://www.awa.com/stories/>

Under the auspices of Charles Deemer, this project divides the story space into distinct, simultaneous neighborhoods, with their own characters and situations.

Storyweb
<http://ourworld.compuserve.com/homepages/Poetry_Machine/storyhom.htm>

An interactive literary adventure begun by Martin Auer. You are invited to read, be inspired, create a story or poem as a page at your own home page, and link to all the other Storyweb sites in the world proliferating in like fashion.

WebRings
<http://www.webring.org/orig/>

Similar to StoryWeb, the WebRings phenomenon was begun in the summer of 1995. Any single WebRing site can link to all the others, and any addition brings exponential growth to the ring. The original now has 300 pages.

Cafi Utne
<http://www.utne.com>, in the Literature section of Cafi Utne

Utne readers decided to write a novel together at the magazine's online forum, Cafi Utne. Each person assumed a fictional persona and posted entries from that character's diaries. In nine months, they'd accumulated 1,000 entries, plus 1,200 posts discussing the chain novel itself.

And, as *The Hate Parallax* demonstrates, writers don't need the Web to collaborate. Screenwriting teams have collaborated from disparate land-based locations using e-mail.

E-mail can be the basis for collaboration upon which hypertext and interactive multimedia can be added later. I participated in such an e-mail collaboration in the summer of 1995. I answered a call posted online, and soon joined nine other writers and the initiator who then became the coordinator. We each wrote a chapter and then sent it to the coordinator. A week later, she sent each of us someone else's Chapter 1, from which we'd continue a new chapter. A week later, we'd all get someone else's Chapter 2, and so forth, until we'd each completed ten chapters, ten weeks later. (The result is to be the basis for a multimedia interactive CD-ROM.)

It was a good way to work, especially given the subject: a character with multiple personalities. In fact, it was an excellent example of form as an extension of content; hopefully future readers will experience much of the surprise and excitement the authors experienced in receiving and dealing with a new installment every week.

THE ART OF HYPERTEXT

I've already indicated that using the Net implies being creative as much as it's about learning the technology. A Web site can be "authored" in just a few minutes, yet the creative implications run deeper. Although originally created for scientists, not writers and artists, the Web does come with many design amenities built in, such as rule lines, boldface, italics, bulleted lists, extracts, and six different levels of headings. Now, what shall writers make of these tools, plus the interactivity, nonlinearity, networking, and linking?

This section touches on the key introductory points you'll need to learn to pack the tool of hypertext in your kit and put it to use. These approaches are useful to consider no matter what kind of writing you do. As you'll see, interactivity isn't only about doing old things in a new way — it's also about doing new things differently.

To use an analogy commonly evoked in connection with New Media (namely, film), hypertext is the biggest widespread application of nonlinear presentation since a filmmaker first crosscut footage of a woman tied to a train track, thieves blowing up a bank safe, and a cowboy on a galloping horse — to invent cinematic montage. Similarly, Net writers are now inventing hypertext.

How Is Hypertext Different?

Many readers (and writers) aren't ready for a thing with no beginning, no middle, and no end. Yet the developmental peaks and valleys of traditional dramatic exposition now compete with the flashes of recognition that accompany TV channel surfing — little flashes of "Aha!" rather than one, big, climactic, "Oh, wow!" This is typical of the new landscape of hypertext.

Audience identification with hypertext characters is also different. Manipulating events is as if in a computer game; the audience feels more intensely inside the characters while also outside them, leading to a different kind of character development. And, because the outcome isn't fixed, the audience, in a way, is narrating, making choices with a power greater than in traditional storytelling.

Once a writer opens out linear character development, cause-and-effect interaction, and dramatic closure into multiplicity, simultaneity, interpenetration, and nonlinearity, readers are afforded possibilities of new dimensions, delving deeper — or at least alternatively to our conditioned perception of the world. One of the best cases to be made for hypertext is that it can replicate for the reader not just a particular thought but the process of thought itself. Here an idea can not only be stated, but the thought process out of which it arises can be experienced, too.

There are precedents reaching back to the very origins of literature, such as metaphor and polyphony. (Think of Homer's rosy fingers of dawn. Think of Proust comparing the street cries of a dog groomer, birdseed seller, and scissor sharpener to mezzoArabic medieval chant and fragments of Debussy.) More recently, Arthur Koestler defined the act of creation as the bi-association of ideas.

As mentioned already, a common analogy for New Media is the early days of Hollywood, where each week they tried something new (close-up, pan, cross-cut, two-reelers), until, eventually, a vocabulary, a grammar, and an industry were born. Perhaps hypertext still awaits its D.W. Griffith, Sergei Eisenstein, or John Ford. But maybe hypertext will never evidence that level of "higher unity" which cinema can create out of juxtaposed short strips, and may be awaiting instead its Michael Jackson and Jay Leno, and its "killer" application for TV commercials and news reports.

Hypertext is also a proving ground for all the academic critical theory in the air at its birth — Barthes, Derrida, Kristeva, Foucault, Deleuze and Guattari — exemplifying fluid boundaries between different texts (slipstream), and between author and reader (interactivity), multiple spheres of meaning (hypertext), etc.

Certainly, hypertext is a powerful way to structure a biography or a historical account, allowing the reader to braid relevant strands rather than hammer them into one, narrow, linear progression. One fine example of hypertext storytelling in fiction is Rick Pryll's short story *Lies*. Two lovers keep diaries, and the reader has the choice between two versions: "truth" and "lies." The choice doesn't affect the outcome of the story, only the reader's perception, which makes all the difference.

Lies
<http://www.users.interport.net/~rick/lies/lies.html>

Poetry, drama, fiction, or prose — hypertext may reanimate your sense of these vehicles of expression and communication. Here follow a few special samples for your consideration.

Hypertext Criticism

The World Wide Web was invented, in part, for scientists to interlink cited texts, within and across the heavily annotated world of physics. We're starting to see how this applies to literature as well.

Pride and Prejudice
<http://uts.cc.utexas.edu/~churchh/pridprej.html>

Henry Churchyard's online edition of *Pride and Prejudice*, for example, is more than a digitized text. Here, Jane Austen's novel has five options of hyperlink annotation throughout (the links go into or out of the main text, either to or from words pertaining to any of these five categories):

1. cast of characters
2. chronology of events
3. comments on random topics
4. index to the motifs of "pride" and "prejudice"
5. important places (with a map)

This site was made not only for scholars, but for midget-brains like me; if I'm not reading an illustrated version, or haven't seen Greer Garson and Sir Laurence Olivier in the movie, then visualizing and keeping track of everything can be taxing. All those different people stopping to sit on park benches gets so confusing! And it has its uses for the rest of us.

The art of hypertext thus opens new dimensions to criticism. A must-see in this regard is:

The Victorian Web
<http://www.stg.brown.edu/projects/hypertext/landow/victorian/victov2.html>

Curated by George Landow, Brown University scholar of both Victorian and hypertext literature. Whereas the hypertext *Pride and Prejudice* never left the book, here the links take you to other critical areas of the Web site. You can start at any one of ten top-level buttons and eventually hyperlink to the rest of the material. The initial topics are: Victorianism, literature, and Victorian authors; art, architecture, and design; social and political contexts; economic contexts; religion; philosophy; and science. In short, a whole universe.

Web denizens refer to "experiencing" a site, rather than "visiting" or "seeing," and that's appropriate here. The cornerstone of the site was laid in 1985, and a noble edifice is being built upon it as various scholars and students from Brown and other universities add new essays, questions, images, and so forth. Way at the "bottom" there are links to over twenty other related sites of hypertext criticism (Lewis Carroll, Disraeli, Gilbert & Sullivan, Sherlock Holmes, Victorian women, and more), but this one wins the *writers.net* Dancing Footnote Award for Best Demonstration of Hypertext in Action.

Gravity's Rainbow
<http:/www.hyperparts.com/gravity/gravity.html>

For an example of hypertext footnoting a modern work, see Tim Ware's brilliant hypertext concordance to Thomas Pynchon's *Gravity's Rainbow*.

"It's Not What You Think"
<http://www.charm.net/~sam/inwyt/inwyt.html>

For an example of a hypertext "rant" (with 150 links), see Stuart Molthrop's review of *Newsweek*'s 1995 "TechnoMania" issue, entitled "It's Not What You Think."

We've noted that the Web was made for annotation. Perhaps the most concise and the most poetic hypertext experience on the Web today is the annotation to the title of The Voice of the Shuttle's Web site.

The Voice of the Shuttle
<http://humanitas.ucsb.edu/shuttle/the_myth.html>

Below the logo there's an epigram from Aristotle: "And there is 'the voice of the shuttle' in Sophocles' *Tereus*." Clicking on the hyperlinked words doesn't hop to Sophocles but, instead, to four texts, ancient and modern, all hyperlinked together by key words. It is, as the site's Web weaver Alan Liu describes it, "a commentary with no voice other than the pattern of the links themselves."

And it makes a suitable transition to our next new hypertext genre: poetry.

Hypertext Poetry

The Cyberspace Sonnets
<http://www.teleport.com/~cdeemer/cyberson.html>

Charles Deemer has been "weaving' *The Cyberspace Sonnets*, which has five decision points, each offering between two and four choices, culminating in a range of 250 sonnet possibilities.

Hunger
<http://www.nua.ie/worsmith/Maighread Medbh/index.html>

A series of poems by Méighréad Medbh, following a poor Irish farming family through the Great Irish Famine of 1845–49. Hyperlinks expand and explain the text.

Julie Peterson
<http://awaken.org/museum/resume/poetry/ploop.html>

Julie Peterson, at *HotWired*, has created a very rudimentary poetry loop.

Jim Rosenberg
<http://cnsvax.albany.edu/~poetry/rosen.html>

Jim Rosenberg works with self-styled integrams and diagram poems.

Diana Slattery
<http://raven.ubalt.edu/guests/alphaweb/intro.htm>

Diana Slattery's graphics-rich Alphaweb site is navigable either by alphabet, first lines, or topical headings.

Haunting Grounds
<http://marie.az.com/~fenmere>

Jonathan Sodt's Haunting Grounds includes a series of poems all hyperlinked into each other, a hyperlinked table of contents, and a proposed hyperlinking of poems from various sites.

The Virtue of What Is
<http://www.marlboro.edu/~nweiner/>

The fourteen poems on Neal Weiner's Web site are hyperlinked to each other, illustrated, and read aloud "to slow things down and provoke the heart and mind to make comparisons."

Hypertext Drama

Elliptical storytelling verging on hypertext became a recent fad in cinema, from *Pulp Fiction* to *Usual Suspects* to *Lone Star*. For some time, Alan Ayckbourn has crossed the boundary of linearity in such stage plays as *Intimate Exchanges* (filmed as *Smoking and No Smoking* by Alain Resnais — himself a pioneer of such hypertextual cinema as *Last Year at Marienbad*). In *Intimate Exchanges*, there are four pivot points: five seconds, five days, five weeks, and five years after the beginning, resulting in a total of sixteen endings.

Charles Deemer's Hyperdramas & Essays
<http://www.teleport.com/~cdeemer/chile/chile-m.html>

I've already mentioned Charles Deemer's megasource jumpstation for stage and screenwriting. Later, I spotlighted his collaborative hypertext space, Downtown Anywhere (where the reader can choose the point of view and what to do next). But

---

OBSERVER AS PARTICIPANT

The script excerpt (opposite page) from Charles Deemer's *Château de Mort* has two "decision moments" for the audience in less than a minute of action. Putting it another way, the story "branches" twice in less than a minute.

(Jack, Polo, Heather, and Medalion are in an upstairs bedroom.)

HEATHER: Want to go downstairs for a drink?

MEDALION: Why not?

HEATHER: Jack? I'm really sorry about your dad.

JACK: Thanks, hon.

(The women leave to go downstairs.)

READER INTERACTION:

Do you want to follow the women
or stay here with the men?

Make your choice below:

|<<<<<<<<<>>>>>>>>>|

(After the women are gone:)

JACK: Polo, I know that you—

POLO: Hey, man, for the last time, it's not my concern that you got a weirdo for an old man. Hear what I'm saying? So where's the stash?

(etc.)

(The women head downstairs, running into Brown.)

BROWN: Hello.

HEATHER: Have you seen Dr. Brodey?

BROWN: I think he's in the dining room.

HEATHER: Thanks.

READER INTERACTION:

Do you want to go:

|<<<<>>>>|

(new scene)   (new scene)   (etc.)

New Writing

Deemer's greatest accomplishment thus far may be his hypertext playscripts, wherein many scenes occur at the same time. The audience, like the reader of hypertext, must decide "what happens next." Deemer's one-act hyperdrama, *The Last Song of Violeta Parra* (1996), for example, takes place in a two-story house of six different rooms.

Hypertext drama may take a quantum leap with the popularization of 3-D (VRML, or Virtual Reality Markup Language) on the Net, enabling the user to explore virtual worlds such as buildings and landscapes. And, as we've said, there's untapped dramatic potential in multi-user environments: the Electronic Visualization Laboratory (EVL) at the University of Illinois at Chicago, Seattle's Worldesign, and Alternate Realities of Research Triangle Park, North Carolina, are researching the possibilities of using these "immersive" virtual reality environments for presentations and entertainment for groups — with multiple users internetworked from remote locations. Writing for them sounds challenging and fun.

Hypertext is an elusive bird, but I hope that by now your interest is sufficiently aroused to pursue it further. Here are gateways for more information, online and off.

For More Information

"Hypertext Sources"
<http://www.eastgate.com>

A hyperlinked bibliography of authors, articles, and books, compiled by Mark Bernstein at Eastgate Systems, makers of Storyspace software and leading publishers of hypertext fiction.

"In Defence of Hypertext"
<http://www.geocities.com/Athens/1114/defence.html>

A fine survey of the field by Alon Bochman.

"As We May Think"
<http://www.isg.sfu.ca/~duchier/misc/vbush/>

The seminal hypertext essay by Vannevar Bush, which appeared in *The Atlantic Monthly*, July 1945, anticipates the Network Computer, and proposes a personal

Memex (Memory Expander) computer in which material can be filed by association rather than hierarchical index. This version has been appropriately annotated and hyperlinked.

"Writing for the New Millennium: The Birth of Electronic Literature"
<http://ourworld.compuserve.com:80/homepages/rkendall/pw1.htm>

This informative article by Robert Kendall includes hypertext publishers besides Eastgate (the foremost publisher of hypertext fiction).

"The Color of Television"
<http://raven.ubalt.edu/features/media_ecology/lab/96/cotv/>

A work in progress by Stuart Moulthrop and Sean Cohen, 1996.

"Tree Fiction on the World Wide Web"
<http://www.cl.cam.ac.uk/users/gdr11/tree-fiction.html>

By Gareth Rees; includes an excellent hyperlinked bibliography of sources.

Writing Lives: Technology, Creativity, and Hypertext Fiction
<http://www.duke.edu/~mshumate/fiction/htt/mals.html>

Hypertext master's thesis by Michael Shumate.

MEGASOURCE JUMPSTATIONS
Collaboration

Collaborative Software Resource Clearinghouse
<http://www.ics.hawaii.edu/~csrc/>

Daniel LaLiberté World Wide Web Collaboration Projects
<http://union.ncsa.uiuc.edu/HyperNews/get/www/collaboration.html>

W3C Collaboration Resource Page
<http://www.w3.org/hypertext/WWW/Collaboration/>

Many of these collaborative examples are hypertext, enabling the reader to interact as well as the authors.

Interaction

Hyperizons: The Hypertext Fiction Home Page
<http://www.duke.edu/~mshumate/hyperfic.html>

Hyperizons was created by Michael Shumate, a fiction writer, graduate student at Duke, and manuscripts archivist/cataloger at Duke's Special Collections Library. Awarding it the Best of the Net '95 award, GNN (Global Network Navigator) said: "Chock full of resources on postmodern fiction and its computerized cousin, hypertext fiction, this site links to a wonderland of Web sites, including The Hypertext Hotel begun by Robert Coover at Brown University; *Victory Garden* and *Marble Springs*, hypertext novels from Eastgate Systems, and inside information on the history and structure of hypertext fiction." The 250 links include about seventy original works. From this site you can hop to:

- CyberPort, featuring interviews with hyperfiction authors and collaborative hypertext science fiction
- Postmodern Theory, Culture Studies, and Hypertext, a carefully arranged and annotated jumpstation
- The Search for Some Hypertext Fiction, a little collection originally created by Prentiss Riddle for *City of Bits*
- The Web Hyperfiction Reading List, Carolyn Guyer's fine annotated bibliography of hypertext fiction to her article in *Feed*.

Hyperizons wins *writers.net*'s esteemed Gold-Plated Channel-Zapper for Best Hypertext Megasource Jumpstation.

Hypertext and Literary Things
<http://www.aaln.org/~kmm>

Hypertext and Literary Things has 200 external links featuring forums and even some archives of forums, such as Ht_Lit. It organizes this interdisciplinary topic in a simple but thorough interface. The host, Kia Mennie, also manages the Ht-Lit list.

Hypertext Fiction
<http://www.cel.sfsu.edu/msp/Instructors/kurtz/Fictionpage.html>

Professor Glenn A. Kurtz created this rich megasource jumpstation for the San Francisco State University Multimedia Studies Program.

The Voice of the Shuttle
<http://humanitas.ucsb.edu/shuttle/techwrit.html#hypertext>

Some "meta" sites span a number of categories. This one wins the *writers.net* Jade Hat Pin for Intense Literary Megasource Jumpstation. I list it here, under hypertext, but its wide-ranging, eclectic mix of resources spans New Media cyberculture and traditional humanities, which each have something to say to each other.

Just scrolling through the main menu of options under any one topic can be like attending a Chinese opera — midway, you can slip out for dinner and come back for more.

19
Net Censorship and Copyright

He who receives an idea from me, receives instruction himself without lessening mine, as he who lights his taper at mine receives light without darkening mine.
— Thomas Jefferson

The good news is that the NII [National Information Infrastructure] allows for quick, efficient, and technically perfect reproduction and distribution of copyrighted works worldwide. The bad news is that the NII allows for quick, efficient, and technically perfect reproduction and distribution of copyrighted works worldwide.
— Hon. Bruce A. Lehman, addressing George Mason University, February 28, 1996, on "Copyright, Fair Use, and the National Information Infrastructure"

It is impossible for ideas to compete in the marketplace if no forum for their presentation is provided or available.
— Thomas Mann

The onus is on us to determine whether free societies in the twenty-first century will conduct electronic communication under the conditions of freedom established for the domain of print through centuries of struggle, or whether that great achievement will become lost in a confusion of new technologies.
— Ithiel de Sola Pool

Now that anybody can be a publisher, can anyone publish anything at all?

And who owns words: their author or their publisher?

Will protection of copyright limit the free flow of information?

This chapter looks in more detail at these fine points of censorship and copyright. I'll also highlight organizations that act as advocates for writers' rights as the Internet moves through its formative development. The most important new communications medium of the next century is in our hands, and together we can define its future — and ours.

NET CENSORSHIP

Question: If you're publishing your own home page, what's one sure-fire way to elicit "hits"?

Answer: Include as many of the "Big 7" Words (banned from radio and TV) as possible, to trigger hits from search engines.

Any communications medium has its taboos as to what is and isn't said or done within it, as well as people who push those limits, many of whom are often artists. Dante's works were burned by Savonarola's "bonfire of the vanities" (along with Ovid, Propertius, and Boccaccio). In 1555, Queen Mary banned the *Bible* in English.

This eternal conflict may exist in any new medium. Much of what we know about Gutenberg, for example, comes from evidence recorded in trial proceedings against him for counterfeiting. Today's Internet is still a fledgling medium, yet it has already been the subject of trials and legal scrutiny regarding censorship. Thus far, the Net is proving resilient and resistant to censorship, though not on all counts, and certainly not with any definitive outcome as yet.

One salient factor is the Internet's internationalism. The U.S. cannot prevent Scandinavians from producing erotic postcards, for example, and putting them on the Net. A striking case occurred in 1995 when CompuServe in Germany temporarily shut down 200 pornographic newsgroups on Usenet, acceding to demands privately lodged by law enforcement officials. Except in the case of five sites under investigation for child pornography, the purge lasted only five weeks, however, in the face of the difficulty of enforcing such restrictions on a global medium: what's on CompuServe is available internationally, and censoring content for one country would censor it for subscribers in all countries.

This is an internationalization of the problem of community standards, which may vary from community to community. Thus, too, are America's decisions as to Internet censorship doubly important, as they're being scrutinized by people grappling with these issues in foreign countries, many newly emergent to the comity of world nations.

Furthermore, an online service such as CompuServe should not reasonably be expected to monitor everything crossing its cables, routers, and servers. After all, if you were to receive an obscene phone call, you would not sue the phone company. And now there are technologies such as caller ID that enable you to block or monitor your calls; the Internet can be similarly regulated by each user, with software such as Net Nanny (<http://www.netnanny.com/netnanny/>) and SafeSurf (<http://www.safesurf.com>). CompuServe offers its members use of Cyber Patrol software that automatically restricts access to forums and files containing material to which the user might object. Cybersitter, however, has been found to come with a pre-programmed agenda; it blocks all content from The WELL, for example. On the horizon is a system of ratings, much as currently exists for American movies. A viable approach in this regard appears to be the Platform for Internet Content Selection (PICS), <http://www.w3.org/pub/WWW/PICS/>.

One night, with no warning, America Online acceded to pressure from conservative Christian fundamentalists and made a sweep of its forums. A retired Baptist minister replaced the moderator of the atheist forum and blanked out numerous postings. Other forums suffered arbitrary erasure, as if by a global search for a key word — women discussing breast cancer, for example. And poets at AOL's Poets Corner found their work purged, often by no discernible criteria, on a continuing basis. Requests for written guidelines went unanswered. One poet, Isa Sadiq, wrote, "It seems ironic to me that a service which names itself after America has sought to take away the First Amendment rights of its consumers." (The poet happened to be a writer in political asylum from her native Somalia.) Meanwhile, AOL's chat rooms continued to exhibit questionable language, even people looking to expose children to sexual situations.

This issue is important to any writer thinking of maintaining a forum. The current legal standards are, basically, that the owner of a forum is liable for the content of its users therein if it is a moderated list. If it is unmoderated, then forums members are bound by their own discretion, and the forum host is not liable for its content (such as offensive material, hate mongering, etc.).

The Law

America had no laws regarding obscenity for eighty years. Then, suddenly, after but a few minutes of debate, Anthony Comstock (founder of the Society for the Suppression of Vice) pushed through our first obscenity laws, establishing a legal precedent still used today. The Comstock Law of 1873 (the Federal Anti-Obscenity Act) banned the mailing of lewd, indecent, filthy, or obscene materials. From that point on, publishers had to submit their manuscripts to the Comstock Society.

After 1915, test cases began to shrink the boundaries of suppressible obscenity. The Comstock Law, however, still remains on the books. In fact, on February 8, 1996 (ironically, the same day as "24 Hours in Cyberspace"), President Clinton signed the "Communications Decency Provision" of the Telecommunications Reform Act (the Communications Decency Act, or CDA) which specifically applied part of the Comstock Law to computer networks, suddenly thrusting the Internet into this legal arena. Despite its laudable intention of making the Internet safe for children, the unfortunate result of the CDA would have been to raze the entire Internet to the standards of kindergarten.

The CDA would have had a chilling effect on all writers, as well as all users. While the First Amendment protects a print version, but publishing an electronic copy of the same text could constitute a federal felony, editors and publishers would inevitably measure print copy against the constraints of the CDA, rather than consider two versions, electronic and print. Indeed, Jim Warren had his regular column for *Boardwatch* magazine censored by a print editor who cited the CDA as the reason, causing Jim to quit his post.

The CDA was overturned in its initial trial. Federal Judge Dalzell (who unanimously joined Judge Buckwalter and Judge Sloviter on June 13, 1996, in supporting the injunction to overturn the CDA) wrote:

> . . . the Internet may fairly be regarded as a never-ending worldwide conversation. The Government may not, through the CDA, interrupt that conversation. As the most participatory form of mass speech yet developed, the Internet deserves the highest protection from governmental intrusion. . . .
>
> Just as the strength of the Internet is chaos, so the strength of our liberty depends upon the chaos and cacophony of the unfettered speech the First Amendment protects.

As of this writing, the Supreme Court has not entered a decision on the CDA. But however the CDA is resolved, the impulses toward censorship and freedom of expression will continue to coexist in a dynamic tension on the Internet. At the end of this chapter, I've listed some resources which allow writers to not only remain current with the issues, but also take a proactive role in shaping the outcome.

I should add that, in addition to censorship by law and self-censorship, there is economic censorship, as in countries that make the Internet prohibitively expensive. This brings us to a related question: ownership of literary property in cyberspace.

NET COPYRIGHT

If you were just starting out and planning a lucrative career, you'd do well to consider going into intellectual property law. The Information Economy is, in large part, fueled by the development of packages of software demanding canny understanding of copyright laws to ensure their profitability. There is also the entertainment industry, with its properties vulnerable to pirated duplication.

The Internet poses a particular problem. Today's lawyers are attempting to copyright, license, and howsoever protect everything their clients own. In an editorial entitled "Infohighwayman" in the *New York Times*, Nicholson Baker defined the sweep as including "slogans, facial and vocal likenesses, melodic snippets, genetic sequences, bits of mathematical reasoning, unpublished letters and the look and feel of software programs."

As writers, we're concerned with how copyrights affect our words — including words we might cull from the Internet, and our words being made available over the Internet. The parameters appear to be simple. On the one hand there's copyright, and on the other there's fair use.

LIMITATIONS ON EXCLUSIVE RIGHTS: FAIR USE (11 U.S.C. §107)

Notwithstanding the provisions of Sections 106 and 106A, the fair use of a copyrighted work, including such use by reproduction in copies or phonorecords or by any other means specified by that section, for purposes such as criticism, comment, news reporting, teaching (including multiple copies for classroom use), scholarship, or research, is not an infringement of copyright. In determining whether the use made of a work in any particular case is a fair use the factors to be considered shall include:

1. the purpose and character of the use, including whether such use is of a commercial nature or is for nonprofit educational purposes;
2. the nature of the copyrighted work;
3. the amount and substantiality of the portion used in relation to the copyrighted work as a whole; and
4. the effect of the use upon the potential market for or value of the copyrighted work. The fact that a work is unpublished shall not itself bar a finding of fair use if such finding is made upon consideration of all the above factors.

Just because you can copy something doesn't mean that it isn't protected by copyright. Copyright is written into the Constitution to promote "the progress of science and useful arts."

Fair use arose out of tensions between copyright law and the First Amendment, in situations wherein scholars, critics, writers, and others upheld their right to speak and write freely, even while using copyrighted material. Fair use entitles you to use someone else's material if the purpose is for critical comment, news reporting, research, education, or scholarship. Besides purpose of use, another factor is how much is used. You wouldn't be using material fairly if you used more than necessary to make your point. A sample excerpt would suffice; copying the entire text would be going overboard.

Fair use also allows you to use someone else's published information as a fact, as long as you don't copy the manner in which it was presented or expressed. Facts cannot be copyrighted, only the way in which they're presented.

How fair use and copyright apply to the Internet remains to be seen. While the Internet is comparable to the Wild West in its prospects of instant material wealth, another resemblance is its relative lack of clearly defined laws. As attorney Karl Olson of Cooper White & Cooper puts it, "Trying to define what law applies to the Internet is a little bit like trying to nail a jellyfish to the wall. There's a lot of wriggle room right now."

Questions are still being raised, answers are still being determined, and there are still no hard-and-fast facts. Rather, we're making it up as we go along. And the arena is the negotiating table as well as the courts, not to mention organizations for collective bargaining. Presented with a contract, there are often very few precedents. And big businesses favor monopoly ownership, as reflected not only in their contracts but also their lobbying of the government.

Despite the old saw, "Don't worry; it's our standard contract," there is no Standard Writer's Contract, despite what publishers might tell you. These days, a publisher's right to exclusive first English rights is often being erased and replaced with a blanket contract buying all rights, for media known and unknown. That is, instead of one-time rights, many publishers are seeking blanket rights, via a work-made-for-hire contract. While rookie freelancers might be happy to get exposure, not to mention a lump sum of money, this is a serious blow to more seasoned freelancers who make their living by parceling out rights to their work amongst various purchasers.

Moral: Rights are not always freely given but must be won, constantly.

The question of protecting our copyrights has a flip side, which is likewise being tested at this very moment. That question is: can work be protected from unlimited free distribution? As it stands now, you can surf the Net and redistribute copyrighted material as long as it's for fair use, for free. Yet such a standard was created independent of the major players in the information industries, and thus might not withstand the test of time.

In addition to the Communications Decency Act, another salvo triggered under the Clinton Administration has been the white paper entitled "Intellectual Property and National Information Infrastructure (NII)," by "Hon. Bruce A. Lehman, Assistant Secretary of Commerce and Commissioner of Patents and Copyrights, <gopher://ntiant1.ntia.doc.gov:70/00/papers/documents/files/ipnii.txt>. While it attempts to uphold the commercial viability of a national information infrastructure, critics argue that it would diminish fair use and confer full control over digital transmission to publishers — and deny the reader the ability to freely browse before deciding to peruse.

In a similar vein, in December of 1996, the World Intellectual Property Organization (WIPO) met in Switzerland to consider the draft of a new treaty that would require countries, including the U.S., to limit the public's right to use public-domain materials stored in databases.

Next, I'll focus on how writers are banding together to keep each other informed and to express an organized, collective voice in the electronic copyrights arena.

Professional Organizations

Up until now, electronic rights clauses were often ignored in contract renegotiations by traditional guilds. Today these clauses are coming to the foreground. It may be recalled that a five-day work week, paid vacations, and medical insurance were not freely dispensed by employers, but rather battled over by workers who joined in common cause. Here are three organizations at the ramparts of the Information Age.

The National Writers Union
<ftp://ftp.netcom.com/pub/new/nwu>
<http://www.nwu.org/nwu>

Today, an author's articles and essays become grist for database "indexes" that, in effect, use people's faxes and modems as their printing presses. The Magazine Index, for example, charges $8 per fax or $43 per online retrieval — even to the original author — but pays no royalties on such sales.

Jonathan Tasini, President of the National Writers Union, filed a suit with ten other union members against the New York Times Company, Time Warner Inc.'s magazine group, and four other newspaper and magazine publishers and database companies, protesting the unauthorized and uncompensated distribution and reselling of authors' works via computer access to commercial databases. The NWU alleges that the *New York Times* has even blacklisted any freelancer who refused to sign away all electronic rights. As National Writers Union Assistant Director Irving Muchnick has put it, "Before there is an online highway there has to be a donkey trail of rights and dignity," referring in part to the European concept of "moral rights."

In August, 1995, the National Writers Union signed an agreement with UnCover, which they say is the world's largest database of magazine and journal articles. By so doing they launched their collective licensing organization, called the Publication Rights Clearinghouse (PRC). This bolstered their position in their Tasini v. NYTimes suit, by establishing the "full-text database industry," a valuable market in and of itself.

This also serves as a model for a potential revenue stream for the Union's members. Thus, any time someone accessed and paid for an article a Union member had written in a magazine in the UnCover database, the writer would be reimbursed through PRC if it was a magazine with whom the writer hadn't signed an all-rights contract. Since the arrangement was made, UnCover's owner, CARL, was acquired by Knight-Ridder, which might give the collective licensing arrangement more muscle.

Publishers could object that we're painting a one-sided picture. Through no fault of their own, they might argue, they're simply attempting to resolve electronic rights at purchase, rather than be frustrated by being unable to find an author to get a signature at some later stage. And the publisher's in-house legal department, in drafting such a contract, might be not so much greedy as simply lazy, working on a salary rather than on billable hours, and so going for the easiest solution. Moreover, if a publisher were to license electronic rights separately, who would keep track of, collect, and distribute payments? They might have to hire more employees, or shovel the new responsibilities under somebody's preexisting job description.

On balance, we might consider yet another perspective. Computer guru Esther Dyson points out that, beyond a certain point, money is not the issue. If someone is making adequate revenue, investing time to police possible additional revenue, such as copyright infringements, might be time better spent in other ways. In a highly competitive marketplace, she asserts, intellectual property is going to be less and less important an asset. To her, the trick is how to leverage one's product as an asset through which some other service, product, or income stream can be defined.

The commodity in diminishing supply, she argues, won't be money or information but, rather, attention. "In my case," she says, "my newsletter [*Release 1.0*,

$595/year] is an advertising for my conferences [PC (Platforms for Communication) Forum, $2,000/ticket]. With Sun Microsystems, their Java software is really advertising for their hardware. We have a lot of cases where content ends up being like beer in a bar: it's what you serve to get people in." See <http://www.edventure.com> or <info@edventure.com>

Her paradigm is not unlike the San Francisco Gold Rush, during which fifteen breweries and 300 saloons opened up almost overnight. Free lunch was offered for the price of a schooner of beer; oysters and game with a shot of whiskey or a flute of champagne. And a ragtime pianist might cut a few piano rolls for a chance to have his compositions heard — assuming, in the first place, that he had a way of keeping a roof over his head, such as a job in a saloon. Thus, for most writers, Dyson's analogy will seem theoretical and a luxury. Yet in that analogy we can locate the National Writers Union as being like ASCAP (the American Society of Composers, Authors, and Publishers), founded fifty years after the Gold Rush, which would act as a clearinghouse for the rights to songs such as those of the ragtime pianist. Or so the NWU hopes; ASCAP started out small, but is now a $400-million-a-year operation.

The National Writers Union has 4,000 members in thirteen locals — not only freelance journalists and book authors but also poets, kids' book writers, publicists, and technical writers. Union Secretary-Treasurer Bruce Hartford states, "From the NWU's perspective, the challenge of a coherent national new technology policy breaks down into four areas: access, commerce, end-user issues, and illegal sales." They publish a fifty-three-page booklet, *Authors in the New Information Age*, for $3.00, spelling out such matters and their position on them. For this or other materials:

National Writers Union (UAW Local-1981)
873 Broadway, #203
New York, NY 10003
Phone: 213-254-0279
E-mail: <nwu@nwu.org>

The American Society of Journalists and Authors (ASJA)
<http://www.asja.org>

The American Society of Journalists and Authors is a national organization of leading freelance nonfiction writers . The membership requirement is either one published book with at least one more under contract, or six recent articles in major periodicals. As its name states, it's a society, not a union. As such, it's a structure wherein members can help other members. They publish a regular newsletter,

CYBERFABLES

"E-Wrongs About E-Rights" lists over a dozen common "cyberfables," followed by the ASJA's rebuttals, such as:

"Databases like Lexis-Nexis are just another way of distributing our magazine. You wouldn't expect more money if we signed up 1,000 more newsstands, would you?"

A database is not simply another means of distributing a magazine, because a database doesn't distribute magazines at all; it distributes individual articles. Online services collect a per-article fee from database users and pass a piece back to the publisher. It's as if a reader could go to a newsstand, slice your article out of a magazine, and pay for the clipping alone. It is, in effect, an electronic delivery system for a reprint service.

Other "cyberfables" include:

- "We don't 'cherry-pick.' We use the article only as part of the whole issue in which it appears. It's simple archiving."

- "This is just like microfilm."

- "But no publisher is making a dime at this."

- "We don't charge download fees on our Web site. If we start charging, then we'll pay authors."

- "We don't know which articles are accessed. It would be too expensive to keep track."

- "It would be too expensive to write a lot of small royalty checks."

- "The exposure will be good for you. It'll get your name around. It'll sell books."

- "We can't delete a single article."

- "If you make us delete this article, you'll be interfering with the flow of information, research, scholarship, the future of the Western world. . . ."

- "We ask for only nonexclusive e-rights; you can resell the work yourself any way you want."

- "The business is new. Let it shake down a few years, then renegotiate."

- "All the other writers are signing."

- "Our lawyer won't allow any changes."

Contracts Watch, (highly recommended) available by e-mail, and a number of papers on their Web site.

Among other helpful documents on electronic rights issues, they have a two-page paper, "E-Wrongs about E-Rights." To such classic fables as "Wow! It fits you like a glove," "It's our standard contract," and "Our check is in the mail," this document adds newer "cyberfables." (See the sidebar, "Cyberfables," opposite.)

ASJA welcomes inquiries to:

Contracts Committee, ASJA
1501 Broadway
New York, NY 10036
Phone: 212-997-0947
E-mail: <75227.1650@compuserve.com>

The Authors Registry
<http://www.webcom.com/registry>

In mid-1995, the Authors Registry launched with a model similar to, but in some ways different from, the NWU Publication Rights Clearing House (PRC). Whereas the PRC is a division of one group (NWU), the Authors Registry began with the American Society of Journalists and Authors (ASJA), the Authors Guild, the Dramatists Guild, and the Association of Authors' Representatives (AAR) as first signatories. In its first year, thirty groups joined, including the American Book Producers Association, the Editorial Freelancers Association, and the National Book Critics Circle, as well as the National Writers Union, plus nearly a hundred literary agencies.

The Registry is compiling a master referral list of writers and their works so that publishers and others desiring to reach writers to license work will contact the Registry, which has contact information for over 50,000 writers so far. Perhaps more importantly, however, they've put in place the mechanism for collective licensing and for the collection and distribution of payments for New Media and other re-uses of written work.

For a moment, let's look at the other side of the coin. Big companies lacking a payment policy for electronic rights might argue that they're being unfairly demonized. It's valid to consider, they might say, that New Media may be as much of a black hole for them as a potential gold mine. A Web site requires large start-up and maintenance expenditures, and only a few are starting to make money. Even if they wanted to pay for electronic rights, they might say, how could they do so, having considerable investments already at stake?

Nevertheless, sites with databases or archives that are heavily researched are making considerable sums. *The New York Times* estimated in 1995 that its revenues from Nexis searches alone would reap $80 million over a five-year period. But the issue of profitability obscures the issue of new ventures expecting to get raw materials (content) for free.

So if the publisher's question is, "If we invest in New Media, who'll handle rights? Will we have to create a new job description just for that?" then the Authors Registry has the answer. By offering publishing companies relief from the minute bookkeeping and distribution of payments for such things as electronic rights, the Authors Registry has begun to bring previously reluctant publishers to the licensing table.

In February of 1996, *Harper's* became the first periodical to say that it would systematically pay authors for electronic rights on a per-access basis, with the Authors Registry as clearinghouse, and *Publishers Weekly* and *The Nation* quickly followed suit. In August, 1996, the Registry began writing the first $150,000 in royalty checks to authors. (See update at the Registry's Web site.)

You can contact The Authors Registry at:

The Authors Registry
330 West 42nd Street
New York, NY 10036
Phone: 212-563-6920
E-mail: <registry@interport.net>

Paul Aiken is the managing director.

ADDITIONAL RESOURCES

In addition to the above-mentioned organizations, the Net is a hive of individuals and groups disseminating information and activism regarding the related issues of censorship, authorship, and copyright. Some, such as the Electronic Freedom Foundation, straddle all these topics; nevertheless, here is a survey of major outposts divided according to the twin lights of censorship and copyright.

Anti-censorship Resources

Banned Books Online
<http://www.cs.cmu.edu/Web/People/spok/banned-books.html>

From Milton to the *Bible*, *Ulysses* to *Little Red Riding Hood*, various works have been banned throughout history. This site curates many such texts.

Banned Books Bookmarks
<http://box.hotwired.net/banned.html>

Links to two dozen major sites of cultural significance that are objectionable under the CDA, including condom use and breastfeeding, a hate group, and clearly indecent material, as well as relevant legislation.

Bonfire of the Liberties
<http://www.d-a-c.com/exhibit.html>

A fascinating gallery of symbolic book burnings through the ages, organized by rationale.

The Center for Democracy and Technology

An advocacy group for policy research, public education, and coalition-building for civil liberties and democratic values in computer telecommunications. For more information, e-mail <info@cdt.org>.

Computer Professionals for Social Responsibility
<http://www.cpsr.org/cpsr/nii/cyber-rights>

A Cyber-Rights home page dedicated to privacy, free speech, universal access, and related issues in cyberspace.

The Electronic Frontier Foundation
<http://www.eff.org>

Concerned about copyright, censorship, and other social issues of new information technology. For more information, e-mail <info@eff.org> or visit their Web site.

Free Expression Network
<http://www.freeexpression.org>

A megasource jumpstation representing a joint venture of over thirty groups (such as the American Civil Liberties Union, the American Booksellers' Foundation for Free Expression, the American Libraries Association, the National Campaign for Freedom of Expression, and PEN American Center) whose mission is the protection of the First Amendment rights to free expression, and who provide action alerts, legislative updates, legal briefings, community news, and links to member and related sites.

Index on Censorship Magazine
<http://www.oneworld.org/index_oc/index.html>

Reprints many of its excellent articles online, with international perspective; also has a Netwatch section.

Voters Telecommunications Watch
<http://www.vtw.org>

Based in New York City, Voters Telecommunications Watch is a national activist group. Their site features their Congressional BillWatch, the Citizens' Guide to the Net, an Internet parental control FAQ, and a CDA FAQ.

Copyright Resources

Copyright & Fair Use Web Site
<http://fairuse.stanford.edu/>

In July of 1996, Stanford University Libraries & Academic Information Resources, in collaboration with the Council on Library Resources and FindLaw Internet Legal Resources, put up this latest and greatest of megasource jumpstations devoted to copyright and particularly fair use. Immaculately laid out, it provides an overview of and access to the laws, the documents of relevant U.S. court cases, and related commentary, all full-text searchable. Plus it furnishes an impartial, copious, and expanding list of links to relevant governmental and nongovernmental organizations, other Web sites, mailing list forums, and online articles on these issues.

Copyright Clearance Center
<http://www.copyright.com>

A nonprofit collective licensing system for corporate clients.

The Copyright Web Site
<http://www.benedict.com>

P.J. Benedict Mahoney's charming megasource, with some solid pipeline on fundamentals, registration, public domain, sample infringements. Special emphasis is given to song lyrics.

Ivan Hoffman
<http://home.earthlink.net/~ivanlove>

Attorney Ivan Hoffman specializes in authors and publishers and publishes his work on copyright, electronic rights, and Internet law.

"10 Big Myths about Copyright Explained"
<http://www.clarinet.com/brad/copymyths.html>

Brad Templeton's (publisher of ClariNet) essay is highly recommended.

Library of Congress
<telnet://marvel.loc.gov> (log on as "marvel," then select the "Copyright" menu)
<gopher://marvel.loc.gov>
<http://lcweb.loc.gov/copyright>

* * *

This is an historic moment. You are witnessing the birth and evolution of a major new communications medium whose impact is on the order of magnitude of Gutenberg's movable type. Our active participation and commitment to the Net's promise will shape its future and the future transformation of the world we live in. The Net's potentials for fertilizing the free flow of information and the commerce of ideas are clearly present. The rest is up to us.

My deepest hope is that *writers.net* increases your abilities to network so that you may work well, write good things, and thrive.

Appendix

An Internet Primer for Writers

It is said the Internet is like high school sex. Everyone thinks everyone else is doing it. Everyone wishes they were doing it. Only a few are actually doing it. And of the few that are doing it, all aren't doing it very well.

—Kate Muldoon

If a generation is roughly twenty years, it took:

- *1,275 generations to move from cave drawings to writing,*
- *250 generations from writing to the printing press,*
- *19 generations from the printing press to photography,*
- *7 generations from photography to desktop computing,*
- *and less than half of one generation from desktop computing to the World Wide Web*

—Paul Lester

With an emphasis on writers' needs, this appendix provides:

- a mini-tutorial for beginners (newbies)
- a brush-up for Internauts (Netizens)
- a reality check for Net vets (knowbies)

People approach the Internet with varying levels of preparation and awareness. As the Internet population mushrooms, newcomers are continually climbing on board. Meanwhile, intermediate and even advanced users have often settled into a niche and rarely venture out of their chosen comfort zone, still hazy about the particulars of the terrain beyond their pasture. And there are many — often teenagers — for whom the whole thing is as familiar as wallpaper.

Beginners find that the Internet combines the simplicity of the telephone with the complexity of the computer. Plug a phone into a wall and it's ready to use. With computers, on the other hand, we usually have to try something a number of times, maybe even bump our heads on it first, before it clicks and we clue in. Not to worry: the Internet is easier to master than word processing software. But it does require a certain literacy, akin to the early automobiles: you not only have to know how to crank it up and steer, but be prepared to get out, open up a tool kit, and tinker. And because the Internet has evolved totally ad hoc, there's no official Internet literacy certification. Hence this appendix.

This appendix attempts to bring even the most computer-illiterate writer up to speed with the basic vocabulary of the Net. If you are moderately Net-savvy, you will probably pick up a few new points that will improve your online effectiveness. For a fuller version, I can shamelessly refer you to my *Pocket Guide to the Internet*: <http://www.pocketbooks.com/netguide.html>.

Caveat: Don't be alarmed if you don't "get it" all, here. Shoehorning so much into twenty-some pages, some things are bound to remain hazy. And some of it you won't really "get" until you actually go online and see for yourself.

As a brief primer, here is an outline of the Internet ABCs, as covered in the following pages:

A. What is the Internet, and how can I get there?
B. What are the five major Internet applications?
  1. E-mail
  2. Forums
     a. Via e-mail
     b. Via Usenet
     c. Other (online services, real-time, etc.)
  3. FTP
  4. Telnet
  5. Information resources and resource guides

      a. Gopher
      b. The World Wide Web
   C. How to put all of this in perspective?

WHAT IS THE INTERNET, AND HOW CAN I GET THERE?

First, what is a network? A network is a connection of systems that work together. A network can be a group of people, such as a work team or a special interest group. Or it can be two or more computers connected by a wire. Offices often have a computer network — a Local Area Network (LAN) in-house, and/or a Wide Area Network (WAN) between branch offices. Human resources departments now hire from computerized job banks, payroll is administered by computer, management incorporates groupware programs like Lotus Notes, and you might hear someone say, "Whose computer is down? The printer won't work!" Security can even monitor remote video cameras by computer network.

Hobbyists and entrepreneurs can configure some software in an "el cheapo" computer in the basement to set up an easy-to-maintain network for profit or play, called a Bulletin Board System (or BBS). There are over 180,000 BBSs in the U.S., accessible directly via a local number with a computer and a modem — for dating, jobs, games, hobbies, etc. These, in turn, could be part of a network of BBSs (such as a genealogical association, for example).

Next, consider contemporary research. When paper-based (hard copy) text is made digital, via a word processor or scanner, it can more easily be edited, printed, distributed, and otherwise manipulated. More and more libraries, for example, have replaced their card catalogs with computers that pool various holdings, such as the stacks, periodicals, and special collections, into one common database of information. Just as you can search for words in a document with a word-processing program, so can you search a computerized library database by author, title, or subject. Such a library computer might also network with other libraries and related resources. And many people can search that networked database at once.

The Internet

Now, let's take a step back. Each of these networks — whether for work, play, or research — interweaves various departments and far-flung branches. What if they were all interconnected — the libraries, the hobbyists, the businesses — *internetworked* into one all-encompassing, multipurpose network of networks?

Hence the word "Inter-net." Simply put, it's all of these computers hooked up to each other. It's commonly called the network of networks; plug into any part, and you plug into the whole. (As an open system, however, this doesn't mean that anyone can then access files on your hard disk. And you're not suseptible to viruses unless you take some software from the Net and run it with your computer, which you might not ever do.)

Right now, the Internet (or "Net," for short) interlinks 6.6 million computer hosts, or hubs, interconnecting over fifty thousand networks, bringing tens of millions of people into arm's reach from over 160 nations around the globe. And a new network gets added about every thirty minutes. For nearly the past decade, the Internet population has doubled annually, which means that at any given time half the people online are relative newcomers.

Now, why did I say, "Plug into any part, and you plug into the whole"? Because there's no center to it. Just as there's no global central bank or post office, yet bankers accept all currencies and post offices accept all stamps, the Internet accepts all participants. Thus the technology carries with it a certain philosophical perspective and culture: a do-it-yourself, anarchic, "bottom-up," fluid, horizontal interdependency, rather than a canned, top-down, rigid, vertical hierarchy.

This is part of what makes it so attractive to so many, but also very discouraging to people who expect to jump right in. To be a successful Netizen means realizing that, along with a relatively simple set of computer rules, the Internet has its own culture. Writers, being cultural workers by definition, are thus at a natural advantage in scoping out and clueing in to the Internet culture.

ASCII.   A basic example of Net culture is found in the adoption of ASCII (the American Standard Code for Information Interchange; pronounced "ass-key"). ASCII eliminates all the variables in the different programming code of various software applications (word-processors, desktop publishing programs, etc.) and uses a one-size-fits-all solution (code) that is universal for the character set found on all English-language keyboards. The neat thing about ASCII is that it is displayed exactly the same, no matter what the monitor or the make of computer.

Tip: Knowing how to work with ASCII can come in handy, especially if you have a deadline. To create an ASCII file, ask your word processor to save your text using the "Save As . . . " command from the File menu. From the dialog box that follows, choose "Text Only," rather than the Normal default (which is the application-specific file format).

Furthermore, when saving a document in ASCII format, it's best to first save your text in a nonproportional font (such as `Courier`), with a line length of 5½". (This text you're now reading is typeset in a proportional font, New Caledonia — the "M" character, for example, is wider than the "t". In a nonproportional font [a.k.a. "monospaced"], every character is of equal width.) By using a nonproportional font with a limited line-length, you'll do a great favor for the Internet recipient of your document: you'll prevent awkward and unwanted paragraph breaks and word-wrapping when the recipients open the document with their (often different) software.

Getting Online

All you need to get online are five things:

1. a central processing unit (CPU) and screen
2. a transmission medium
3. a modem
4. connectivity
5. telecommunications software

A Central Processing Unit (CPU) and Screen. To get online, you'll need a central processing unit, or CPU — simply, a mechanical-electrical device that can read, write, and process digital data — which can be a computer or other variant like a set-top box for a TV. If you're just getting your first personal computer (PC), you may be confused about whether to get a less expensive network computer (NC), or even just a converter for your TV (such as WebTV). WebTVs usually lack a disk drive, so you would have to investigate what options, if any, they have for storing, editing, and printing text. If you're getting a PC and want to use the Web's multimedia applications (graphics, sounds, etc.), you'll need *at least* a 386 PC or a Macintosh LC-II.

A Transmission Medium. The most common transmission medium (today) is a telephone-line connection (transmitting data via twisted copper wire, with a modem as the intermediary between CPU and the phone line).

The carrying capacity of transmission media is called "bandwidth" — just imagine filling a pail with water from a hose: the wider the hose, the faster the pail fills up. Copper wire connections (phone lines) are the most commonly used medium, but the bandwidth is relatively low when compared to other media.

Other transmission media options, with far greater bandwidths, include: fiber optic cable; coaxial cable (as found with cable TV), and wireless (like a cellular phone, but potentially wider).

A Modem. A modem translates (MODulates-DEModulates) signals between your computer, which is digital, and an analog transmission medium, such as a phone.

Connectivity. Connectivity (connecting to the Net) is facilitated via a complicated computer program (or protocol) called TCP/IP (Transmission Control Protocol/ Internet Protocol), which provides the basic, universal language for telecommunication from one machine to another. It's not likely that ordinary consumers will install and use it. Instead, most people either access it through a workplace or campus computer, or dial up someone else who has it and use theirs — either an Internet service provider (ISP), (such as Earthlink, Netcom, Whole Earth Networks, Mindspring, the telephone companies' Internet services, etc.) or a commercial online service (such as America Online, CompuServe, Prodigy, etc.).

An online service differs from an ISP in that it provides special features in addition to Internet access. For example, an online service may offer members-only access to certain software, databases, content, games, or forums.

Regional computer magazines often list local Internet service providers. If you want full, multimedia access to the Web (sounds, pictures, movies, etc., rather than text-only), you'll need an online service provider that can give you either a SLIP or a PPP account.

Starving artists, note: some cities have Free-Nets — local providers that offer free e-mail service and sometimes even free (text-only) Web access.

Telecommunications Software. Many ISPs are accessible via generic telecommunication programs, such as Procomm for PCs and Z-Term or Microphone for Mac. These can come in handy, and it's how I dial my local public library, not only to search its card catalog but also to surf the Web (in text-only format) for free. Most online services and many ISPs have their own, proprietary software, on floppy disk or CD-ROM, but having a generic telecommunications software program gives you the additional option of local services such as libraries and BBSs.

Additionally, multimedia access to the Web requires software called a "Web browser," such as Microsoft Internet Explorer or Netscape Navigator. Basic versions of these browsers are available for free downloading from the Net.

Many providers offer free, introductory Net access for a limited time period, distributing their software by mail, magazine insert, or bundling with your computer. If you're completely new to the online world, you might give any of them a try. But which provider you'll want to stay with depends on a number of criteria, as outlined in the sidebar below. After all, if there were one answer, there wouldn't be intense competition. And the Internet remains a moving target, making inroads within word-processing and desktop publishing software, not to mention phones, cars, and stoves.

So that's what the Internet is and how to get there. But actually it's like a highway, connecting all these resources. So read on to learn how to use the highway, with different vehicles.

HOW TO EVALUATE AN INTERNET ACCESS PROVIDER

Ask yourself:

- Is access provided via a local phone number? Is the number frequently busy?

- Do I like the system's visual organization and navigation (interface)? Do I need no-brainer navigation, or can I learn commands or tools?

- Is the help desk helpful? Are they prompt? Intelligible? Does their support team respond by e-mail or by phone? Which do I prefer? If by phone, is there an 800 number?

- Can I talk with others who've already tried this provider?

- For an online service, what's the culture of the members like? Are they more interested in talking about writing or about the singles' scene? Is there a prevailing political ideology? Are there "live" forums? Are there private rooms? Might my publisher read something I write about them there?

- Will I want to host a mailing list? An infobot? A Web page? Will the provider include means to do this in the base price?

- How much storage will the service provide? (Over two megabytes is great.)

Remember: a perfect pizza is more of an ideal than a reality.

WHAT'S OUT THERE? — A GUIDED TOUR

Knowing how to connect to the Internet only brings us to the gate. Just as we don't get in our car to visit Highway 101, but take Highway 101 to visit Aunt Em or the campus or the mall, so do we use the Internet as a means of visiting particular destinations.

Originally, the Internet didn't encompass the profuse variety it does today. The Net evolved with relatively little planning, and continues to do so. Beginning as an experiment, it continues to be a work-in-progress.

After a quarter century of incubating new applications for itself, the Net has evolved a complex infrastructure. Downtown Internet is different than uptown, which is unlike the wharves, which stand apart from the stadium, the campus, the mall, the chestnut trees, or the wishing well.

Hence this guided tour.

You can count on the fingers of one hand the major Internet applications. (Applications are like vehicles on a road — car, bike, trailer — or software programs on a computer — word processor, spreadsheet, game. They're ways of applying the medium.)

1. e-mail
2. forums
3. file transfer protocol (FTP)
4. remote log-on (telnet)
5. information resources or resource guides, such as gopher and the World Wide Web (WWW)

These five functions exist simultaneously and independently. Before I describe each one, let me give you an overview of how they compare and contrast.

E-mail is one-to-one, me-to-you, you-to-me, person-to-person. But it is also one-to-many and many-to-one (for example, you can write one piece of e-mail, and send it to many people with the click of a button). Forums — group communication — are many-to-many. There are two primary kinds of forums: mailing lists and conferences.

E-mail and forums involve numbers of people. The third kind of Internet application deals with volumes of information. File transfer protocol (FTP) provides open libraries, archives, or warehouses full of files (usually free) and provides a means of transmitting large files.

Remote log-on (a.k.a. telnet) allows you to operate other computers from your computer. (Actually, FTP is one form of remote log-on.) Here, the variable is the number of different kinds of applications you can access and use (databases, library catalogs, full-text books, job banks, games, weather satellites, etc.).

Finally, there are information resources, or resource guides, such as gopher and the World Wide Web ("Web," for short). Consider information as facts made meaningful by being organized: facts in formation. These resource guides help us organize and find things throughout this big, amorphous haystack, and even customize things for our own preferences and needs.

E-mail

E-mail ("e" for electronic) is the most ubiquitous feature of the Net, used by about fifty million people. As such, it is the glue of networked communications. It is also the Internet's primary support system, whereby you can always send a query for help or a request for more information.

Learning the mechanics of e-mail will teach you basic Internet skills, such as sending and saving files (a.k.a. uploading and downloading, respectively), keeping an online address book, storing information in file folders, closely following one subject (a "thread") over a period of time, respecting the rules of the road ("Netiquette"), and so on.

E-mail helps create communities of interest. Professor Sherry Turkle has remarked to Howard Rheingold, in an interview at his home page, that newcomers to the Net "discover a new kind of conversation, one that opens out to a new kind of relationship. They are not simply going to be developing new pen pals."

For people whose major media were telephone and TV, e-mail has created a significant revival of interest in the written word in general, and letter-writing in particular. You'll find that e-mail's combination of anonymity and immediacy can induce spontaneity and informal directness. Thus, Netizens often write in a shoot-from-the-hip, colloquial style, somewhere between speaking and thinking styles. Netiquette advises that you not correct others' grammar or spelling, even if you're compulsive from years of freelance proofreading. Similarly, compose important messages offline before posting, just as you might write a postcard but not a business proposal while standing at the post office. To get S. Hambridge's thorough *Netiquette Guidelines*, e-mail <rfc-info@isi.edu>. Leave the subject line blank; in the message body, put two lines:

Retrieve: FYI
DOC-ID: FYI 0028

Along with its elimination of envelopes, stamps, and mailboxes, e-mail erases the burden of toll charges and overseas rates. The costs are for access charges levied by your provider, and telephone toll charges if your access number is not local. Some providers charge you for each piece of mail, but no one discriminates in regard to whether you're communicating down the hall or around the world.

THE ANATOMY OF AN E-MAIL ADDRESS

Beginners are often thrown off by the special language of an e-mail address. But it's really quite simple. Let's take a hypothetical e-mail address:

<writer@avalon.net>

Everything to the left of the "@" sign is the person's ID — their screen name, how that person logs on to his or her Internet connection (not including their secret password).

If you're communicating with someone who has the same Internet access provider as you, then you can just use this ID (in this case, "writer"). If not, then you have to specify their Internet access point — their "domain" or "site." Everything to the right of the "@" sign is the domain. Domain names work the same way that an envelope address does: from specific to general. I live at 2001 (very specific) Main Street (more panoramic), San Francisco (bird's-eye view), California (satellite view), U.S.A., earth, and so on.

So consider this four-part domain:

<writer@igor.cs.ucsd.edu>

The terminal suffix "edu" — the most general part of the address — means that the domain is at an educational institution. Reading from right to left (general to specific), the address then says that it's at the University of California San Diego, at the Computer Science department, where Internet access is made through a computer designated as "igor." (Computers on networks are often assigned names.)

Other possible terminal suffixes are ".com" for commercial company, and ".org" for nonprofit organization. Terminal suffixes can also be country codes: ".cn" for China, ".ca" for Canada, and so on. The United Kingdom likes to combine the two: ".co.uk" for a British company and ".ac.uk" for a British academy.

There are no spaces in an e-mail address, but special characters can be used, such as the tilde (~) or the underline (_). And some e-mail addresses are case-sensitive; they have to be typed exactly as required — all lowercase, for instance.

If you're sending a message to someone who is on the same network as yourself, whether they're across an ocean or down the hall, the message appears in their e-mail in-box in seconds. Between two different networks it might take a few more seconds, or even an hour or two. That's still fairly fast. Such speed seems to erase the boundaries of time and space, although it can also make you more aware of international time zones.

This combination of speed and convenience is luxurious. Your dialogue with a key-pal can go back and forth several times in one day. And if your correspondent is an editor who's sufficiently hardwired and you have already written your query letter, proposal, and article, you might move your ball through all those croquet hoops of submission, agreement on terms, and revision in less than a day.

For writers, e-mail offers many new ways of being in the world. In many instances, for example, it can be an ideal way of querying publishers and editors, of transmitting proposals and writing, of interviewing sources, and of interacting and collaborating with others.

Learning the basic mechanics of e-mail can take five minutes. But learning when and how to send e-mail, rather than "snail mail," fax, or phone, can take six months. Here are some of the basics.

There are a number of e-mail programs — such as Pine, Mush, Elm, Pegasus, Claris Emailer, and Eudora (named after a short story by Eudora Welty, "Why I Live at the P.O."). They are all generically called "readers." Each offers a range of formal options.

For example, one reader might enable you to store mail in folders online, according to subject, and filter your mail so that incoming mail is automatically sorted into these folders. Other readers let you to check whether someone has read your e-mail yet, indicating whether they've downloaded it and forwarded it to anyone else, and, if so, to whom.

Aside from such particular features of each reader, there are also universal features:

- E-mail enables you to send a short line (the subject line) that will appear in the mail menu of the recipient(s); subject lines allow you to display your creativity (low-key, or all-caps; succinct, or teaser; etc.).

- You can forward e-mail you receive with the tap of a finger. And others can forward your forwarded mail, too — creating circles of correspondents.

- If you choose to reply to an incoming message, the sender's address and subject line will automatically be copied for you, streamlining response.

- With most e-mail software, you can automatically quote the incoming message you're replying to (usually with ">"s in the left-hand margin — Internet quotation marks). Using this feature (with judicious editing) is an essential and powerful skill, allowing for quick, tight, focused, gears-meshing dialogue in a way that is not possible by phone or fax, and frequently difficult even face-to-face or on paper.
- When writing, forwarding, and replying, you can make cc's ("courtesy copies," formerly known as "carbon copies"). That is, you can add dozens of addressees to a file and send it to all of them at once with the tap of a finger (unlike a fax, for which the machine would have to dial each number separately).

This instantaneous multiplicity of recipients brings us to the next kind of Internet function: group communication unlike most anything else you've ever experienced.

Forums

As mentioned earlier, *forums* are a form of group communication. It's a generic term, interchangable with "conference" and includes a variety of specific applications. Along with e-mail, forums are the most dynamic, exciting, and popular feature of the Net. People naturally like to communicate. Thanks in part to forums, the Internet is not only a community of networks; it's also a network of communities.

Forums can fulfill various functions and needs. They can be one-way, such as to deliver a series of lessons, a newsletter, or a custom newspaper. Or they can be two-way: a shared, public space like a café or a commons for round-robins of back-fence chat. Imagine a radio talk show in which no one is ever put on hold, multiple topics are discussed simultaneously, and people talk with each other, not just to a host.

Forums can be moderated (hosted) or free-for-alls. They can be public (most are), private (such as for sensitive topics), free (most are) or for a fee.

There are several different formats for forums. Some are real-time ("live"), sometimes called "chat rooms," Internet Relay Chat (IRC), or "talk."

Online services (America Online, CompuServe, Prodigy, the Well) provide members-only forums. You can also find conferences on the Internet outside of online services, in an area called Usenet. And some forums are conducted by e-mail. E-mail forums are also called "mailing lists."

E-mail Forums (Mailing Lists).   Ordinary e-mail mediates tens of thousands of online affinity groups, through forums called mailing lists, reflectors, and aliases. To get the basic idea of an e-mail forum, consider a "telephone tree," in which one person phones a message to twenty-five people, who, in turn, each phone it along to twenty-five more people, and so on. Now, what if that entire list of people could be stored in one place? And what if members could join in and leave at will? And what if all the members could receive any other member's message all at once? That's what happens in an e-mail forum.

Here's how it works. Suppose you want to join a new mailing list, Writers' Anonymous (I'm making this up, of course). Following the instruction you'd seen somewhere, you send e-mail to <listserv@anon.org>, leaving the subject line blank and typing in the message body the command: Subscribe Writers Anonymous Jane/John Doe.

Within a few minutes or hours, you'll receive a welcome message containing instructions, including other commands you can send to <listserv@anon.org>. Now you can send a message to <writ@anon.org>, introducing yourself. If there are seventy members forming this new group, you'll soon get seventy self-introduction messages in your e-mail box, including your own. Reading writing-addiction confessions from seventy writers is sure to break the ice and get the conversation going. And maybe there's a moderator to facilitate the process. Now there's a twenty-four-hour support center — a resource bank, a virtual watering hole, a shared affinity network.

Tip: When you join an e-mail forum, be sure to save the Welcome message, with its instructions. Also, be sure to distinguish the address that is for sending commands (here, <listserv@anon.org>) and the address that is for communicating with the group (here, <writ@anon.org>).

Conferences and Newsgroups. Now that you've seen what a forum is, let's turn to a variant in the way the information is displayed and accessed. Besides being in our e-mail box, online forums can have their own area. The most commonly used is called Usenet, which calls its forums "newsgroups." They can also take place in special areas at online services. For example, when I joined the Books conference at the WELL, my first posting (message to the group) was in an ongoing discussion topic there called Computers & Metaphor. Having followed the discussion thus far, I added my two cents and mentioned the recent spate of neo-Luddite, anti-Internet backlash books. (I typed my message on the screen and selected a "Send" option that added it to the scroll.) The conference hosts immediately decided to make that a separate topic. During the next few weeks, 431 postings were made on the new topic of Internet Backlash Books, while Computers and Metaphor continued to be discussed in its own, parallel, separate area. (Talk about a pebble, dropped in a pond, casting ripples!)

In an e-mail forum, I would have received 431 separate e-mail messages in my e-mail box, each with the same subject line. But there all the messages with a common topic are "threaded" together as they are posted, one after another, to be read sequentially when one visits that conference area.

So where else are conferences to be found? Conferences are relatively recently starting to appear within Web sites (for example, at *Salon* and *Utne Lens*). But the largest "space" for online conferences is at Usenet, which calls its conferences "newsgroups" because their news is about (and by) us. About eleven million people participate in Usenet, generating about 1.5 gigabytes of text a day.

The first newsgroups were initiated for the discussion of scientific topics, but scientists also have hobbies and pets, and they created newsgroups to chat about them, too. Today, there are hundreds of thousands of newsgroups, but only ten thousand might be remotely of interest to nonscientists. If an online service or ISP hosts two thousand, that's a very representative range to have available to choose from. You'll find that you have time to participate in only a few at a time, unless you become a Netaholic.

Newsgroups are named in progressions of phrases that go from general to specific, the reverse sequence of domain names (example: lovely.metermaid.rita). With this nomenclature, interest groups can be targeted as generally or specifically as you please.

In newsgroup names, "comp" stands for computers; "news" designates Usenet newsgroups. "Soc.culture" designates nationalities, ethnic groups, and gender groups (for example, males, females, and "motss" for "members of the same sex"). The prefix "misc" stands for miscellaneous and is similar to "alt," meaning alternative. News.announce.newusers has basic information about Usenet. Alt.best.of.the. internet, alt.culture.internet, and alt.internet.guru are groups whose members ask Net questions and post Net news.

Selecting and Participating in a Forum. You'll naturally want to evaluate a forum first to see if you'll visit it frequently. Measure the "signal-to-noise ratio" — the proportion of worthwhile messages to pointless ones. If you visit a number of forums, you'll find one or two that are just your style.

The last thing you want to do is jump in "out of the blue," immediately discussing a topic you happen to see on day one. Instead, it's wise to hang out silently for about two weeks without contributing anything (a practice known as "lurking"). In forum jargon: lurk before you leap.

Forums often provide an invaluable file of answers to Frequently Asked Questions (a "FAQ"). By finding and consulting it, you'll avoid bringing up topics that are too elementary or that have already been discussed. In and of itself, the FAQ will typically provide valuable information about the topic, serving as a handy crash course. It's truly a unique form of literature: a collective text, authored by a group of experts/natives/fans, and revised over time, up to the minute. The FAQ concept acts as a portable community memory, self-service education, and collective courtesy.

Forums hold many possibilities for writers. They break down the traditional eight degrees of separation between us and anyone else in the world. Forums put worlds of experts, field informants, and human interest sources right at our fingertips — sometimes even writing assignments. They further provide an escape hatch from the solitude and "cabin fever" common to our trade. And they're an effective form of publishing, easily reaching tens of thousands of readers, and more.

Some people are put off by the fact that everyone can become their own publisher. The *writers.net* motto here is: THE NET IS AN ALTERNATIVE CHANNEL OF MAINSTREAM CULTURE AND A MAINSTREAM CHANNEL OF ALTERNATIVE CULTURES. Another way of expressing it is that not only are writers readers on the Net, but readers here are writers, too.

Two-way forums allow us to both produce and consume our own texts. (Think of the telephone, originally conceived as a one-way medium: people could pick it up and hear an opera singer or a preacher. Its users discovered they preferred to "create their own content" and it became two-way.) The Internet thus can blur the borderline between producer and consumer (writer/"content provider" and reader/"end user"), and so is said to "disintermediate" by eliminating the intermediary of publisher or broadcast network.

Breaking down the walls between writer and audience, readers can respond directly to our published work so that we can better know for whom we are writing. Some writers use forums for research, particularly among natives "in the field"; others, for advance feedback; still others, for post-publication feedback, for the next time. Authors who think of themselves as professional experts may be uncomfortable here, finding their authority challenged, their viewpoints vacuumed, their voice but part of a larger chorus.

And there are additional writerly benefits from an online community formed by a private, members-only forum. For example, contributors to an anthology can form their own mailing list to discuss work in progress, share ideas about drafts, express other ideas about the topics at hand, and create conversational connections between separate articles.

The forums I am describing are not "real time." For real-time ("live") forums, you might want to visit an Internet Relay Chat (IRC), such as the writers' chats mentioned in Chapter 2. (For more information on IRC, there's a FAQ at <http://www.kei.com/irc.html>.) Some online services, such as AOL, have "live" chat rooms. And the Web is starting to support "live" forums.

Plus, there's real-time videoteleconferencing over the Net: you can buy a tiny hundred-dollar video camera that perches atop your computer, download free CU-SeeMe software, and conduct one-on-one interviews: <http://goliath.wpine.com/cu-seeme> <http://www.noshame.com/cuseeme-friends>.

FTP

While e-mail and forums are wildly popular, the next two applications are more ho-hum. But they're useful, and they teach useful skills in the process, too. FTP (file transfer protocol) is a way of quickly sending, and accessing, large amounts of data (text, multimedia, software). Imagine if you could access a CD-ROM at another computer, either to send it data or to take some off it. That's what FTP is like. FTP is the application to use when sending large files (long texts, or files rich with graphics) to a publisher or to a Web site. FTP is generally faster than other types of data transfers. And if you visit a computer with an archive, it probably uses FTP to make that archive available (like newspaper archives or online book libraries).

Whether one user or 200,000 users grab a copy of a given file at such a computer's archive, the digital "master copy" remains "on the shelf," as it were, available twenty-four hours a day, for as many people who want it. And copies-of-copies-of-copies are all just as good as the "original."

While some FTP sites have text files, other sites have gigabytes of software (such as time managers, bibliography templates, fonts and font managers, or linked haiku display programs and e-mail programs like Eudora). If not free, software offered at these sites is usually *shareware*; if you use it often enough, you're on your honor to make a nominal contribution (typically $15 to 35), which might entitle you to extra features as well as a user's manual and updates. Like giving away a sample chapter to sell a whole book, the motto is: TRY IT BEFORE YOU BUY IT. Besides the inexhaustibility of "digital master copies" and shareware, FTP introduces three more important concepts: "paths" and "URLs," "compression," and "search engines."

FTP sites are arranged in directories with subdirectories, and even subsubdirectories, which contain files (much like DOS, Mac, or Windows folders, which can nest files within many layers of a hierarchy of folders). As an example, the "address" or citation for finding the Canonical Collection of Light Bulb Jokes (circa 1980s) is: <ftp://wiretap.spies.com/Library/Humor/Jokes/litebulb.jok>. The entire "address" is called a Universal Resource Locator (*URL*, pronounced "earl"), and indicates the domain and the *paths* of subdirectories within that domain for getting to the particular file. Here, the URL specifies the FTP server at a company called Spies, which maintains a library in which there's a directory (folder) for humor, in which there's a subdirectory (folder) for jokes, and so forth. In an URL, the text preceded by slash marks indicates the names of folders. The final *suffix* has no slash at the end, and is a file name, not a folder name.

If the final suffix were "lightbulb.sea" or "lightbulb.zip" instead of "lightbulb.txt," that would indicate that it is a file that has been *compressed*. A compressed, or *archive* file is smaller (fewer bytes) and therefore has a shorter transmission time. The ".txt" extension denotes a text file. The suffix ".sea" stands for "self-extracting archive," which is a common compressed-file format for the Mac. If you're using a Mac, clicking on the ".sea" file will expand it to its full size and be readable. The extension ".zip" is the most common Windows-based archive file, which can be "unzipped" (decompressed) with appropriate software. In order to compress and decompress archived files, you need a software program (freeware) such as StuffIt Expander for the Mac, or WinZIP for PCs.

Last but not least, the Net has search tools called "search engines," which help us find needles in haystacks, at our command.

Archie
<http://pubweb.nexor.co.uk/public/archie/servers.html>

Archie ("archive" without the "v") is a search tool for FTP sites. As you'll see when you go to and access the Archie program, to use Archie to locate documents you enter one or more keywords into the designated blank line. Archie then searches a majority of FTP sites for those words and returns with a list of subject lines that contain your words, the names of the sites where they were found, and paths for getting to the files containing them.

Remote Log-on (telnet)

Telnet allows you to log on to any number of remote computers out there in Internetland. It's as if your computer now operated another computer by remote control. Typing a command on your keyboard becomes like typing a command on its keyboard — activating software programs and databases of which FTP is but one of many, many options.

For example, now that computerized catalogs are becoming commonplace in libraries around the world, those libraries' computers have telnet capabilities and can be searched from your computer. (One of the trade terms for these digital catalogs is "Online Publicly Accessible Catalogs," or OPACS).

Remote log-on happens in real time, "live." For example, when you log in to a weather satellite via computer, you see on our screen the exact same picture appearing on the host (or "remote") machine.

With telnet, it's not the amount of people being networked or the amount of data, but rather the number of different computer applications — not just library databases but also:

- Online books, searchable by key words (author, title, subject). For instance, it took three centuries for the writings of Dante to be disseminated across Europe. Today, to add just one scholarly monograph to the body of Dante studies via paper might take six months to two years. But now a joint site (Dartmouth Dante Database) houses a universally accessible, definitive edition of Dante, collating 600 years of line-by-line commentary into one master, searchable nexus. <telnet://lib.dartmouth.edu>, and type "connect dante."

FORGOTTEN PATHS

<telnet://fp.castlefur.com:8888>

This is a multi-user remote login of the variety known as a MUCK, and is a community of particular interest to writers. A MUCK is a text-based, virtual world that tends to be oriented toward socializing (whereas MUSHes tend toward role-playing and MUDs toward combat). MUCKs are usually populated by "furries" (totem animals with human characteristics). Regularly scheduled Forgotten Paths events include Storyteller's Circle (collaborative, improvisational storytelling), a variety of word games, Short Short Story Night, and the occasional Gawd-Awful Pun Night.

- Employment databases, searchable by job description, location, and salary.
- Multi-user environments, where a number of people who log on at the same time can interact in a thematic environment, to play a game, say, or build a city, or tell stories together. Some offer physical environments in which you can perform actions while talking with other people. They have a variety of flavors, the most common being MUD (Multi-User Dimension) and MOO (Multi-Object-Oriented); the acronyms are not self-explanatory, but visiting, experiencing, and interacting at some of these sites will open your eyes. For a list of some multi-user environments, visit <http://www.css.neu.edu/home/fox/moo.www.html>.

Telnet introduces us to two more basic Internet concepts: "links" and "the client-server relationship." A practical example will help illustrate both telnet in actual usage and these related concepts.

Links. In many instances, one domain is linked to another. This allows you to "teleport" between telnet sites. For example, imagine you're at the front door lobby, the entrance, home page, main menu of a telnet site — you might log in from your telnet menu displayed on your screen just as you'd see it if you were there — and in this session you've logged in to the library of Trinity College, Dublin, to do some research on James Joyce. Perhaps you find some material you like there and download it (save it) to your hard disk. Then, the bottom of the Trinity College menu may provide an option enabling you to telnet to other libraries. So you might pop over to the Bibliothèque Française in Paris to do a bit more research. From there, you might hop to the library at Beijing University for a little research on Joyce in Chinese. When you're all through and you log out from Beijing, you'll see the main menu at Paris. Logging out from there, you'll see the Trinity College library menu. Log out, and you're back home.

So, in other words, a site may not just offer resources native to it, but also can act as a launch pad, as it were, to other sites; or "links." And the way it allows us to link from anywhere to anything brings up the basic telecommunication model of the client-server relationship.

The Client-Server Relationship. The client-server relationship is not only the underlying structure of remote login, but also the basis for the Internet itself, and so it's nice, at some point, to understand — not essential, but helpful. It's an easy concept to grasp. When you log on to a distant site, you are the client, and the remote host is the server.

The client asks the server, "Can you do/find/get such-and-such?" and if the server can, it does.

This is basically the relationship you have with your dial-up Internet service providers. A provider has a computer that you interact with, called its server; the server is connected to the Internet twenty-four hours a day. You, the client, send a command asking the server for e-mail, Usenet, FTP, or whatever, and it serves you those items. Simple.

However, sometimes the server becomes a client to another server in order to fulfill your request. Here's how that would work. Let's say that you walk up to the counter of my café and ask if I can make you a cappuccino. You're the client, I'm the server. I'll say "Yes" and make you one. (The client asks, "Can you do/make/get/find such-and-such?" and if the server can, it does.) But instead, you might ask if I can make you an espresso romano. I say "Yes," but I don't have any lemon peel. I duck out the back door, slip over to the corner market, buy a lemon, and dash back, and make your espresso romano. In that case, I (the server) become the client to another server. but you didn't have to know that. All you know is, you got what you asked for.

This client-server relationship enables us to directly link to a site, a subdirectory, or a file. So if you, as client, specify a particular file at a distant domain, including its path (as you discovered with FTP), the server could take you directly to that file without, say, your having to "slip out a back door," log on to another computer, and navigate the menu.

Tip: telnet requires careful, patient watching for commands, passwords, and other instructions, as well as observation to see whether the commands are taking effect or require pressing a Return key.

Information Resources and Resource Guides

With all these resources out there — e-mail forums, FTP, and telnet — how do we make sense of it all? Indeed, as I've noted, the Internet is comparable to the largest library ever known, but it often resembles the library of a war-torn city, with books scattered all over shelves and on the floor, some with pages torn, and some fallen through holes in the floor on down to the basement.

Enter the dynamic resource guides of gopher and the World Wide Web. They are both programs that make accessing remote files much simpler. Essentially, they have to do with what's called "interface" in computerese — how the user interacts with information at screen level. (The Web also shapes the file itself, adding multimedia and interactivity.)

Gopher. The gopher display and retrieval format, though being eclipsed by the Web, is still very useful — both in and of itself, and as a stepping stone to the Web. If you don't have gopher available at your Internet connection, <telnet: consultant.micro.umn.edu>, log in as "gopher," and operate the gopher program running there. You will see that gopher's interface has two aspects: one is *hierarchical*, and the other involves *linking*.

"Hierarchical" simply means that gopher enables you to navigate remote sites using a universal menu interface. A menu is a list — 1, 2, 3, 4 — and each item may, in turn, produce another list until you come to the end of the branches. This is helpful because, otherwise, each remote site can have its own interface: in one system you have to enter an "e" to edit, but in another "e" means Exit. Then, there's *linking*.

You've seen how you can teleport from one telnet site to another. Gopher can do this, too. Moreover, gopher can hop not only from one main menu to another main menu, but from anywhere on one menu to anywhere on another menu. If a library in Romania, for example, lacks files about women writers, it could link to a folder of files about women writers at a site in Cleveland so that you are automatically teleported from Romania to Cleveland, seamlessly. The menu never even states that this is happening (thanks to the client-server relationship).

This possibility led some intrepid Internauts to create innovative and highly useful *subject trees*. That is, they'd created a site that just linked to resources on other sites, all organized with a main menu by topic. (This is the forerunner to Yahoo! and similar sites.) For example, try out the mother of all "subject trees":

Gopher Jewels
<http://lmc.einet.net/GJ/> or <gopher://cwis.usc.edu>,
under "Other Gophers and Information Resources".

Gopher has two other noteworthy features besides its easy navigation interface and its linking ability: *searching* and *bookmarking*.

All sites that run gopher automatically pool together into one big gopherspace. That entirety is searchable (by subject header) with an engine called Veronica (Very Easy Rodent-Oriented Net-wide Index to Computerized Archives). Enter a word or phrase to search for in gopherspace, and Veronica brings back a menu of what it has found. That returned menu is a "hot list," linking directly to what it's found and remaining linked during your search session. So you can go to an item that Veronica has found, browse it, download it if you wish, and then return to the list and surf some more links. If you don't have Veronica, <gopher://veronica.scs.unr.edu> and look under "other gophers."

This linking ability leads us to gopher's ultimate feature: the ability to fix "bookmarks" at places you want to visit again. They're like the bread crumbs that Hansel and Gretel laid on the trail through the forest, except that the crows won't eat these. You can log off, and your bookmarks will still be there for you next time you turn on your computer. What might have been a subsubsubdirectory in the arrangement of files at an obscure site can now be a primary resource on your personal gopher bookmarks menu. (Your personal gopher bookmarks menu might link to reference books, journals, research sources, libraries, newspapers, etc.)

If you think that computers become obsolete quickly, check out the pace of change on the Internet. During 1992, the first year gopher was introduced, gopher traffic increased 600 percent. One year later, gopher was eclipsed by the Web, whose traffic increased by a whopping 341,000 percent and a healthy 2300 percent the year after that.

The World Wide Web.   To help understand the Web, first compare it with gopher. Like gopher, the Web:

- links to other Web sites and Internet sites, as well as to internal documents
- forms a totality with other Web sites
- has search engines (such as HotBot and Alta Vista) that can search within text as well as within subject headings
- has proliferated the equivalent of subject trees in the form of directories, like the world-famous Yahoo! site, also known as "metasites" or "megasource jumpstations"
- supports bookmarks

Two things make the Web different from gopher:

- the interface is interactive multimedia
- it is easy to create your own presence on the Web (a home page, a.k.a. a Web site)

Multimedia is simply any text merged with audio (sound effects, spoken word, music) and/or graphics (such as charts, cartoons, photos, video). Interactivity, here, is achieved via hypertext ("hyper" meaning nonlinear). In the Web, a word, phrase, or picture can be a link to any other word, phrase, or picture. Move your cursor (portable tracking spot) to the link, click (press the mouse or touchpad), and you're taken to the hyperlink (via client-server) — elsewhere within the same file, or to another file at that domain, or anywhere on the Internet.

"Interactive" means that it's "pull" rather than "push": you pull the information in as you choose, rather than be pushed down one preset path, 1-2-3-4.

Whereas gopher has a tree hierarchy, the Web is like a crystal: there's no top nor bottom, and any facet can reflect all the other facets. Thus, it's associative rather than hierarchical.

Unlike gopher, no technical expertise is necessary to create for the Web. Web sites can be created using a simple programming language called HTML (HyperText Markup Language), which is easy as pie. Now anyone can be a publisher or a self-publisher.

The Web is increasingly being used to access the various other Internet functions — e-mail, FTP, newsgroups, telnet — via the interface of Web browsers like Netscape Navigator and Internet Explorer.

For a great megasource of Web information and links, head for <http://www.w3.org/pub/WWW/WWW> — about as close to the center of the Web as you can get.

For More Information About the Net

Science-Fiction Author Bruce Sterling's History of the Net
<http://www.lysator.liu.se/etexts/the_internet.html>

Other Histories
<http://www.isoc.org/guest/zakou/Internet/History/HIT.html>
<ftp://umcc.umich.edu/pub/users/seraphim/doc/nethist8.txt>.

Top Ten Documents about the Internet
<http://www.sips.state.nc.us/docs/top-10.html>

The Library of Congress
<http://lcwels.loc.gov/global/explore.html>

A good jumpstation of online Internet tutorials.

Understanding the Internet
<http://www.screen.com/understand/explore.html>

Another megasource jumpstation.

Internet Web Text
<http://www.december.com/web/text/about.html>

John December's amazingly pliable megasource; highly recommended.

For a practical and interactive spin, an excellent mailing list for asking questions about the Internet ("How can I find/do/get suchandsuch?") is Help-Net, currently numbering about 750 members from around the world. To subscribe, leave the subject line blank, and e-mail the command "Sub Help-Net *YourFirstName YourLastName*" (without the quotation marks) to <listserv@vm.temple.edu>. Save the Welcome message you'll get, and just "lurk" for a week or two at first.

PUTTING THE NET IN PERSPECTIVE

Most newbies, at some point, wonder how to incorporate the Net into their everyday lives, and rightly so.

First, how long does it take to learn your way around? Well, you can learn practical Internet literacy in about a week; it will take a few months to become acclimated to Internet culture. But writers are usually quick to perceive the ideology that accompanies technology (like appreciating how a flashback can affect a narrative). Keep an eye peeled, keep an open mind, and exercise your imaginative, empathetic muscle of creativity.

How often will you use the Internet? Checking your e-mail once a day isn't a bad idea if you're awaiting responses. Otherwise, it's up to you.

How much time you spend in cyberspace is also up to you, of course. But remember: online time is intensified time. Five hours can fly by, seeming like a half hour. And online time can entail additional offline time for reading files you've saved and composing files to send. Ask yourself in advance how much time you'd like to devote to the Net, then see later on how well you're sticking with your intentions. If you're spending much more time than you'd initially estimated, be careful.

The Net can be time-consuming — even downright addictive. (What two fields call their patrons "users"?) For a rule of thumb, the national average for Net use is believed to be an hour or two a day. Practice seeing how long you spend online, and work at formally budgeting your time.

The Three Ss

Because the Internet is colossal, decentralized, multifaceted, and a moving target, you should budget fifteen percent of your online time for the "Three Ss": Searching, Surfing, and Staying Up-to-Date.

- *Searching:* Decentralized, the Net requires that you find and customize resources that are right for you.
- *Surfing:* Vast but interconnected, it requires surfing — point your arm, follow your shoulder, paddle your board across flat water until there are swells, and ride the wave to where it takes you.
- *Staying Up-to-Date:* Always evolving, you have to scout out and stay on top of new additions, new features, new resources.

Two years from now, the Net and your relationship with it will have changed considerably. Pledge that fifteen percent of your online time to these Three Ss, and you'll stay a happy camper.

Getting information from the Internet can be like trying to get a glass of water off an open fire hydrant. You couldn't keep up with all the Internet even if you spent the rest of your life trying; there's more to it than any one person can ever grasp, and more is on the way.

On the other hand, you might zip through all the sites mentioned in this book in just a few weeks and come away convinced that the Internet is not for you. But I suggest that you give it time. Bracket off a section, explore it, lay down some stakes, and spend time cultivating a particular niche. Give yourself a graduation party. Then move on to explore another section when you're ready.

Map Your Orientation

By all means, sample as many of the available resources as suits your fancy. But, just as most people have to decide how much of the *New Yorker*, the *Economist*, or the daily paper they're going to read regularly, so will you have to make similar decisions online. Which brings me to the next-to-last of my tips: map your orientation.

Six months from now, say, after you've found some comfort zones, make a list of the five Net regions (e-mail, forums, FTP, telnet, and resource guides). Below each one write down what you're using it for: general uses and even some specific sites.

("E-mail is how I communicate with my faculty department chair, my editor, my sister, and some information sources; forums are where I do more research, show drafts for feedback, and goof off; I've marked the following Web sites because . . . ") After your first pass at this, go through again and cross-reference some things. For example, under "e-mail" you might want to note that you use e-mail to communicate with individuals you met in a forum rather than take up time of the whole group. And e-mail might be the way you've asked for help regarding a telnet site, by sending a query to an address you saw listed there. Likewise, you might note how certain forums are where you hear about new additions to FTP sites. And so on.

This way, you'll appreciate the right Net tools for the right jobs, and how one Net tool can lead to another.

* * *

Congratulations!

Now you know your Net ABCs and are *writers.net*-Certified Internet Literate.

Well, maybe you've only understood seventy-five percent of this. That's OK. You just have to fill in the remaining twenty-five percent by doing — practicing your Netizenship. My final advice: engage the Internet as an ally with which to create. Here's how:

Keep a file open in your subliminal awareness as you surf the Net; and as you move through life, remember that you'll be seeing combinations and patterns that no one else is seeing, has ever seen, or ever will. Consider these unique patterns. Leverage these situations to create new opportunities or situations for yourself, for your writing, and for others.

And have a bundle of fun!

BIBLIOGRAPHY

General

Gach, Gary. *Pocket Guide to the Internet.* New York: Pocket Books, 1996
   <http://www.pocketbooks.com/netguide.html>

Hafner, Katie and Matthew Lyon. *Where Wizards Stay Up Late: The Origins of the Internet.* New York: Simon & Schuster, 1996.
   A book-length history of the Internet.

Mandel, Thomas and Van der Leun, Gerard. *Rules of the Net: On-line Operating Instructions for Human Beings.* New York: Hyperion, 1996.

Romance

Paludan, Eva. *Romance Writer's Pink Pages.* Rocklin, CA: Prima, 1996.
   Has added a section for the online world.

Children's Literature

Bix, Cynthia. *Kids Do the Web.* Cupertino: Adobe, 1996.

Journalism

Garrison, Bruce. *Computer-Assisted Reporting.* Mahwah, NJ: Lawrence Erlbaum Associates, 1995.

Houston, Brant. *Computer-Assisted Reporting.* New York: St. Martin's Press, 1995.
   Covers the nuts and bolts of spreadsheets and databases, and comes with a disk of exercises.

Internet Newsroom, bimonthly, Dick Maloy Editors' Service, PO Box 737, Glen Echo, MD 20812.

Paul, Nora. *Computer Assisted Research: A Guide to Tapping Online Information*, 3rd edition. St. Petersburg, Florida: Poynter Institute for Media Studies.
> Focuses on researching stories and locating and interviewing sources. Available in looseleaf form alone or in a three-ring binder for quick, convenient updates. Phone 813-821-9494 to order.

Reddick, Randy and Elliot King. *The Online Journalist*, 2nd ed. New York: Harcourt Brace College Publishers, 1996.
> Expanded section about the Web; extensive discussion of how to find documents and people on the Net, and a focused discussion on getting more out of e-mail discussion lists and their archives. Indispensable.

Ullman, John. *Investigative Reporting: Advanced Methods and Techniques*. New York: St. Martin's Press, 1995.

Wendland, Mike. *Wired Journalist: Newsroom Guide to the Internet*, Washington, DC: Radio and Television News Directors Foundation, 1996.
> A plain-speaking, comprehensive beginner's guide; available free to accredited broadcasters. <rtndf@rtndf.org>

Self-Promotion

Kremer, John. *1001 Ways to Market Your Books.* Fairfield, IA: Open Horizons, 1993
> Available from the author: <JohnKremer@aol.com>

O'Keefe, Steve. *Publicity on the Internet.* New York: John Wiley & Sons, 1996.
> Highly recommended. <http://www.olympus.net/okeefe/pubnet>

Web Site Design

Dayton, Linnea. *Photoshop WOW Book*. Berkeley: Peachpit Press, 1996.

Laurel, Brenda, ed. *The Art of Human-Computer Interface Design*. Redding, MA: Addison-Wesley, 1990.

_____ *Computers as Theatre*. Redding, MA: Addison-Wesley, 1993.

Mok, Clement. *Designing Business*. Cupertino: Adobe Press, 1996.
> This is the benchmark for online design books in the nineties. A truly stellar book; serious practioners will find it well worth its $60 pricetag.

Norman, Donald. *Design of Everyday Things.* New York: Doubleday, 1990.

Sano, Darrell, and Kevin Mullet. *Designing Visual Interfaces: Communication Oriented Techniques*. SunSoft Press, 1995.

Siegel, David. *Creating Killer Web Sites.* New York: Hayden, 1996.

Waters, Crystal. *Web Concept & Design.* Indianapolis: New Riders, 1996.

Williams, Robin. *The Non-Designer's Design Book.* Berkeley: Peachpit Press, 1994.

New Writing

Barrett, Edward, Editor. *The Society of Text*. Cambridge: MIT Press, 1989.

Berk, Emily and Joseph Devlin, Editors. *Hypertext/Hypermedia Handbook*. New York: McGraw-Hill, 1991.

Bolter, Jay. The Writing Space: The Computer, Hypertext, & the History of Writing. Mahwah, NJ: Lawrence Erlbaun Associates, 1991.
   A classic in the field.

Borges, Jorge Luis. *Ficciones*. New York: Grove, 1962.

Boyd, Greg. "Hypertext & the Way We Read." *Central Park*, Spring/Fall 1990.

Calvino, Italo. *If on a Winter's Night a Traveler*. New York: Harcourt Brace, 1981.

Coover, Robert. "Hyperfiction: Novels for the Computer." [Cover story] *New York Times Book Review*, August 29, 1993.

Cortázar, Julio. *Hopscotch*. New York: Random House, 1966.

Jennings, Humphrey. *Pandaemonium: The Coming of the Machine as Seen by Contemporary Observers, 1660–1886*. New York: The Free Press, 1995.
   Historical interpretation as hypertext.

Landow, G.P. *Hypertext: The Convergence of Contemporary Critical Theory and Technology*. Baltimore: Johns Hopkins, 1992.

Motte, Warren. *Oulipo [Ouvroir de Literature Potentielle]*. Lincoln: University of Nebraska, 1986.

Perec, Georges. *Life: a User's Manual*. Godine, 1987.

Roubaud, Jacques. *The Great Fire of London*. Elmwood Park, IL: Dalkey Archive, 1991.

Spencer, Michael. *Letters from the Antipodes*. Athens: Ohio University Press, 1981.

Miscellaneous

Hart, Anne. *Cyberscribes.1: The New Journalists*. San Diego: Ellipsys International Publications, 1997.
   "How to write yourself a career in online journalism, netcasting, content authoring, and scriptwriting." <http://www/ellipsys.com> The Web site offers a free, interactive career classifier.

GLOSSARY OF INTERNET TERMS

© 1995 Internet Advertising Southwest
<http://www.iasw.com/glossary.html>

56K line A digital phone-line connection (leased line) capable of carrying 56,000 bits-per-second. At this speed, a megabyte will take about 3 minutes to transfer. This is 4 times as fast as a 14,400bps modem. (See also: bandwidth, T-1)

ADN Advanced Digital Network. Normally refers to a 56K/bps leased-line. (See also: 56k line)

alpha numeric paging Oh boy! Now when you get e-mail you can receive a page! Pretty cool idea though. Allows you to forgo long bouts of busy signals just to check your e-mail. (See also: e-mail)

America Online A popular commercial online service with an easy to use graphical interface. (See also: AOL)

AOL America Online. If you want to sound hip, always refer to America Online as AOL!

Archie A software tool for finding files stored on anonymous FTP sites. One must know the exact file name or a sub-string of it. (See also: FTP, Veronica)

ARPANet Advanced Research Projects Administration Network. The forerunner to the Internet. Developed in the late 1960s and early 1970s by the U.S. Department of Defense as an experiment in wide-area networking that would survive a nuclear war. (See also: Internet (uppercase "I"), network, WAN)

Anonymous FTP See: FTP

ASCII American Standard Code for Information Interchange. This is the accepted world-wide standard for the code numbers used by computers to represent all the upper and lower-case Latin letters, numbers, punctuation, etc. There are

128 standard ASCII codes. Each code can be represented by a seven-digit binary number: 0000000 through 1111111.

backbone   A high-speed line or series of connections that makes a large pathway within a network. The term is relative to the size of network it is serving. A backbone in a small network would probably be much smaller than many non-backbone lines in a large network. (See also: network)

bandwidth   How much information (text, images, video, sound) you can send through a connection. Usually measured in bits-per-second. A full page of English text is about 16,000 bits. A fast modem can move approximately 15,000 bits in one second. Full-motion, full-screen video requires about 10,000,000 bits-per-second, depending on compression. (See also: 56K, bit, modem, T-1)

baud   A method of measuring modem speed that is equal to one signal per second. Rhymes with "Maude." (See also: modem)

BBS   Bulletin Board System. A computerized meeting and announcement system that allows discussions and the exchange of files (uploading and downloading) without users being connected to the computer at the same time. There are thousands (maybe millions?) of BBSs around the world. Most are very small, running on a single computer with one or two phone lines. Some BBSs are very large. The difference between a BBS and a system like America Online is not clearly defined. (See also: America Online, upload, download)

binary   Any file that contains data that is not text. Image files like GIFs and JPEGs, and applications are examples of binary files. (See also: GIF, JPEG)

binhex   Binary Hexadecimal. A way of converting non-text files (non-ASCII) into ASCII. This is necessary because Internet e-mail can only handle ASCII. (See also: ASCII, e-mail)

bit   Binary Digit. The smallest component of computerized data, a single digit number in base-2 (either a 1 or a zero). Bandwidth is generally measured in bits-per-second. (See also: bandwidth, byte, kilobyte, and megabyte)

BITNET   Because It's Time Network. A network of educational sites autonomous of the Internet. E-mail is freely exchanged between BITNET and the Internet. Listservs, the most popular kind of e-mail discussion groups, started on BITNET. BITNET machines are IBM VMS machines, and the network is likely the only international network that is getting smaller. (See also: e-mail, listserv, network)

body   The message area in an e-mail, as opposed to the signature or header. (See also: e-mail, signature, header)

bounce E-mail is just like a check. When it does not go through, it bounces! (See also: e-mail)

bps Bits Per Second. The standard measure of transmission speed through a modem. After 300 bps, its not comparable to baud. (See also: baud, bit, modem)

browser Client software that is used to look at various kinds of Internet resources. The most popular Web browsers are Netscape Navigator, Internet Explorer, and Mosaic. Like most things on the Internet, there are few standards here. What looks good on one browser might look awful on another. There are browsers that will read graphics and some that will read text only. (See also: client, Netscape, Mosaic, URL, World Wide Web)

BTW Online speak for "By the way."

byte A set of bits that represent a single character. Generally there are 8 or 10 bits to a byte, depending on how the measurement is being made. (See also: bit)

Call For Votes What happens after discussing a creation of a new newsgroup. (See also: newsgroup)

CERN The genesis of the World Wide Web. This high energy physics research laboratory is located in Geneva, Switzerland. (See also: World Wide Web)

CFV See: Call for Votes.

connect time The amount of time a computer is connected to an online service. Because many services charge by the amount of time a user is connected, it is important to keep a close eye on the amount of connect time you use.

.cpt Compact Pro's filename extension. (See also: Compact Pro)

CGI Common Gateway Interface. An interface-creation scripting program that allows you to make Web pages on the fly based on information from buttons, checkboxes, text input, etc. The pages can contain pictures of your product, your specific message to the world, secure online order forms, etc. . . . this list goes on and on. Transferable by the Web. (See also: page, World Wide Web)

CIM See CompuServe Information Manager.

CIS CompuServe has all kind of acronyms associated to it. Here is another, it stands for CompuServe Information Service.

Clarinet A commercial form of newsgroups. Clarinet carries information from UPI and other news organizations. Clarinet uses the same transmission routes as Usenet, but providers or users must pay for accessing it. (See also: newsgroups, provider, Usenet.)

client A software program used to contact and download data from a server software program on another computer (like Netscape finding information for you across the globe). Each client program will work with one or more specific kinds of server programs, and each server requires a specific kind of client. (See also: data, Netscape, server)

Compact Pro A widely used compression software program for Macintosh. File names created by it usually have the letters .cpt at at the end of them.

compression An action taken by a software program that reduces the size of a file. Compressed files take up less space on computers and transfer to other computers more quickly.

CompuServe One of the largest and the oldest commercial online service. Contains the most business information of all the major commercial services. CompuServe is sometimes abbreviated CIS. (See also: America Online)

CompuServe Information Manager CompuServe's software; the graphical interface for Mac and Windows. Usually abbreviated CIM.

cross-posted When several newsgroups receive the same posting. This is more efficient than posting thousands of separate copies. Be careful, messages that are cross-posted must be relevant to all the newsgroups they are sent to. If those messages are not relevant, prepare for some major flaming! (See also: newsgroups, post, spam, flame)

CU-SeeMe CU-SeeMe is a free video-conferencing program (under copyright of Cornell University and its collaborators) to anyone with a Macintosh or Windows and a connection to the Internet. With CU-SeeMe, you can videoconference with another site located anywhere in the world, or by use of a reflector, multiple parties/locations are able to participate in a CU-SeeMe conference, each from his or her own desktop computer.

cyberspace Originated by author William Gibson in his 1984 novel *Neuromancer*, the word cyberspace is now used to describe the complete range of information resources available through computer networks. (See also: network)

database A large file that can contain any type of data — usually created and accessed by spreadsheet programs like Excel and Lotus. A database allows quick and easy access to a tremendous amount of information.

domain name The exclusive name that identifies an Internet site. Domain names have two or more parts, separated by dots. The part on the left is the most specific, and the part on the right is the most general. One machine may have more than one domain name, but a given domain name points to only one machine. Generally, all machines on a given network will have the same letters on the right-hand portion of their domain names. For example: "gateway.iasw.com", "mail.iasw.com", or "www.iasw.com". A domain name can exist without being connected to an actual machine. This way a group or business can have an Internet e-mail address without having to establish a real Internet site. In these instances, a real Internet machine must handle their mail on behalf of the listed domain name. The great thing about having your own domain name is that no matter where you go in the world, no matter what provider you choose to use, you will always have the same Internet address! Domain names are going fast! In July of 1995, InterNIC had about 5,000 domain names waiting to be registered. In August of 1995, that number had increased threefold to 15,000! Even if you do not want to establish a Web site for your company right now, it is worth the small investment to get your company a domain name immediately, before your competitor does! (See also: Internet, IP number, NIC, site, World Wide Web)

domain name server   A computer that tracks other machines and their numeric IP addresses. When a computer is referred to by name, a domain name server puts that name into the numeric IP address necessary to make a connection. (See also: domain name, IP addresses)

download   Importing files from one computer by connecting to another.

downstream   Usenet neighbors who get their news from you are considered to be downstream from you. (See also: upstream, Usenet)

e-mail   Electronic mail. Messages, usually text, sent from one person to another through a computer. E-mail can be sent automatically to a large number of addresses (mailing list). (See also: listserv, mail list)

Ethernet   A popular way of networking computers in a LAN. Ethernet will handle about 10,000,000 bits-per-second and can be used with almost any kind of computer. (See also: bandwidth, LAN)

Eudora   A great e-mail program for Windows and Mac users. It is available in shareware. A full commercial version that allows filtering of messages and encryption was recently introduced. (See also: e-mail, Eudora`)

FAQ   Frequently Asked Questions. Documents that list and answer the most common questions on a particular subject. There are thousands of FAQs on subjects as different as personal finances and ostrich breeding . FAQs are generally written by people tired of answering the same question over and over.

FDDI   Fiber Distributed Data Interface. A standard for moving data on optical fiber cables at a rate of approximately 100,000,000 bits-per-second (about twice as fast as T-3, 10 times as fast as Ethernet). (See also: bandwidth, bit, Ethernet, T-1, T-3)

finger   An Internet software program used to locate people on other Internet sites.

Finger can also be used to access non-personal information. The most common use is to determine if a person has an account at a particular Internet site. Many sites do not allow incoming Finger requests. (See also: site)

firewall   A firewall is any one of several methods of protecting one network from another untrusted network. The actual mechanism that makes this happen varies widely, but in principle, the firewall is as a pair of mechanisms: one which exists to block traffic, and the other which exists to let traffic through. Some firewalls place a greater emphasis on blocking traffic, while others emphasize permitting traffic to flow through it. (See also: network)

flame   A nasty e-mail you might receive if you posted a message that has nothing to do with the mail list or newsgroup it was sent to. (See also: mail list, newsgroup)

Freenet   Provides free Internet access, many times through schools and libraries. Freenet also limits what users can access on the Internet.

freeware   Free software! You can get tons of it on the Internet. You can use it and distribute it, but you cannot modify it because the author usually retains the rights to it.

FTP   File Transfer Protocol. A common method of moving files between two Internet sites. FTP is a unique way to log in to another Internet site to retrieve and/or send files. There are many Internet sites that have publicly accessible FTP sites storehousing material that can be downloaded using FTP. Users normally log in using the account name "anonymous." That is why these sites are called anonymous ftp. (See also: log in, download, server, site)

FYI   Online speak for "For Your Information."

gateway   A machine living on two networks that can transfer e-mail between them. Like the Internet and AOL.

gopher   A very popular and successful way of making menus of material available over the Internet. Gopher is a client-and-server style program, which requires that the user have a gopher client software. Although gopher spread rapidly across the globe in only a few years, it is being largely replaced by hypertext, used extensively on the Web . There are still thousands of gopher servers on the Internet, and they will probably remain for a while. (See also: client, gopher, hypertext, server, World Wide Web)

hacker   A person who is a computer guru. Hackers are able to almost Zen through programs that gives a less experienced person major brain cramps. Hackers can be good or bad guys. If a hacker using the Internet broke into your computer and killed your hard drive, that person would be bad. If a hacker came over to rescue your dead hard drive, that person would be good!

header The area in an e-mail message that contains information about who that message came from, when it was sent, etc. (See also: e-mail)

homepage Usually the first part of a Web site. From there you interactively explore that site. (See also: interactive , page, site, World Wide Web)

host Any computer on a network that is a storehouse for services available to other computers on that network. It is common for one host machine to provide numerous services, such as Web and Usenet. (See also: node, network, Usenet, World Wide Web)

HTML HyperText Markup Language. The coding language used to make hypertext documents for use on the Web. HTML resembles old-fashioned typesetting code, where a block of text is surrounded with codes that indicate how it should appear. Also, you can specify in HTML that a block of text, or a word, is "linked" to another file on the Internet. HTML files are designed to be viewed using a Web client program, such as Netscape Navigator, Internet Explorer, or Mosaic. (See also: client, HTTP, hypertext, Netscape, Mosaic, World Wide Web)

HTTP HyperText Transport Protocol. The way hypertext files move across the Internet. Requires a HTTP client program on one end, and an HTTP server program on the other. HTTP is the most important protocol used on the Web. (See also: client, hypertext, protocol, server, World Wide Web)

hypertext Usually any text that contains words or phrases in the document (links) that can be chosen by a reader and which cause another document to be retrieved and displayed. (See also: links)

IMHO In My Humble Opinion. A shorthand added to a remark written in an online forum. IMHO indicates that the writer knows they are expressing a debatable idea, probably on a subject already under discussion. One of many such shorthands in common use online, especially in discussion forums.

interactive An interface that allows for an immediate response to information. The raw marketing power of the Internet is that it allows a customer to view a business's information and immediately interact with it in some way. Maybe a prospective customer wants to view pictures of your product, or download detailed information about it. Or maybe that customer has a question about your product or service — if so, they can quickly and easily e-mail you and you would receive their query in seconds. It doesn't matter if that customer is located across the street, or on the other side of the globe! (See also: e-mail, interface)

Internet (upper case "I") The huge collection of interconnected networks that use the TCP/IP protocols and that evolved from the ARPANet of the late 1960s and early

1970s. The Internet now connects approximately 60,000 independent networks into a giant global internet. (See also: ARPANet, internet (lower case "i"), protocol, TCP/IP)

internet (lower case "i")   Any time two or more networks are connected. (See also: network)

Internet Advertising Southwest   The Web design and marketing group who compiled this fine glossary.

IP number   Every machine on the Internet has a unique IP number — if a machine does not have an IP number, it is not really on the Internet. Most machines also have one or more domain names that are easier for people to remember than the IP numbers. IP numbers are also called a "dotted quad." A unique number consisting of four parts, separated by dots. For example: 182.981.525.9 (See also: domain name, Internet)

IRC   Internet Relay Chat. A huge multi-user live chat area. There are a number major IRC servers around the world linked to each other. Anyone can create a "channel" and anything typed in a given channel is seen by all others on that channel. Private channels are created for multi-person "conference calls," which is perfect for businesses that have clients or employees in different locations. (See also: server)

ISDN   Integrated Services Digital Network. A way to move greater amounts of data over existing regular phone lines. ISDN is slowly becoming available in the United States. ISDN can provide speeds of 64,000 bits-per-second over a regular phone line at nearly the same cost as a normal phone call. (See also: data)

JPEG   Joint Photographics Experts Group. Like a GIF, a compression software program that allows for the exchange of graphics between computers.

kilobyte   A thousand bytes. Exactly 1024 (2^10) bytes. (See also: byte, bit)

LAN   Local Area Network. A computer network limited to the same area, normally in the same building. (See also: network)

leased-line   A phone line that is rented for exclusive 24-hour, seven-days-a-week use from one location to another. The highest speed data connections require a leased line. (See also: 56K, T-1, T-3)

link   The power of HTML. A link allows a viewer to tap on a highlighted item on a Web page and immediately link to whatever the HTML programmer wants them to see. (See also: HTML, page, World Wide Web)

listserv   The most widespread of mail lists. Listservs started on BITNET and are now common on the Internet. (See also: BITNET, e-mail, mail list)

login   Noun: The account name used to access a computer system. Not secret (like a password.) Verb: The act of connecting to a computer system; for example, "Login to the Internet and see how many of your competitors (and maybe, your customers) are already taking advantage of its marketing power." (See also: password)

lurkers   A group of old guys who sneak around at night and peek into your bedroom window! No . . . really, "lurker" is a non-derogatory term for a person who views newsgroup discussions but does not participate in them. (See also: newsgroups)

mail list (or mailing list)   A (usually automated) system that allows an e-mail to be sent to one address; then that message is copied and sent to all of the other subscribers to that particular mail list. Mail lists allow those with different kinds of e-mail access to participate in discussions together. (See also: e-mail)

megabyte (MB)   A million bytes. A thousand kilobytes. (See also: Byte, Bit, Kilobyte)

MCI Mail   An efficient commercial e-mail system by the mega telecommunications guys from MCI. (See also: e-mail)

mirror site   A site that exactly matches the contents of another site. Used to lessen the load, or traffic, on a popular site. (See also: site)

MOO   Mud, Object Oriented. One of many types of multi-user role-playing environments, at this point text-based only. (See also: MUD, MUSE)

modem   Modulator – Demodulator. A device connected to a computer and a phone line. The modem allows the computer to talk to other computers through the phone system.

moderator   The person who reads all the posts to a moderated newsgroup before they are posted to that newsgroup. The big job for this person (99.9% are volunteers) is to decide if a particular message is appropriate to the newsgroup they are moderating. (See also: newsgroups, post)

monospaced fonts   Fonts whose characters all have the same width. Monaco and Courier are examples of two monospaced fonts. Monospaced fonts are usually used when reading text on the Internet. Also known as "non-proportional fonts." (See also: proportional fonts)

Mosaic   The first Web browser available for the Macintosh, Windows, and UNIX with the same interface. Mosaic popularized the Web to the non-technical users of the Internet. The source-code to Mosaic has been licensed by several companies, and there are several software programs as good or better than Mosaic — most notably Netscape Navigator and Internet Explorer. (See also: browser, client, Netscape Navigator, UNIX, World Wide Web)

MUD   Multi-User Dungeon or Dimension. A (usually text-based) multi-user simulation setting. Some are just for fun; others are used for serious software development, or education purposes. Users can create things that remain after they leave. Other users can interact with these things in their creator's absence, allowing a "world" to be built gradually and collectively. (See also: MOO, MUSE)

MUSE   One kind of MUD — usually with little or no violence. (See also: MUD, MOO)

news   Same as Usenet news. (See also: Usenet)

newsgroups   The name of discussion groups on Usenet. (See also: Usenet)

newsreader   A software program used to read newsgroups and to follow and delete threads. (See also: newsgroups, thread)

network   When two or more computers are connected and sharing resources. Connect two or more networks together and you have an internet (lowercase "i"). (See also: Internet, internet)

NIC   Network Information Center. Any office that handles information for a network. The most famous of these on the Internet is the InterNIC, where new domain names are registered. (See also: domain names, network)

nickname   An easy way to remember an e-mail address. Also referred to as an alias. (See also: alias, e-mail)

node   A single computer connected to a network .(See also: network, Internet, internet)

offline   Actions taken with a computer when it not connected to another computer.

online   Actions taken with a computer when it is connected to one or more computers.

packet switching   The technique used to move data around on the Internet . In packet switching, all the data coming from a computer is broken up into chunks; each chunk has the address of where it came from and where it is going. This allows chunks of data from many different sources to share the same lines, and to be sorted and directed to different routes by special machines along the way. This allows many people to use the same lines at the same time.

page   One section of a Web site. A page can contain one word or a million words. Pages can also include sounds, videos, animations, etc. (See also: World Wide Web, HTML)

password   A (usually secret) code used to gain access to a locked system. Good passwords contain letters and non-letters and are not simple combinations such as Bill2 . A good password might be: good9-7 (See also: login)

PGP Pretty Good Privacy. A way of encrypting information sent through the Internet to secure privacy. Definitely better than no security at all, but a competent computer hacker could get through PGP. (See also: hacker)

POP Post Office Protocol. A protocol for storing and receiving e-mail. Eudora uses POP. (See also: e-mail, Eudora, protocol)

port 1. A place where information goes into or out of a computer, or both. For example, the "serial port" on a home computer is where a printer would be connected. 2. On the Internet, "port" often refers to a number that is part of a URL, appearing after a colon (:) right after the domain name. 3. "Port" also refers to translating a piece of software to bring it from one type of computer system to another; for example, to translate a Macintosh program so that it will run on a Windows machine. (See also: domain name, server, URL)

post To send a message to a newsgroup or a mailing list. (See also: mailing list, newsgroup)

PPP Point-to-Point Protocol. A protocol like SLIP that allows a Mac to mimic a full Internet machine using only a modem and a regular phone line.(See also: modem, protocol, SLIP)

Prodigy A popular commercial online service.

proportional font A font whose characters have different sizes. Where an "X" is wider than an "l". Many times, a proportionally spaced font does not work well when reading text on the Internet. (See also: monospaced font)

protocol One language computers use to talk to each other.

public access provider A group that provides Internet access, often for a fee. Both individuals and organizations use public access providers. Also called simply "provider."

public domain Free (software) to be used, distributed or modified. (See also: freeware, shareware)

QuickTime An Apple software program used for QuickTime movies. These files can contain text, sound, animation, and video but are often too large to be used on the Internet. For instance, depending on the speed of your modem and the speed of your Internet connection, it could take up to 20 minutes to download a one-minute-long QuickTime movie from the Internet. (See also: connection, download, modem)

quoting Including a part of an original message in the reply to that message. The ">" ("greater than" symbol, in mathematical terms) is placed to the left of a quote in a reply. You can refresh the memory of the person who wrote the original message by quoting that message in your reply to it. This is great because an average Internet user can send and receive hundreds of e-mail messages over a short period of time. (See also: e-mail, site, World Wide Web)

RealAudio   A commercial software program that plays Internet audio on demand, without waiting for long file transfers. For instance, you can listen to National Public Radio's entire broadcast of "All Things Considered" and the "Morning Edition" via the Internet. (These and other audio news programs are updated daily. You can also tailor news broadcasts to your specific needs using RealAudio!

RFC   Request For Comments. The result and the process for creating a standard on the Internet. New standards are proposed and published on the Internet, as a Request For Comments. The Internet Engineering Task Force is a opinion-building body that enables discussion, in which eventually a new standard is established.

router   A special-purpose computer (or software package) that facilitates the connection between two or more networks. Routers look at the destination addresses of the packets passing through them and decide which route to send them on. (See also: network, packet switching)

self-extracting archive   A compressed file that needs no special software to decompress it. You can decompress it just by clicking on it. (See also: compression)

search engines   A software program that allows a user to search databases by entering-in keywords. A search engine or vehicle quickly finds any item pertaining to those keywords. This powerful tool is like the Yellow Pages to the Internet. For instance, if you were traveling to another city and wanted to find interesting places to visit, you might enter the key words, "entertainment" and "the name of the city your are visiting." The search engine might return several possibilities that you had no idea existed. To be successful marketing your product or service on the Internet, make sure your provider or Web page creator lists you on as many search engines as possible. (See also: databases)

server   A computer or software package that provides a particular kind of service to client software running on other computers. The term "server" can pertain to a particular piece of software, such as a Web server, or to the machine on which the software is running. One server machine might have several different server software programs running on it, giving many different services to clients on that network. (See also: client, network, World Wide Web)

shareware   Software that can be downloaded for free. The creators of shareware sometimes provide an abbreviated form of the actual program (called a demo), or they allow use of a full version of that program for a short period of time before they require you to register it and pay for it. Your payment is usually sent directly to the shareware author.

signature   A space that automatically includes several lines of text on an e-mail or newsgroup post. Signatures are easily created by the user and can include e-mail addresses, snail mail addresses, and phone numbers. Often, signatures will include graphics created in ASCII. A signature is a good area to include the name of your business (and its Internet address) so that when you post to a newsgroup you can unobtrusively advertise your product or service to whoever reads your message. If you do this, just make sure that your post pertains to the specific subject matter that the group discusses. Otherwise you will probably get flamed, or worse . . . spammed! (See also: ASCII, e-mail, flame, newsgroup, snail mail, spam)

.sit   The extension used for files created by Stuffit compression software. (See also: Stuffit)

site   The spatial location of any Internet resource (like a Web site, a gopher site, etc.) (See also: gopher, World Wide Web)

SLIP   Serial Line Internet Protocol. A standard for using a standard telephone line (a "serial line") and a modem to make any computer a real Internet site. SLIP is slowly being replaced by PPP. (See also: Internet, modem, PPP)

SMDS   Switched Multimegabit Data Service. A new standard for extremely high-speed data transfer. (See also: data)

smileys   Computer speak for describing tone, body language, or feelings. Smileys are simple graphical representations (usually of faces) created from keyboard characters like colons, hyphens, parentheses, etc. For example: :-)   a smile, or :-(a frown

snail mail   Traditional methods of sending information. It could take a few seconds to send an e-mail across the globe. The same message sent traditionally (for example, by postal service) could take a week or longer. (See also: e-mail)

Stuffit   A group of software programs developed by Raymond Lau and now published by Aladdin Systems. Stuffit is available in a full commercial package(Stuffit Deluxe) and in shareware form (Stuffit Lite).

systems administrator   Treat this person with the same respect you would show a police officer. The system administrator is responsible for running your host computer. This person decides whether your connection to the Internet is dead or alive! Also known as "network administrator" or simply "administrator."

T-1   A leased-line connection carrying data at up to 1,544,000 bits-per-second. At maximum capacity, a T-1 line could move a megabyte in less than 10 seconds. Although still not fast enough for full-screen, full-motion video (for which you need at least 10,000,000 bits-per-second), T-1 is the fastest speed commonly used to connect networks to the Internet. (See also: 56K, bandwidth, bit, byte, Ethernet, T-3)

T-3 A leased-line connection that can carry data at 45,000,000 bits-per-second. This is four and a half times more than is needed to do full-screen, full-motion video. (See also: 56K, bandwidth, bit, byte, Ethernet, T-1)

TCP Transmission Control Protocol.

TCP/IP Transmission Control Protocol/Internet Protocol. The group of protocols that defines the Internet. Originally for the UNIX operating system, TCP/IP software is now usable for every major kind of computer operating system. To be truly on the Internet, a computer must have TCP/IP software. (See also: IP number, Internet, protocol, UNIX)

telnet The program and command used to login from one Internet site to another. The telnet command/program points to the login prompt of another host. (See also: login, site)

terminal A device that sends commands to another computer. At a minimum, this generally means a keyboard and a display screen and some simple circuitry. Usually terminal software in a personal computer — the software pretends to be ("emulates") a physical terminal and sends typed commands to a computer somewhere else.

terminal server A special-purpose computer that connects many modems on one side, and connects to a LAN or host machine on the other side. The terminal server answers calls and passes the connections on to the appropriate node. Most terminal servers provide PPP or SLIP services if connected to the Internet. (See also: LAN, modem, host, node, PPP, SLIP)

text A file that contains only the ASCII characters. FTP, for example, would know that the file you will be transferring contains only text, if you activate this FTP option by using the ASCII command. (See also: ASCII, file, FTP, transfer)

thread A group of messages on a newsgroup that relate to each other. Depending on the newsreader, these threads can be read or deleted. (See also: newsgroup, newsreader)

timeout In a SLIP connection, after a certain amount of idle time, depending on the software being used, the connection will disconnect. Some software programs allow you to adjust the amount of idle time before disconnect. (See also: SLIP)

Turbogopher A fast, rodent-like software program that allows you to browse through gopherspace. Born at the University of Minnesota. (See also: gopher)

.txt The file extension usually used for a a text-only file (ASCII) that you can read. (See also: ASCII)

UNIX A computer operating system (the basic software running on a computer, underneath things like databases and word processors). UNIX is designed to be used by many people at once (it is "multi-user") and has TCP/IP built-in. Unix is the most prevalent operating system for servers on the Internet. (See also: TCP/IP)

upload   To transfer a file to another computer.

upstream   Senders of your Usenet news are "upstream" of your computer. Recipients of your news are "downstream" from you. (See also: downstream, Usenet)

URL   Uniform Resource Locator. The standard method of address of any Internet resource that is part of the Web. A URL looks like this: http://www.iasw.com or telnet://indirect.com or news:new.newusers.questions The most common way to use a URL is to enter it into a Web browser program, such as Netscape Navigator, Internet Explorer, or Mosaic. (See also: browser, Mosaic, Netscape, World Wide Web)

Usenet   A world-wide network of discussion groups, with comments exchanged among hundreds of thousands of computers. Probably only half of all Usenet groups are on the Internet. Usenet is completely decentralized, with over 10,000 discussion areas, called "newsgroups." (See also: newsgroup)

userid   User IDentification. The name you use when you log on to another computer (Also called "username.")

username   See: userid. They are the same thing.

.uu   A file extension used by uuencode. (See also: .uud., uudecode, .uue, uuencode)

.uud   Usually used as a file extension for files used by UUencode. (See also: UUencode)

UUdecode   A conversion software program used for decoding UUencoded files. UUdecode turns ASCII files back into binary files. (See also: ASCII, binary)

.uue   A file extension name used by UUencode.

UUencode   This Unix program turns binary files into ASCII files that can be sent as e-mail or as posts to newsgroups. (See also: ASCII, binary, e-mail, post, newsgroup, UNIX)

Veronica   Very Easy Rodent-Oriented Net-wide Index to Computerized Archives. Developed at the University of Nevada, Veronica is a continuously updated database of the names of almost every menu item on thousands of gopher servers. The Veronica database can be searched from almost all major gopher menus. (See also: database, gopher)

WAIS   Wide Area Information Servers. A commercial software program that indexes huge quantities of information. WAIS then makes those indices searchable across networks like the Internet. A crucial feature of WAIS is that the search results are ranked ("scored") according to how relevant the "hits" are, and subsequent searches can find "more information like that last search" and thus refine the search process.

WAN   Wide Area Network. Any network or internet that includes an area larger than a single building or campus. (See also: Internet, internet, LAN, network)

worm   A program sent through a network that infiltrates hard drives, reduplicates itself over and over until it fills up the drive, uses all memory, and crashes your computer. A worm can take down an entire network.

World Wide Web (WWW)   The macrocosm of hypertext servers (HTTP servers) which allow text, graphics, sound files, etc., to be integrated. (See also: browsers, Internet, FTP, gopher, HTTP, telnet, URL, WAIS)

XMODEM   A file transfer protocol. (See also: protocol)

YMODEM   A file transfer protocol. (See also: protocol)

.zip   Filename extension used by files compressed in the PKZIP format.

ZMODEM   The most popular file transfer protocol. It is also the fastest. (See also: protocol)

INDEX

A
Aaronson, Larry, 97–98
Above Ground Press, 71
The Academy of American Poets, 64, 71–72
Adam's Poetry Page, 67
Addison-Wesley, 222
Adobe
Acrobat, 261
    as sponsor, 110
Advanced Usage, 263
Adventures of Sword & Sorcery, 34
Advertisers, 110
Adv-HTML, 263
Against All Odds Productions, 144–145
Agents, 179–182
    intelligent agents, 180–181
    offline agents, 179–180
"Agents of Alienation," 182
Agnieszka's Dowry, 71
Akropolis Magazine, 92
Albany Poetry Workshop, 66
Alex, 241
AliWeb, 177
Alix of Dreams, 231
Alliance for Computers and Writing, 11
All-in-One, 186
AlphaPoint, 268
Alta Vista, 164, 172, 174
Alt.binaries.zines, 210
Alt.law-enforcement, 63
Alt.zines, 210
Amazon.com, 233–234
The American Amateur Press Association (AAPA), 145
American Book Producers Association, 303
The American Book Review, 240

American Bookseller's Association (ABA), 223
    BookWeb, 243
    CD–ROMs at convention, 276–277
American Cybercast, 102
American Film Institute, 88–89
American News Service (ANS), 134
American Reporter, 111, 121–123
    book reviews, 240
    distributing text on, 250
The American Society of Journalists and Authors (ASJA), 301, 303
America Online (AOL), 22–23, 314
    censorship, 295
    Digital City, 144
    e-zines, 210
    for journalists, 130
    Mercury Center, 119
    as subscription model, 112
Amos, Tori, 17
Andrian Kreye, 146
The Angel, 181
Angelfire, 268
Anime Crash, 279
Ansible, 34, 203
Antiquarian Booksellers Association of America, 236
Anuff, Joey, 201
A1 Index of over 200 Free Web Page Promotion Sites, 255
AP Breaking National News, 132
Apel, Warren S., 68
AP Online, 132
The Arachnoid Writer's Alliance, 269
Archie, 325
Archieplex, 166
The Armchair Detective, 57

ArrowWeb, 269
ArtCommotion, 204
ASCAP (American Society of Composers, authors and Publishers), 301
ASCII, information on, 312–313
Ashbery, John, 278
Asher, Levi, 207
Asian Poets' Page, 67
Ask An Expert, 161
Associated Press (AP), 133
Association of Authors' Representatives (AAR), 303
Association of Progressive Communicators (APC), 142–143
The Association of Research Libraries, 210
"As We May Think," 288–289
Athene, 206
Atlantic on the Web, 191, 192–194
　book reviews, 240
AT&T
　800 telephone numbers, 159
　Hometown Network, 144
Auer, Martin, 280
Auletta, Ken, 194
Austen, Jane, 239, 283
Authorlink!, 22
Authors Guild, 303
Authors' home pages
　for booklovers, 239
　children's writers, 80
　fantasy writers, 39–40
　mystery writers, 59
　for poets, 71–73
　resources, 264–269
　romance writers, 50
　science fiction writers, 39–40
　screenwriters, 88
　for technical writers, 97–98
Authors in the New Information Age, 301
The Authors Registry, 303–304
Author's Showcase, 249
Autonomy Web Researcher and Autonomy Press Agent, 181–182
Avec, 67
Ayckbourn, Alan, 286

B

Baden, Steven L., 148
Baen Books, 36
Baker, Nicholson, 297
Balan, Bruce, 80
Bandwidth, 313–314
Banned Books Bookmarks, 305
Banned Books Online, 305
Bantam/Dell/Doubleday, Isn't It Romantic, 48
Banyan Tree Friends, 79
Barbraud, Pascal, 231

Bare Bones guide to HTML, 262
Barker, Mike, 17
Barnes & Noble, 237
Bartlett's Familiar Quotation, 2, 182
Barton, Howard, 179
Basement Full of Books, 35
Baughen, Barbara, 253
BBC film resources, 89
BBEdit, 256
Beat Page, 153
Beaucoup, 186
Beginner's Guide to HTML, 262
Being Digital (Negroponte), 223–225
Bengali poetry, 72
Benson, David, 280
Bentson, Randolph, 98
Berchtold, Catherine, 17
Berger, Guy, 151
Berkana Productions, 262
Bernstein, Mark, 288
Berry, Michael, 267
The Best News on the Net, 153
Best-Quality Audio Web Poems (BAWP), 68
Bezos, Jeff, 233
Biblio, 236
Bibliobytes, 234
Bibliography, 335–337
Biblomania, 230
Big Ten Plus NewsNet, 162
The Biz, 84
Blackwells, 236
Bless this Food (Butash), 223
Blister, 238
The Blue Penny Quarterly, 200
Bochman, Alon, 288
bOING bOING, 204
Boller, Gregory, 141
Bonfire of the Liberties, 305
Book Links on the Internet, 244
Booklist, 240
Book Lovers: Fine Books and Literature, 244
Bookmarks, 167
BookPage, 240
Books, 215–244. *See also* Publishers
　bound books, online bookstores for, 233–237
　for children's writers, 78–79
　digitized books, 225–231
　discussion lists, 238
　original online-only books, 230–233
　paperless books, 225–233
　resources for book lovers, 237–240
　reviews, 239–240
Books AtoZ, 271
Bookserve, 236
Book Stacks Rants-N-Rave, 240
BookStacks Unlimited, 234–235

Fiction Writers' Workshop, 7
Bookstores
   bound books, online bookstores for, 233–237
   for fantasy writers, 35–36
   genre bookstores, 235–237
   local bookstores, 237
   megasource jumpstations, 243–244
   for mystery writers, 58
   for science fiction writers, 35–36
   for technical writers, 97
BookZen, 269
"Boolean Logic Defined," 184
Boolean operators in search, 173
Borders, 237
Borders as sponsor, 110
Boston Book Review, 240
Boston Globe, AP Breaking National News, 132
Boulter, Jeffrey, 138
Bound books, online bookstores for, 233–237
Boutell, Thomas, 201
Bowling Green State University OWL (Writime), 3
Brackett, Charles, 83
Brady, (inits?), 219
BradyGAMES, 217
Bragg, Katt, 49
Brainstorms, 267–268
Branding, 109
Branwyn, Gareth, 204
Breaking the News: How the Media Undermine American Democracy (Fallows), 139
Bricolage, 27
British Poetry, 1780–1910, 72
Brock Meeks, 147–148
Broken Pencil, 210
Bruce Balan, 80
Brumback, Charles, 153
Bryce, James, 98
Buckingham, D., 101
Bulletin Board Systems (BBSs), 311
Burke, Fauzia, 253
Burt, Andrew, 33
Bush, Vannevar, 288–289
Business Wire, 133
Butash, Adrian, 223
°*Bylines*° magazine, 112–113
Byron Poetry Server, 66

C

Cadigan, Pat, 39
Caffeine Destiny, 104
Cafi Utne, 280–282
Cain, James M., 55
Callie's WritePage, 27
Calvin, William H., 267
Cameron, Jim, 129–130

The Canadian Broadcasting Company's Journalists' & Broadcasters' Resources, 130–131
The CAR/CARR Links, 153
Card, Orson Scott, 39
CareerPath, 150
Carnegie, Dale, 219
Carnegie Mellon University
The English Server at Carnegie Mellon University, 72, 229–230
   Sudden, 70
Carter, Chris, 41
The Case, 59
Caser Star-Tribune, 122–123
Casey, Patrick, 131
Casey's Reverse Dictionary, 184
Cassingham, Randy, 251, 252
Castle Phrodesia, 51
CataList, 164
Catbird Press, 225
CD-ROM, 275
   as new market for writers, 276–277
Celebrity Lounge at Mr. Showbiz, 84
Censorship, 294–296
   anti-censorship resources, 305–306
   legal issues, 295–296
The Center for Democracy and Technology, 305
Center for Living Democracy, 134
Center for Talented Youth at Johns Hopkins University, 79
Central processing unit (CPU), 313
Central Source, 159
Century — The Magazine of Speculative Fiction for Adventurous Readers, 34
Chandler, Raymond, 55
Chapped Lips, 71
Charles Brumback home page, 153
Charles Deemer home page, 286
Charoy, François, 211
Château de Mort (Deemer), 286–287
Cheap Truth, 34
Cheat Sheet, 174
CheckFree, 110
Chidaya, Farai, 146
The Children's Book Counsel, 78
Children's Book Insider magazine, 81
Children's Literature Newsletter, 240
Children's Literature Web Guide, 81
Children's Publishers & Booksellers on the Net, 78
Children's Theatre Resource, 81
Children's writers, 77–82
   forums, 78
   for kids by kids, 79–80
   magazines for, 78–79
   megasource jumpstations, 81–82
   personalized literature for, 78
The Children's Writing Mailing List, 78

The Children's Writing Resource Center, 81
The Choice (Woodward), 218–219
Christian Science Monitor, 111, 132
Churchyard, Henry, 283
Cinema screenwriters. *See* Screenwriters
CineMedia, 88–89
City of Bits, 232
CitySearch, 144
Civic journalism, 139
Clancy, Tom, 24
ClariNet, 132–133
Classic Mystery Authors, 59
Classics, 93
The Clearinghouse for Subject-Oriented Internet Resource Guides, 186
The Clearinghouse Guide to Theatre Resources on the Net, 91
Clickshare Corporation, 111
Clinton, Bill, 296
Close, Sandy, 134
ClueLass, 61
C|Net, 202
C|NET-TV, 184
Cody's Books, 97
Cohen, Jodi, 124
Cohen, Sean, 289
Colgate University, 12
Collaboration, 274–281
 list of experiments in, 279–281
 literary collaboration, 278–281
 megasource jumpstations for, 289
 multimedia collaboration, 274–278
Collaborative Software Resource Clearinghouse, 289
Collinge, Pat, 52
"The Color of Television," 289
Columbus Dispatch, 206
The Columns, 146
Comet.Net, 28
Commerce Business Daily, 133
Commercial online services, 22–25
Common Movie Clichés, 86
Commonplace Book, 243
Communet, 125
Communications Decency Act, 296, 299
CompuServe, 23–24, 314
 censorship, 295
 e-zines, 210
 for journalists, 129–130
 Romance Reviews (CRR), 49
 Screenwriting section, 84
The Computer-Assisted Research & Reporting List (CARR-L), 125
Computer Book Publishing, 96
Computer Literacy Books, 97
Computer Professionals for Social Responsibility, 305

Comstock, Anthony, 295
Comstock Law of 1873, 295–296
Conferences, 321
Connectivity, 314
Conroy, Gary, 99
Contracts Watch, 303
The Convention Connection, 56
Cook Robin, 24
Coover, Robert, 290
CopNet, 62
Copyediting, 96
Copyediting-L, 126
Copyright Clearance Center, 307
Copyrights, 297–304
 cyberfables, 302
 legal issues, 298–299
 professional organizations, 299–304
 resources, 306–307
The Copyright Web Site, 307
Cornell University Romance Writer's Mailing List (RW-L), 46
Council on Library Resources, 306
Coursepacks, 246
Cowles Business Media, 198
Craft of the Screenwriter (Brady), 219
Crash, 213
Creating a Successful Web Page, 263
Creating HTML in 11 Easy Stages, 262
Creative Freelancers Online, 20
Credit cards online, 110
Crime Scene Evidence File, 103
Critiques. *See* Forums
Critters, 33
CROW (Capsule Reviews of Original Work), 85
Crumlish, Christian, 205
CTheory, 204–205
The Curmudgeon's Stylebook, 99
CyberCash/CyberCoin system, 110
CyberDewey, 188
Cyberdock, 223, 225
CyberLope, 111
CyberMad, 88
Cyber Park, 38
Cybersoaps. *See* Serials on Web
The Cyberspace Sonnets, 285
CyberTeddy-Online, 164
CyberTeens, 79
CyberWire Dispatch, 147

D

Dahlby, Mark, 8–10
Dale Furutani home page, 266
Daniel LaLiberté World Wide Web Collaboration Projects, 289
Daniels, Kate, 34
Dan Pynter's Book Publishing Resources, 271

"Dark Alliance," 119–121
David Rand home page, 98
The David Siegel Project, 264
Davis, Glenn, 179
Dawn'I, 126
De Abreu, Carlos, 85
Dead Write, 57
December, John, 100, 332
Deemer, Charles, 10–11, 94, 280, 285, 286–288
Deeper: My Two-Year Odyssey in Cyberspace (Seabrook), 158
Deja News, 159
Delirium, 230
Del Rey books, 36
Deltapoint, 256
Densmore, Bill, 111–112
Denton, William, 62
Deputy Kills Man With Hammer (Cassingham), 252
Derie, Kate, 61, 62
Derk, James, 155
Desktop publishing, 249
De Sola Pool, Ithiel, 293
DeVry's Online Writing Support Center, 9
Diana Slattery home page, 285
Dickens, Charles, 101
Digerati, 269–270
DigiBox, 111
DigiCash, 110
DigiCoin, 111
Digital Edge, 152
Digital Guru, 97
Digital Ink, 123
Digitized books, 225–231
    megasource jumpstations for, 241–242
Discovery Channel Net, 186
Distance learning, 8–9
    megasource jumpstations, 12
    teaching writing through, 11
Distance Learning Directory, 12
Distance Learning Laboratory, 12
Distance Learning Resource Network, 12
Distribution online, 249
Documents in the News, 131
Dogwood Blossoms, 74
The Dominion, 40
Dom's Domain: Media Sites and Strategies, 124
Doom, 37
Dornfest, Asha, 252
DorothyL, 56
Dr. Klopfenstein's Help for HTML Tools, 263
The Dragon Project, 38–39
The Dramatic Exchange, 92
Dramatists Guild, 303
Drew, Ivan, 270
Drew's Scripts-O-Rama, 87
Drucker, Peter, 157

Druk, Vladimir, 207
Dueling Modems, 34
Dungeons and Dragons, 38
Durant, Ariel, 219
Durant, Will, 219
Dyson, Esther, 107, 113, 232, 300–301

E

Earthlink, 314
Eastgate Systems, 290
East Village, 103
Ecola's Newsstand, 149, 211
E-credit, 110
Editorial Freelancers Association, 303
Editorial Inc. (EI), 222
Editor & Publisher, 149, 151
    Interactive, 124
Educational options, 1–3
    fee-based services, 8–9
Edupage, 126
"The Effect of the Net on the Professional News Media: Will This Kill That?," 152
Ego Interactive, 136–137
ELAC (East Los Angeles College)
    Play and Monologue Collection, 93
    Theatre Arts, 93
The Electric Library, 182, 227
Electric Newsstand, 1098
Electric Pencil, 211
Electronic Book Aisle, 235
The Electronic Frontier Foundation, 305
Electronic Poetry Center (EPC), 74
The Electronic Text Center, 241
Elements of Style, 2
E-mail, 316, 317–320
    addresses, 159–161, 318
    collaboration through, 281
    forums, 320–321
    self-publishing via, 250–251
    sources, 160–161
    universal features of, 319–320
E-Mail Discussion Groups, 164
The E-Mail Zines List, 211
Emerson College's "New Media" students' page, 153
Encarta encyclopedia, 182
Encyberpedia, 183
Encyclopedia Britannica, 2, 183
Encyclopedia Mythica, 183
The English Server at Carnegie Mellon University, 72, 229–230
Enterzone, 205
Enzian Theater's Filmmaker's Resources, 89
Eon 4, 104
The Eris Project, 228
Erlindson, Mike, 124
eSCENE, 205

Esch, Jim, 209
ESPN's *SportsZone*, 109
Essays on the Craft of Dramatic Writing, 86
The Essential World-Wide Web Site Design Guide 1.1, 264
Etext, 211
Eureka!, 186
European Center for Nuclear Research (CERN), 171
Evans, Paul Peter, 137
Excite, 170
Exclusive rights limitations, 297
ExperNet, 162
The Exploratorium, 40–41
E-zines, 210–213
The E-Zines Database, 212

F

FacsNet, 133–134
Fact Sheet Five, 212
- Electric, 212
Fair use limitations, 297
Fallows, James, 139, 261
Fallows Central, 139
The Family Jewels, 103
Fantasy writers, 31–43
   authors' home pages, 39–40
   bookstores, 35–36
   forums, 32–34
   games, 37–39
   magazines and newsletters, 34–35
   megasource jumpstations for, 42–43
   publishers, 36–37
Farai Chidaya, 146
Fat City News, 141
Fattal Collins, 102
Fawn Fitter home page, 266
Federal Anti-Obscenity Act, 295–296
Fee-based learning services, 8–9
Feed, 200
Fees, 109–110
Fenn, Evonne, 210
Ferndale, 103
Fiction Addiction, 240
The Fiction Writers' Workshop, 7
Fillmore, Laura, 221–225
Finding an e-Mail Address, 159
Finding Data on the Internet, 153
FindLaw Internet Legal Resources, 306
Fine Press Bookshop Online, 71
Firefly, 180
First Virtual Holdings, 110
Fischer, Elizabeth, 208
Fitter, Fawn, 266
Florida Times-Union, 151
FOI-L, 126
Ford, Henry, 15

Foreign Affairs, 143
Foreign-language repositories, 242
Forums
   for book proposals, 240
   for children's writers, 78
   for fantasy writers, 32–34
   FAQs, 165–166
   finding forums, 163
   introduction to, 320–324
   for journalists, 125–129
   for mystery writers, 56–57
   participating in, 322–324
   for playwrights, 91–92
   for poets, 66–67
   research via, 163–166
   for romance writers, 45–47
   for science fiction writers, 32–34
   for screenwriters, 84
   selecting a forum, 322–324
   for technical writers, 95–96
   writers forums, 16–22
Foster, Alan Dean, 37
Fought, Barbara, 126
The Foundation for American Communications (FACS), 133–134
Four-One-One White Page Directory, 159
Fowler, John, 68
François Charoy's home page, 211
Franklin, Jon, 112, 128
Frauenfelder, Mark, 204
Free cuisinart, 205
Freedom Forum, 148
Free Expression Network, 306
Free Internet Encyclopedia, 182, 183
The Free Internet Encyclopedia, 212
Freelance Online, 151
Freelancers
FAQs on, 21
   mailing list, 20
Free Web pages, 268–269
Friends of Mystery Newsletter, 57
From the Heart, 51
FrontPage, 256
FTP, 166, 324–325
Archie, 325
   paperless books on FTP site, 226
Fulkerson, Robert, 207
Furutani, Dale, 266
Fusion, NetObjects, 145, 256
Future Fantasy Bookstore, 235
Fuzzy logic, 181

G

Gach, Gary, 268
Gaia's Lover, 232
Galaxy, 170

Games
    fantasy games, 37–39
    science fiction games, 37–39
Games Domain, 38
Garland, Joseph E., 335
Gary Conroy's Technical Writing Resources, 99
Gary Gach home page, 268
Gary Kline home page, 266
Gaslight, 56
Gatti, Rosanna Madrid, 266
Gay Daze, 104
Geddes, Eric James, 233
Geek Girl, 205
Genesis Press, 48
GEnie, 24
    Romance Writers' Newsletter, 48
    RomEx, 47
    Science-Fiction Round Tables, 34
    "Theme Park," 5
Genre bookstores, 235–237
GeoCities, 268
George Jr., 206
George Mason University, 2
Gibson, William, 31, 40
Gillmoor, Dan, 154
Gleick, James, 267
Global Information Services, 168
Global journalism, 142
The Glocester Guide (Garland), 225
Gopher, 167–168, 329–330
    search engines, 167
    subject trees, 167–168
Gopher Jewels, 168, 329
Gothic Journal, 51
Gothic Tales, 33
Grant, Jo, 269
Grantt, Lou, 84, 88
Graphics on Web site, 261
Gravity's Rainbow, 284
Gray, Terry A., 185
Greenberg, Susannah, 253
Green Mile (King), 101–102
Grist, 68
Guerrilla marketing, 253
Guides to Writing HTML Documents, 271
A Guide to Classic Mystery and Detection, 60
Guide to Lock Picking, by Ted the Tool, 63
Guide to Web Publishing, 270
Gulf + Western Industries, 216
Gumball Machine Billing, 223, 224–225
The Gumshoe Site, 59
Gunarat, Shelton, 154
Guyer, Carolyn, 290

H
Hacking, 178

The Haiku Server, 74
Halberstadt, Alex, 207
Hall, Justin, 109, 270
Hall, Karen, 266
Halperin, Jim, 231
Hard line returns in HTML, 257
HardPress, 71
Harlequin/Silhouette Publishers, 49
Harold D. Underdown, 81
Harper's, 304
Hart, Michael, 226, 227–228
Hartford, Bruce, 301
Harvard, Nieman Foundation, 139
Hass, Robert, 65
Hatrack River, 39
Hauben, Michael, 152
Haunting Grounds, 286
Heller, Steve, 98
Hermans, Bjorn, 191
Hewitt, John, 28, 85, 89, 100, 212
High, John, 10
Hines, Tracie, 83
Hipschman, David, 273
Historical Library, 51
Histories of the net, 331
Hoffman, Ivan, 307
Hollywood Scriptwriter, 86
Hootenanny, 68
HotBot, 174–175
HoTMetaL, 256
HOTT, 126
HotWired, 109, 148, 201–202
HotBot, 174–175
House of Speculative Fiction, 35, 40
Houston Chronicle, NIT, 127–128
"How Reporters Use the Net," 152
"How to Find an Online Journalism Job on the Web," 151
"How to Search the Web — A Guide to Search Tools," 184–185
"How to Set Up and Run Your Own Internet Mailing List," 252
"How to Widely Publicize Your Site," 255
HTML Demonstration of Basic HTML Tags, 262
HTML (Hypertext Markup Language), 256, 257, 331
    authoring tools, 256
    enhancements for Web site, 260
    links, 258
    navigation on Web, 258–259
    online resources for, 261–263
    tags, 257–261
    writing hypertext, 256
HTML Transit, 256
Human Languages page, 2
Human Resources (Kemske), 225
Hume, Ellen, 152

Hunger, 285
Hungry Mind, 240
Hwang, David, 271
Hyperizons: the Hypertext Fiction Home Page, 290
Hypertext, 260–261
    criticism, 283–285
    differences of, 281–282
    drama, 286, 288
    introduction to, 281–289
    megasource resources for, 290–291
    poetry, 285–286
Hypertext and Literary Things, 290
Hypertext Fiction, 290
The Hypertext Hotel, 290
Hypertext Shakespeare, 93
"HyperText Sources," 288
Hytelnet, 166

I

Ian Hoffman home page, 307
IBM
    InfoSage, 180
    News Rack, 149
Icon CMT, 197
iDirect, 255
Il Postino, 65
Incognito Cafe, 72
"In Defence of Hypertext," 288
Indexes and copyrights, 299
Indexing for paperless books, 226
Index of HTML Tags, 262
Index on Censorship Magazine, 306
Inference Find, 176
InfoChase, 268
Infomine, 187
Information agents, 138–139
Information farming, 137–138
Information SuperLibrary, 217–221
InfoSage, IBM, 180
Infoseek, 160, 174–175
Ingle, Robert, 115
Inklings, 26
Inkspot, 12, 81
Inktomi, 172, 174–175
Insane Search, 176–177
The Institute for Alternative Journalism's First Media and Democracy Congress, 140
The Institute for Global Communications (IGC), 140, 142–143
INTCAR–L, 127
"Intellectual Property and National Information Infrastructure (NII)," 299
Intelligent agents, 180–181
"Intelligent Software Agents on the Internet," 181
Interactive Media, 279
Inter@ctive Week, 148

International Affairs Net, 143
The International Interactive Communications Society (IICS), 276
Internationalism of the Net, 294
Internet
    connectivity, 314
    explanation of, 311–312
    getting online, 313–3151
    guided tour of, 316–332
    information resources on, 328–332
    mapping orientation on, 333–334
    telecommunications software, 314–315
    transmission medium for, 313–314
The Internet: a Goldmine for Editors & Reporters, 151
Internet Address Finder (IAF), 160
Internet Book Fair, 244
The Internet Book Information Center, 242
The Internet Bookshop, 235
The Internet Companion: a Beginner's Guide to Global Networking (LaQuey with Ryer), 222
Internet Crimewriting Network, 62
The Internet Crimewriting Network, 56
Internet Directory of Literary Agents, 29
Internet Directory of Published Writers, 29
The Internet Entertainment Network, 85
Internet Journalism Resources, 154
Internet Links for Technical Communications, 100
Internet Newsroom, 132
Internet Poetry Archive (IPA), 72
The Internet Public Library (IPL), 170
Internet Relay Chat (IRC), 25, 324
Internet Research Pointer, 187
Internet Resources for Technical Communicators, 96
The Internet Screenwriters' Network (ISN), 85
Internet Service Providers (ISPs), 314, 315
    choosing a provider, 315
The Internet Sleuth, 187
Internet Web Text, 332
The Internet Writers' Guidelines, 212
The Internet Writing Workshop, 5
InterNIC Scout Toolkit, 179
InterNovel, 279
InterText, 33, 35, 206
Intimate Exchanges (Ayckbourn), 286
Intrigue Press, 58
Inventing an Online Newspaper, 123–124
Investigative Database, 60
Investigative Reporters and Editors (IRE), 127, 152
    WWW.Reporter.Org, 156
IQuest InfoCenter, 130
IRE-L, 127
isibongo, 68
Isn't It Romantic, 45
IT Informer, 133
It's a Bunny, 206
"It's Not What You Think," 284

J

Jacobs, David, 207
Jacobsohn, Rachel, 219
James Bryce home page, 98
James Gleick home page, 267
Jane Austen's Writings, 239
Janssen, Michael, 207
Järvinen, Petteri, 32–33
Järvinen's List, 32–33
Java software, 301
Jefferson, Thomas, 293
Jenks, Ken, 109
JetPack, 206
Jim Rosenberg home page, 285
Jinn, 135
J-Jobs, 151
Job banks for journalists, 150–151
Joe Burns' HTML Goodies, 263
John December home page, 100
The John F. Kennedy School of Government, 131
John Hewitt home page, 100, 212
John Labovitz home page, 213
John Makulowich home page, 131
Johns Hopkins University, Center for Talented Youth at, 79
Johnson, Bill, 8
Johnson, Samuel, 157
Joiner, Leila B., 26
Jolly Roger, 206–207
Jones, Mary Harris, 141
Jones Digital Century, 183
Jossey-Bass, 218
The Journal, 92
Journalism, 115–156. *See also* Magazines and newsletters
  case studies, 118–123
  of cyberspace news, 144–145
  civic journalism, 139
  feeds and leads, 132–136
  forums for journalists, 125–129
  global journalism, 142
  information agents, 138–139
  informational resources, 123–125
  information farming, 137–138
  job banks in, 150–151
  local news, 143–144
  megasource jumpstations for, 153–155
  new journalism, 141–142
  new skills in, 137
  online newsstands, 149–150
  online services, 129–130
  professional organizations, 148–149
  progressive media, 140–141
  research resources, 130–132
  self-publishing journalists, 145–148
  transition to digital news, 116, 118
  trends in, 136–145
  Usenet newsgroups for journalists, 129
Journalism Bookmarks, 153
The Journalism List, 154
Journalism Resources, 154
The Journalist's Toolbox, 132, 154
The Journal of Buddhist Ethics, 202
JourNet, 127
Joyce, James, 239
The J.R.R. Tolkien Information Page, 39
JStarr's Poetry Forum, 70
Julie Peterson home page, 285
Junker, Howard, 261

K

Karen Hall home page, 266
Keith Mays home page, 146
Keith Soltys' Internet Resources for Technical Communicators, 100
Kelly, T. L., 251
Kemske, Floyd, 225
Kendall, Robert, 289
Kent, Janet, 7
Kerlin, Scott, 47
Kershaw, Derek, 207
Kettell, Jenn, 47
Khargie, Mignon, 195–196
KidPub, 79
KidsWeb, 268
Kidworld, 79
King, Peter, 271
King, Stephen, 101–102, 222
Kinko's, 249
Kinsley, Michael, 194, 195
Kissane, Dan, 174
Kline, Gary, 266
Knopf Publishing Group, 36
Kreye, Andrian, 146
Kroker, Arthur, 205
Kroker, Mary Louise, 205
Kunkin, Art, 140–141
Kurtz, Glenn A., 290
Kyosaku, 207

L

Labovitz, John, 202–203, 213
LaFayette, Madame de, 45
Laguna Life, 240
Lail, Jack, 128
Landow, George, 284
Language of Life television series (Moyers), 65
Lanier, Jaron, 181–182
Lankford, J. R., 4, 5
Lappé, Frances Moore, 134
LaQuey, Tracy, 222
Larry Aaronson home page, 97–98

The Last Song of Violeta Parra (Deemer), 288
Last Year at Marienbad (Resnais), 286
The Launchpad for Journalists, 131, 132
Lavaccari, Tom, 197
Lee, Patrick, 117
Leen, Mary Soon, 42–43
Le Grand Secret, 231
Lehman, Bruce A., 293, 299
L'Engle, Madeleine, 77
Lenov, 279
Leppik, Peter, 33
Lerner, Marcia, 247–248
Lester, Paul, 309
Lethin, Rich, 251
Lewis, Bill Dallas, 80
Lexis-Nexis
   for journalists, 129
   as subscription model, 112
   Library of Congress, 2, 307
   film resources, 89
   Global Electronic Library, 168
   histories of the net, 331
   paperless books and, 226
LibWeb, 187
Lies (Pryll), 283
Lin, Nancy, 280
Lingo, 69
Linklater, Richard, 86
Linkmaster aids, 254–255
Links
   in HTML, 258
   Telnet links, 327
Links from the Underground, 109
Links to Higher Online Higher Education, 12
Lippert, Eric, 39
Listproc, 164, 252
Listserv, 163, 164
   self-publishing and, 252
Liszt, 164
Literary Kicks, 207
Literary Science Fiction & Fantasy Discussion
   Forum, 33
The Literary Times, 48, 203
Lithuanian Poetry, 72
The Little Planet Times, 79
Liu, Alan, 285
Local area networks (LANs), defined, 311
Local news, 143–144
Location, printing on, 248–249
Locus Solus, 278
Los Angeles Times, 111
   AP Online, 132
Losito, Lisa, 108
Lotus Notes, 311
Lou Grantt's home page, 88
The Lurker Files, 104

Lycos, 175
Lynx, 261
Lynx of the Week, 179
The Lysator Science Fiction & Fantasy Archive, 42

M

McAdams, Melinda, 123–124
McCarthy, Nan, 250, 265
McCoy's Guide to Theatre and performance
   Studies, 92
McCullagh, Declan, 142
McIntosh, Shawn, 153
McLuhan, Marshall, 157
McNamee, Jim, 207
McNeese State University, 174
McQuarrie, Christopher, 84
Magazine Index, 299
Magazines and newsletters. *See also* Money issues
   children"s writers, 78–79
   editorial direction, 113
   e-zines, 202–210
   for fantasy writers, 34–35
   for mystery writers, 57–58
   for playwrights, 92–93
   for poets, 67–70
   for romance writers, 48
   for science fiction writers, 34–35
   for technical writers, 96–97
   webzines, 191–214
   writers' magazines, 25–26
Magellan, 170
Magnifying Glass Mystery Newsletter, 57
Mahoney, P. J. Benedict, 307
Mailbase, 252
Mailing lists, 320–321
   self-promotion and, 253–254
   self-publishing via, 250–251
Mailserv, 252
Majordomo, 164, 252
Make Your Own Home Page, 261
"Making the Hollywood Film," 86
Mako, Suzette L., 51
Mako's Angel, 51
Makulowich, John, 131, 155
Malloy, Judy, 279
Mandel, Lisa, 219–220
Manderley, 49
Mandy's Film and TV Production Directory, 89
Mangan, Tom, 146
Mann, Thomas, 293
Marble Springs, 290
The Marexx, 37–38
Market guidelines, 51
Martin, Teresa, 179
Mason, Matthew, 207
Mason West home page, 267

The Matrix (Quarterman), 222
Mayhem, 60
Mays, Keith, 146
Medbh, Méighréad, 285
Media, 127
MediaCentral, 198
MEDIANet, 89
MediaNet, 162
Media Search and Techno3, 104
Medill School of Journalism, 198
Meeks, Brock, 147–148
Megasource jumpstations
    for booksellers, 243–244
    for children's writers, 81–82
    for collaboration, 289
    for digitized books, 241–242
    for distance learning, 12
    for fantasy writers, 42–43
    for journalists, 153–155
    for mystery writers, 60–63
    for online writing laboratories (OWLs), 12
    for playwrights, 93–94
    for poets, 74–76
    for research, 186–189
    for romance writers, 52–53
    for science fiction writers, 42–43
    for screenwriters, 88–89
    for self-publishing, 271
    for technical writers, 99–100
    Web pages, creating, 271
    for writers' forums, 26–30
Megasources Journalism Resources, 154
Mellish, Xander, 264–265
MelrosEast, 105
Melville, Herman, 15
Mennie, Kia, 290
Mentoring
    classes, 8–10
    for screenwriters, 84–85
Mercury Center, 118–120, 143
Metacrawler, 177
Metzger, Deena, 140
Meyer, Eric, 149
Michael Berry's Cheat Ironies, 267
Micropayments, 111–112
Microsoft
    Sidewalk, 144
    Slate, 191, 192–194
    as sponsor, 110
Microsoft Internet Explorer, 257, 315, 331
Microsoft Network (MSN), 24
    Encarta encyclopedia, 182
MSNBC, 135
Mike Erlindson home page, 124
Mike Vidal's Independent Filmmaker's Internet Resource Guide, 89

Mike Wendland home page, 145–146
Milwaukee Journal, 121
Mind's Eye, 109
Mindspring, 314
Mirman, Brad, 85
Misc.Writing, 18–20
The Mississippi Review Web, 200
Mitchell, William, 232
Modems, 314
MojoWire, 141
Mola, 279
Molthrop, Stuart, 284
Money issues, 107–114
    advertisers, 110
    branding and, 109
    fees, 109–110
    free exchange and, 108
    online currency, 110
    payment models, 111–112
    sales, 109–110
    self-promotion, unpaid, 108–109
    sponsors, 110
    subscriptions, 109–110
Monitors, 313
Monsterboard, 150
Montezuma's Return, 38
Morgan, Bev, 46
The Morpo Review, 207
Moscow Channel, 207
Mother Jones, 141
The Mother Load, 171
    Insane Search, 176–177
Moultrop, Stuart, 289
The Movie Critic Rate O'matic, 180
The Moviemaker's Home Page, 89
The Movie Review Query Engine, 87–88
Moyers, Bill, 65
Mr. Showbiz, Celebrity Lounge at, 84
MSNBC, 135
MTV, 219
MT Void, 35
Muchnick, Irving, 299–300
MUCs, 326
Mueller, John, 188
Muldoon, Kate, 309
Multimedia Developers' Group (MDG), 276
Multisearches, 176–177
Murderous Intent, 57
MUSHES, 326
Myers, George, Jr., 206
My Name is Scribe, 279
Myst, 37, 260
Mysterious Bytes, 57, 203
The Mysterious Page, 59, 61, 63
Mysterious Press, 59
Mystery Connection, 63

Mystery Corner, 60
Mystery (mailing list), 56
The Mystery Page, 60
Mystery Readers Journal, 58
Mystery writers, 55–64
    authors' home pages, 59
    bookstores, 58
    forums for, 56–57
    magazines and newsletters, 57–58
    publishers, 58–59
    technical information resources, 62
The Mystery Zone, 58
My Yahoo!, 180

N

Naropa Institute Poetics Program, 65
The Nation, 304
National Book Critics Circle, 303
National Diversity Journalism Job Bank, 151
National Freedom of Information Coalition, 126
National Institute For Computer-Assisted Reporting (NICAR), 156
    forum, 127
National Newspaper Association, 148
The National Poetry Association, 74–75
National Poetry Month (April), 73
National Press Club, 148
    Journalism Resources, 154
The National Writers Union, 96, 299, 300–301
National Writing Centers Association, 12
Navigate, 201
NBNews Daily Electronic Journal, 179
NCSA (National Center for Supercomputer Applications), 262
Neal Weiner home page, 275
Nebraska Center for Writers, 27
    for poets, 65
Negroponte, Nicholas, 223–224
Nelson, Ted, 111
NESFA Press (New England Science Fiction), 36
Netcom, 314
NetDirectory, 170
NetGuide, 172
    subject directory, 171
Netiquette, 317
netMEDIA, 149
NetObjects' Fusion, 145, 256
Netscape Navigator, 257, 315, 331
NetSearch, 170
Network, defined, 311
Networking, 276
Neuromancer (Gibson), 40
N.E.W. Base Internet Directory Service, 161
Newcomb, Jonathan, 217, 218
New journalism, 141–142
Newsbytes, 133

New School for Social Research, 8
Newsgroups, 18–20
News in the Future, 136
News in the Next Century, 152
Newsletters. *See* Magazines and newsletters
Newslink, 149
News Mait Writers' Cooperative, 151
Newspaper Association of America (NAA), 118, 148, 153
    Digital Edge, 152
Newspaper & Journalism Links, 150
News Place, 154
News Research, 127
Newsstands, 149–150
    webzines and e-zines, 210–213
New York Times, 299–300, 304
    "Bosnia: Uncertain Paths to Peace," 143
NICAR-L, 127
Niche marketing, 111
The Niche Resource Directory, 178
Nightmares and Dreamscapes (King), 222
NIT, 127–128
NIVA Writer's Block, 97
No Dead Trees, 280
No Martyrs, 233
Noth, Dominque Paul, 124
NWHQ, 208

O

OASYS Network, 21
OBscure, 208
Ocain, Pat, 47
The Occasional Screenful, 69
Ockerbloom, John Mark, 241
The Official Page of the Hopelessly Romantic, 51
Offline agents, 179–180
O'Keefe, Steve, 253
Oklahoma State University, The Technical Writers List, 96
Olson, Karl, 298
Omni, 35
OMNI Internet, 198
On-demand book industry, 247
101 Hollywood Blvd., 105
OneLook Dictionaries, 183
One World News Service, 143
"Online: Will It Hurt or Help Newspapers?," 124
The Online Book Initiative (OBI), 229
The Online Books Page, 241–242
Online Career Center, 150
Online currency, 110
Online Literary Resources, 242
Online magazines and newsletters. *See* Magazines and newsletters
Online-News, 128

Online Newspapers: The Newspaper Industry's Dive into Cyberspace, 124
Online Newspapers on the Web, 150
The Online Word Biz, 278
Online workshops, 4–8
Online writing laboratories (OWLs), 2–3
   megasource jumpstations, 12
   virtual writing courses, 3–4
Online Writing Workshop, 8
Open Book Service (OBS), 221–225
OpenMarket, 110
Open Text, 176
Operators, search engines and, 173
Oregon University's Writing Online Resource Directory (WORD), 3
Outing, Steve, 124
Over My Dead Body, 58
OWLs. *See* Online writing laboratories (OWLs)
OZ Poetry Page, 69

P

Pacific Book Auction, 237
Pacific News Service (PNS), 134
Packer, Ann, 10
PageMill, 256
Painted Rock Readers and Writers Colony, 47
Paperless books, 225–233
Parallel, 208
Paramount Communications, Inc., 217
Parr, Christopher, 88
Pat Cadigan home page, 39
Paul Phillips' One Book List, 238
Payment models, 111–112
PBS film resources, 89
PC Gamer, 38
PC (Platforms for Communication) Forum, 301
Pelson, Dan, 197
Penguin USA, 223
Pen & Sword Hypersite, 208
People, locating, 158–163
People Finder, 161
Peress, Gille, 143
Periodicals. *See* Magazines and newsletters
Peripatetic Eclectic Gopher (PEG), 168
Permut, David, 84
Personalized children's literature, 78
Personal Mystery Home Pages, 59
Peter Jennings' World News Tonight, 139
Peterson, Julie, 285
Pew Center for Civic Journalism, 139
Phenix & Phenix, 253
Phone numbers, finding, 158–159
The Pickwick Papers (Dickens), 101
Playbill Online, 92
Playwrights, 91–94
   forums for, 91–92

   hypertext drama, 286, 288
   magazines for, 92–93
   megasource jumpstations for, 93–94
   scripts for, 93
   technical information, 92
The Pocket Crime Series (Australia), 59
The Poems Gallery, 66
Poems-Poetry-Poets, 75
Poetic Immolation Press, 71
The Poetry Exchange, 69
The Poetry Reading Room, 73
Poetry slams, 73–74
Poetry Slams!, 73–74
Poetry Web Spotlight, 75
Poets, 65–76
   authors' home pages, 71–73
   forums and critiques for, 66–67
   hypertext poetry, 285–286
   magazines and newsletters, 67–70
   megasource jumpstations, 74–76
   publishers, 70–71
Poets' Corner, 73
Poets of South Africa's Western Cape, 72–73
The Poet's Workshop, 66–67
Poets & Writers Online, 26
Poet Warrior Press: Writer's Resource Center, 28
Point, 179
PointCast Network (PCN), 138–139
Pore, Jerod, 203, 204, 210
Pornographer's Handbook: How to Exploit Women, Dupe Men, & Make Lots of Money, 147
Porteous, James, 179
Potash, Steve, 233
Poynter, Dan, 271
Poynter Institute, 149
PPS Online, 139
The PRC Home Page, 98
Prentice Hall, 217
Presslink, 135
Pride and Prejudice, 283
Print's Appeal, 248
Procomm, 314
Proctor, Roger, 187
Prodigy, 24, 314
   for journalists, 130
Prof. Randolph Benston home page, 98
Professional Communication Society, 99
Professional organizations for journalists, 148–149
ProfNet, 162
Progressive media, 140–141
Project Bartleby, 229
Project Cool, 179
Project Crayon (CReAte Your Own Newspaper), 138
Project Gutenberg, 2, 182, 226, 227–228
Promoting yourself on the Net, 253–255
Protean Press, 335

Pryll, Rick, 283
Public Affairs Web, 162
Publication Rights Clearinghouse (PRC), 300, 303
Public-domain titles, 228
Public information officer databases, 161–163
Publicly Accessible Mailing Lists, 164
Public Relations on the Web, 270
Publishers. *See also* Self-publishing
   of fantasy, 36–37
   mystery, 58–59
   for poets, 70–71
   for romance writers, 48–49
   of science fiction, 36–37
Publishers Weekly, 304
   Bookwire, 244
Publish Yo'self, 270
Pulpless.Com, 231
Purdue University OWL, 2, 3–4
   for technical writers, 100
Purely Academic, 187
Putnam Berkley (Ace), 36
Pynchon, Thomas, 284

Q

Quanta, 35
Quantum Books, 97
Quarterman, John S., 222
QuickSite, 256
Quiet Americans, 231

R

R. R. Donnelly, On-Demand Printing Division of, 247–248
Radio and Television News Directors Foundation, 152
Radosh, Daniel, 195
Rainwater Press, 265
Rand, David, 98
Rapture, 208
Rashkin, Peter, 209
Rasley, Alicia, 52
Rawhide and Lace, 51
A Reader's Guide to Romance & Women's Fiction, 52
ReadersNdex, 242
Realist Wonder Society, 230
Real Poetik, 69, 250
Real-time forums, 324
Rec.Guns FAQ, 62
Red Alert Internet Strategy Guide (Wong), 38
Reddick, Randy, 154
Redrum Coffeehouse Horror Zine, 35
Red Sage Publishers, 49
Rees, Gareth, 289
Reference Information, 155
Reid, Joanne, 52
Reid's Page for Writers, 52
Release 2.0, 232

Remote logon, 316–317, 326–328
The Reporter's Guide to Internet Mailing Lists, 165
The Reporters Internet Guide (RIG), 131
Reporter's Internet Survival Guide, 131
Research, 157–189
   agents, 179–182
   conducting Web research, 169
   e-mail addresses, 159–161
   forums for, 163–166
   hacking, 178
   megasource jumpstations for, 186–189
   multisearches, 176–177
   online reference shelf, 182–183
   people, locating, 158–163
   phone numbers, finding, 158–159
   reference list, 185
   scouting, 178–179
   search engines, 172–173
   subject guides, 169–172
Researching the Internet (Rowland), 161
RES-Links (The All-in-One Resource Page), 187
Resnais, Alain, 286
Resource Selection and Information Evaluation, 184
Resources for Journalists, 154
Resources for Romance Writers, 52
Resources for Romance Writers (WWW Virtual Library), 53
Reuters, 133, 135
Reviews
   of books, 239–240
   for romance writers, 49–50
Rex Adaptive Newspaper Service, 181
Rex (Resource EXchange), 178
Rheingold, Howard, 24, 165, 267–268, 317
Rice, Sudama, 207
Rice Subject Gopher, 168
Richard Toscan's Playwriting Seminars, 92
Roberts, Carol, 96
Roberts, Janine, 201
Robots. *See* Search engines
Rodgers, George, 112
Roget's Thesaurus, 2
Romance Authors Page, 50
Romance Forum, 46
Romance Novelists Author's pages, 50
The Romance Novelist's Home Page, 52
The Romance Pages, 52
The Romance Reader, 49
Romance Readers and Writer's Guides, 49
Romance Readers Anonymous, 46
Romance Readers' Corner, 50
Romance & Women's Fiction/Readers' Groups, 46
Romance writers, 45–53
   authors' home pages, 50
   forums, 45–47
   magazines and newsletters, 48

megasource jumpstations for, 52–53
publishers, 48–49
reviews, 49–50
Romance Writer's Mailing List (RW–L), 46
Romance Writers of America (RWA), 52
Romancing the Web, 53–54
Romanos, Jack, 218
Romantic Notions, 50
RomANTICS, 46
RomEx (the Romance & Women's Fiction Exchange), 46–47
Rosanna Madrid Gatti home page, 266
Rosenberg, Jim, 285
Roswell Electronic Computer Bookstore, 97
Rothman, David, 139
Rowland, Robin, 161
run on, run along, 280
Ryan, Bob, 120
Ryer, Jeanne, 222

S

Sadiq, Isa, 295
St. Martin's Press, 59
Sales on Net, 109–110
Salon, 110, 191, 195–196
   book reviews, 240
Sanders, Bernard, 140
San Diego Technical Bookstore, 97
San Francisco Bay Guardian, 143–144
San Francisco Review, 240
San Francisco State University
   Poetry Center, 75
   Way New Journalism, 125
San Jose Mercury News, 118–120
Savvy, 177
Scandinavian Mystery News, 58
Scheer, Robert, 140
Schiller, Stephen, 100
Schulman, J. Neil, 231
Schuster, Max, 216
Schweitzer, Susan, 280
Science-Fiction Author Bruce Sterling's History of the Net, 331
Science Fiction Fantasy Writers, 33
The Science Fiction Resource Guide, 42
Science Fiction Weekly, 35
Science fiction writers, 31–43
   authors' home pages, 39–40
   bookstores, 35–36
   forums, 32–34
   games, 37–39
   magazines and newsletters, 34–35
   megasource jumpstations for, 42–43
   publishers, 36–37
Science Fiction Writers List, 6
Sci-Fi Channel, 37

The Dominion, 40
Scoop CyberSleuth's Internet Guide, 155
Scott, Peter, 166
Scott's Theatre Links, 93
Scott Yanoff's Internet Services List, 189
Scouting, 178–179
   with agents, 179–182
The Scout Toolkit, 179, 188
Screenwriters, 83–89
   film reviews, 87–88
   forums for, 84
   megasource jumpstations for, 88–89
   scripts, 87
   technical information, 86
Screenwriters FAQ, 86
Screenwriters' Homepage, 85
Screenwriter's Master Chart, 86
The Screenwriter's Nebula Drive, 85
Screenwriter's Online: the Insider Report, 85
Screenwriters & Playwrights Home Page, 88–89, 94
Scriptito's Place, 80
Scripts
   for playwrights, 93
   for screenwriters, 87
The Scrivenery, 26
Seabrook, John, 158
Searchable Index Newsgroups and Mailing Lists, 165
Search.Com, 188
Search engines, 172–173
   advanced strategies with, 172–173
   Gopher search engines, 167
   multisearches, 176–177
"Searching Boolean," 184
"Search the Web in Style: Seek Right & You Shall Find," 184
Search Tools and Master Sites, 188
Select Fiction, 240
Self-promotion on Net, 253–255
Self-publishing, 245–271
   autobiographical Web site, 261
   distribution online, 249
   e-mail and, 250–251
   home pages for, 250
   location, printing on, 248–249
   mailing lists for, 250–251
   megasource jumpstations for, 271
   miscellaneous resources, 269–270
   news, 145–148
   notable self-publishers, 247
   online-only digital self–publishing, 249–252
   paper, digital self-publishing on, 246–249
   payment for writers, 251
   short printing runs, 247–248
   subscription models, 112
   visibility on the net, 250
   Webtop publishing, 249–250

Sentry Box, Alberta, 35Future Fantasy bookstore36
Serials on Web
   beginnings of, 101–102
   samples of Web serials, 103–105
SFF Net, 40
SFnF-WritersWorkshop, 33–34
SFRT on the Web, 43
Shadow Underground (Parr), 88
Shakespeare, Hypertext, 93
Shannon, Gabrielle, 210
Shannon, Kyle, 210
Shaw, George Bernard, 245
Shea, Joe, 121–123
Shinder, Debi, 16
Shockey, B. Clifford, 232
Shorenstein Center, 149
Shortmystery-L, 56
Shumate, Michael, 289, 290
Siegel, David, 261, 264
The Silence, 208–209
Silly Billy Page, 80
Sim-City, 37
Simon, Richard, 216
SimonSays, 218–219
   book reviews on, 240
Simon & Schuster Online, 216–217, 218–219
Sinclair, Carla, 204
Singer, Shelley, 10
"Sink or Swim: Internet Search Tools & Techniques," 186
SLAKE, 50
Slam poetry, 73–74
Slate, 110, 191, 194–195
Slattery, Diana, 285
SLIPP/PPP, 314
The Slot, 99
The Small Business Publicity FAQ, 270
A Small Garlic Press, 71
Smoking and No Smoking (Resnais), 286
Smolan, Rick, 144–145
Soap operas on Web. *See* Serials on Web
Society for Professional Journalists (SPJ), 128
The Society for Technical Communication (STC), 99
Soda Creek Press, 49
Sodt, Jonathan, 286
The Softer Side of Murder, 60
SoftLock, 230
Solock, Jack, 173
Soltys, Keith, 100
SomePIG, 69, 203
Spamming, promotion without, 253–254
Spanish Dagger, 209
Sparks, 209
Spectrum, 38
Spectrum Virtual University, 4
Speculative Fiction Clearinghouse at Carnegie-Mellon University, 41

The Speculative Fiction Page, 42–43
Speculative Fiction Writing Resources, 41
Spencer, Stephen, 29
Spiders. *See* Search engines
Spilled Ink, 209
SPJ-L, 128
Sponsors, 110
Sports-Ticker, 133
The Spot, 102
Spratt, Lee, 19
Spratt, Steven, 19
Spriggs, William A., 265
The Spring, 150
Spyglass Mosaic, 257
Stacey's Bookstore, 97
Stack, Charles, 234
Stale, 195
Stanford University Libraries & Academic Information Resources, 306
Stanley, Jack, 86
Stars in the Night, 70
Star Trek: WWW, 41
Star Trek books, 220
Star Trek Nexus Top Picks, 41
State & Screen Writing Resources, 94
Steadman, Carl, 201
Steeldragon Press, 36
Steffensen, Jan B., 61
Stephen Schiller's Technical Communications Resources, 100
Sterling, Bruce, 331
Sternberg's Daily News, 135
Steve Heller home page, 98
Steve Outing's FAQ, 124
Stone Soup magazine, 78, 79
Stories from Downtown Anywhere, 280
Story of Civilization (Durant & Durant), 319
Storyweb, 280
Strangelove, Michael, 232
Straub, Peter, 24
"Structuring Simple & Complex Keyword & Phrase Queries," 184
Studio Briefing, 111
Stumpers, 163
Style sheets for HTML, 256
Subject guides, 169–172
Submit-It, 254
Subscriptions, 109–110
Sudden, 70
Suh, Chan, 210
Sun Microsystems, 301
SunSites' LibWeb, 187
SuperSearch, 177
Surround tags, 257
Swaine, Alex, 203
Sweet, Jeffrey, 10

Sweig, David, 196
Switchboard, 158
Syracuse University
　National Freedom of Information Coalition, 126
　Plethora Writing Consultant Page, 3

T

"Tabloids, Talk Radio, and the Future of News: Technology's Impact on Journalism," 152
Tags in HTML, 257–261
Talbot, David, 196
Talk.Com, 32
Tangled Web, 60
TapRoot's Electronic Edition (TREE), 71
T@P Virtual Dorm, 105
Tartar, Stacy, 209
Tasini, Jonathan, 299–300
TCP/IP, 314
Technical Authors on the Web, 98
Technical writers, 95–100
　bookstores for, 97
　megasource jumpstations for, 99–100
　periodicals for, 96–97
Technical Writer Salaries, 99
The Technical Writers List, 96
Teen Writers, 80
TeleCafe, 18
Telecommunications Reform Act, 296
Telephonebook, 159
Telnet, 166–167, 326–328
　client-server relationship, 327–328
Templates for HTML, 256
Templeton, Brad, 133, 307
Tempo magazine, 142
"10 Big Myths about Copyright Explained," 307
Terminal X, 41
Texas A&M Subject Gopher, 168
Theatre Central, 94
Theatre Insight, 93
Theatre Network Magazine, 93
Theatre People, 92
There's a FAQ, How to Find E-Mail Addresses, 160
This is True, 251–252
3-D Language. *See* VRML (Virtual Reality Markup Language)
THUNDER (THe UNstoppable DreamERs), 70
Time CyberPorn cover article, 147
Time Warner
　Delirium, 230
　Electronic Publishing Search Engine, 181
　Quick Read program, 223
Tolstoy, Leo, 1
Tom Mangan home page, 146
Tompkins, Liz, 179
Tools for Aspiring Web Weavers, 262
Tor Books, 37

Toscan, Richard, 92
Touch Today, 135
Trafford Publishing, 248
Transit, 256
"Tree Fiction on the World Wide Web," 289
Trinity College's Purely Academic, 187
Tritter, Michael, 195
Truepenny Books, 71
Truth Machine, 231
Tudor, Dean, 153, 154
TuLiP Project, 270
Turbogopher, 167
Turkle, Sherry, 317
Tutoring classes, 8–10
20 Consonant Poetry, 73
Twilight, 209
Twists, Slugs, and Roscoes — a Glossary of Hardboiled Slang, 62
Two Tickets to Rio and Product Placement, 104
Tyner, Ross, 185, 186
Tyson, Laura D'Andrea, 116

U

The Ultimate Collection of Newslinks, 150
The Ultimate White Pages, 160
"Umney's Last Case" (King), 222
UnCover database, 300
Underdown, Harold D., 81
Understanding Internet: the Democratization of Mass Media and the Emerging Paradigm of Cyberspace, 232
Understanding the Internet, 331
Under the Covers, 50
Union2, 105
University at Albany, 279
University at Stony Brook, 162
University Books, 237
University of California, Santa Barbara, 168
University of California Virtual Library, 171
University of Florida Writing Environment, 3
University of Illinois Writer's Workshop Online Handbook, 3
University of Michigan OWL, 3
University of Missouri's Writery, 2
University of Nevada, 167
University of Sheffield, 262
University of Texas at Austin's Writing Lab, 3
Unknown Children's Book Writers, 81
Unlimited Vision Online Network, 123
Urban Desires: An Interactive Journal of Metropolitan Passions, 210
Urchin Reefs, 80
URLs, 139
　hacking with, 178
U.S. Fish & Wildlife Services Forensics Lab, 62
Useful PR Links, 270

Usenet newsgroups. *See* Forums
 for journalists, 129
Utne Reader, 197–198
Utopia Technologies, 38

V

Van Leeuvwen, Steven, 229
Vaughan, Chris, 17
Ventura, Michael, 140
Verbiage Magazine, 201
Veronica, 167
VH1, 219
Viacom, 218–331
The Victorian Web, 284
Victory Garden, 290
Vincent, Charlie, 109
Virtual Communities (Rheingold), 24
Virtual Reference Desk, 182, 188
Virtual writing courses, 3–4
The Virtue of What Is, 286
Vivian Neou searchable index, 164
Voice of America, 135
Voice of the Prisoner, 74
The Voice of the Shuttle, 285, 291
Von Rospach, Chuq, 6
Voters Telecommunications Watch, 306
Voyager, 37
VRML (Virtual Reality Markup Language), 219, 260
 hypertext drama and, 288

W

WAIS, 168–169
Walentynski, Liz, 18
Wall, David, 201
Wall Street Journal Interactive Edition, 109
Ware, Tim, 284
Warner Aspect, 37
Warren, Jim, 296
Washington Post, 123
The Washington Post Online book reviews, 240
Way New Journalism, 125
Webb, Gary, 119, 120–121
Web browsers, 257, 315, 331
Web Builders and Multimedia Resources, 264
Webcatcher, 180
Web Concept & Design and Web Access Design, 264
Webcrawler, 175
Web crawlers. *See* Search engines
Web del Sol, 213
The Web Inquirer, 201
WebKids, 80
WebMaster Magazine, 155
Webmasters, 275
Webmaster's Guide to Search Engines and Directories, 185
Webmasters Reference Library, 263
WebOvision, 155
Web Poetry Corner, 70
The Web Poetry Kit, 64
WebRings, 280
Web sites. *See also* Authors' home pages; HTML (Hypertext Markup Language)
 creating your own, 255–270
 design resources, 264
 enhancements, 260
 free Web pages, 268–269
 hypertext, 260–261
 megasource jumpstations for creating, 271
Webster's Dictionary, 182
Webtop publishing, 249–250
Webzines, 191–214
 newsstands, 210–213
The Wedding, 103
Weil, Debbie, 155
Weiner, Neal, 275, 286
Weintraub, Pamela, 198, 199
Weise, Elizabeth, 147
The WELL, 24–25
 censorship, 295
 e-zines, 210
 reference shelf, 182
 Whole Earth 'Lectronic Link, 168
Welles, Orson, 37
Wendland, Mike, 116–117, 145–146
Werbach, Kevin, 262
West, Mason, 267
"Where To Find Anything on the Internet," 184
Whole Earth Networks, 314
Who's Afraid of C++ (Heller), 98
WhoWhere? PeopleSearch, 160
Wide area networks (WANs), defined, 311
Wilder, Billy, 83
William, Jeff, 210
William A. Spriggs home page, 265
William H. Calvin home page, 267
Williams, Ed, 5, 26
Willson, Meredith, 91–94
WiReD, 109, 148
Wistar, Caleb, 232
Wong, Roger, 38
Woodward, Robert, 218–219
Word, 191, 197
Wordbiz.Net, 155
Working Writers, Inc., 99
Work in Progress (WIP), 239
World E-mail Directory, 160
World Free Press, 140–141
World Intellectual Property Organization (WIPO), 299
World Media Link, 135
World Wide Web, 330–331
WR-Eye-Tings, 67
The Write Page, 50, 53

Writer's Block, 97
Writer's block suggestions, 47
Writer's Conference, 8
Writer's Digest, 25
Writers forum, 16–17
Writers Free Reference Desk, 189
The Writer's Guild of America, 278
Writer's Guild of America, 86–87
Writers' Internet Exchange (WRITE), 6–7
WritersL, 128–129
°*Bylines*° magazine, 112–113
The Writer's Market Board, 28
WritersNet, 29–30
Writers on the Net, 8–10
Writer's Page, 213
The Writer's Planet, 7
Writer's Resource Center, 28
Writers Resource for poets, 85
Writer's Resources, 28
Writers Studio Utne Reader, 197–198
Writer's Workshop, 7
@*Writers*, 25–26
The writing center at Virginia Tech, 2
WritingChat, 16
Writing for Stage & Screen, 89
Writing for the Net, 273–291
"Writing for the New Millennium: The Birth of Electronic Literature," 289
Writing for the web, 264–281
Writing for the Web: a Primer for Librarians, 263
The WritingLab, 4
Writing Livevs: Technology, Creativity, and Hypertext Fiction, 289
Writing Speculative Fiction, 41
Writing Your Own Web Page, 271
WS Gopher, 167
W3C Collaboration Resource Page, 289
W3 Consortium, 171
wURLd Presence, 254
WWW.Reporter.Org, 156
WWW Virtual Library, 188
    Fantasy and Science Fiction Writers, Resources for, 43
    HTML Style, 271
    Journalism, 155
    Mysteries, 63
    Poets, Resources for, 75
    Romance Writers, Resources for, 53
    as subject guide, 171

Theatre and Drama, 94
Wyan, Michele, 48
WYSIWYG, HTML requiring, 258

X

Xanadu Project, 111
Xander Mellish home page, 264–265
The X–Files, 41
The X-Files Official Web Site, 41

Y

Yahoo!
    advertising on, 110
    Announcement Services Page, 255
    Author's Pages, 239
    Children's Books, Guide To, 79
    HTML Guides and Tutorials, 271
    My Yahoo!, 180
    Personalized Children's Literature, 78
    Poetry
    forums, 67
    Resources, 75
    regional pages, 144
    Screenplays, 87
    security companies, index to, 63
    subject guide, 171–172
    Web searching, 185
    Writing resources, 30
Yahooligans, 82
Yahooligans, 82
Yanoff, Scott, 189
Yard Show, 40
Yellow Pages Online, 159
Yoohoo Inc., 71
YO! (Youth Outlook), 134
Yudkin, Marcia, 21, 270

Z

Zeno's Forensics Page, 62
Zero City e-zine, 75–76
Zine News, 213
Zine Online Newsstand, 213
Zines Zines Everywhere, 213–214
ZipZap, 210
Z-Term, 314
Zuzu's Petas, 30
Zyzzyva, 261
@*Cloud9*, 198

ABOUT THE AUTHOR

Gary Gach (pronounced like "Bach" or "gawk") is also the author of the bestselling *Pocket Guide to the Internet*, based on a class he's been teaching for a couple years. A technopeasant (VCR blinking 12:00 o'clock), he has found the Internet a vital subject with important aspects in need of communicating. He has recently created a five-hour video teaching the Internet for use in China.

Former Editor-in-Chief of *CV Guide* (cable-tv), Gach has also worked as a hospital administrator, waterfront stevedore, second-hand bookstore clerk, paralegal, typographer, and actor. His prose, poetry, and translations have been published in a few chapbooks, more than a hundred magazines, and a dozen anthologies, including *American Book Review*, *American Cinematographer*, *American Poetry Review*, *American Reporter*, *The Book of Luminous Things*, *A Brotherhood in Song*, *City Lights Review*, *Exiled in the Word*, *New Asia Review*, *Poems for the Millennium*, *San Francisco Review of Books*, *Shambhala Sun*, *Technicians of the Sacred*, and *Zyzzyva*. Among his forthcoming titles are: *What Book!? Buddha Poems from Beat to Hiphop*, *The Last Emperor 2*, and *Adventures in Haikuland*. He lives in San Francisco, reads books at City Lights' library, and swims in the Bay. His Web address is: <http://www.geocities.com/Athens/Acropolis/2730>. E-mail: <writersnet@hotmail.com>.